The Pulitzer Diaries

Inside America's Greatest Prize

John Hohenberg

 Syracuse University Press

First Edition 1997
96 97 98 99 00 01   6 5 4 3 2 1

The paper used in this publication meets the minimum requirements of American National Standard for Information Sciences—Permanence of Paper Printed Library Materials, ANSI Z39.48-1984. ∞™

Library of Congress Cataloging-in-Publication Data

Hohenberg, John.
    The Pulitzer diaries : inside America's greatest prize / John
Hohenberg. — 1st ed.
      p. cm.
    Includes bibliographical references and index.
    ISBN 0-8156-0392-4 (cloth : alk. paper)
    1. Pulitzer prizes—History. 2. Hohenberg, John. I. Title.
AS911.P8H625   1996
071'.3—dc20   96-34121

Manufactured in the United States of America

For JoAnn

John Hohenberg, a distinguished journalist and political and diplomatic correspondent in New York, Washington, D.C., the United Nations, and abroad, was Professor of Journalism, Columbia Graduate School of Journalism, from 1950 to 1976. From 1954 to 1976, he also served as the Administrator of the Pulitzer Prizes and Secretary of the Pulitzer board. He is the author of *The Bill Clinton Story* (Syracuse University Press, 1994), *Foreign Correspondence: The Great Reporters and Their Times,* 2d edition (Syracuse University Press, 1995), *The Professional Journalist, Free Press/Free People,* and three books on the Pulitzer Prizes among others. He also holds a Pulitzer Prize Special Award for his services to American journalism.

The Pulitzer Diaries

Contents

The Art of the Diarist   xi

PART ONE   **Expanding Horizons**

1. The Big Prize   3

2. My View of the Prizes   8

3. An Atomic Crisis   13

4. New Times for the Prizes   21

5. Test for a Teacher   29

6. With Hearst in Moscow   39

7. The Kennedy Prize   47

PART TWO   **The Best of Times**

8. A Question of Funding   59

9. The University Experience   68

10. In the Public Interest   74

11. Shuffling the Prizes   80

12. Presidential Politics   88

13. Press versus Government   95

14. The Soviet Challenge   103

15. Showdown   109

PART THREE   The Prizes as History

16. The Greatest Sacrifice   121

17. Asian Dilemma   128

18. The Prizes and Vietnam   136

19. Honors for the Duke   145

20. Fifty-Year Reckoning   152

21. The Grand Show   161

22. Losing a Prize   169

PART FOUR   Surviving the War

23. The Oldest Rebel   181

24. Turnabout   189

25. The War at Home   196

26. Another World   204

27. The Peace Riots   212

28. Tragedy at Kent State   220

29. Rommy   227

30. Saigon Revisited   236

PART FIVE   The Trials of Peace

31. Life after Vietnam   247

32. Turmoil at Columbia   257

33. Watergate in Retrospect   265

34. The Awards under Fire   273

35. A Prize Solution   283

36. Beyond Defeat   290

37. Auld Lang Syne   297

Southern Exposure   304

Notes   313

Bibliography   331

Index   335

The Art of the Diarist

After a lifetime's contribution of memorable lyrics to the American theater, Oscar Hammerstein II concluded, "There is no invariable or inevitable method in writing songs." [1]

That also is true of the art of the diarist. Just as a change of a few notes or words in a song may warm the heart, the perceptive diarist sometimes can vary his method or add new material to give a more valid picture of the society about him.

That has been my purpose in this work, based on the diaries and notebooks covering my twenty-two years as administrator of the Pulitzer Prizes. What I have done in effect is to complete the public record of the years of struggle for control of the prizes and the system through which they are selected. That applies as well to my activities and my close-up view of such combined awards as those for the Pentagon Papers, Watergate, and the Vietnam War together with individual prizes such as those for John F. Kennedy and William Randolph Hearst Jr.; nor do I overlook the denial of a similar honor to Duke Ellington.

It was my decision entirely to delay my public accounting even if what I did or did not do was no secret to my superiors either at Columbia University or on the Pulitzer board.

This is not to say that we diarists as a rule take ourselves as seriously as our more austere associates—the historians, biographers, and social scientists among them. The prince of diarists, Samuel Pepys, wrote once after a difficult weekend three centuries ago:

"After dinner, we all went to the church stile, and there we ate and drank, and I was as merry as I could counterfeit myself to be." [2]

Does the diarist, then, often counterfeit himself into merriment? I can observe only that pretense and cajolery, like outright lying, nullify the basic purpose of keeping a diary, which is to try to be honest with oneself. True, Pepys felt, in some of his sharper observations, that it would be prudent for him to resort to code, but he nevertheless had his say.

Code is not, however, something I have been obliged to use in this work about my long association with the Pulitzer Prizes. Nor was I ever handicapped, as my predecessors sometimes were, by the refusal of an earlier Columbia president, Nicholas Murray Butler, to consider Pulitzer Prizes for books, plays, or journalistic feats of which he disapproved. And usually, he carried with him the Pulitzer board of his time.

Fortunately for me, I never had to contend with such moral problems as the administrator of the prizes. Nor have I, in these eminently personal reflections on my years at Columbia, adhered to the convention in American journalism under which the writer refrains from serious personal commentary as I was bound to do in my earlier work, *The Pulitzer Prizes: A History,* for which some of my superiors acted as editors before publication in 1974. A lot of changes have occurred since, as these pages now demonstrate in my ninth decade.

To give the background of my diaries, they were begun toward the conclusion of my second year as a tenured Columbia professor in 1952 when I hadn't the faintest inkling of a future association with the prizes. I find the first notation of the Pulitzers in these hastily scrawled pages in 1953:

> April 23—The Pulitzer Prizes were decided upon today behind closed doors in the Journalism building. My friend Professor Richard T. Baker, who was in the room with the Pulitzer board and its secretary, Dean Carl W. Ackerman, offered to tell me in confidence who won in advance of the formal announcement, but I said no thanks. I didn't see much point in knowing about the Pulitzer winners when the news would become public shortly.[3]

I wasn't prepared for my unexpected appointment as the prize administrator as well as board secretary in 1954, therefore. And I was even less certain how I would be able to handle work that was so new to me in addition to my usually full academic load of instruction as a university professor. Such feelings were reflected in the opening pages of the diaries which, from then on, became more concerned with the Pulitzers than anything else at Columbia.

In addition to the long row of hard-backed red diary books, all except the first in 1952 measuring about 5 by 9 inches, I also accumulated a large box of smaller paper-backed notebooks that I used for many of my more or less official government trips on which I was sent during summers and other breaks in the academic routine. I have identified quotations from both by date and circumstance where necessary.

For this unique experience, longer than that of anybody else concerned with the prizes, except Nicholas Murray Butler, I am grateful first of all to the members of the Pulitzer board—what was then known as the Advisory Board on the Pulitzer Prizes—for maintaining me as their secretary and to Columbia University and its presidents for my added appointment as their prize administrator on a day-to-day basis. I also give thanks to the family of the first Joseph Pulitzer, the donor of the awards and the supporting Pulitzer Prize Fund; to his son, Joseph Pulitzer II; and to a grandson, Joseph Pulitzer Jr., the chairman of the Pulitzer board for all save the first year of my service. I was responsible at one time or another to all of them, except for the first Pulitzer and a surviving grandson, Michael E. Pulitzer, the current head of the Pulitzer Publishing Company.

In addition to Oscar Hammerstein II, Ralph McGill, and so many other Pulitzer Prize winners whose experience and example have been so important in the design and content of this work, my gratitude as always goes to JoAnn F. Hohenberg for having stimulated my interest, offered precise editorial suggestions when I needed them most, and guided me with wisdom and patience to see this book through to completion.

John Hohenberg

Knoxville, Tennessee
September 1996

PART ONE

Expanding Horizons

1   The Big Prize

Toward the end of my fourth year as a Columbia University professor, my dean asked me to join him at a meeting of the Advisory Board on the Pulitzer Prizes.

I wouldn't have much to do, he said. In my diary, I wrote that he'd suggested, "Maybe you can help me by taking a few notes."

It sounded interesting, particularly because I had no classes that sunny April morning in 1954, but I still had a large pile of student papers to read. No matter. The dean's business came first.[1]

The dean, Carl W. Ackerman, had been running the Graduate School of Journalism for twenty years while also serving as the Pulitzer Prize board's secretary. He always said he liked the work, but now he was in poor health and near retirement.[2]

On the way from our fifth-floor offices in the Journalism building to our ceremonial World Room two floors below, he explained that this session was to be the first of a two-day meeting of the Pulitzer board and probably would be devoted more to discussion than to voting. Most voting, he suggested, would come on the morrow.

At the time, he was carrying an armful of manila folders—the Pulitzer jury reports, he said—and a large book with the notation typed across its faded red cover on a white rectangle, "Minutes of the Advisory Board on the Pulitzer Prizes."

Once inside the World Room, I saw a group of men at an oval table in front of a stained-glass replica of the Statue of Liberty, set into a wall like a window. That, at least, was familiar to me. I'd obtained it as a deed of gift to Columbia from the mayor of New York City.

One of my earliest assignments after coming to Columbia at the end of a quarter-century's newspaper work had been to secure the Liberty Window for the journalism school. The gift was delivered before a city wrecking crew razed its home, Joseph Pulitzer's old New York *World* building, to broaden the approach of traffic to the Brooklyn Bridge.

3

Mayor Robert F. Wagner, so the dean reminded me as we entered the World Room, would be with us on the morrow to re-dedicate the Window.[3]

But now, at their oval table, it was clear that the dozen members of the Pulitzer board wanted to get to work. I had a brief introduction from Dean Ackerman as the day's note-taker, then retired on a chair next to his beside the chairman, the second Joseph Pulitzer, a son of the donor, who was large, aging, and wore thick glasses.[4] Like the chairman, ten of the others were newspaper executives who paid little attention to me. The only familiar face was that of the twelfth member, the Columbia president, Grayson Kirk.

Once Chairman Pulitzer called the meeting to order, the morning passed quickly enough in a discussion of various aspects of the jury reports Dean Ackerman summarized from the folders he had been carrying. Among the few arguments, various board members commented on the sickness that seemed to have overtaken American literature with the decline of the American novel—a supposition based on the fiction jury's failure to recommend any novel of the previous year for an award. But no matter how many board members offered proposals about books that few if any of the membership had read, the jury's "no award" remained intact.

There was similar dissatisfaction with the drama jury's recommendation of a light comedy, *Teahouse of the August Moon,* by a little-known playwright, John Patrick, which had been shown to a half-empty theater. But that jury report, too, remained firm.

Such details as these are not based on any miracle of total recall after so many years; instead, whatever notes I took for Dean Ackerman also were summarized in my diaries, from which this account is derived. In any event, all too often, I found myself so interested in the give-and-take around the table that my secretarial work suffered. But nobody except Dean Ackerman seemed to notice.

In a kindly way, now and then, the dean would murmur a reminder that he was depending on me to produce the minutes of this meeting, even though no voting would take place until the morrow. Still, before I quite realized it, the first day's session was over, the members of the board scattered, and the dean and I started for our offices after Chairman Pulitzer politely dismissed us with thanks.

Then, in the elevator that took us to the fifth floor, a curious thing happened—a scene so inexplicable at the time that I made no note of it when it happened but it still is vividly engraved in my mind. Instead of taking his manila folders of Pulitzer jury reports and the faded red book of Pulitzer board minutes back to his office, Dean Ackerman suddenly thrust the lot in my arms without a word. Just then, the elevator doors opened on the fifth floor and he scurried off along the corridor to his office as if the devil had been after him.

Not knowing what else to do, I took the documents and the minute book to my office, set them aside, and tried to fix my attention on reading and grading my latest set of student papers. But my mind wandered and I couldn't help wondering about the dean's behavior.

Next morning, when I joined the Pulitzer board in the World Room again, Dean Ackerman was nowhere in evidence and his chair was vacant. Chairman Pulitzer, seeming not at all surprised, motioned to me to sit beside him. As I took the seat the dean had occupied the day before, I felt others glaring at me suspiciously, except for President Kirk, who cheerfully nodded in seeming encouragement.[5]

Then, as recounted in my notes, Chairman Pulitzer said without emphasis, "Proceed, Mr. Secretary." I didn't know what to do, and so I asked, as deferentially as I could, "How do you wish me to proceed, Mr. Chairman?" There was a ripple of amusement among the membership, in which the chairman seemed to share.

Pointing with a thumb and forefinger to his thick eyeglasses, the second Joseph Pulitzer explained something I should have known about his ancestry but didn't: "My eyesight is poor, a family failing, so I must depend on you to announce each subject for a vote, briefly summarize the pertinent jury report, identify any member with a conflict of interest, and ask him to leave the room. Then I shall do the rest."

Again, I saw President Kirk nod smilingly and proceeded to follow the chairman's directions, but scarcely with the aplomb of Dean Ackerman. For by this time, it had occurred to me that the dean's casual invitation to be a note-taker at the Pulitzer board meeting had developed into something more important, perhaps by chance, perhaps with serious intent. But there was no time now for philosophizing.

Mainly because of a quarter-century's tough discipline in reporting the news or batting out a breaking story on deadline, I followed Chairman Pulitzer's orders in introducing the essentials for each prize. Then, he took over for final discussion and a vote with graceful but praiseworthy firmness.

I had no problems, except for the fiction prize, which eventually was passed as the jury had proposed, and the drama award to the jury's choice, *Teahouse of the August Moon,* which was grudgingly accepted. There were, however, unanimous votes for such favorites as *A Stillness at Appomattox* by Bruce Catton for the history award, and *The Waking* by Theodore Roethke for poetry.

But the biography jury's nomination of *The Spirit of St. Louis* by Charles A. Lindbergh touched off a brief but uncomfortable silence that seemed for the moment, alas, to stump the chairman, who was also the editor and publisher of the St. Louis *Post-Dispatch*. I couldn't help him; in fact, I wondered vaguely whether he might be an interested party to the jury's nomination, but decided not to act unless he voluntarily left the room.[6]

The book in question featured the aviator's pioneering nonstop trans-Atlantic flight from New York to Paris on May 20–21, 1927, described twenty-seven years later in the book named after the little aircraft he had piloted. But at a quick glance around the table, I saw doubts about the jury's selection, and I'm sure Chairman Pulitzer hesitated for the same reason.

At a guess, I suspected the reaction had to do with Lindbergh's ambiguous views as an isolationist before World War II; either that, or his undisguised annoyance with American newspapers. Of the former, I had but a vague memory; having covered the 1935 trial of Bruno Richard Hauptmann for the murder of the Lindbergh baby, however, I had a lively recollection of the aviator's antipress attitude.

At Flemington, New Jersey, the scene of the trial, I remembered that the press photographers had been tireless in their daily pursuit of Lindbergh and his wife, the former Anne Morrow, before and after court sessions. One scene in particular lingered in my mind—Lindbergh backing away between a double line of press photographers, bent down with an overcoat covering his head, until he noticed all cameras were at the feet of the photographers. Angrily, he walked off in a huff—scarcely grounds for opposing his book any more than were his prewar visits to Nazi Germany. Whatever the reasons for Lindbergh's often irritating public behavior, particularly toward the press, the editors swallowed their undoubted prejudices and voted his book the biography award. The music prize went to Quincy Porter.

As for the press awards, some did not follow juries' recommendations, but the end results seemed creditable. Long Island *Newsday*'s disclosure of a race-track scandal was given the public service gold medal. A newspaper in Vicksburg, Mississippi, won for its tornado coverage, the Philadelphia *Bulletin* for a numbers racket exposé, and the Des Moines *Register* for the results of an FBI loyalty check. Three individuals also were given prizes—the veteran, Jim Lucas, for his war reporting; Herblock (Herbert A. Block) of the Washington *Post* for cartoons, and an amateur photographer for snapping a waterborne rescue. In my diary, I concluded:

> April 23—Sometimes you have good days. Today was one of my best. In Dean Ackerman's absence, I acted as secretary of the Pulitzer board and ran the meeting for Joseph Pulitzer II, the chairman. President Kirk sat across from us at an oval table in the World Room.

It seems as if I'd done well enough because they elected me as secretary succeeding Dean Ackerman. It's only a one-year appointment, but I'm grateful for that. Chairman Pulitzer said I'd taken hold nicely, and Dr. Kirk seemed pleased. But most remarkable of all, I talked back to Arthur Krock of the New York Times—and got away with it.

As was explained to me later, I had an additional appointment as the day-to-day administrator of the awards for which I was at the time responsible, not to the dean, but to the president of the university.

Dean Ackerman never did explain why he decided the best way to break me in was to shove his papers in my hands in the elevator and let me struggle through the board meeting, not knowing what was to happen next. I suppose he wasn't sure whether I would qualify and didn't want to raise my hopes.

Anyway, as the board's records were to show, it was the first of fourteen such appointments annually for me, after which both jobs became mine permanently along with the tenured professorship. My Pulitzer service lasted until my departure from Columbia in 1976 for another honor at the University of Tennessee in Knoxville—the occupancy of an endowed professorship there.

When Dean Ackerman finally turned up with a big grin that first year, it was as Mayor Wagner's escort into the World Room with his City Hall entourage after the board meeting. But neither took notice of me among the board members who were invited to the ceremonial dedication of the Statue of Liberty Window.

The mayor's address was eloquent, there were tears in Chairman Pulitzer's eyes, and President Kirk congratulated all of us at the Graduate School of Journalism on the tribute to our founder and the donor of the prizes bearing his name.[7] After it was over, I made one more note in my diary. "It turned out to be a good day for the dean, too. He thoroughly enjoyed it."

2   My View of the Prizes

"I've been given a 10 per cent pay increase," I noted in my diary the day after the Pulitzer board meeting, "but the university people are very emphatic that it is for one year only. Unlike most newspapers, where a $10-a-week raise causes a great to-do, Columbia carefully refrains from giving professors big ideas."

It didn't matter to me. Like most newspaper people with literary interests, I'd followed the Pulitzer Prizes for years in celebrating the rise of writers, dramatists, and musicians as well as journalists. To me, many a Pulitzer laureate had whetted my own ambition while brightening American public life.

True, there also had been regrettable oversights for such honors, Theodore Dreiser for one, and unnecessary delays in prizes for others, notably Ernest Hemingway and William Faulkner as novelists. But now, for one year anyway, I would be on the inside, watching how these honors were decided upon and distributed. It was, to me, the chance of a lifetime.

Sometimes, in my early struggles as a journalist, it had given me more pleasure to follow trends in the nation's letters, drama, and music than it did to report on the usually dismal consequences of our political, economic, and social failings. And yet, now and then, a winner of a journalism award also was inspiring.

My favorite was Herbert Bayard Swope, when he was a red-headed, 200-pound battering ram of a reporter. He was still in his twenties when he electrified New York by developing the evidence that convicted a New York police lieutenant and four gangsters of the murder of a notorious gambler.[1] He went on to win the first Pulitzer Prize for reporting in 1917 for his correspondence from Germany in the New York *World*, Pulitzer's paper, which also had carried his crime reporting. Later, he won still more Pulitzers for exposing the Ku Klux Klan's barbarous conduct and smashing Florida's peonage system by disclosing whippings and murders in the state's prison camps.

After Swope left the *World*[2] as its executive editor, the paper finally died in 1931, when it was merged with Scripps's New York *World-Telegram;* but his enthusiasm for journalism and public service never diminished. Although I'd worked briefly on the *World* during his regime, I came to know him best while he was at the United Nations years later as the chief of staff for Bernard Baruch, then the US delegate to the UN Atomic Energy Commission.

Swope was still as interested as ever in the Pulitzer Prizes and investigative reporting, always favorite topics of his for my Columbia students and me in the UN Delegates' Lounge while foreign dignitaries also were trying to attract his attention. Undoubtedly, they preferred discussions about how to control the big bomb that destroyed Hiroshima and Nagasaki, but most of the time he kept them waiting—a break for the young people who were in training as journalists.

Another who attracted the attention of Pulitzer Prize juries, George Gershwin, never won an award. But he came to the notice of serious American music audiences in 1923, when he was only twenty-five, with his first performance of his *Rhapsody in Blue.* I heard him do the same work brilliantly at the piano the following year at Carnegie Hall with Paul Whiteman's orchestra, a masterly performance in the jazz age.

While Gershwin was still just a kid from Brooklyn, banging out jazz rhythms for a music publisher in Tin Pan Alley, he wrote his first hit, *Swanee,* and followed with Broadway acclaim for such shows as *Girl Crazy,* in which Ethel Merman sang *I Got Rhythm,* words by his brother, Ira. But once he composed his jazz masterpiece, the *Rhapsody,* he plunged headlong into music in its larger forms—*Piano Concerto in F* in 1925, *An American in Paris* in 1928, and his most memorable work, the folk opera *Porgy and Bess* in 1935.

It is all the more remarkable, in between, that he also was able to compose the music for the Broadway classic *Of Thee I Sing,* which won a Pulitzer Prize in 1932, not for him but for his three coworkers, George S. Kaufman, Morrie Ryskind, and brother Ira. As the involuted reason for his exclusion was handed down to me when I became the Pulitzer administrator, there was no music prize at the time, so George Gershwin couldn't be honored.[3] It was, of course, a typical Butlerean cop-out. If there had been no Gershwin music, there could not have been as great a show as *Of Thee I Sing.*

Another among the early winners, Archibald MacLeish, became in succession a Phi Beta Kappa scholar and a football player at Yale, a practicing Boston lawyer after taking his law degree at Harvard, and in between he was a captain in field artillery in the American Expeditionary Force in World War I. At thirty-one, however, he decided he wanted to be a poet, closed his law office, and for five years he traveled the earth with his wife and two children while writing poetry as he went.

One result, in 1933 when he was forty-one, was his first Pulitzer Prize for a long poem, *Conquistador,* inspired when he followed the route in Mexico of the Spanish conqueror, Hernando Cortez. Being a poet of independent means, MacLeish's pleasant life might have gone on indefinitely; but in the middle of Europe the Nazi storm was rising, freedom once again was in danger, and his work from then on developed a strident political character. His 1936 volume of poetry, *Public Speech,* became in effect a rallying cry among the arts in the cause of freedom. When in 1939 he saw a chance to join the Roosevelt administration as the Librarian of Congress, he did so. And two years later, just before Pearl Harbor, he ran the Office of Facts and Figures until it turned into the Office of War Information and he became its assistant director. He concluded World War II in 1944–1945 as an assistant secretary of state, then became one of the founders of the UN Educational, Scientific, and Cultural Organization.

But he never stopped writing poetry, won a second Pulitzer for his *Collected Poems* in 1953, and a third six years later for a poetic drama, *J.B.*[4] Throughout, he was ever the inspired poet of action, typefied by his definition. "A poem should not mean / But be."

Just as MacLeish was a predictable Pulitzer Prize winner, for he seemed to excel at everything he tried, Margaret Mitchell was probably the unlikeliest laureate of them all.[5] As Ralph McGill so often told me while he represented the Atlanta *Constitution* on the Pulitzer board, she was a small, rather timid reporter on the *Constitution* during the early 1930s and always was scribbling in a series of thick notebooks when she wasn't doing news assignments.

After a while, instead of sitting around the newsroom between assignments, she'd often work on her own stuff at a typewriter. And whenever she was asked what she was doing, she'd reply shyly that she was working on a story. That went on for some years until one day in 1936 a book came out in her name as author, *Gone With the Wind.* After publication in June, it was twice reprinted that month, three more times in July, six more times in August, and twice in September for the better part of its first million copies. It was submitted for a Pulitzer Prize in 1937 and won the award for the best novel of the year—one of the most popular romances ever published in the United States.

Margaret Mitchell was thirty-seven years old when she won her Pulitzer. She lived to see it transformed into a film about the love life of Rhett Butler and Scarlett O'Hara in the Civil War period that charmed movie-goers all over the world. And after her death in 1949, *Gone with the Wind* became a major attraction on TV schedules for succeeding generations here and abroad. In Japan, with an all-Japanese cast singing a score written by the American composer, Harold Rome, Rhett Butler still was making love passionately to Scarlett O'Hara.

But after *Gone With the Wind,* the Pulitzer Prize in fiction went to toughness in 1940 by honoring John Steinbeck for *The Grapes of Wrath,* an angry and often profane account of the suffering of millions of poor Americans during the Great Depression. A distinguished jury headed by Joseph Wood Krutch called it "the most powerful and significant of all the works submitted for our consideration." And yet, when Steinbeck first came to New York in the early 1930s, he couldn't hold a job as a $25-a-week reporter on Hearst's New York *American* and was forced to return to his native California to make a living. He finally came into his own with a Pulitzer at the age of thirty-eight.

Another 1940 Pulitzer, this one to Carl Sandburg, crowned the career of the son of a Swedish day laborer who had begun life as a day laborer himself after becoming a college dropout. He made an uncertain living thereafter as a labor reporter and film critic in Chicago until, as a stunning surprise, he won his first Pulitzer award as a poet in 1919 at age forty-one. For the rest of his life, he devoted himself to writing poetry, entertaining audiences by singing some of his verse while strumming a guitar, and working all the while on a four-volume life of Abraham Lincoln. The first two volumes, *The Prairie Years,* were published in 1926 and did so well that he was able to quit newspaper work. Thirteen years later, with the publication of *The War Years,* the last two volumes of the Lincoln biography, he won the 1940 Pulitzer Prize in history. And to cap the climax, his *Complete Poems* in 1951 brought him his third Pulitzer and nationwide acclaim. For Sandburg, in his own way, also was a man for the ages.[6]

With the coming of World War II, a quite different kind of Pulitzer winner emerged from the fighting on so many fronts involving millions of people of diverse races in the Atlantic and Pacific. In the wake of the first American defeat in the far Pacific, the fall of Corregidor and the Bataan peninsula in the Philippines to the rampaging Japanese early in 1942, the two highest ranking officers had been flown to Australia by order of President Roosevelt. And there one day, General Douglas MacArthur summoned his aide, Brigadier General Carlos Peña Romulo, a smiling little Filipino, to a makeshift American military headquarters office in Melbourne and sternly ordered, "Sit down, Carlos!"

Romulo sank wonderingly into the nearest chair, prepared for the worst since their escape from Corregidor. The general announced with a big grin, "Carlos, you've just won a Pulitzer Prize!"

The 1942 award had been voted by the Pulitzer board in New York for Romulo's forecast, published in the *Philippines Herald* of Manila toward the end of 1941, that the Japanese were preparing for a Pacific war against the United States. Just a month after the last article was published, the account of his 20,000 mile Asian journey, Romulo left his editor's job with the Japanese assault on Pearl Harbor and put on an

American uniform. Years later at the UN, when he was elected president of the General Assembly as the representative of the independent Philippines, he told me the story of MacArthur's surprise announcement in Australia and commented, "The general always had a great sense of the dramatic but he scared me half to death before he gave me the big news."[7]

For Ernie Pyle, a scrawny little war correspondent, fortyish and never very healthy, there never were any heroics—just a lot of foot-slogging with his beloved infantry from the Normandy beaches to Paris, then on into the Pacific. There, he was with the infantry again at the battle of Ie Shima and fell with a bullet in his right temple just six days after the nation had mourned the death of President Roosevelt on April 12, 1945. And once again there was mourning wherever American soldiers and war correspondents gathered because Ernie Pyle had been one of them—"the greatest," they called him. He earned his Pulitzer Prize at the cost of his life.[8]

Joe Rosenthal, an Associated Press combat photographer, was luckier. He crawled up the slopes of Mount Suribachi with the Marines under fire on Japanese-held Iwo Jima toward the end of the war in 1945, saw the Marines about to raise the American flag at the peak, and focused his camera just in time to snap the greatest picture of the war. He never knew what he had on film until the congratulations began coming to him, plus a 1945 Pulitzer Prize.[9]

Demonstrably, then, for more than three decades before I began my record of the Pulitzer Prizes in my diaries, the awards and those who had won them had made an enormous impact on American life. Perhaps Joseph Pulitzer might not have expected as much from his "germ of an idea" when he had first outlined it in 1902. But his son and his grandsons all had reason to be proud of the results of his benefaction.

3   An Atomic Crisis

I noted in my diary for February 2, 1955, "We just have to consider the Formosa Strait problem a major crisis. It's that serious." [1]

The tension soon became worse for our graduate journalism students at Columbia, particularly the young men of military age who were in good health. The first army reserve already had been hauled out of class early in that academic year of 1954–1955, a signal that trouble with China lay directly ahead.

Dean Ackerman, however, hadn't helped any in his opening greeting to the incoming class the previous fall. As I noted in my diary:

> Sept. 23—We opened the school year at Columbia with Dean Ackerman cheerfully predicting that some of our students in the Class of 1955 would survive an atomic global war to report what happened. The students seemed rather appalled at the prospect, but then this was the first time they'd heard from our dean.

Four days later, in my own greeting to a Columbia night class, I don't believe I did much better. Nor was I any more self-assured the next night at the first meeting of a university Seminar on Peace. This was the dismal record:

> Sept. 27—My first night lecture that year in the School of General Studies before a class of 22, half of them graduate students. It was a scary time but at least I didn't talk to them about covering a global atomic war.
>
> Sept. 28—Attended Professor Philip Jessup's Peace Seminar for faculty people and he and Professor Jim Hyde asked us, their fellow faculty members, 'Is it possible to build a trusted world authority which will be able to prevent a global war that would destroy humanity?' The dean's opening address to our incoming students seemed to have one answer to the question, to wit: Anybody who survived could write a

13

news story about a global atomic war . . . Anyway, it was an interesting evening.

Once Congress passed the Formosa Strait resolution giving President Eisenhower the power to employ the armed forces of the United States "as he deems necessary," all of us at Columbia knew perfectly well that anything could happen in this dangerous game of one-upmanship we were playing with China.

In any hostile move by the Chinese toward Taiwan, the Nationalist Chinese refuge across the Formosa Strait, it was clear that the United States Seventh Fleet, still being stationed there, would be seriously involved. The president himself said as much when he warned, in a news conference, that the Communists would have to "run over the 7th Fleet" to attain any objective in this high-stakes game of chicken.

Laying it on the line still more in response to a reporter's question over whether he was ready to use tactical atomic weapons "in a general war in Asia," Ike promptly responded, "Yes, against strictly military targets."

A few days later in answer to a similar query, he added for good measure, "Every war is going to astonish you in the way it occurred and the way it was carried out. So that for a man to predict . . . what he is going to use, how he is going to do it, would I think exhibit his ignorance of war. . . . You just have to wait."

That was the most damnable part of our academic dilemma of 1954–1955, the most difficult as well for both students and faculty: the waiting—waiting—waiting.

It fell to me also, standing before several score young Americans of military age in a Columbia University classroom, to be torn by conflicting emotions as the days slowly dragged by without any sign that tensions were easing.

As a teacher and old army type of World War II vintage, I couldn't help warning my charges continually not to overreact in anything they wrote for publication or reported over the air that had to do with the crisis. But as the administrator of the Pulitzer Prizes, I constantly had to repel the urge before these young people to praise the heroics of the war correspondents of the past who had made such great names for themselves by their bold conduct under fire.

What all of us realized, those who faced the reality of military service in this China crisis and their elders in university classrooms, was that this test of strength with China had burst upon us almost without warning.[2]

Early in Ike's first term as president, the Chinese Communists had killed thirteen Americans—eleven of them airmen in uniform—whom a Chinese court had sentenced to prison as spies. At about the same time, the Nationalist Chinese who'd fled to Taiwan had called for a "holy war" against Mao Zedong in Beijing and his Communist forces.

Next thing we knew, the Chinese Communists were shelling Quemoy and Matsu, the island groupings just off the Chinese coast that could be used as stepping stones in any general offensive against Taiwan. Nor did the Chinese commanders pay any attention to Ike's warning not to try to "run over the 7th Fleet" to press their attacks against their Nationalist enemies.

It did appear, therefore, to the Pentagon's military strategists that the Chinese apparently had decided after the drawn Korean War to maintain the pressure on the United States to withdraw across the far Pacific. But President Eisenhower gave no sign that the United States could be licked without an atomic war.

Turning up the heat, Premier Jou En-lai in Beijing then demanded the "liberation" of Taiwan, to which Chiang Kai-shek's people responded with their plea to the United States for a "holy war" against their Communist foe. As a relatively new Pulitzer Prize administrator, I was sufficiently concerned before the first student appeared in the late summer of 1954 to have my 1955 journalism juries approved by the Pulitzer board. After that I filled out the letters, drama, and music juries with the intention of getting the nonjournalism entries to their judges as I received them.

It seemed to me that an earlier preparation for the prizes in such threatening circumstances might ease our collective burden toward the end of the 1955 jury verdicts on the products and issues of 1954. At any rate, that is how I decided to operate before the 1954–1955 academic year began.

Because of these preparations, fortunately, I was able to respond to an invitation by the Air War College for an early fall symposium on public affairs and the Formosa Strait crisis.[3] With Robert U. Brown, the publisher of *Editor & Publisher* magazine, and the Hearst columnist, Bob Considine, the three of us spoke for about two hours before 160 senior Air Force officers at Maxwell Air Force Base in Alabama, then answered questions about the public's attitudes toward Air Force intervention for another 75 minutes.

I am not sure what all this proved, but our Air Force sponsors seemed satisfied and saw us off back to New York. Still, all we actually knew then in the early stages of the crisis was that our naval and Air Force positions off the China coast were vulnerable, as witness the Quemoy/Matsu attacks. Also, in the case of the Columbia J-school, neither I nor anybody else in our faculty could be certain from then on how many male students with 1-A military draft numbers or reserve classifications would be snatched from us without notice.

There was one other interruption just before classes began for the

1954–1955 academic year when a terrific Long Island hurricane isolated me and a few prospective students near me for the better part of three days 90 miles from New York City. I noted in my diary:

> Aug. 31—The gale howled with enormous force that bent our old elm trees in Aquebogue and dashed great sheets of rain against our 1827 house. It rained so hard at times that we couldn't see the old red barn only 30 yards away. Toward noon, the storm ended and we began cleaning up but we were isolated without electric power.
>
> Sept. 1—We fixed a garden hose so we could draw water from the Hallocks' next door, but we were without lights for three days. The whole area was in the same fix, which I'm sure affected some of our incoming students. By the time I called the Pulitzer Prize office, my secretary told me I'd already lost a fiction juror—Professor Irwin Edman, who died of natural causes during the storm. It took me another two weeks to locate a proper replacement and obtain all the necessary Pulitzer board clearances.

Once I returned to Columbia and Dean Ackerman opened the school year with his proposed coverage of an atomic disaster by our incoming students, my secretary in the Pulitzer office and I had almost daily interruptions, as is usual during a Pulitzer season, from jurors who asked for a particular book, or tickets to a new show, a copy of a major feat of newspaper coverage at home or abroad, and so on. Of course, such services for jurors were by no means as important as the work of the Pulitzer board. But providing for the needs of the juries, too, soon required the addition of another secretary in the Pulitzer office for as long as I was expected to continue to be a full-time teacher.

The tensions over the Formosa Strait, added to all else, intensified the faculty's problems at the outset of the school year before we even saw our first incoming student, as witness the following:

> Sept. 15—I attended a UN luncheon for Secretary General Dag Hammarskjold during which he seemed quite nervous. He admitted to us that he had no hope of reducing East-West tensions, doubted that the incoming General Assembly could do anything worth mentioning, reminded us of the Chinese veto in the Security Council and in effect apologized because he had been able to do so little to keep the peace. Then, he put the whole sad business off the record, which didn't matter, because he had accomplished zero.
>
> Sept. 16—For the first time in two years, I called on Bernard M. Baruch at his home, 4 E. 66th St., in New York, but he apparently was no longer advising Presidents. At least, he said he hadn't heard from Ike, whom he supported for President, about the Formosa crisis and admitted he didn't know what could be done about it. Anyway, he autographed a copy of his latest book for me.[4] At 84, he still was tall

and straight, spoke quickly but wandered a little toward the end and seemed more deaf than usual.

Sept. 22—The Overseas Press Club invited Harrison Salisbury, just back from Moscow as a New York Times correspondent, and I went as Bob Considine's guest to hear the latest on Soviet-Chinese relations in connection with Formosa Strait. He wasn't given much time for that, however, when an old line anti-Communist, Max Eastman, criticized his Moscow coverage. Anyway, we gave Salisbury an ovation after he defended himself—but, no news from the Strait.[5]

Oct. 7—I also had no luck when I went to Arden House today for the 6th American Assembly, President Eisenhower's own creation while he was at Columbia, and I'd hoped he might have something special for us. But he didn't even send us a greeting. Anyway, the food was good.

Oct. 12—The Peace Seminar again but there was no peace in sight. We spent the evening arguing whether an institution could also be a concept or whether a concept could become an institution. Phil Jessup told us off as we wound up by telling us we'd all danced gracefully on the head of a pin.

For the Columbia J-school class of 1955, there also were changes in form and substance as the year continued and I managed to maintain my teaching schedules along with my Pulitzer work. I still ran my Washington and Foreign Correspondence seminar and tried as often as I could to cover a UN session at least once a week with four or five students on a rotating basis. The Formosa crisis was always prominent in the news, which sharpened the students' interests.

In addition to my regular night class in journalism in General Studies, I also had a twice-a-week session on journalistic ethics in the Journalism building. But my greatest effort there was the all-morning writing program once a week. I'd become the newly appointed director of a group of faculty people and outside professionals who helped me conduct a three-hour class in writing for all our students. It had been the heart of our program during my student years and, to me at least, it retained its importance.

It pleased me that the 1955 students, for the most part, felt as I did. With few exceptions, they seemed to respond to the challenge of the weekly writing class under deadline pressure. And because it was the first major course at Columbia that I'd supervised, I put myself under the same pressure as the students. Sometimes, when I spotted one who had a writing block, I'd take over his or her typewriter for a few minutes to provide a fresh start.

Cruel and inconsiderate procedure? Perhaps it was. But I was never a teacher of theoretical writing and the interventions, such as they were, seemed to do the students no harm. Some of the young men and women kept in touch with me for many years after they left Columbia and the Pulitzer Prizes.[6]

Toward the end of October, while the students and I were planning their election night coverage in the first week of November, there was an unexpected diversion from the Air Force once again. An Air Force officer, Colonel Max Boyd, came to see me at Columbia at just about the time of the first break in the Formosa Strait affair and proposed a Far East tour of duty for me. What apparently was being asked of me was an impartial, non-service-connected estimate of the reactions of China's neighbors in East and Southeast Asia to the developing crisis into which the United States was being drawn.[7]

It was something I felt I could do, mainly because of the five years I'd spent in UN and foreign coverage before coming to Columbia, but I told Colonel Boyd I couldn't get away until the academic year was over. He expected it, said the latest encounter with Communist China wasn't expected to end for a long time, and concluded that I'd hear from him. With that, he returned to Washington and the Pentagon to report to his superiors while I went back to finishing the election-night schedule for my students.

For the weekend, Columbia was celebrating Charter Day, the founding of our predecessor, King's College, in 1754. Britain's Queen Mother, the widow of King George VI, was to be the guest of honor at a Waldorf dinner on October 30 and a convocation next day at the Cathedral of St. John the Divine in New York City. Bob Harron, our University public affairs director, urgently needed help with the turnout of TV, radio, and press people and photographers, so I filled in as a diversion from all else that preoccupied me.

As I noted in my diary for the ceremonial at the cathedral and elsewhere, "The Queen Mother saw so much of me that she finally seemed to recognize me with those glacial blue eyes. And another distinguished guest, Adlai Stevenson, began grinning whenever he saw me surrounded by cops, reporters and photographers."

Despite the extra engagements of their supervisor, the students stayed late the night of November 2–3 to get out their election-night extra and the video reportage that accompanied it. It pleased me enormously that they correctly called the two closest and most important races. One was a narrow victory by a Democrat, Averell Harriman, for governor of New York State, the other another close one in favor of a Republican, Jacob Javits, for attorney general. Once we'd analyzed what had been done and how it had been accomplished, I tried to give credit to everybody involved for a professional performance. And all the time I was wondering how I'd be able to work with the Pulitzer board if the Formosa crisis deepened, as people in Washington seemed to expect.

More because of my own concern than anything else, I issued a public notice of the coming February 1 deadline for journalism entries for the 1955 Pulitzer awards. The letters, drama, and music juries all had earlier deadlines and some had already reported their recommendations.

I remember my surprise when the fiction jury that year came with a report favoring a first novel about the extinction of the buffalo over William Faulkner's latest, *A Fable*. At that time, Faulkner had never won a Pulitzer Prize and I wrote in my diary, "I think they [the fiction jurors] are out of their minds but I must send their report to the Pulitzer board as drafted whether it makes sense or not. There's so little nowadays that makes sense in any case."

The drama jury at about the same time had presented the Pulitzer board with another problem by recommending a play about Noah's Ark by Clifford Odets, done partly in dialect. It was called *The Flowering Peach*, but on Broadway the trade already was referring to it as *The Greenberg Pastures*. It was obvious, however, that the joke, if any, would be on the Pulitzer Prizes if it won an award.

It was in this confused manner that the year ended for me with the Christmas break and a prolonged argument with a draft board that had insisted, to our faculty's annoyance, on plucking one of our students directly from class. Having been deputized to oppose so arbitrary a decision, I did my best for the victim but came off with little satisfaction. I conduced in my diary:

> Dec. 2—A Brooklyn draft board has summoned another of our students for immediate duty. He was told he'd have to leave school in four days. I told the Selective Service attorney in charge of draft deferment cases, in a phone conversation, that our faculty very probably would admit no more 1-As for 1956 and would give preference instead to men who had had previous military service. The only satisfaction I could report to my faculty colleagues was a deferment for the Brooklyn student until January, then it was shoo-shoo, baby. The draft boards mean business and there isn't much a university can do about it.

A week later, during one of my regular UN sessions with students, all of us were sobered by a chance remark from a UN official about the secretary general's worries over an atomic confrontation in the Formosa Strait between China and the United States. There is only a note in my diary about it, but that day even the possibility of nuclear warfare hit me hard:

Dec. 9—To the UN with my foreign seminar and I detect a very uneasy feeling there about the beginning of a new offensive by China in the Formosa Strait. I saw Ralph Bunche, the UN's Nobel Peace Prize winner for his work in Palestine, and I was told he's now been assigned to a UN atomic research project. Coming at the time of the latest moves in Formosa Strait, I could understand the Bunche appointment. If anybody can bring about a settlement there, he can.[8]

It was in this manner that the year ended for us at Columbia with my time divided between a full schedule of instruction for graduate students, interceding in vain for at least one candidate for the military draft, preparing for the possibility of a conflict with China in the Formosa Strait, and assembling jury reports for the next meeting of the Pulitzer board to vote on the 1955 prizes.

It was scarcely the kind of sheltered academic life I'd envisioned when I accepted a tenured professorial appointment in 1950. Even so, when a friendly city editor of the New York *Times* invited me not long afterward to leave Columbia to join his staff, I thanked him but decided to stay put. Regardless of military crises, nuclear threats, and academic problems, the Pulitzer Prizes had become a part of my life.

4   New Times for the Prizes

The second Joseph Pulitzer, who had welcomed me to the Pulitzer board as secretary and day-to-day administrator, died in St. Louis on March 30, 1955, at the age of seventy.

In the last months of his life, so I was told later, he often expressed the hope that his oldest son, Joseph Jr., would succeed him as the chairman of the Pulitzer board as well as the publisher of the St. Louis *Post-Dispatch*.

Although we at Columbia had not expected the second Pulitzer's death fewer than four weeks before the 1955 Pulitzer board meeting, it did not upset our arrangements as much as it saddened us. While Professor Baker as associate dean prepared to attend the funeral in St. Louis as the representative of the university and the J-school, I was asked by President Kirk to send formal notification to all other board members of the chairman's death.

After a decent interval once that was done, again at President Kirk's suggestion, I took an informal poll of the board members I was able to reach about a new chairman and reported that there would probably be enough votes for Joseph Pulitzer Jr. to replace his father. What President Kirk had wanted was an orderly transfer of authority at so uncertain a time for the nation, and it seemed likely to me that the board would react accordingly.

The third Joseph Pulitzer then was forty-three, a graduate of Harvard who had spent most of his life working on the St. Louis *Post-Dispatch* editorial staff. He already had taken over the management of the newspaper, so I was told, and was proceeding as his father had wished. There also was a younger half-brother, Michael Pulitzer, also a Harvard graduate and a lawyer, who was taking over another family newspaper in Arizona and was expected later in life to be next in line for leadership at the *Post-Dispatch*.

Over the more than twenty years that Joseph Jr. and I worked together on the Pulitzer board, I came to know him fairly well, but we associated and consulted each other only in connection with the prizes. He was nearly always pleasant to talk to, rather small and distinguished in appearance, with a handsome face set off by a mass of curly brown hair and a trim, lithe body.

During all the years Joseph Jr. had served as an apprentice to his father and the top editors of the *Post-Dispatch*, he had learned the know-how of the news business and became a working newspaper editor. I could make no mistake about that, despite what seemed to me like his much greater interest in the rather stiff-necked world of modern art. But then, my own special interest was the even more snobbish world of modern music in its larger forms, so I could scarcely hold Joseph Jr.'s involvement with modern art against him.

It also was no surprise to me to discover early in our long association that he, like his father and grandfather, was an articulate and devoted liberal Democrat of the old school. He habitually inquired into the political leanings of new candidates for the board to replace those who retired after a maximum of three successive three-year terms, but I never knew him to make political considerations a condition for a vote on a prize. He did have a problem, however, a distinct form of ancestor worship that caused him to oppose any major change in the annual decisions on Pulitzer Prizes that deviated from the conditions in his grandfather's will.[1]

As might have been expected under such circumstances with the accession of a new board chairman, the approach to the prize selections that year of 1955 was one of the strangest within memory and is worth expanding on through the entries in my diary just before the meeting of the Pulitzer board:

> April 12—There were a lot of administrative chores at Columbia today in addition to Pulitzer affairs. I was stuck with handling the arrangements for the selection of a student sports writer for the annual Grantland Rice Award, another student as the winner of a cash prize offered by the old newspapermen in the Society of Silurians, an Admissions Commitee meeting on the Class of 1956 and so on. I'd rather have continued my regular teaching and board preparation, but somebody had to take care of these other matters and I was selected. My luck.
>
> April 13—It looks like "The Flowering Peach" will have unexpected competition for the Pulitzer Drama Prize from a new play that has just opened and technically shouldn't be considered until next year, but the rules on eligibility are vague. Anyway, I saw the new show

tonight—Tennessee Williams's "Cat on a Hot Tin Roof"—and it is superb theater even if it is also very depressing. Burl Ives as "Big Daddy" gave the best acting performance of the season in my judgment even if Barbara Bel Geddes, as "Maggie," seemed to me to be just another debutante trying to be an actress. Still, on the whole, I think it's no wonder that "Cat" already has won the Critics' Award and maybe the board will have to take notice of that.

However, in a sudden shift of attention from the Pulitzers that was typical of my Columbia experience, I had to deal once again with events that were transpiring in Formosa Strait within ten days of the 1955 meeting of the Pulitzer board. Secretary of State John Foster Dulles had warned once more of the seriousness of the Formosa Strait crisis by insisting, as he had earlier in the year, that there was "at least an even chance that the United States will have to go to war."[2]

By evil chance that day, my annual discussion of war correspondence was due in my Foreign Seminar and there was no way I could substitute for it at the last minute because I had to work on arrangements for the prize meeting. And so I made this entry in my diary following another disturbing meeting with my students:

> April 15—My usual seminar on foreign affairs, but I had to talk on war correspondence and assign each student to do a piece on a correspondent of note—a typical library research project. Having heard or read of Dulles's latest threat, most of the students were thoroughly nervous, especially the men of military age who knew of the trouble we'd been having with the Brooklyn draft board. I tried to explain that I wasn't taking up where Dulles had left off, that this was in effect the same lecture and the same assignment I gave every year but they didn't believe me. Anyway, the Formosa situation is heating up again and most of the students still remember Dean Ackerman's opening lecture of the school year when he predicted an atomic war that some in the class would survive to cover.

This was the position as it existed with the opening of the last week of April, during which I would meet the Pulitzer board for the 1955 prizes. I didn't know what to expect from Joseph Pulitzer Jr., how the older members of the board would receive him, and what unexpected proposals he might make that would create unanticipated difficulties. In retrospect, I'd guess that Joseph Jr. was almost as uncertain as I was because I have a disturbing memory of how tense and shrill he was from the moment he reached Columbia at the beginning of the week.[3] The diary entries tell their own story without much elaboration:

April 25—First thing this Monday morning, Joseph Pulitzer Jr. was on the phone from St. Louis and didn't get off for much of the morning. I did my best for him but he's pretty nervous about whatever actions the Pulitzer board may take on Thursday. So, for that matter, am I. I worked on my presentation to the board and got the Columbia public information office busy on the publicity background. Also, I took time out to introduce Leonard Lyons, the New York Post columnist, for a lecture before my news writing class on his operation and the work of his rivals. At least, it wasn't war talk.

April 26—Did a lot of phoning for the new Pulitzer, who is still in St. Louis. He seems to be curious about the way the board lines up politically, wanted to know how the members voted for president in 1944, 1948 and 1952. How would I know? Anyway, most of them are Republicans, I'd suppose, but if there are any Democrats outside the Pulitzers they're undoubtedly on the conservative side except for Ralph McGill.

April 27—I'm told that Arthur Krock of the New York Times, the most imfluential member of the board as well as the White House Press Corps, intends to retire after this year and eventually will be replaced by Turner Catledge the Times's executive editor. At least, I know I can depend on Krock for 1955, which is a relief. Other than that, I've finished my arrangements for tomorrow's board meeting but can't quite figure out Joseph Pulitzer Jr., who was on the phone again to me this morning.

April 28—The first business of the opening day of the Pulitzer board meeting was to elect the third of the Pulitzer line as chairman. After the meeting was called to order by a senior board member, Arthur Krock moved Joseph Jr.'s nomination, it was seconded and I announced a unanimous vote had been cast. The new chairman, who had been waiting outside the World Room, then was summoned and took over while I handled the agenda as his father had asked me to do. There were no speeches, no hoopla. It was strictly business from then on.

However, we ran into trouble with the first item, the Fiction Jury recommendation for Milton Lott's first novel, "The Last Hunt." In a brief but eloquent speech, Hodding Carter nominated his fellow-Mississippian, William Faulkner, for his latest novel, "A Fable." I needed only a glance around the table to determine that Faulkner, after being ignored for his greatest works, finally would be given a Pulitzer Prize as our great living novelist. And so it turned out, by a unanimous vote.[4]

Directly afterward, I had to talk our new chairman out of upsetting the Drama Jury's verdict for "The Flowering Peach" in favor of the Williams play, "Cat on a Hot Tin Roof," mainly because nobody around the table had seen it yet—an embarrassing circumstance. The board quickly decided to ask the chairman to name a committee of two to see the "Cat" that night as an unexpected contender for the 1955 drama award and report to us tomorrow.

The rest of the awards followed jury recommendations except for the cartoon jury when the board voted a prize for the St. Louis Post-Dispatch cartoonist, D. R. Fitzpatrick, which we were told had been a last wish of the second Joseph Pulitzer.[5]

My own favorite for a prize, Gian-Carlo Menotti's opera, "The Saint of Bleecker Street," won the music award. There also were two journalism awards that interested me—a national prize for Anthony Lewis of the Washington Daily News, who had just applied to the New York Times, and a local award for Roland Kenneth Towery, the editor of the Cuero (Texas) Record, whom I'd known in World War II while we both were in the Army,[6]

April 29—This was the board's formal meeting in the Columbia Trustees' quarters where I read my proposed citations for all the awards after the board voted the drama prize to "Cat on a Hot Tin Roof" on the recommendation of our instant two-member substitute Drama Jury. Otherwise, instead of going into executive session to adopt all the prizes, a formality, I recorded a unanimous vote for them in the minutes.

On Arthur Krock's motion, I was re-elected secretary and prize administrator for the ensuing year after a second from John S. Knight. A few others offered complimentary remarks that made me feel good, which ended my second year with the Pulitzers. The rest was now up to the university's public information office, which had to run off a press release on the 1955 awards over the week-end and make it public once the university Trustees gave their final approval on Monday afternoon, May 2.

May 2—The Pulitzer Prize announcement was delayed more than an hour because the Trustees couldn't muster a quorum to approve the work of the Pulitzer board before the awards could be made public at 4:22 p.m. It was a comment on the manner in which the first Joseph Pulitzer had designed the control for the prizes that were established at Columbia in 1911 after his death and were awarded beginning in 1917. As Columbia had interpreted the donor's intentions the Trustees were given the options of approving or disapproving the prizes as voted by the Pulitzer board—known then as the Advisory Board on the Pulitzer Prizes. Otherwise, the board's decisions could not be changed, which was what led to the Trustees' concluding vote on the day the awards were announced.

I wish I could report that the second announcement of the Pulitzer Prizes in my administration received massive coverage and touched off salvos of applause for the wisdom of the juries and the board. But that was reserved mainly for the winners, the organizations they represented, the newspapers that were favored, and others who were interested in the awards for letters, drama, and music.

Instead of compliments from the public, my phone in the Pulitzer office that first Monday in May was burdened mainly with complaints from juries that had been reversed and prospective candidates for prizes who had been disappointed.

Francis Brown of the New York *Times,* one of my fiction jurors, told me how disappointed he was that Milton Lott had not won the fiction award, and I replied quite frankly that it finally had been Faulkner's year. Professor Carlos Baker of Princeton, the other fiction juror, said he'd been so upset at the Lott reversal that he worked in his garden for an hour with his rapid-digger, felt better, and said he'd write an encouraging letter to Milton Lott.

When Professor Oscar Campbell, the drama jury chairman, called, he said emphatically that he didn't think much of Tennessee Williams's play and wasn't impressed when I told him how *Cat* had been picked for the prize.[7]

The most difficult call I had to handle was one from an old friend, Sylvan Byck of King Features, who had been a member of the cartoon jury and wanted to know how Fitzpatrick had won when his work hadn't been recommended. It was the first and last time I ever risked a personal friendship in offering my annual jury appointments.

When Joseph Pulitzer Jr. and I met later that day for a review of his first prize session and my second, both of us agreed almost without discussion on a one-day session of the Pulitzer board from then on and no overnight inspections of last-minute proposals for a change in jury recommendations. My attitude was not altogether based on principle because I realized at once, in the case of my friend, the cartoon juror, that if such jury reversals continued to any great extent in years yet to come, I would have great difficulty in persuading distinguished authorities to serve as Pulitzer jurors. Nor was this likely to affect only artists and experts in the fields of letters, drama, and music, who served on juries that worked for almost an entire season for only a token compensation. That was true even of journalists, most of whom still traveled and consulted as jurors at the expense of their news organizations.

It was, as I explained to the new board chairman, a very real weakness in the Pulitzer system that was likely to hurt the awards and undercut their prestige with the public. I am not sure that the third Pulitzer agreed, for he made no comment of substance on my observations. But his approval of a one-day session, at the very least, would make it impossible for another board committee to inspect a new play overnight and cause a jury's decision to be reversed. And with that I had to be content.

There was a much happier reaction to the 1955 awards on the night after the annual announcement for the nationwide viewers of the Edward R. Murrow TV program, *See It Now.* This was how I recorded it:

May 4—Ed Murrow's "See It Now" program on TV last night surprised us all with the complete story of Ken Towery's expose of a Texas scandal in his little paper, the Cuero Record, which won a Pulitzer Prize on Monday. Even more remarkable, Murrow had captured a TV sequence of Towery getting the news that he'd won a Pulitzer Prize.

As I understand it, Murrow's crew had been shooting the story of Towery's expose on the spot in Texas, knew he'd been nominated for a Pulitzer and took a chance that he'd actually win an award. It was a fine job anyway both for Ken and Murrow. I'd thought so little of Towery's prospects when his exhibit came in that I hadn't even guessed that it had a chance of an award and had promptly forgotten about it. Then Ken's face flashed on the tube at the climax of 'See It Now' in an expression of tense anticipation, wonderment, then dawning realization of a big break followed by a burst of sheer joy.[8]

It was worth all the difficulties we'd been through in the judgment by juries of more than 1,600 exhibits in all categories. Once all the loose ends had been gathered, the checks and certificates sent to the winners together with notes of thanks to the jurors, President Kirk gave me permission to attend the Air War College at Maxwell Air Force Base and also, later in the summer, to circle the Pacific for the Air Force from Hawaii through Taipei, Manila, and Tokyo—an assignment that had come to me late in the academic year through the Air Force secretary's office and Colonel Max Boyd.

As I began planning for my examination of the Air Force's position during the long confrontation with Communist China over Taiwan and the Formosa Strait, I had the satisfaction of knowing that we had lost only two members of the class of 1955 to the armed forces and had a full complement of seventy acceptances, a majority being young men of military age, for the class of 1956 beginning in the fall.

By early June after commencement at Columbia, the crisis seemed to have abated in the Formosa Strait. Premier Jou En-lai had been quoted at an African-Asian conference at Bandung on April 23 as saying that China had no intention of fighting the United States and was ready to negotiate the problems of Taiwan (Formosa) and the Far East. Three days later, Secretary Dulles had come right back, after consulting President Eisenhower, with a proposal for a cease fire. Jou thereupon announced at Bandung that China was prepared for a peaceful settlement of outstanding issues.[9]

As I left for my swing around the Pacific for the Air Force, I knew that an informal cease-fire prevailed, but nobody could predict how long it would last. Nor did Secretary Dulles or anybody else guess how long the Soviet Union would stand by as China's armoror in this deadly contest of threat and bluff in the Far East. Early in June, I noted that there had been a bit more assurance of a truce, this time from India. Its envoy, Krishna Menon, had been sent to Beijing to intervene in the crisis and luckily obtained a Chinese pledge to release four of the American airmen who had been seized as hostages nine months ago.

In embarking from Hawaii on my projected six-week, 20,000-mile inspection of the Air Force's position in the far Pacific, therefore, I had reasonable assurance that I would be able, upon my return, to prepare for a more peaceful year at Columbia with the class of 1956 and my third annual experience with the Pulitzer Prizes.

5   Test for a Teacher

If I ever had decided to leave Columbia and the Pulitzers in the early years of this dual responsibility as teacher and prize-giver, it would have been to join the Air Force as a civilian executive.

I hadn't given second thought to a prospective return to newspapering. Teaching at the university level had seemed to me to be much more important, a judgment I shared with those teachers in New York who remembered me as a student.

But the Air Force was different. It was a new and challenging experience that I couldn't easily turn aside (and eventually I served as a special consultant to three Air Force secretaries in the Eisenhower administration). So at the beginning, the swing around the Pacific that I was asked to do in the summer of 1955 became in effect a test of my future.

It was clear enough to me at the outset that the people at the Pentagon were testing me; for what purpose, I did not really know. But I also was testing myself on that trip, continually asking, "Do I belong as a teacher at the university level? Am I at the same time capable of administering the Pulitzer Prizes?"

I expected the Pacific flight would help produce some answers for a rather puzzled forty-nine-year-old professor who had, by good fortune, been accepted by a great university as a qualified instructor for the next generation of journalists in national and international affairs.[1]

What had made this self-examination possible in the first place was a tantrum at the White House—one of President Eisenhower's fits of temper that plagued his associates. I find the following record in my diary for the early spring of 1955:

> March 29—Ike is in a bad mood.
> He's rebuked Defense Secretary Wilson, ordered a cut of one-third
> to one-half of the personnel in the armed forces' information staffs and

isn't accepting any arguments from the service chiefs. Also, he wants civilians put in charge of all military press operations, no matter what they're called.

The reason for Ike's annoyance is certainly clear enough to anybody who knows the Pentagon even slightly. For example:

1. The Air Force recently put out data on the restricted Falcon rocket, a no-no if there ever was one.

2. The Navy at about the same time leaked estimates that the Chinese planned to invade the island groups of Quemoy and Matsu (which have small American garrisons) after April 15 and a Navy captain had an article in a major magazine about the new atomic submarine. That one's supposed to be top secret.

I'm afraid under the circumstances I was cold comfort for Air Force Secretary Talbott (I'm an occasional consultant) because I told him he was way overstaffed in his information services. Before he could renew our conversation about a civilian chief for his information services, I begged off and caught the next plane for New York.[2]

Having seen Ike in action at Columbia, I knew enough not to try to second-guess him on his own turf in Washington.

To explain the last cryptic reference, the Air Force secretary, Harold Talbott, had asked me as early as 1954 to become his director of public information. I had noted in my diary:

April 14—Secretary Talbott abruptly told me today that he wished I would accept a post of chief of information services for the Air Force, currently occupied by a two-star general. It was so unexpected that I gulped and finally gained presence of mind enough to say that I couldn't leave Columbia. He said somewhat grumpily that he supposed I couldn't leave—but that he could very easily put a civilian in that two-star general's job and would prefer to do it. Anyway, I flew back to New York on the 5:30 plane, worried and confused.[3]

My Pacific trip in the summer of 1955 developed soon afterward, and now I really was tempted to trust my future to the Pentagon. My mission had to do with a management report on the Air Force's Far East information services, a survey last produced by an eight-member team of civilian examiners in forty-five days.

Patently, my conclusions would be matched against those given by my predecessors and the judgment of the Air Force secretary's military and civilian staff people. But I knew perfectty well now that I, too, would be testing myself at the same time to determine, at least for the next few years, where I really belonged in my early fifties.

In World War II, while in the army, I had had a similar though more limited responsibility in accompanying American troops across the submarine-infested Atlantic on a great British transport before D-Day. My report then had been for the army's transport service and had to do with the readiness of the ship's British officers and crew to handle emergencies in the case of a U-boat attack, which was narrowly averted one clear day in mid-Atlamtic while several thousand American troops were aboard.

That, at least, wasn't currently anticipated during my Pacific flights. The Chinese Communists had shown no disposition to follow up their threats with actual combat against the Seventh Fleet. Nor was the home front braced for a repetition of Rear Admiral Patrick. Bellinger's eight-word radio flash from Pearl Harbor on December 7, 1941:

AIR RAID PEARL HARBOR THIS IS NO DRILL.[4]

Whatever civilian concern there was appeared for the most part to be limited to the electronic media and the editorial pages. Beyond a few intemperate anti-Communist outbursts here and there on my trip from New York and Washington to Oahu, I had noticed no signs of rising war fever in public places.

To nearly all outward appearances, it had seemed to me to be the start of what was likely to be a relaxed and prosperous summer at home. Except for the unlikely possibility of an all-out Chinese attack in the Formosa Strait,[5] the policy of the Eisenhower administration appeared to be to keep it that way.

After my arrival at Hickam Air Force Base on Oahu, I had to wait a few days for the return of my passport with the required visas and other documents for so long a trip to Asian lands. I made these notes:

> Hickam AFB, July 1—My first assignment is a headquarters report for Major General Sory Smith, the Air Force information director for the Pacific. What he wants of me is more than I anticipated. And no wonder! Defense is a bigger industry in Hawaii than both sugar and pineapple so anything that sends shock waves through the air base is likely to have repercussions in the islands—and that goes for the Formosa Strait affair even if everything now seems relatively quiet. It's still taken very seriously here.
>
> July 5—I have completed a variety of inspections at Hickam over several days before today's takeoff for the long flight to Taiwan via Wake Island. I have the best of company—General Smith, who relieved me of the concern I'd had from the start that I'd have a hard time gathering information. In fact, because of my work since coming here, I have begun to see rather dimly the scope of the Air Force's headquarters problem in the Pacific even if the Formosa Strait challenge by the Chinese could be settled shortly. The area is so large and varied and is inhabited by so many rival peoples that a commander is likely to have to cope with the unexpected more often than not. Getting reliable information will always be a problem.

Taipei, July 7—Taiwan surprised me from the moment I spotted it from the air. It really is an enormous island, half again the size of the state of Maryland, with about 20 million people. The Chinese, that is the two million who fled from the mainland, are a minority but they're the dominant military power and have President Eisenhower's support. No matter how well the White House has managed to play down the very real danger involved in this contest with China over the mastery of 90 miles of open water, the stakes still remain very high.

Taipei, July 8—The surface air of good cheer, the theme of most meetings after my arrival with General Smith, has lasted only as far as the dining room door. Beyond, wherever I've been in a private conference between the American command and our Taiwanese hosts, I've nearly always felt the tension quite as much as the uniformed officers around the table. That was the way our visit began, General Smith's and mine, when we were met at the airport here by General Tiger Wang of the Taiwan Air Force and Brig. Gen. Ben Davis, commander of our Taiwan installation, the 13th Air Force.

We drove through Taipei, its crowded streets, stall shops and pedicabs, to the big Taipei Guest House where we had an enormous lunch, Chinese style, with General J. L. Huang, General Wang's colleague. For the time being, I'm rooming with Colonel Pug Evans, who had flown from Tokyo with the American Far East Air Force Commander in Tokyo, General Lawrence Kuter. There's also a general officer here from Manila in the Philippines so I have, in one room, the responsible military authorities who will have to face any renewal of the Chinese threat except, of course, the admiral in charge of the 7th Fleet. I may not get to see him this trip.

It was an altogether strange position in which I found myself as a Columbia University professor on summer's leave who had agreed to try to do a study of the Air Force's position among the peoples of the Pacific. I had only a six-week limit for travel and conferences with the requisite military and civilian authorities who were available in the area.

My first reaction after arriving in Taipei, quite honestly, was shock. What I had to do, almost at once, was to control my emotions and school myself to listen to both my Taiwanese hosts as well as the American military commanders who had come here.

No matter what I heard in these initial conferences, my instinct as a journalist was to ask questions—and still more questions—but I soon realized that playing the role of a visiting reporter would get me nowhere. The questions served only to divert the attention of these high-ranking American and Taiwanese military people and interfere with an orderly presentation of their concept of the problems facing them in the Asian Pacific. I decided reluctantly that there would be ample time for questions later in my visit, which ended my interruptions and cleared the atmosphere. I resumed my note taking:

Taipei, July 8—Taipei is far less hopeless than I'd thought before arriving here and its defending Chinese commanders have a hard-won knowledge based on somewhat less than brilliant military experiences on mainland China plus the creation of a military establishment here in Taipei. With the backbone of American strength, both the Far East Air Force and the 7th Fleet, this island could put up a strong defense if it had to and I believe the one military theorist who told me quite seriously that we didn't have to depend entirely on a last-ditch atomic defense. If there is ever a chance for peacetime development here, U.S. money is bound to make a whale of a difference.

I was up early, had a breakfast discussion with General Huang that didn't get me very far and better luck with others who were willing to level with me. It became a matter of intense interest to me to run into a crew of working journalists I'd known for years, first of all Tad Szulc of the New York Times who was most helpful, and later Spencer Moosa of AP among others. Then I met unexpectedly with Nancy Yu, a former student from Columbia, who runs the local China Post.

Later at dinner at the Grand Hotel, I was the guest of General Shu, the Chinese chief of staff, who had a number of his fellow-officers with him, an affair that turned into a working session in the absence of our superiors who spent their time calling on Chiang Kai-shek. After a little experimentation, General Shu and I found we could get along very nicely in German so the evening was reasonably productive.

Taipei, July 9—Breakfast with General Huang, which was long on food and short on information. Frankly, I did better with another former student, Gene Loh, city editor of the China Daily News, and Commander Barney Solomon, U.S.N. These talks led to a working lunch at General Tiger Wang's home in a beautiful Japanese-style cottage at which General Ben Davis also sized up the position as he saw it. During the afternoon, I attended a Chinese Air Force military display, plus marching band, in honor of General Kuter just before he took off on a return flight to Tokyo. A short time afterward, I checked some of my facts and observations with Gen. Smith before leaving with him for Manila, my next stop.[6]

Clark AFB, July 9—As Carlos Romulo once said to me at the UN, "Our national interests and those of the United States aren't necessarily identical any more." It was evident in almost everything I saw, heard and experienced in my brief visit to Manila from and back to Clark AFB. In particular, young Filipinos I met and talked to seemed much more nationalist than their elders, but it is not something I'd want to accept other than as a quick impression on short acquaintance. For the area and for the region, I had some frank appraisals from the base commander here, his PIO and the few correspondents I was able to see. Stayed at the BOQ.[7]

Manila, July 10–11—Before leaving Clark AFB, General Kuter extended my travel orders for Tokyo. Then at lunch at Clark, before leaving General Smith, I put in a good hour or so discussing some of the matters that deeply interested us both. After General Kuter took off, I made arrangements for the Japanese part of the trip at the Japanese consulate. The clerks may not have been overly cooperative but our arrangements finally were completed, after which I checked into the Manila Hotel for the night. Mr. and Mrs. Ford Wilkins—he's the editor of the Manila Bulletin—had me to dinner at their home and we talked a long time about current Filipino attitudes—the fate of our bases here, troop arrangements, etc. To me, it was a quite different attitude toward the Philippines—nothing at all like the 'Little America' of my days in Seattle as a schoolboy. Now, I dealt with Asians.

Taiwan, July 12–13—There was a typhoon off Okinawa so I had to lay over in Manila but finally arrived back in Taipei before noon on the 13th. I talked for quite a time with Colonel Kreider of the American command and several others, checking my facts and my impressions, then put up for the night at the Grand Hotel in Taipei.

Tokyo, July 14—It was a long day, beginning with a flight from Taipei to Kadena Airport in Okinawa, which is big and modern and efficiently run by the acting CO., Colonel Curtis D. Sluman, who took me to the Officers' Club for lunch and gave me a strictly professional view of conditions in the region, the state of affairs with Japan, a distant view of the Chinese in the Formosa Strait. From Bobby Vermillion, a correspondent I'd known well and favorably, there was the journalist's view as well. At 2:40 p.m. I left Kadena on the last leg of the Tokyo flight, saw Fuji-San against a setting sun from 75 miles out and landed at Haneda Airport at 7:25 p.m. Colonel Evans picked me up, checked me in at the Sanno Hotel, gave me a fleeting view of the Ginza on our way to the University Club for dinner and assured me that all arrangements for the Tokyo phase of the trip had been completed.

Tokyo, July 15—A full day of all-American conferencing plus a trip to Stars and Stripes, Pacific Edition, and dinner at the Washington Heights Officers' Club before returning to the Sanno Hotel. You could live this way in Tokyo for years without meeting Japanese socially or knowing very much about them. From what little I was able to see of American military life in Tokyo, we had built a small community for ourselves outside the Japanese world, typically American in every respect. One senior officer I met, who remarked on the position, told me quite frankly that he'd never even been in the Tokyo subway, didn't think it was safe.

Tokyo, July 16—My job is almost done. General Kuter discussed the position with me in a thoroughly frank but friendly manner and seemed to support most of the conclusions I laid before him, something that was expected of me. With somewhat less confidence, I made tentative proposals that I thought might help bring Japanese-American relations out of the deep freeze without making us seem like impatient foreigners knocking at the front door. General Kuter was non-commital on some, approved of others, but suggested it would be best for all concerned after so long and difficult an experience to speak my mind about the current position in Taiwan, in the Far Pacific and especially for the situation of the Far East Air Force at a time when the Formosa Strait problem seemed to be easing.[8]

Tokyo, July 17—At last, a day completely for myself. After breakfast, I left the Sanno Hotel with two fellow-guests, officers of the Philippine Air Force—Colonel Godofredo M. Juliano and Colonel Jose L. Ranuedo. We rode the Tokyo subway, taxicabs, shopped the big stores and specialty shops on the Ginza, had a big lunch at the University Club and loaded up on gifts for our wives. We were, unabashedly, tourists and I loved it. So did they, even though we never saw each other before or after our experience. For dinner, Colonel and Mrs. Evans were my guests at the University Club roof.

Tokyo, July 18—The windup. Although there was a summit conference in Geneva on the Formosa Strait problem, my Air Force people here in Tokyo took no chances on an immediate settlement and proceeded as if the conflict was about to escalate. I began with an FEAF staff conference, next was given a security briefing on bases, then a briefing by a two-star general on Japanese politics and current economics.

There was time out for a lunch with the wire service people including some I know—Bob Eunson, AP; Rutherford Poats, UP and Marvin Stone, INS. Afterward, I was given a private briefing by another two star general on American ties (or lack of them) with the Japanese educational establishment, the universities and the press. I also was able to enjoy a reunion with Marv Stone at the Press Club, dinner with the Evanses and back to the Sanno Hotel late, exhausted.

Tokyo, July 19—The flight back to San Francisco from Haneda was aborted, spark plug trouble. Back at the Sanno Hotel, I cut a slice in my head by failing to duck low enough through a junior size Japanese door and bled profusely before the medics got to me. They even called in Chaplain Propst for me.

Tokyo, July 20—Quite an experience in moving time backward. We took off from Haneda at 2:40 a.m. today (Wednesday), crossed the international dateline and landed at Midway at 4:17 p.m. (Tuesday) among the goony birds. A Navy captain toured the island with me, fed me and got me back to the airport in time for a takeoff at 5:37 p.m. (Tuesday) and we landed at Hickam AFB in Oahu at 11:37 p.m. (Tuesday), a little more than three hours before our takeoff from Tokyo.

After being escorted through Customs with my Hong Kong suit, new shirts and sports jacket, together with silks and silver for Dorothy, I was put to bed at Wheeler AFB for a very short night's sleep. Then, on my second July 20, I attended General Smith's morning staff conference, cleared with him the broad outlines of my report for him and for the FEAF in Tokyo and prepared to leave for home.

What I knew now was that we were in the Asian Pacific to stay but not, supposedly, on the Asian mainland.

The last stage of the homeward journey from Hickam AFB, completing the 20,000-mile, six-week Pacific trip, had been time-consuming but otherwise uneventful. For the mid-1950s, the time was a normal 9.25 hours to Travis AFB in California, flying at a 300-mile-an-hour average at 9,000 feet and landing at 12:45 A.M. July 23. By 8:00 A.M. after a few hours' sleep, I was at San Francisco International Airport being put aboard United flight 700 to Idlewild at New York, where Dorothy met me shortly before 8:00 P.M. and drove me home to Aquebogue, L.I.

All Dorothy and I were interested in just then was being together again, getting my things in the car, and driving the last 90 miles to eastern Long Island and the old homestead. By the time we arrived, I was too tired to do more than sit at the table, make a few ceremonial passes at Dorothy's dinner, point to my presents for her, and stumble off to bed. Mercifully, I had a few days off then before catching up on the few summer's developments at Columbia and the Pulitzer office, then taking off for the Pentagon to discuss my report with John McLaughlin, senior adviser in the Air Force's front office, and arrange for its form and distribution. As I noted our conclusions in my diary:

> July 27—Brigadier General Bob Scott, chief of Air Force information, and John McLaughlin, the top civilian in the front office, were glad to see me. We agreed on the scope of the classified report, its distribution to General Kuter in Tokyo-and General Smith in Hawaii among others and my comments on public understanding of the United States position among publics in Taiwan, Manila and Tokyo.
>
> I also was given a copy of the last management report by my predecessors, the eight-man team that took about as much time as I did to make the swing around the Pacific. While I was at the Pentagon, I was told I would soon be dealing with Donald Quarles as Air Force Secretary replacing Harold Talbott, who was resigning over what politely called a conflict of interest between his private business and his official duties.[9]

I never did see Secretary Talbott again. While I was preparing my Pacific report at home in Aquebogue, he resigned and Secretary Quarles replaced him on August 15 at just about the time I'd forwarded my report to Bob Scott and McLaughlin. President Eisenhower, still busy with the fallout from his attendance at the Geneva summit with the heads of the British, French, and Soviet governments, called the Talbott resignation "the right decision."

Of course it was. While my meetings with the secretary had been infrequent, I had seen enough of him to realize that he was headstrong often to an irrational degree. And while he never interfered in any of my assignments, he did seem to like bossing the military, which sometimes brought him into conflict with many in the uniformed service. To the end, he was his own headstrong, irascible self.

By coincidence also on August 1, the Chinese Communists freed eleven American airmen they had been holding since the previous September 3, when they first began shelling Quemoy and Matsu and touched off the Formosa Strait crisis. It was their way of casting aside the last pretense of struggle, which caused President Eisenhower to reflect long afterward:

> For nine months, the administration moved through treacherous cross-currents with one channel leading to peace with honor and a hundred other channels leading to war or disaster. . . . In the Formosa Strait in 1955, we refused to retreat and the enemy, true to his formula, for a while tried harassment but refused to attack. The crisis . . . cooled; it would not heat up again for three years.

President Eisenhower had every right to be pleased with the outcome of the tensions in the Pacific in 1955. As he observed in retrospect, he had had "the courage to be patient." By contrast, the big show at Geneva in the latter half of July that year produced little but ill will between the new Soviet dictator, Nikita S. Khrushchev, on the eve of his assumption of power in Moscow, and the leaders of the West—British Prime Minister Anthony Eden, Premier Edgar Fauré of France, and President Eisenhower. The only new event of importance at Geneva was the introduction of what Ike called his "open skies" plan for the Soviets and the West, which Khrushchev rejected.

My Air Force service continued from time to time under Secretary Quarles until he was promoted to deputy secretary of defense and later under his Air Force successor, James H. Douglas Jr.[10] Meanwhile, President Eisenhower's heart attack on September 23, 1955, put him out of action for much of the rest of that year; but his reelection in 1956, given a decent time for recovery, already was a virtual certainty. Once again, he had demonstrated his mastery of the military art. With patience and faith in the use of American air and sea power, he had turned aside a Chinese Communist challenge to the United States in the Pacific. Despite the military draft, no substantial use of ground troops had ever been necessary.

Had his successors followed his lead in keeping American ground forces out of mainland Asia, the home of 60 percent of humankind, the United States might have been spared the shameful humiliation and ultimate tragedy of the Vietnam War—a defeat by a fourth-rate Communist military power.

As for myself after that summer's difficult experience in dealing at first hand with an international crisis in the Pacific as an Air Force consultant, I no longer had to undergo self-induced testing to decide what I wanted to do with the most precious years of a long and varied career. I settled down for good on Morningside Heights, with weekends usually at our home on eastern Long Island, to teach at Columbia and administer the Pulitzer Prizes.

For all else, as I wrote in my diary after the end of my last year as a Pulitzer Prize juror in the 1980s, "I'll be passing by."

6   With Hearst in Moscow

There was a brief period early in the cold war when the masters of the Soviet Union seemed to be offering to modify their hostility to the United States and Western Europe. At the time, it made headlines and electronic gossip.

But in the end, it failed, and the cold war continued until the Soviet Union collapsed toward century's end. And so, except for the purposes of history, it matters little that Nikita Khrushchev offered the West an ill-defined "peaceful coexistence" in 1955.

What remains of interest is that the proposal was made through a visiting team of Americans headed by William Randolph Hearst Jr., like his father an outspoken anti-Communist. To be sure, the character of the "peaceful coexistence" that Khrushchev offered through the Hearst team was really little more than an uncertain truce with the United States and the West on Soviet terms.

Still, it was a sign, however vague, of Soviet uncertainty about the future and it deserved to be explored even if the Hearst team had no illusions about its essential character. That was why the American ambassador to Moscow, Charles (Chip) Bohlen, welcomed Hearst's interviews with Khrushchev and his two premiers, Georgy Malenkov and Nikolai Bulganin. It was in our interest to determine how far the Soviets would go toward seeking peace with the United States. It turned out to be a hesitant first step. Beyond working on an Austrian State Treaty, Khrushchev didn't put much substance behind his offer of "peaceful coexistence," made through the eldest son of William Randolph Hearst Sr. and his associates, Frank Conniff and Joseph Kingsbury-Smith.

The interviews granted by the masters of the Soviet Union at the time, therefore, remain as a symbol of the cold war era. Their views in that winter of 1955 were considered so vital that the Hearst team's output was widely published and broadcast in and outside the United States beyond their original source, the Hearst newspapers. I well remember that I read these accounts closely because I expected Bill Hearst would be after a Pulitzer Prize, the award created by his father's bitterest journalistic foe.

The mass-circulation London *Daily Mail* already had given this estimate of the Hearst team's reporting:

> No Western journalist—in fact, no Western minister or ambassador—has talked to so many top figures on both sides of the Cold War front in so short a time. No man has been granted such insight into high places in both Eastern and Western policies." The *Mail*'s editors then concluded, "It was . . . the most remarkable mission in post-war journalistic history."[1]

The interviews captured national and world attention from the outset because the United States at that time was still facing a crisis with Communist China over the use of the Formosa Strait as a threat to Taiwan and the American-Nationalist Chinese forces there. Under the circumstances, it was appropriate that the Hearst team's first interview was with Vyacheslav Molotov, the veteran foreign minister, and the Formosa Strait confrontation became the first subject to be discussed.

Although the Soviet Union wasn't involved, what the Americans asked Molotov to do was to assess the problem. At the time, President Eisenhower was planning to rescue the small American garrisons in the offshore island bases of Quemoy and Matsu, despite the Chinese threat. What Molotov concluded was that he couldn't speak for his Chinese allies, but he himself would not try to harm the Americans. As it turned out, whether or not he had anything to do with it, the Chinese Communists also weren't looking for a fight when Ike evacuated his few soldiers from the islands soon afterward.

The discussion of the Austrian State Treaty was more direct. In response to Molotov's complaint that American bases seemed to be encircling the Soviet Union, it was suggested to him that an Austrian pact might open the way for talks on other base issues. And so, to many of us, it seemed a hopeful sign when the Soviets completed the Austrian negotiations in 1955.

It also helped that Khrushchev decided on an interview with the Hearst team after Molotov's talk. This was the point at which the new boss of the Soviets, then the leader of the Communist Party, made his offer to the West of "peaceful coexistence." The Hearst team's response was to suggest a cultural exchange program at the outset, beginning with a visit of the Bolshoi Ballet to the United States and followed by other Soviet artists. To some extent, that also led to the appearance of a few of the greatest of Soviet classical artists in the United States. But after the defection of one visiting dancer, Aleksandr Godunov, the program lagged.

Premier Georgy Malenkov and his replacement, Premier Nikolai Bulganin, had little to offer The Hearst team but pleasantries because Khrushchev still was the director of Soviet policy and Soviet forces. Even Marshal Georgy Zhukov, who contributed so mightily to the defeat of Hitler's Nazi armies before Stalingrad, could suggest no new course toward the improvement of Soviet-American relations.

Others whom the Americans interviewed while Khrushchev still was in an agreeable mood included the composer Dmitry Shostakovich; Stalin's daughter, Svetlana Stalin; Galina Ulanova, the prima ballerina of the Bolshoi Ballet; and several of the monks of the monastery of St. Sergei, seat of the Russian Orthodox Church.

The Hearst team made several other visits to Moscow in subsequent years, with Bob Considine substituting for Kingsbury-Smith, including the one featuring a kitchen debate between Vice-President Richard Nixon and Khrushchev. But the follow-ups never attained the impact and unexpected success of that first venture. It was the product of a long chance that Bill Hearst took only a few years after the death of his father, and it paid off.

I first became aware of the Hearst organization's bid for a prize for Bill Hearst and his two associates when one of them, Kingsbury-Smith, turned up at the Pulitzer Prize office at Columbia with two assistants on January 5, 1956. What he wanted to do more than anything else was to examine some of the prize-winning Pulitzer exhibits of past years and plan for the one he told me the Hearst organization would be entering for the Hearst team before the February 1 deadline.

I gave him the entry papers for his exhibit, tried to answer his questions about the preparation of the material, and looked forward to its arrival, which occurred toward the end of the month. It was complete in every respect—the texts of the major interviews, the account of how the venture originated, and how it was carried out in style.[2]

The preparation of a catalogue covering all the submitted exhibits for letters, drama, music, and journalism was my first concern, for which my secretary required extra student help. Once that was completed and made available to the members of the Pulitzer board and its juries, the next step was to prepare for the appearance of the journalism jurors in mid-March 1957.

There was, however, a brief exchange with the new chairman of the Pulitzer board, Joseph Pulitzer Jr., after he came to Columbia on February 10 to speak at a memorial for his father, Joseph Pulitzer II, in the World Room. When I gave the third Pulitzer his catalogue of all the entries, which then consisted of more than a thousand books and newspaper exhibits (I could only guess at the number of shows the drama jury had seen and the concerts the music jury had attended), I mentioned Kingsbury-Smith's visit and the nomination of the Hearst team through the receipt of its exhibit.

Pulitzer Jr. was immediately interested. There is a note in my diary under that date, "JP Jr. thinks Bill Hearst may be elected to the Pulitzer board. Also, that Bill's series on the Hearst team's visit to Moscow may win a Pulitzer Prize." To that I added, after listening to JP Jr.'s memorial address before the Statue of Liberty Window in the World Room and attending Dean Ackerman's luncheon for him, "Anyway, it was a mild and beautiful day and I relaxed." [3]

That, briefly, is how I knew even in early February that we were in for a struggle in the Pulitzer board over a prize for Bill Hearst and his team.

Although I was greatly attracted to the administration of the awards, there was another esteemed academic institution at Columbia that was of more immediate concern to me that year. I refer to sabbatical leave, through which tenured Columbia faculty people are given their choice every seventh year of a semester's leave on full pay or an academic year's leave on half pay.

Since I was now midway through my sixth year at the J-school, I had already elected to take the first semester's leave in the 1956–1957 academic year which, added to my free summer months, released me from my regular academic function from early June and commencement in 1956 until the opening of the second semester in early 1957.

In authorizing a modest pay increase for me, President Kirk had approved my return to the university on February 1, 1957, at the Pulitzer Prize deadline, so that I would be available not only to teach my classes but also to handle the Pulitzer jury reports, the secretarial function at the annual Pulitzer board meeting, and the announcement of the prizes. The outgoing and incoming deans seemed to have paid little attention to these matters, so I anticipated no problems as far as the university was concerned. As for the Pulitzer board, the position there was somewhat different, but it didn't concern me after President Kirk told me to proceed with whatever plans I had for my sabbatical.

Dorothy already had elected for passage to Europe in June on the *Queen Elizabeth II;* upon arrival of the tickets early in the new year, we had gone around the old homestead in Aquebogue making noises to each other that resembled our concept of steamship sirens—something like "woo-oo—ooh" or a variation, "wee-eee—eeyah!" Even if we had nothing better to do, what I had counted on was a pleasant visit in the English countryside, to be followed by a swing through Scotland and Wales and a leisurely auto trip through France after a visit to Paris, with a windup in the Spanish countryside for the year-end holidays.

To both of us, the arrangements sounded marvelous. And since I'd covered the territory in past years, I expected few arguments and no trouble. We had even decided on selling our well-worn Ford and buying a small British car, a Hillman, which we hoped would carry us through the summer in Britain and Europe until we disposed of it.

All this had so intrigued us both that I had resolutely refused still more offers to return to newspaper work, an experiment in TV, and consideration for another job running a newspaper. Somehow, the notion of a sabbatical leave from a great university appealed to us both at that juncture.

But as the weeks passed, the Air Force began intervening, tentatively at first and later with what seemed like a firm offer to work in Europe. I was told that Secretary Quarles would like me to study American bases in Europe where there had been problems with surrounding communities, that the engagement would last only a few weeks, and I would be free to go ahead with whatever plans I already had made.

In view of my previous Air Force service during the Formosa Strait crisis, I couldn't very well refuse. And so, as a first step, we gave up the notion of selling our Ford and buying a Hillman for our European tour because we had no idea how long the Air Force would keep me busy. What I had to wait for were orders from Washington and acceptance of my mission by the theater commander, Bill Tunner, a three-star general, whom I knew.[4]

Meanwhile, I had been engaged by Saul Padover of the Carnegie Endowment for International Peace to inquire into the effectiveness of the UN Department of Public Information and make recommendations for its future. All I knew at the outset was that most correspondents either had little use for the UN's information services or thoroughly mistrusted them. It was not a very favorable situation but, international sensibilities being what they are, it also would be difficult to change without a lot of hurt feelings among mainly Asian UN staff people.

In every respect, that spring was one of my busiest. In addition to my regular classes at the J-school and the night class in General Studies, I was expected to produce an Air Force report for Secretary Quarles on the conduct of his Public Affairs office; another for the Carnegie

Endowment on the UN Department of Public Information; prepare for the receipt of the letters, drama, music and journalism jury reports for the Pulitzer Prize board; and make arrangements for my sabbatical leave.

The following entries from my diary in the spring semester are a fair reflection both of my activities and my state of mind:

March 12—The Pulitzer jurors for journalism arrived—a merry, healthy, wonderfully competent crew of old pros and I felt very much at home with them. Half of them finished in one day, the rest wound up next day. In international reporting, the Hearst team was the first recommendation followed by two others. Meanwhile I also ran my all-day national affairs seminar today, my night class in General Studies and wound up with a first class headache.

March 15—At the UN in the morning doing Carnegie interviews with correspondents and others. Lunch with Saul Padover and George Beebe to discuss my work to date, then back to the school to take up where I left off. Tonight we saw "The Matchmakers"—a play by Thornton Wilder that closed in three days in 1938 and should never have been revived.

March 16—A howling snowstorm, three to five inches, and Douglas Moore, his two daughters and his son-in-law couldn't make it for dinner so we were stuck with a 12-pound roast beef. I'll be going to the Pentagon later this month.

March 19—Worst snowstorm of the year and my General Studies class was canceled but Dorothy's bridge club met at the Women's Faculty Club and she was there. Bridge players don't give up.

March 20—Spent the day at the UN interviewing correspondents on the Carnegie report but found nobody with a good word for the Department of Public Information, sorry to say. I suggested to Padover that Secretary Hammarskjold, at the very least, should try to find a senior UN official who was sympathetic to the requirements of the news media. The UN, as far as news processing is concerned, is taking a bad rap for no good reason. It was the first day of spring and the city was paralyzed by 13.5 inches of snow for a few hours.

March 26—I saw Air Force Secretary Quarles. He said he was glad I was going to Europe on my sabbatical to do the Air Force information study there and directed me to report to him. He has grown vastly in assurance since I first met him last year and now seems like a tough little grey rooster. I still must wait for the approval of the theater commander.

April 3—To the UN and picked up completed copies of my questionnaire for the correspondents and others. Also had a note from President Kirk giving me a pay rise. In the evening, I attended a university Peace Seminar session and listened to a lecture on Russian economics that left me a little limp. I was never one to enthuse about economics, especially Russian economics.

April 4—My orders arrived from USAFE (US Air Forces, Europe). As Secretary Quarles's consultant and special assistant, I am to visit Air Force installations in Europe and am due to begin work the day after I reach Paris once the university semester ends. Canceled the Hillman auto deal, also hotel reservations in London and sent passport to be stamped for government service plus necessary visas.

April 12—I made my oral report on the Carnegie project at Endowment headquarters . . . I spoke too long but I think the report was effective. What I recommended was a complete reorganization of the UN Department of Public Information. It is long overdue. What is needed more than anything else, so I said, was an honest day's work in that office.

April 16—Secretary Quarles has circulated my headquarters report on Air Force Information Services to General Twining, the Air Force chief of staff, and the Department of Defense. General Scott writes that 'without my assistance the program would not have gotten off the ground.' Sometimes you make the right call.

April 21—I finished the UN job for the Carnegie Endowment for International Peace. It was difficult and I did my best for the UN. The report ran to 70 pages, close to 20,000 words. I'm awfully long-winded.[5]

April 23—President Kirk told me Ed Barrett of Newsweek would succeed Carl Ackerman as dean but asked me to stay on to run the Pulitzers after my sabbatical . . . I mailed a $461 check for our passage, Dorothy's and mine, on the QE II for Europe directly after commencement.

April 25—Dorothy and I attended a matinee of "My Fair Lady" and thoroughly enjoyed it. It's a handsome musical version of Bernard Shaw's "Pygmalion"—not as lovely a score as "The Chocolate Soldier," but Shaw's "Arms and the Man" is better material for a big musical. Still, "My Fair Lady" is memorable.

April 27—Joe Pulitzer Jr. must have made his grandfather twirl in his grave by leading the fight for a Pulitzer Prize for Bill Hearst and company for their Moscow exclusives. The Pulitzer board fought all day and Joe and Bill Mathews finally convinced the majority, so Hearst at last wins a Pulitzer Prize.

It's quite a contrast. Joe is a liberal, Bill is not. Joe is Harvard and Bill is Toots Shor's. Joe collects art and Bill collects datelines. And they're both too nice to be newspaper publishers.[6]

In all the excitement, the other letters and journalism prizes were barely discussed, mainly because there was no disagreement with jury choices. Only I must add, to preserve my own self-respect, that "The Diary of Anne Frank" is American only because the the two dramatists who based their play on her book are American.

April 28—The Pulitzer board ratified its choices, then re-elected me as secretary and administrator on President Kirk's motion even though I'm going to be on my sabbatical in Europe. The president also told the board about Ed Barrett as the new dean and Joe Pulitzer said rather testily that he "didn't know the man." Ah, well, Harvard to Princeton.

May 7—After the Columbia trustees ratified the Pulitzer board's choices this first Monday in May, the results were made public and tonight Bill Hearst was simply crowing over winning one. But I really meant my congratulations. I like young Bill and I like young Joe, who fought for him. On the 10th by invitation, I showed up at Toots Shor's for Bill's celebration and saw a lot of old familiar faces, including Frank Conniff and Joe Smith, Bill's partners on the Moscow trip. We all sat around and talked and had a few drinks (mine, a Coke as usual), then had a buffet supper.

June 1—My passport and extended orders have arrived by registered mail from Washington. In 12 more days we sail for Europe.

June 9—The end of commencement week and all the news is about Ike's monumental tummy ache and his operation. While his doctors have renominated him for president, to be ratified no doubt by the Republican National Convention later this year, it seems a peculiar way of conducting the nation's political future. But then, these are strange times. What Dorothy and I are about to do now is to leave our '1827 House' here in Aquebogue until we return from Europe next year. Our grouds are beautiful. I saw the first red rose blooming in our garden. The first strawberries have come from the fields. It's June—and soon we'll be in Europe."

I was able to complete the Air Force's requirements in Europe first of all in that European sabbatical year, file my report to Secretary Quarles, and obtain clearance for the remainder of my stay in Europe with Dorothy. It was her first visit to Paris since my Indian trip—and to one with a French heritage, Paris always was heaven to her.[7]

Toward early fall, we began a 9,000-mile European tour by car, paused at Lake Lucerne in Switzerland, circled through Italy, and back through France. Then, by October, we were in the English countryside at the lake district around Keswick and the Shakespeare country, lovely as always. During the following month we returned to France and decided to spend the rest of our time in Spain.

First of all, across the Spanish border, there was a rest stop at a resort, Parador d'Ifach. From there we drove south and fell in love with a sunny fishing village, Benidorm, where we remained much longer than we'd planned because of the friendliness of the people. The Spanish expedition wound up with a trip from Madrid to Toledo and back. For all my happy years at Columbia, I never did seem to get in enough travel time to satisfy me. So, as always, it was with reluctance that we returned to New York by the February 1 Pulitzer Prize deadline.

7   The Kennedy Prize

One of the first books I picked up on my return to the Pulitzer Prize office early in 1957 was Senator John Fitzgerald Kennedy's *Profiles in Courage*, an entry for the biography award. It attracted my interest at the outset; I not only read it but thoroughly researched the tremendous amount of work he'd done on it.

The senator from Massachusetts was not then being referred to as a likely Democratic successor to President Eisenhower, who was starting his second term with Richard Nixon as his vice-president. If anything, Nixon seemed a stronger possibility to succeed his chief on the theory that the Democrats, as usual, would be fighting each other instead of the Republican foe.

However, politics aside, *Profiles in Courage* already had made a strong impression on the reading public. The publisher, Harper, had sent in the requisite four copies of the work, which had been distributed well in advance to the biography jury. Certainly, the members of the Pulitzer board also were well aware of the Kennedy work.

Together with my classes for the second semester at Columbia, therefore, I made it my business in the Pulitzer office to consider the ever-widening field of Pulitzer Prize contenders along with *Profiles* and other standouts in letters, drama, journalism, and music.

The effort to catch up with events took time after an eight-month absence. Although Dorothy as always took over the reopening of our Columbia apartment on Morningside Heights and our old home in Aquebogue, I had yet to meet what I was told was a bright and enthusiastic class of 1957 at our school. But a number of the students didn't wait to be sought out. They came in of their own accord for interviews, and some returned several times because I never tried to keep exclusive office hours.

So before the month of February was over, the Air Force inquiry in Europe and our sabbatical trip that followed became only a distant memory.

.   .   .

In almost a quarter-century of journalism in New York, Washington, and abroad, I'd done my share of national reporting and recognized the importance of the Kennedy clan in Boston, of which Senator Kennedy now was the newest leader.

The senator already was a national figure. In World War II in the Pacific, he'd won a great reputation as a PT-boat commander. During a battle off the Solomon Islands in the South Pacific in August 1943, his fragile craft had been sliced in half by an enemy boat. Still, he had been able to save one of his crew members as well as himself with a swim to a rescue vessel, during which he used a rope gripped in his teeth to pull the wounded crewman to safety.

On the basis of his wartime record, once the conflict ended, Kennedy won a seat as a Democrat in the House of Representatives in 1947 and was successively re-elected in 1949 and 1951. Clearly, he was a comer. And in 1952, he ran for the Senate from Massachusetts and defeated another of Boston's great names, the Republican incumbent Senator Henry Cabot Lodge Jr. However, Kennedy's wartime experience had left him with a painfully injured back, and in 1954 he underwent a spinal operation to correct it. During the long convalescence that followed, it occurred to him to do a book about the great men of history in the Senate who had contributed to the America of their times.

That, briefly, was how *Profiles in Courage* had been conceived, why Kennedy had worked on it in bed sometimes during his long convalescence, and how it happened that his work had been submitted for a Pulitzer Prize.[1]

The year, it seemed to me, promised to be outstanding for American letters. Eugene O'Neill's greatest play, *Long Day's Journey into Night,* seemed a virtual certainty for the playwright's fourth Pulitzer award. Similarly, George Kennan's history, *Russia Leaves the War,* would be an important work for the history jury to consider. It was, sorry to say, another barren year for the American novel, but I hoped the jury might still come up with a worthy contender. As for the rest, like the possibilities in journalism, it was mainly up to the juries.

Well before the jury reports came in, I was reasonably certain that *Profiles in Courage* would be a contender if not the jury's choice in biography. I'd admired the author's selection of his senatorial role models of courage and the manner in which he'd written about them. Also, the book was a quick and easy read—a part of its attraction for a mass public.

As a matter of caution, I also looked into the manner in which Kennedy had gone about researching and writing the book.

In his prefatory remarks, the senator gave credit to those who had helped him do the book. It was obvious, as an invalid recovering from a major operation, that he couldn't have done much interviewing of sources in Washington. But I was also aware that he couldn't have won the endorsement of Professor Allan Nevins of Columbia University if this had been a ghosted book.

Early in that judgment year of 1957, I put a note of self-instruction in my diary, "Must make sure that 'Profiles in Courage' is Kennedy's work before the verdicts of the Biography Jury and the board. Every author I know of who does non-fiction needs help with sources, but make sure the Senator did the writing." I tried.

From the outset, Kennedy gave handsome credit to the staff of the Library of Congress, to Arthur Krock, and to Ted Sorenson, then a member of Kennedy's staff. That, certainly, was honest.

There also were a number of others whom the senator consulted, including academic authorities from Harvard, Williams, Georgetown, the Universities of Minnesota and Chicago, and the Nebraska State Legislature. Some were sources of information, others were listed in his introduction as critics of specific chapters, and sometimes both.

From the very nature of the book, a lot of research had been required. Only then could Kennedy have reflected in print on the courage, the devotion, and the strength of such senators of the past as John Quincy Adams, Sam Houston, Thomas Hart Benton, George Norris, and Robert A. Taft. The author also named a number of prominent people who had helped him prepare some of the chapters or criticize them, including such respected figures as Professors Arthur Meier Schlesinger Jr. and Arthur Holcombe of Harvard and Walter Johnson of the University of Chicago.

From my experience with writers and as the author of a number of books, I have seldom seen so complete a characterization of sources and assistance as Senator Kennedy offered the public for his *Profiles in Courage*. To have consulted so wide and distinguished a variety of academic and professional figures in itself would have been a creditable feat for any author.

In any event, I satisfied myself well before the jury reports came in that Kennedy's work in producing *Profiles in Courage* had been both extensive and laudatory.[2] I was thereby prepared for whatever findings the jury might make in awarding the biography prize for 1957.

During my time as the administrator, fiction had nearly always been a problem for most Pulitzer Prize juries and the 1957 report was no exception. I considered myself lucky to have been able to secure acceptances

for jury service from two of the leading critical experts in the field—
Francis Brown, the editor of the *New York Sunday Times Book Review*
and Professor Carlos Baker of Princeton.

Had there been the slightest hope for an American novel worthy of
the Pulitzer Prize that year, Messrs. Brown and Baker would have identified it. Of that I was sure. But when their report came in, it called the
previous year "a poor one for the American novel" and declined to name
any "serious contenders" for a Pulitzer award. If the board insisted, the
jurors offered *The Voice at the Back Door* by Elizabeth Spencer or *The
Last Hurrah* by Edwin O'Connor. Accordingly, the board passed the
novel prize.

After accepting O'Neill's play *Long Day's Journey into Night* for
the drama prize and George Kennan's work for the history award, the
board deadlocked over biography. The jury, Professor Julian Boyd, editor of the Thomas Jefferson Papers at Princeton, and Professor Bernard
Mayo of the University of Virginia, had ranked Kennedy's book third.
They had recommended Alpheus T. Mason's *Harlan Fiske Stone: Pillar
of the Law,* with *Roosevelt: The Lion and the Fox* by James MacGregor
Burns of Williams College as the alternate choice.

The board had seemed to me to be ready to accept the book about
Justice Stone when there was an unexpected intervention. One of the
board members, J. D. Ferguson, the editor of the Milwaukee *Journal,*
raised his hand somewhat hesitantly, and Chairman. Pulitzer recognized
him. Don Ferguson wasn't usually very active in Pulitzer affairs, but now
he wanted to tell his fellow members how he had come across Kennedy's
Profiles in Courage soon after it had been published in 1956, how he
had admired the work, and what he had done to test its effect. To quote
from my diary:

> The white-haired veteran of many a journalistic conflict sighed
> deeply, then murmured of the Kennedy book, "I read it aloud to my
> 12-year-old grandson and the boy was absolutely fascinated. I think we
> should give the prize to "Profiles in Courage." [3]
>
> Then, suddenly, the atmosphere changed. Others who had read the
> book agreed with Ferguson. Now few among the rest had to be told
> about the author's background as a U.S. Senator and World War II
> hero, the title of his first book, "Why England Slept," which had been
> an adaptation of a thesis he had done at Harvard, and his reporting for
> the New York Journal-American of the United Nations conference at
> San Francisco. As for the 'Profiles' book, Arthur Krock, not then a
> member of the board, had been recommending it widely and it also had
> been at the top of most best seller lists.

Among its other admirers, Erwin Dain Canham, editor of the *Christian Science Monitor* and not then a board member, had written, "That

a U.S. Senator, a young man of independent means with a gallant and thoughtful background, should have produced this study is as remarkable as it is helpful. It is a splendid flag that Senator Kennedy has nailed to his mast. May he keep it there."

When the board voted on the biography prize, Don Ferguson and his twelve-year-old grandson carried the day for Kennedy. But once the Columbia trustees ratified this and the rest of the slate voted by the Pulitzer board, in making public the awards, I heard rumors that Kennedy hadn't actually written the book. However, I did nothing about it until Drew Pearson, a columnist and TV figure specializing in sensation, broadcast the accusation over the ABC network that the Kennedy book had been ghosted. Both Kennedy and ABC promptly issued denials.

Still, the gossip continued until I checked my sources once again, then wrote to Senator Kennedy: "I have received several inquiries regarding Drew Pearson's remarks over the ABC-TV network. Beyond answering them with a copy of the enclosed statement given to me by the American Broadcasting Company, I have taken no action and do not intend to do so. I thought you would like to know about this."

Kennedy replied with a brief note and a handwritten scrawl beneath his signature that he was meeting Pearson shortly. The upshot was a statement in Pearson's column that John F. Kennedy had indeed written *Profiles in Courage*.[4] The first draft, as I later learned, was done in part while he was still abed recovering from surgery and it was concluded at Kennedy's home in Palm Beach, Florida, where he used a hard-covered notebook and thick white paper. The dictated final version was then completed after his widespread consultations.[5]

About a month later, I had an unsolicited note from Martha McGregor, a New York *Post* reporter, which I included in my diary:

> Martha McGregor said she'd been gumshoing around Senator Kennedy and the charges that he'd had a ghost writer for his Pulitzer Prize biography. She concluded over the phone that he'd had assistance from Ted Sorenson, his secretary, but had actually written the book himself. Nice of her to say so.

There was one other development after Kennedy's award of a Pulitzer Prize for *Profiles in Courage*. One of the unsuccessful contenders for his literary honor who later became his biographer, Professor James MacGregor Burns, believed it significant that a recent Gallup Poll had shown a four-point increase in Kennedy's lead over Senator Estes Kefauver for the Democratic presidential nomination in 1960 after the 1957 Pulitzer victory. The new figure gave Kennedy 45 percent of the sample, a jump from 41 percent the previous January. All of which caused Burns to observe, "Since the only relevant and significant event in the four-month interim was the Pulitzer Prize award, it seems possible that literary honors carry more weight with the public than has been commonly thought."[6]

The idea is interesting. Of course, the Kennedy clan's advertising and public relations activity also had something to do with his increasing prominence in national affairs, particularly after his election as a senator. Still, in the extremely close elections that featured Kennedy's rise to power, it's possible that literary skills do help a politician to a limited extent. Winston Churchill, for one, would not have dismissed the notion out of hand.

In any event, the argument over Kennedy's authorship of *Profiles in Courage* also led to another modest change in the procedures of the Pulitzer board. At my suggestion, the board agreed to divide itself into small, informal committees to do more of the necessary investigating, reading, play going, and concert attendance to backstop its own juries.

Although I was perfectly willing to continue to try to cover so wide a field by myself, I did suggest that the assignment was impossible for any one person to complete successfully during every prize year. In fact, even the informal committees, so I suggested, would find that the inquiries into various jury recommendations might take a great deal more time and care than any board member expected.

Anyway, the informal committees were formed, except in music, until Vermont Connecticut Royster of the Wall Street *Journal* disclosed, as a board member, that he once had played the trumpet in a brass band. He thereupon became the all-America concert-goer and backstop for the music jury's choices during his tenure on the Pulitzer board.

The rise of the first Pulitzer Prize-winner to run for president of the United States also is worth chronicling, for the youthful Senator Kennedy had his troubles when he first sought to join his colleagues in the upper house of Congress. The tale is still told in the nation's capital, especially by veterans of the political wars, that the new senator wasn't quickly recognized by all concerned with the operations of Congress.

When Kennedy first sought to board the little subway car in the tunnel linking the Capitol and the Senate Office Building, so the story goes, a self-important guard held him back with one long arm and warned him to wait, saying, "Senators go first, young man. You come later if there is room."

The truth is that Kennedy had been lucky to beat so well-established a Republican as Lodge in 1952 when the Eisenhower boom had boosted so many other Republican candidates to victory. Lodge lost to Kennedy by only about 70,000 votes out of 2.3 million, a bit more than 3 percent of the total. At the same time, Ike won the state from Democrat Adlai Stevenson by 208,000 votes, so Kennedy was indeed a child of good fortune that year.

Now, Kennedy faced an uphill battle—Pulitzer Prize or not—to gratify his ambition to become the first Catholic to be elected president. In addition to his base of support in Boston, what he had to do was something more to attract the votes of America outside Massachusetts. For his supporters, who rallied to boost his chances in the nation, that meant a national campaign to make him better known to people at large. And in this, the prize for *Profiles in Courage* undoubtedly helped because it increased the sales of an already popular work.

The trial of his popularity in 1956, when he tried for the vice-presidential nomination to link himself with Adlai Stevenson's presidential candidacy, had turned out to be a disaster. Senator Estes Kefauver had beaten him, but Kefauver also lost in turn when Stevenson was defeated by Eisenhower.

However, after his literary success in 1957 with the Pulitzers, Kennedy ran for reelection to the Senate in 1958, this time against a relatively obscure senatorial Republican nominee, Vincent J. Celeste, and won easily. As James Reston later wrote in the New York *Times* in an assessment of Kennedy's presidential chances:

> Senator Kennedy is on the make; he makes no pretense about it and he dismisses out of hand the suggestion that he is young enough to wait for some other Presidential campaign when newer and perhaps tougher competition will arrive. He is swinging for the fences now.

This is where Kennedy found another outlet for his undoubted literary skill. He began a continual campaign display of copies of his handwritten first draft of *Profiles in Courage* to dispel any remaining doubt about his authorship.

And although he hadn't been able to attract major newspaper and magazine editors to his work until he won a Pulitzer Prize, he now was besieged by editorial offers for articles. His name began appearing over pieces published in outlets as diverse as the *Saturday Evening Post, McCall's,* and the scholarly quarterly, *Foreign Affairs.* He also was popularized in newspaper supplements ranging from *Parade* and the *American Weekly* to the *New York Times Sunday Magazine.*

Between this background and his own vigorous appearance at speaking dates all over the country, he really was "swinging for the fences" now. By winning reelection to the Senate in 1958 by a record 874,000 votes, he managed to put a big one out of the ball park. From then on, he and Senator Lyndon Johnson became the major rivals for the 1960

Democratic presidential nomination and the prospective challengers to the probable Republican nominee, Vice-President Nixon.

The question Kennedy had to answer first of all was the one a reporter had asked him in his 1956 failed campaign to run with Adlai Stevenson as the vice-presidential nominee against President Eisenhower and Vice-President Nixon. "Conceivably, there could be a situation in which the dictates of your church and the demands of your country would conflict. In such a case, where would your higher loyalty be?" Kennedy responded:

> In the first place, I can't think of any issue where such a conflict might arise. But suppose it did? Nobody in my church gives me orders. It doesn't work that way. I've been in Congress for ten years and it has never happened. People are afraid that Catholics take orders from a higher organization. They don't. Or at least, I don't. Besides, I can't act as a private individual does. My responsibility is to my constituents and the Constitution. So if it comes to a conflict between the two, and not just a personal moral issue, I am bound to act for the interests of the many.[7]

He also was ready with a prompt answer to a lighthearted question by another reporter after he'd given a talk at the Los Angeles Press Club. "Do you think a Protestant can be elected President in 1960?"

Amid laughter, a smiling Kennedy replied, "If he is prepared to answer how he stands on the issue of the separation of church and state, I see no reason why we should discriminate against him."

There also seemed to be much more discussion within the Catholic hierarchy about Kennedy's definition of his duties as a Catholic as compared to his obligations as an American citizen. The point of contention was raised first in an interview published in *Look* magazine late in 1958 in a survey of the beliefs of several supposedly Catholic candidates for the presidency in 1960. This was Kennedy's response in substance:

> Whatever one's religion in private life may be, for the officeholder nothing takes precedence over his oath to uphold the Constitution and all its parts—including the First Amendment and the strict separation of church and state. Without reference to the Presidency, I believe as a Senator that the separation of church and state is fundamental to our American concept and heritage and should remain so.
>
> The First Amendment to the Constitution is an infinitely wise one. There can be no question of Federal funds being used for the support of parochial or private schools. It's unconstitutional under the First Amendment as interpreted by the Supreme Court. I'm opposed to the Federal government's extending support to sustain any church or its

schools. As for such fringe matters as buses, lunches and other services, the issue is primarily social and economic and not religious. Each case must be decided on its own merits within the law as interpreted by the courts.[8]

That seemed to do it except for his conservative critics among his fellow Catholics. Right off, *America,* the Jesuit weekly, criticized what it called "the earnest senator's efforts to appease bigots" and argued, "A man's conscience has a bearing on his public as well as his private life." To which Senator Kennedy responded, "That's mere academic toe-dancing."

These were the divisive elements against which Senator Kennedy had to struggle in the decisive stages of his presidential bid. These, too, are worth further examination with the passage of time—and not only because Kennedy was the first Catholic to seek the presidency since the 1928 defeat of Alfred Emanuel Smith. I still couldn't help wondering how much validity to attach to Professor Burns's notion that "literary honors carry more weight with the public than has been commonly thought."

PART TWO

The Best of Times

8   A Question of Funding

For many of us who served in World War II and survived, the mid-1950s will always be remembered gratefully as a relatively brief era of peace between the savage conflicts in Korea and Vietnam—the best of times. And that was particularly true of me after I left newspaper work to become a tenured professor at Columbia and the administrator of the Pulitzer Prizes.

What surprised me about my change of status, although it didn't bother me, was the relatively limited funding of the Pulitzer awards and the somewhat restricted manner in which the university had to conduct the greatest of America's literary prizes, as we liked to call them then on Morningside Heights.

In Joseph Pulitzer's will in 1911, when he died, the total bequest to the university was $2 million, to which Columbia added $500,000—a substantial gift to higher education for the time, especially from a newspaper publisher. But of the total, only the income from $500,000 was set aside for prizes and scholarships. The rest was for the funding of the journalism school and scholarships.

I recall my wonderment after fewer than ten years as the administrator of the awards when I was shown the books on the Pulitzer estate's funding of the prizes and the J-school by a new university financial officer, Robert G. Olmsted. I noted in my diary for 1961:

> Feb. 2—I learned that under a program of share allocation and capital gains that the Pulitzer Prize fund of $550,000 since 1932 was now valued at about $867,000 (647,527 units in the allocation program times $1.34 per unit). With interest set at 4.3 per cent, this was expected to bring in about $37,000 for the prizes annually at the time. Formerly, the university had been paying 5 per cent, so I asked for permission to obtain the benefit of interest on my own budgetary savings for that particular year but was told it couldn't be done, that my annual savings if any had to go back into principal.

I finally understood then why the monetary prize awards (except for the gold medal for public service in journalism) began at only $500 each in 1917, increased to $2,000 each in my time, and eventually to $3,000 currently. It became equally clear why I still could pay only a token fee to jurors in letters, drama, and music and nothing at all for the journalism judges, including the cost of their travel expenses to Columbia and back that usually were absorbed by their newspapers.[1]

By contrast, Alfred Bernhard Nobel, the Swedish chemist who invented dynamite, bequeathed $9 million to fund the prizes bearing his name upon his death in 1896, which accounts for the current value of a Nobel award of about $900,000. Truly, dynamite was far more valuable in the twentieth century world than a few newspapers.* And so, while it is still an honor to win a Pulitzer Prize, the monetary rewards have not kept pace with the times. In the visual arts, even the Oscars and the Emmys get more attention, plus extensive TV coverage.

It was mainly through my Pulitzer experiences and my background in university procedures and financing that my career insensibly broadened during the Eisenhower administration in the latter 1950s. It seemed to be taking me far afield when I was asked to investigate charges of excessive spending in the construction of the new United States Air Force Academy at Colorado Springs, but my Columbia superiors expected me to accept —and I reluctantly did so.

Like so much else that seemed extraneous at the time, it used up precious weeks of my summers' vacation periods for purposes that had nothing to do directly with my Columbia assignments. However, some of my friends on the Pulitzer Prize board believed the experience would be broadening, President Kirk agreed, and I therefore took on still another new and interesting assignment.

The Air Force Academy, a partner to West Point and Annapolis in American military education, had been accused by a Congressional committee of enormous waste in the construction of its facilities at Colorado Springs at the onset of my inquiry. Plush houses for professors and a faculty golf course were among the items that were being heavily criticized. The first I knew of it came in a telephone call from the Pentagon to my Pulitzer office that Air Force Secretary Douglas wanted to see me.

---

* The Pulitzer Publishing Company reported a thriving business in 1996 for its nine TV/stations although its flagship newspaper, the St. Louis *Post-Dispatch,* had to lay off 300 employees at the time to cut costs. The report appeared in The New York *Times,* Mar. 27, 1996, C-1.

When I called the secretary's office for specifics, a senior officer was polite but uninformative about the reason for the sudden request. Nor were any of my former associates in the information office any more illuminating.

It wasn't until I received permission from my superiors at Columbia to make what amounted to an emergency trip to Washington (I had to miss a class to do it) that I learned there had been "trouble over spending," as the case was put to me, in the construction of the Air Force Academy.

And could I go to Colorado Springs, do some interviewing, and make an independent judgment on the facts as they were presented to me? In vain I pointed out, as best I could, that I had never laid claim to being an economist, that my financial planning in my own family was so uncertain that Mrs. Hohenberg had to take charge and that, outside examining and approving the site, I'd had no background whatever in the planning of the Air Force Academy.

Secretary Douglas sympathized with my professed weakness in cost accounting but explained, with his usual good nature, that this was mainly a difference of opinion involving academic-minded Air Force planners and a politically-minded Congressional committee. I gave in; with Columbia's permission, I began the survey as requested. [2]

There still were problems. Although the Columbia administration had taken a friendly interest in the Air Force's school, the most we had done previously was to hold a seminar between prospective members of the USAF faculty and a Columbia committee for a discussion of curriculum. That had been in addition to my own site inspection trip.

The related and more important problem, although I didn't say so point blank, was that I couldn't be at all sure I'd be of any help in discussing such grave matters as the funding of a new service academy for the armed forces of the United States. It had been well-nigh four years since I'd had any contact with the project; and I wasn't familiar with the planning, the construction, or the executives in charge. Also, my time rightly belonged first to Columbia.

However, after taking counsel with the respective offices of the president of the university and the journalism dean, I did arrange for a two-day trip to the Pentagon mainly, so I was told by my superiors, to show friendly interest in the Air Force Academy and its academic future. To demonstrate how vague the affair actually was, I quote from my 1958 diary:

March 31—To the Pentagon and a senior officer talked to me in an aimless way about a lot of things he thought the Air Force Secretary might want me to do. I gathered that the Air Force already had agreed to permit the Defense Department to absorb some of the Air Force's information functions, but this was an old battle that dated from the first Eisenhower administration and it had long since seemed to be resolved. So I listened politely and wondered what really was being expected of me when I received an invitation to lunch tomorrow with Secretary Douglas.

April 1—At Secretary Douglas's lunch, there was an impressive gathering of some of the service's civilian and military leadership— Under Secretary Malcolm McIntyre, General Joe Kelly and Colonel Maurice Casey as well as the Secretary himself. The latest Pentagon reorganization was aimlessly discussed, but Secretary Douglas didn't seem particularly concerned by that. Nor was he worried about the latest scrubbing of an Atlas missile firing at Cape Canaveral. What did bother him, it turned out, was the Congressional investigation of spending at the Air Force Academy site—something that had intensely interested a Congressional committee. After he'd talked about it for a while, he turned to me in a matter-of-fact way and asked me in a conversational manner to see what I could do about it.

Well! I hadn't bargained for an individual mission to Colorado Springs and the still temporary Academy operation at Lowry Air Force Base in Denver, especially after Congressional investigators seemed to have done quite a job of their own to the Pentagon's discomfiture.

It was disturbing to me, as well, that I would have to go to Colorado Springs as an independent investigator who couldn't possibly be expected to contend with a Congressional committee report charging overspending. Moreover, if I found and corroborated the Congressional findings, which was probable, how could I possibly reduce the damage? Also, what did that have to do with the Pulitzers?

Obviously, when too much money has been spent on a government project and a private investigation is ordered, there is little reason to expect that there will be a drastic change in the proceedings. Nor was it suggested to me that that would be the purpose of the trip. Secretary Douglas hadn't asked me to combat the Congressional charges. What he'd wanted me to suggest was what the Air Force now should do, assuming the committee's investigative findings were very largely correct.

My first impulse was to try to bow out of the proceedings once more by pleading that I had neither the time nor the engineering background to propose an Air Force response to such criticism other than a *mea culpa,* plus a pledge to tighten up on academy costs.

I doubted, too, that it would have helped if I'd put the burden on my superiors at Columbia to decide what, if anything, I should do. If I did not teach summer school, my time was my own.

There was no help for it. I agreed to see what I could do, provided my visit to Colorado Springs could be postponed until after commencement. To that, Secretary Douglas cheerfully agreed, after which I returned to Columbia, my classes, and the annual Pulitzer Prize ritual.

It should have occurred to me that my role as an agent of the Pentagon, however temporary it might be, would provide me with contacts that would be of infinite use in the event of an extended wartime role for the Pulitzer Prizes. But then, I had missed the Korean War, in which seven awards had been given for frontline service or heroism, sometimes both, during which Pulitzers were awarded to seven reporters and a photographer,

Nor could I guess that my Pentagon experience would lead me to two extended visits to the war fronts in Vietnam within the foreseeable future, when I would be able to witness at first hand some of the exploits that would lead to the award of nineteen Pulitzer Prizes for that tragic nine-year conflict. My experience with the Air Force Academy, briefly put, was the gateway to several unique wartime adventures.

The Academy had been born in 1954 as the gasping, almost helpless survivor of a rousing budget fight between President Eisenhower and an embattled Congress,[3] Out of the debris of this slugging match when Ike sought big military spending cuts, the White House and Congress managed to agree on the creation of the new Air Force school. Its mission in years yet to come, they decided, would be to prepare the leaders of the nation's military aviation for their careers, not so much in a mere flying school, but in a military university. They also agreed it would be dedicated to train the future leaders and developers of the nation's air power in the same manner as had been done by the military academy at West Point since 1802 and the naval academy at Annapolis since 1845.

Still, it was too much to expect that the new institution would take shape at once at Colorado Springs. To begin with, therefore, the government authorized a temporary site for the Air Force Academy at Lowry Air Force Base in Denver beginning in 1955 to allow for the four years that would be required to plan, build, and staff the permanent Air Force Academy.

The champions of the Air Force's school had to be content with that —and the quick adoption of the old war song the Army Air Force had carried into battle when it was first organized:

> Up we go into the wild blue yonder,
> Flying high into the sun;
> Here we go, aiming to meet our thunder:
> At 'em, boys, give 'er the gun . . .[4]

In the mid-1950s, on my first trip to Colorado Springs, construction on the permanent buildings had barely begun, and there was little I could do or say about the way the project was shaping up. In all truth, the place was little more than a grandiose dream over a mudhole at the time.

To some, I am sure, the sight would have been discouraging in the extreme. But somehow, it seemed to me the beginning of a vast experiment in the future of military education. It was high time, so it seemed to me when I first viewed the site, that the importance of military air power in all its phases at last had been recognized both by Congress and academe under presidential pressure.

More than a half-century had passed since the Wright brothers had lifted their primitive biplane off the ground for all of 12 seconds on December 17, 1903, at Kitty Hawk, North Carolina. Less than twenty-five years later, Charles A. Lindbergh's little *Spirit of St. Louis* aircraft had flown nonstop across the Atlantic from New York to Paris on May 20–21, 1927, spanning 3,610 miles in 33.5 hours. The French had gone wild in cheering the young American's great adventure, but no more so than the worshipful crowds in New York City upon his arrival back home.

No less important, in between the feat of the Wrights' and Lindbergh's, one of the first military pilots had wrecked his biplane off the New England coast in 1912 and made a forced landing during which he managed to hang onto a wing until rescued from a watery grave. That was how Henry H. (Hap) Arnold—later to become General Arnold, the father of the Air Force—had begun his career in military aviation. At the time of the wreck, the ambitious West Point graduate had been the supply officer of a newly founded aviation school in San Diego. [5]

During World War I, except for the Fokker fighter aircraft that gave Imperial Germany air superiority at the outset in 1914, much of the Allied effort had gone into scouting planes. So for the United States, it had been a year, from the time of our declaration of war on Germany on April 6, 1917, before American troops had reached Europe in significant numbers to offset the combined German air and trench defenses.

However, in the lull between the wars, there was no real effort to achieve air power in the United States until President Franklin Roosevelt, on November 14, 1938, ordered a massive aircraft buildup. This time, he told his uniformed military leaders, he was taking no chances against potential enemies that already were fully armed. What he wanted, he said, was a "vast rearmament program" including 3,700 combat aircraft, 2,500 others for training, and 3,750 in reserve. [6]

It was too much for the infant American aircraft industry to produce before World War II burst upon an unprepared United States in 1939. At the time, we had only 940 military aircraft. Even after Pearl Harbor at the end of 1941, there was a lot of contract trouble in the industry as it tried and failed once again to meet the President's latest goal of 50,000 aircraft.

In 1942, General Eisenhower wrote in despair, "If we're to keep Russia in, save the Middle East, India and Burma, we've got to begin slugging with air at West Europe to be followed by a land attack as soon as possible."[7]

It took a lot of hard work and heroic effort for the American military, backed by the country's industrial capacity, to produce the essentials for victory in Europe and North Africa as well as the two atomic bombs that knocked Japan out of the Pacific war. But those in uniform, especially the aviators, knew all too well when it was over that victory had been a near thing.

Therefore, when President Eisenhower produced his first military budget with huge Air Force cuts, he was careful to inform Congress that the Air Force still was receiving more than 40 percent of the budget's military funding.[8] So it seemed, at the outset, that the Air Force Academy was little more than a blink in Ike's supposed "new look" for the American military presence in a dangerous world. Still, with the coming of the Academy and its plans for an integrated program of instruction in flying, science, and engineering, some of the leaders of the aircraft industry also began moving in the same direction. What seemed to be forming was an altogether new and formidable academic/industrial complex for the nation.

Something of this nature had developed in the Northeast early on when institutions like the Massachusetts Institute of Technology, Harvard, and others helped draw defense plants to their part of the country. The same thing had happened later on the Pacific coast, especially in California, when there was a mix of new defense plants there among great institutions of learning like Stanford, the University of California, and the California Institute of Technology.

Now, it seemed likely in due course that the Mountain states might well be able to maintain their own scientific and military mix stimulated by the new Air Force Academy among others. To carry so great an experiment inland was a gamble, to be sure, but that would have been the case with any new private institution of higher learning that was being put together under such pressure from Washington. What the infant Academy would have to do first was to prove itself capable of supplying the nation with new air leadership.

Once I reached Colorado Springs after finishing my 1957–1958 academic year at Columbia, it didn't take me long to determine that there was a blunt answer to Secretary Douglas's concern about Congressional charges of too much unnecessary spending at the site of the Air Force Academy. There was substance to the allegations, and some of the evidence was readily available. The first sight that struck me was an elaborate layout of forty-four professors' houses of special construction. Now I'm all for professorial comfort, but I had to think twice about the special provisions for their housing at Colorado Springs at government expense, particularly when I thought of how we were put up at Columbia in old but comfortable and well-managed apartment houses for which we were charged modest rentals. And among Ivy League schools, Columbia made better provisions for its teachers and supporting staff than some others.

The special housing provided at Colorado Springs was, necessarily, a modest item. But I also saw other symptoms of what a Congressional inquiry could well have believed to be unnecessary expense. Still, even if extravagance could be proved, I saw very clearly before I had been at the Academy site for very long that little could be done about money that already had been generously if unwisely spent. A few entries from my 1958 diary illustrate my problem after my arrival at Colorado Springs:

> June 9—A succession of Air Force officers briefed me on various stages of the Academy's operations. I took detailed notes, asked a lot of questions and suspected, from the responses, that I was in for a difficult time in studying the Air Force Academy's construction and outlook in the limited time at my disposal.
>
> June 10—I was given a tour of the Academy's campus including the more than two score professors' houses and other features that had been criticized by the Congressional committee and press reports for weeks before my arrival. One Air Force officer tried to rebut all the charges on a point by point basis. He didn't make much sense, but I didn't argue with him.

From then until June 18, I was given the same treatment and considered the whole sad business a colossal waste of time. The only clue I had for a decent response to the charges was an indication by Major General Buster Briggs, the superintendent, that some thought had been given to spreading the cost of the project among other branches of the Air Force, especially the Strategic Air Command, which was looking for a secondary base and liked Colorado Springs. (Maybe the golf course had something to do with that!)

Anyway, I checked in at SAC headquarters in Omaha, where I saw the first glimmer of light in darkness. The SAC command appeared willing to share expenses on the Academy project in return for space there, something that I decided to check with a few of the other separate commands. That wound up my inquiry.

When I wrote my report for Secretary Douglas back home in Aquebogue on June 25, that was just about the only positive suggestion I could make. As I added, I'd had too little time to check all the Congressional charges, and it wouldn't have done me—or the Air Force—much good if I'd tried.

Rather, it seemed to me, Secretary Douglas might do better to assure Congressional and other critics that he'd see to it no further unnecessary expenses would be incurred at Colorado Springs, also that the Air Force major commands would share costs without undermining the proposed program of instruction. That was the best I could do.

Fortunately, Secretary Douglas decided to follow my line in his own follow-up visit to Colorado Springs. In any event, the Academy's construction was completed without further argument and exists today on a par with West Point and Annapolis. [9]

For the rest of that summer and much of the fall of 1955, I was too busy with my classes and preparations for the next Pulitzer Prize year to be unduly concerned over the millions that were available to a military school run by the government as compared with the relatively small sum set aside for operating the Pulitzer Prizes. Whenever I thought of the elaborate professors' houses and the golf course at Colorado Springs, I got over it quickly enough.

The honor of supervising the Pulitzers would have to suffice. My main duty at Columbia, after all, was the care and instruction of the students who took particular interest in my courses. I owed them my best efforts—something I had in common with the great American teacher, Horace Mann, when he said, "Be ashamed to die until you have won some victories for humanity."

I have tried. The Air Force Academy experience caused me, finally, to appreciate the confidence the university placed in me when I was given the severely limited financial responsibility for the prizes. I never did worry unduly after that about questions of funding.

9 The University Experience

The first night of a Tennessee Williams play usually was an event while Broadway still was a functioning center for the best in the American theater.

More often than not, the drama jury for the Pulitzer Prizes would make arrangements in advance through my office to see the first performance of a new work by a major dramatist, especially if it opened near the deadline for a particular Pulitzer year. And sometimes, if the producer was agreeable, I'd go, too, with a few other members of the Pulitzer board who were able to make it.

This is what attracted a large audience and the Pulitzer drama representatives to one of the season's works by Tennessee Williams, *Sweet Bird of Youth,* on its opening night. My own experience was disastrous. I suffered through what seemed like an interminable discussion of some of the dramatist's special interests—sex life, castration, and the nation's racial problems.

As a result, I awaited the jurors' report on *Sweet Bird of Youth* with some trepidation because the opening was just before the year's deadline for drama entries. My own likes and dislikes didn't count, but I knew the board members well enough to realize this was one play they could scarcely favor. As it turned out, neither did the jurors. John Mason Brown, the chairman, summed up the position in a single sentence: "The play should have been cut, not the hero." [1]

There also were times within my experience when a dramatist accepted his or her award with becoming grace, but some of their relatives still complained at the small cash amount of the prize or, in one famous case, hadn't even heard of the Pulitzer Prizes until a talented family member won one. I'm told that the mother of one of the latter-day laureates, a starchy Southern lady, complained when told of her relative's eminence, "I suppose it's all right that she won that prize but I wish she'd won it for writing about white people." I've wondered since whether the

Southern lady would have approved of separate but unequal white and black Pulitzer Prizes.

And then there was the night after the Pulitzer Prize show, *Fiorello,* won the Pulitzer Prize despite the disappointment of the drama jury's chairman in the performance he saw. Although I never took sides in a dispute between board members and jurors, I wrote in my diary after I saw the show, "As for the essence of the musical theater, from book to music, I've seen better. But then it hasn't been a very good theatrical season." [2]

Despite my deep interest in the Pulitzer Prizes, which must by now be evident even to the most casual reader of these lines, I do not want to leave the impression that the total of my university experience was summed up in the prizes, much less solely in the drama award. It was important to me, certainly, to serve as secretary of the Pulitzer board and administrator of the awards, but it was not the be-all and end-all of my university experience.

My first interest had to be the 5,000 or so students who looked to me for instruction during a critical year toward the end of their academic preparations for a useful career. That invariably gave me the most concern in my daily routine. Because I was at Columbia as a teacher for twenty-six years, regardless of the title I was given or the rank, that became my dominant interest, but it was by no means the only one. I also had some of the liveliest and most vivid experiences with students during more than five years at Tennessee, two at Syracuse, and one each at the Universities of Florida, Miami of Florida, and Kansas. There also were shorter periods at the East-West Center at the University of Hawaii, the Chinese University of Hong Kong, and lectures of varying periods at a score of more of other universities here and abroad including, some at Harvard and Dartmouth.

I don't know what I might have contributed during a course or an academic year to so many former students. They included, to cite only a few that come immediately to mind, a small, graceful girl who became the three-time governor of a great state, a number of Pulitzer Prize winners, the head of the world's greatest news agency, the chief executive officer of the country's most powerful newspaper chain, editors of some of the leading newspapers in the land, as well as anchors and producers of major TV importance, together with those capable of renewing the profession, the deans and professors of numerous J-schools and colleges, including, fittingly, one at Columbia.

There was, however, a vast difference between the world of the journalist, from which I had come, and the affairs of the academic community into which I had plunged with so little preparation. I remember

how difficult it was for me at first to come to terms with university life.
The following diary entries in 1959 are fairly typical of the difference:

> April 2—Dean Acheson was the J-school guest at dinner for a
> small faculty group and students, then afterward before our entire stu-
> dent body. The former secretary of state took pains to define himself
> and his position as a diplomat before a fascinated younger audience.
> He seemed to take delight in creating confusion instead of dispelling it.
>
> In discussing current American problems in foreign affairs, he
> seemed tougher on Republicans at home, especially Senator Robert A.
> Taft, than the successors to Stalin in Moscow. He didn't like Ike, didn't
> even think much of FDR, forgot to mention Truman altogether, thought
> well of Senator Lyndon Johnson and seemed to despise all reporters
> without referring to their professional affiliations.
>
> I'm not sure what our students were able to make of all this, but it
> was an evening that some of them won't forget—an exercise in not
> taking everybody in Washington too seriously.[3]
>
> Nov. 2—Charles Van Doren, who has starred in so many TV quiz
> shows, now has confessed that he is a fraud but no one at Columbia
> seems to be surprised. The trustees have accepted Van Doren's resigna-
> tion from the faculty. The newspapers are acting very holy about all this
> and so is the Congressional committee that investigated him because he
> finally told the truth when he was forced to do so.[4]
>
> For a typical day in our largest class in the Journalism building
> that same year, I picked a random morning a week later when six of us
> in the faculty worked with 80 students in a three-hour news writing
> course. There was nothing very difficult or unusual about the exercise
> —a set of facts taken from the day's news and given orally to our
> writers who worked against a set deadline.
>
> I wish I could claim that the student performance was professional
> but the truth is that nearly all of them need a lot more work. I do not
> know how else to train journalists to write on deadline—and it doesn't
> make any difference if they do it on a beat-up old Remington or the
> latest model of a fancy compuer. (The thought always appalls me that I
> may be tearing apart the beginnings of an American genius, a play-
> wright, a novelist, a TV or movie script writer, whatever. But forgive
> me; it is hard to recognize genius at the university level under the
> methods we have to use to produce professional results in a year's work
> toward a master's degree.

This is at least part of the way it was for a relatively new professor at
Columbia at the time. Perhaps I was overly in awe of academe, having
had a troublesome acquaintance with university life in the 1920s as a
student. It wasn't easy then to pay my way by working nights on a
tabloid as a copy editor, snatching a few hours' sleep whenever possible,
and still regularly attending classes, doing the necessary academic read-

ing, and completing all the written requirements for each course including tests.

In any event, these were some of the people, the scenes, the pleasures, and the pain that I recorded in my diaries in the latter 1950s aside from my work for the Pulitzer Prizes:

> Our students weren't backward about taking on a new dean one day when I was in attendance at a committee meeting. They wanted him to know that his course in Basic Issues—a roundup of national and international problems, was such a mish-mash that they thought it a waste of their time. The dean took it with poor grace, for which he couldn't be blamed, especially when the committee people told him most students wanted more writing and less talk. I doubt if the dean will do anything about it. He doesn't take kindly to students' protests over course work, particularly when the protests are aimed at one of his favorite course contributions.[5]

This, in sum, was the way it was in the Journalism building at Columbia when I taught there toward the end of the Eisenhower administration.

At the Council on Foreign Relations at about the same time, I heard Sir Alexander Grantham, the retiring governor of Hong Kong, tell us in his most benign British manner that we'd better get used to dealing with Communist China because a nation of 1.2 billion people wasn't going to fade away no matter how much we disliked its government. I sat across from Dean Rusk, the president of the Rockefeller Foundation and a future secretary of state, who took it all in without a word.[6]

> A few nights later, there was still another diversion when Dorothy and I saw Sir Laurence Olivier in John Osborne's new play, "The Entertainer." For sheer ability at stagecraft, Sir Laurence was superb—the best I'd seen in several seasons. (And considering the dearth of significant new works for the Broadway stage toward century's end, this play and others of quality at the time remain a shining memory for me after a lifetime of viewing the living theater including several score opening nights.)
>
> There also were engagements outside Columbia that I had to fulfill for the university's sake as well as my own, notably an occasional lecture at the Army Information School and arrangements for the new Air Force Academy. But I drew the line at political engagements although one of a series of new deans did try to twist my arm to help out a friend, District Attorney Frank Hogan of New York County. What happened here, and I doubt if Hogan knew of it, was that this particular dean wanted me to write speeches for his friend, the D.A., who was running for the U.S. Senate, and I impolitely but firmly refused. It was

a short lesson in how not to get along with deans who are a bit shaky on the subject of academic freedom.

What always comforted me, after this kind of an encounter, was the friendship of an old and distinguished Columbian like Douglas Moore, the director of the Columbia Music School, the winner of a Pulitzer Music Prize for operatic composition and the youthful composer of the Yale student anthem, "Boola-Boola."

Of the many New Year's Eves Dorothy and I spent with the Moores and their family at their home near us on eastern Long Island, I shall always remember the onset of 1959. It was then that Douglas serenaded us at the piano with the "Emperor Waltz." I followed with some Viennese music on his piano with everybody else waltzing, if not very convincingly. Then Douglas made scrambled eggs with armagnac and orange peel, followed by coffee at midnight and a climactic singing of "Auld Lang Syne" before we left for home at 2:30 a.m.[7]

Early in 1959, I had my first book-publishing party at the Carnegie Endowment for International Peace with the appearance of my anthology, "The Pulitzer Prize Story." For this, I had my picture taken with Professor Jacques Barzun of Columbia, an honor in itself. But in all honesty, I would suggest that the Pulitzer Prizes and Columbia University also had something to do with my becoming a published author for the first time at the age of 53.

A bit later that year, in token of many a lively evening in the Philippines, I was able to return the favor by giving dinner to the Filipino ambassador to the UN, Salvador Lopez, and his daughter, Rosemary, before all of us, including Dorothy, rode downtown to the Winter Garden on Broadway to watch some graceful Filipino girls performing native dances. It was a fun evening.

At lunch at the Faculty Club one day, I heard a young instructor at a nearby table say bitterly, "Columbia insures you against everything except starvation." Although the speaker didn't seem to be starving at the moment, I was embarrassed because my guest, the son of an old friend, was an assistant professor with a Ph.D. in economics from Harvard who had just begun his first year's service at Columbia. As I recall, he didn't seem to be discouraged in the slightest but continued to broaden an admirable career.[8]

Much the same thing happened when the editor of the Christian Science Monitor, Erwin D. (Spike) Canham, came to the J-school to explain how he kept his much-admired paper running in difficult times. It was the kind of encouragement the students needed—and some continued to stay with newspapers even in a fast-developing TV era because the emphasis of the big tube remains on entertainment—and a lot of the day's news is far more necessary than entertaining.

What it all came down to for me in my shift to a university career in my mid-forties, with the handicap of a 30 percent pay reduction for the privilege,[9] was to do the best I could for the young people who trusted me as a teacher. I never dreamed that I would be associated with the Pulitzer Prizes, writing books, being dispatched on government missions, or even remaining active late in life.

That is why I tried never to offer specific advice to the many students in my classes who came to me for career counseling just before graduation. I do not have the magical insight to determine whether a young person's beginning should by made in wire services, newspapers, or the electronic media; in magazines, the movies, or book publishing; on the business or advertising side, or editorial; or even as a first-year university instructor. Such choices, for the most part, depend on personality, experience, and adaptability as well as the 101 instances in which friendly associations, family ties, and sheer luck play so important a role.

Nevertheless, to those who somewhat desperately insisted on an older person's judgment, all I ever dared to do was to suggest that it is important to make a beginning, to seize the main chance, to start somewhere, and then decide on the next step if any. I cannot undertake the responsibility of trying to run someone else's life in addition to my own in so highly competitive and ever-expanding a field.

True, I have known teachers who also are inclined to act as cheer leaders for their students, but the very thought of so serious an intellectual lapse makes me uncomfortable. For the young person whose blatantly inflated hopes collapse can and sometimes does sink into a serious state of depression. No experienced teacher can afford to take such risks with young lives.

This is not to say that enthusiasm for an active life, a particular line of work, or a profession should be moderated or even concealed; from the time of my first published news interview at age seventeen, my first night class as a teacher at age forty-two, and my first lecture as a Columbia professor at age forty-four, I have always been fascinated by journalism in all its forms and have never gotten over it. But I doubt if that has seriously affected my judgment in the progress of the news business, or lack of it, no matter what form it takes. Whatever mistakes I may have made, and in dealing with a fast-moving chain of events mistakes are inevitable, I hope I have been able to own up to an honest admission of error and profited from the experience. Perfection in journalism is a sometime thing, and that goes double for television. I append a note from my 1960 diary:

Nov. 15—To the CBS Studio on 58th St., New York, in the afternoon to tape two shows for Channel 13. A fine one with Harrison Salisbury of the New York Times was ruined when the tape jammed. A less effective one with Phil Santora of the New York Daily News came through OK and will be shown Nov. 19. That's show business.

10 In the Public Interest

When Ralph McGill came home to his invalid wife in Atlanta one night in mid-October, 1958, she told him that a bomb had ripped apart The Temple, the largest place of worship in the great Southern metropolis.

For McGill, as he later told me the story, something snapped. It was too much for him to face up to the reality that the crimes of Adolf Hitler in Nazi Germany should be repeated in the United States, that some American Jews were marked for violence and perhaps death just as their 6 million co-religionists in Europe had been wiped out in the Holocaust.

Straightaway, as I recorded his story in my diary, the editor of the Atlanta *Constitution* dashed off an editorial in only 20 minutes that ran next day in his newspaper under the heading: "ONE CHURCH, ONE SCHOOL":

> This is a harvest. It is a crop of things sown. It is a harvest of defiance of courts and the encouragement of citizens to defy the law on the part of many Southern politicians.
>
> It is not possible to preach lawlessness and restrict it. When leadership in high places fails to support constituted authority, it opens the gates to all those who wish to take the law into their own hands. The extremists of the Citizens' Councils, the political officials who in terms violent and inflammatory have repudiated their oaths of office and stood against the due process of law, have helped unloose this flood of hate.

For his bravery and his leadership in the face of senseless attacks that followed against his home, abuse of his ill and bedridden wife, and threats against his own life once the editorial was published, McGill was awarded the Pulitzer Prize for editorial writing in 1959. I still remember writing his reaction in my diary, "John, I never really thought I'd make it."

This time he referred to the preservation of his own life, not the Pulitzer Prize that came to him so late in a distinguished career.[1]

At an earlier time, when McGill still was a member of the Pulitzer board before I became the secretary and administrator, he liked to recall that he often published editorials in the *Constitution* headed, "One of These Days It Will Be Monday."

What he was trying to do, as he once told me, was to remind his readers that the US Supreme Court regularly handed down decisions on the first of the week and might one day include an order desegregating the nation's public schools on a Monday.[2]

When that all-important Monday occurred on May 17, 1954, a unanimous Supreme Court headed by Chief Justice Earl Warren outlawed segregated schools by striking down a lower court ruling in favor of "separate but equal" public education in *Brown* v. *Board of Education.* "Separate educational facilities are inherently unequal," the Warren Court decided.

A revisionist high court forty-one years later differed with the Warren court in *Missouri* v. *Jenkins*, a school *pro*-segregation decision, with the lone black member of that court, Justice Clarence Thomas, arguing strangely against the Warren court's finding that "black students suffer . . . harm from segregation [and it] also rests on the assumption of black inferiority."

But *Brown* v. *Board of Education* can't be nullified overnight by outraged conservatives, no matter what the political composition of the high court. Nor can the nation's social revolution easily be reversed so many years after it began with the Warren court's landmark decision.[3] The Pulitzer Prizes provide the evidence.

It must never be forgotten that when white rioters forced the withdrawal on February 8, 1956, of Autherine Lucy, the first black student to be admitted to the University of Alabama, the editor of a small newspaper in Tuscaloosa, Buford Boone of the *News*, wrote, "We have had a breakdown of law and order, an abject surrender to what is expedient rather than for what is right. Yes, there is peace on the university campus this morning but what a price has been paid for it."

The editorial, "What a Price for Peace," won for Buford Boone the 1957 Pulitzer Prize for editorial writing. The reason: he had the guts to support the law against the mob that sought to eject a black woman from a university classroom that was supported at public expense.

As I write, it is difficult to re-create the frantic atmosphere under which white mobs tried to dictate who should be admitted to a university. Boone's then was a lonely voice. Knowing something more about what is expected of journalists rather than what can happen under changing concepts of the law, I would doubt that Boone's conduct under stress would be any less admired today.[4]

It was in this fashion, at any rate, that the campaign for desegregating the Southern schools continued through the rest of 1956.

In 1957, President Eisenhower had to call out federal troops to restore order in Little Rock after rioting broke out there over the enrollment of nine black children at Central High School.

On September 9, 1957, Editor Harry Ashmore wrote still another courageous editorial of protest against racial prejudice that was published in his *Arkansas Gazette* with the approval of its eighty-five-year-old publisher, John N. Heiskell:

> Somehow, some time, every Arkansan is going to have to be counted. We are going to have to decide what kind of people we are—whether we obey the law only when we approve of it, or whether we obey it no matter how distasteful we may find it. And this, finally, is the only issue before the people of Arkansas.

However, the Ku Klux Klan and the White Citizens' Councils weren't reading such newspapers, and there certainly was nothing on the air that disturbed them, either. So it happened on a distressful fall morning only a short time later, September 23, 1957, an Associated Press reporter, Relman Morin, was outside Central High School in a glass-enclosed telephone booth calling his office when all hell broke loose.

A howling mob of white supremacists swirled past him as he dictated his bulletins to the AP and a nationwide audience of newspaper editors, radio and TV stations to report that Central's first little black pupil had been forcibly removed from his class.

That was when federal troops moved into the city as President Eisenhower acted promptly and vigorously to restore order. However, the troops couldn't change all the minds in the South overnight. After Central High School, the center of attack was the Arkansas *Gazette*.

Even though Ashmore left the paper to try to save it for its octogenarian owner, it is reported to have lost at least $2 million through mob boycotts of advertisers. Even so, two Pulitzer Prizes for 1958 went to the *Gazette* and to Ashmore personally because they supported the right. And Relman Morin, who already had one Pulitzer to his credit, was awarded another for his minute-by-minute reporting for the AP of the mob attack at the risk of injury, and perhaps worse, for himself.[5]

In the 1960s, more followed where McGill, Boone, Ashmore, and others had led. They included not only the bravest and wisest of Southern editors but now the might of the Gannett newspaper chain also was enlisted in the battle to restore the rule of law.

The symbol of the kind of savagery in American life that they opposed became a symbol in the cartoons of Herblock, the Washington *Post*'s prize-winning artist—a rotten apple shaped in the features of Senator Joseph R. McCarthy Jr., who had set himself up as the arbiter of American patriotism and those who were unworthy of such recognition.

If the public-spirited newspapers of the South that opposed the growth of mob rule in America did nothing else, they demonstrated once again that no price can be placed on the courage it takes to support the right of a free people to think and act for themselves under law.

However, not every journalist or every newspaper in the 1950s and 1960s was willing to take the chances of a McGill, an Ashmore, or a Buford Boone. Nor were the inquiries of the press, as reflected in the Pulitzer Prize records of the era, limited to such issues as school desegregation and the defense of individual liberty such as freedom of the press and religious thought.

Exposés of corruption in public office and labor racketeering, too, were legitimate matters affecting the public interest but often could be undertaken only at serious risk by crusading newspapers. In 1957, for example, the Chicago *Daily News* won a Pulitzer gold medal for public service with an exposé of a $2.5-million fraud centered in the office of the state auditor of Illinois. And in 1959, the gold medal went to two smaller newspapers in Utica, N.Y., for a cleanup of official corruption in that city.

In such cases as these, it wasn't mob violence that provided the main risk. It was the threat of a multimillion dollar libel suit if by evil chance the information the newspapers published was either incorrect or demonstrably false. The play-it-safe press never took such chances, especially when newspaper circulations for many daily papers were falling and advertisers were deserting to the mighty tube.

Still, the crusading journalist had won an honored place in American public life and there still were newspaper publishers who believed that public service was a part of their responsibilities. In 1958, for example, attacks on labor racketeering and official corruption also won a reporting prize for Wallace Turner and William Lambert of the Portland *Oregonian*. In the same year, another labor racketeering and crime exposé won a national reporting award for Clark Mollenhoff of the Des Moines *Register and Tribune*. And in 1959, Howard Van Smith of the Miami (Fla.) *News* was rewarded with a reporting award for his inquiry into the hardships of a labor camp for migrant workers, part of a national problem facing 1.5 million workers.

Another award for serving the public interest came to George Beveridge of the Washington *Star* for a study of the future of the nation's capital, Washington, D.C. And farther from home, Joseph Martin and Philip Santora of the New York *Daily News* won a 1959 Pulitzer for their accurate forecast, based on an investigation in Cuba, that Fidel Castro was about to overthrow the Batista regime and turn the island into a Communist state.[6]

However, such specialized inquiries at home and abroad, like the self-sacrifice of Southern editors who defied the prospect of mob rule, did not always result in greater public support for daring editors and publishers. Some paid a tremendous price for their ventures in the public interest. More and more newspapers were folding because of declining readership and advertising in the face of TV competition. And many a city, including some of the largest, was now being served by only one newspaper.

Among journalists who watched the seemingly unlimited expansion of TV toward century's end, the question inevitably was raised: "Does public service journalism really pay?" For the masters of the tube, the question was phrased differently by a Columbia University professor, Eric Barnouw, but it was just as meaningful. "In a few decades, television has grown from a toy to a popular diversion, to a pipeline to millions and finally to a watchtower on the ramparts, manned by seers—with independent power. How would it be used?"

The question still begs for an adequate answer regardless of the spread of TV as entertainment, probably matched by a competition in cyberspace, the decline of all save the most influential and well-managed press/TV chains and individual national, regional and local newspapers.

Edward R. Murrow, still the outstanding news broadcaster in TV's relatively short history, phrased the medium's problem in this fashion. "This instrument can teach, it can illuminate; yes, and it can even inspire. But it can do so only to the extent that humans are determined to use it to those ends. Otherwise, it is merely lights and wires in a box."

One of the early presidents of the Columbia Broadcasting System's TV network, James Aubrey, was quoted as follows in 1960 by Fred Friendly several years before Friendly's resignation from CBS as the executive producer of a new project, *CBS Reports:*

> Look, Fred, I have regard for what Murrow and you have accomplished, but in this adversary system you and I are always going to be at each others' throats. They say to me, "Take your spoiled little hands, get the ratings, and make as much money as you can"; they say to you, "Take your lily-white hands, do your best, go the high road and bring us prestige."[7]

It was inevitable, under the circumstances, that Friendly and Murrow would be at a disadvantage for as long as money-making was the prime objective as Aubrey had phrased it so long ago. Murrow wound up as chief of the US Information Agency and Friendly as a Columbia University journalism professor.

"So much of what is wrong with television is due to circumstances beyond somebody's control," Friendly wrote in his letter of resignation to CBS after he was refused permission to broadcast the Senate's hearings on the Vietnam War on February 10, 1966. It also was the title of the book he later wrote about his experiences. [8]

Without doubt, the feeling attributed to Aubrey still exists at the heart of commercial television. But it is also true that TV news has expanded enormously in the 1980s and 1990s, especially through the competitiveness of the Cable News Network, NBC, and others as well as the emphasis given to news reporting and interpretation on noncommercial TV in the Public Broadcasting Service. But it still is rare, despite the presence of many talented journalists, including former Pulitzer Prize winners on TV news staffs, to see and hear anybody on TV take the chances of a Buford Boone, a Harry Ashmore, or a Ralph McGill in the public interest.

I hope there will yet come a time when the bravery and the talent of Peter Arnett and Christiane Amanpour in reporting a small Balkan war under fire for CNN will be duplicated in TV public service journalism. When that happens generally, I shall be among the first to applaud.

11 Shuffling the Prizes

Toward century's end, when the Pulitzer Prize Board rules its own affairs and has been enlarged and diversified in membership, it is easier to understand my concern as an administrator who worked with a smaller board mainly of newspaper executives.

Nowadays, moreover, Pulitzer juries no longer are asked to recommend winners; instead, their task is limited to several choices in alphabetical order for the consideration of the Pulitzer board without indicating preference. And the trustees of the university, for many years the final arbiters, have long since removed themselves from contention in favor of the president of Columbia.[1]

But for all save the last of my twenty-two years with the Pulitzers, my problem as board secretary and administrator was quite different. As the position was outlined in 1954, when I was initally appointed by my colleague, Professor Richard T. Baker:

> There have been many criticisms of the Pulitzer Prizes during their history. Certain American authors, for example, acknowledged leaders in the world of literature, have gone unrecognized by Pulitzer Prizes. . . . There also has been bitter criticism of the number of journalistic awards which have gone to newspapers with members of their staff on the Advisory Board.[2]

Still, at the outset of my twin assignments as teacher and prize executive, I took comfort in the rule that board members involved in a particular award had to leave the room until after a decision had been made on that nomination. However, as I discovered soon enough, members whose cause was lost while they were out of the room did not always accept the result gracefully. Now and then, there were hard feelings that couldn't be smoothed over at once. It wasn't an easy situation for me to handle as administrator, especially when the board permitted its members to be eligible to serve three consecutive terms of three years each. Such lengthy continuities long since have been eliminated, and the prizes are better for it.

During my first six years with the board, I also was disturbed by the large number of jury reversals in letters, drama, and even music as well as journalism. As I already have indicated, even during the board's advisory status when the trustees of the university had the final say on the prizes, I often felt the heat of a reversed jury's objections as I have already indicated. Sometimes, there might have been reasons for a jury reversal if there were developments affecting the entry after the jury had acted. But such notions never were easy for me to justify to angry jurors who never again wanted to serve.

Actually, I was dependent more often than not on the goodwill of expert jurors because the prizes in my time operated on a small budget over which I had no permanent control. But to give the newspaper executives on the board their due, regardless of their jury reversals, I doubt if the Pulitzer awards could have existed for very long earlier in the century without their support, their own generosity, and their trust.

Nevertheless, this sensitive situation reached an unexpected climax in 1960, when the Pulitzer board reversed its juries' recommendations in fiction, drama, history, and biography as well as six out of the eight awards that then were bestowed for outstanding performance in newspaper journalism and wire services. Only the juries' choice in poetry, music, public service, and national reporting survived this outbreak of wholesale damnation.

As I wrote in a note to myself in my diary, "It was a real rampage." What I also realized, with a sinking heart, was that jurors who were reversed (and paid only nominally if at all) would not want to be considered for service in another year.

That, quite honestly, is why I concluded at the end of the board's 1960 session, "The Pulitzer board members made a shambles of their juries' recommendations." [3]

The letters, drama, and music prizes had come in early that year, and the juries I'd assembled seemed to me to be the finest and the most experienced to date in their respective fields. The first choices, except for history, may not have pleased every member of the Pulitzer board, but I heard no strong complaints in advance of the annual meeting.

In fiction, the recommendation was for *Henderson, the Rain King* by Saul Bellow, who was only then beginning to figure in the nation's literature but who would be awarded a Nobel Prize in 1976. The alternative was a popular best-seller, James Michener's *Hawaii*.

The theatrical season that year had not been particularly noteworthy, but the jury chairman, John Mason Brown, had recommended Lillian Hellman's *Toys in the Attic* on behalf of his jury.

I thought there might be a problem with the history prize, mainly
because the outstanding history of the year had been *The Armada* by
Garrett Mattingly, the destruction of the Spanish Armada off the English
coast in 1588. However, the terms of the award called for a history of
the United States.

By contrast there were two contenders for the biography award—*In
the Days of McKinley* by Margaret Leech, who had managed to write
about the causes of the Spanish-American War without reference to the
fierce rivalry between the Hearst and Pulitzer newspapers over "bleeding
Cuba," and Samuel Eliot Morison's *John Paul Jones.*

For poetry and music, the recommendations were *Heart's Needle* by
W. D. Snodgrass for the first and Elliott Carter's *Second String Quintet*
for the latter after Roger Sessions was said to have asked not to be
considered.

The journalism jury recommendations were decided upon March
10–11 without any sign of either argument or dissension but a great deal
of effort. I offer this general record:

> The Pulitzer Journalism Juries came in—all 26 editors arrived on
> time although there was a snow storm that interfered with most travel
> throughout the country. They worked hard. The only untoward inci-
> dent was good-natured laughter when I tried somewhat awkwardly to
> compliment Dean Edward Barrett by introducing him as a scholar.
>
> He was gracious anyway—said I carried a heavy teaching load as
> well as the Pulitzer Prizes and had written and published two books in
> the previous 12 months. After most of the juries finished that first day,
> I went home for a quick dinner, then returned to the Pulitzer office to
> prepare the final jury reports for the Pulitzer board and worked until
> 11 p.m.
>
> March 11—The International and one Local reporting jury stayed
> over and finished. Then my secretary, Mrs. Hewlett Barnes, and I
> worked all afternoon and well into the evening to finish the presentation
> for the Pulitzer board members. I was pleased because everything was
> at the printers' by the time we finished for the week-end.

Ordinarily, between that time and the arrival of the Pulitzer board
on April 28, I would have been able to catch up on some of the class
work I'd been forced to postpone, such as the visits to the UN that
usually were so fascinating to small groups of students who went with
me. But for reasons that never were very clear to me, Dean Barrett
worried continually about the conduct of unspecified members of the
Pulitzer board.

This was a sample of what I happened that year along with all the regular work for my classes and the Pulitzers:

> March 30—Dean Barrett keeps telling me that there have been irregularities in the conduct of the work of the Advisory Board on the Pulitzer Prizes. And I continually tell him I know of no such thing.
>
> It happened again today when he phoned me from his office (it is just down the hall from mine) and told me John O'Rourke of the Washington Daily News had phoned him for permission to enter a news exhibit. I told the dean the deadline had been February 1 for all journalism exhibits, the Journalism Jurors had come and gone and O'Rourke could write a letter to me if he wished but it would be ill-advised.
>
> The dean then suggested there were 'little pieces of paper' that had been produced in the past without the knowledge of jurors. I didn't know what he was talking about and he backed down.[4]

That didn't help me when the members of the Pulitzer board assembled in the World Room on April 28 and began shuffling the recommendations of all the letters and drama juries, except for poetry. This is how I began the record of the confusing decisions of the board that day:

> Instead of "Henderson the Rain King" by Saul Bellow, the Pulitzer board picked "Advise and Consent" by Allen Drury for the fiction prize and brushed off President Kirk's openly expressed dislike of what he called an unfair picture of Washington. The jury's second choice, James Michener's "Hawaii," wasn't considered.
>
> That, however, was just the beginning of the onslaught against jury recommendations. The next to suffer was the recommendation of John Mason Brown's Drama Jury for Lillian Hellman's "Toys in the Attic." Instead, the board's members voted for an amusing new musical, "Fiorello," based on the adventures of a pudgy little New York mayor, Fiorello H. LaGuardia. I was too stunned to say anything.
>
> The big turnover after that came in a switch between the jury recommendations for history and biography. There was some discussion of the Mattingly book, "The Armada," but it wasn't eligible for the History award so the board voted it a Pulitzer Special Award. Next, the board members rejected the first two History Jury choices in favor of Margaret Leech's "In the Days of McKinley," which had been recommended for the Biography Prize. And for Biography, the members voted the No. 2 jury choice in that category, the Morison book, "John Paul Jones."
>
> I suppose, theoretically, I should have reminded Chairman Pulitzer that the new winner in history, Miss Leech, was in private life the second wife of his uncle, Ralph Pulitzer, which technically at least gave

him an interest in the proceedings. But by the time I thought of that, the board already had acted and gone on to start bashing the choices of the journalism juries.

After approving the award of the public service gold medal to the Los Angeles Times for investigating illegal drug sales across the Mexican border, every other recommendation except that of national reporting was upset—six in all. The national award went to Vance Trimble of Scripps-Howard News Service for his series on nepotism in Congress.

Then the board voted its own decisions as follows:

Local Reporting—Jack Nelson of the Atlanta Constitution.

Local Specialized Reporting—Miriam Ottenberg of the Washington Star, the jury's No. 4 choice.

International—A. M. Rosenthal of the New York Times, who risked his life in reporting from Communist Poland and was expelled.

Editorial Writing—Lenoir Chambers of the Norfolk Virginian-Pilot, another jury that was upset.

Cartooning—Instead of the jury's choice, this one was passed.

Photography—Andrew Lopez of UPI for a series on the execution of a Cuban soldier by a Castro firing squad, a jury's third choice.

I was exhausted at the end of this free-wheeling demonstration of authority but the members were chipper. They re-elected me for another year but without enthusiasm. From now on, they decided, the book deadline will be December 1 and journalism will remain February 1. Later, President Kirk and I decided on a March 1 deadline for drama and music, exchanged a few thoughts and called it another year for the Pulitzers.[5]

Except for the trustees' decision to accept or reject the Pulitzer board's choices, the university had no authority to intervene, and protests would only have made the position even more untenable. And so, with a fatalistic mixture of resignation and dread, I awaited the trustees' vote and the announcement of the prizes on Monday, May 2. To my surprise, the immediate reaction was peaceful once the reporters finished phoning the news to their offices. This was what I noted:

May 2—By 4:30, the reporters were out of the building and everything seemed peaceful. The news was accepted quietly and without demonstration at first. Only an editor from the New York Post called, demanded to know the makeup of a jury in which it had had an exhibit and asked if it had qualified. It hadn't been, and I gave him the identities of the jurors.

Next day, Chairman Pulitzer and I exchanged notions about the 1959–1960 year by phone while he was in St. Louis, after which I distributed the list of jury acceptances I already had received for the 1960–1961 year. I thought I'd escaped the pain and the anger of the juries that had been reversed but, beginning the next day, I discovered that I'd been living in a world of illusions. This is how I rounded out the reactions in my diary:

> May 5—A long day of Pulitzer protests. The editorial and drama juries were irked over being reversed and I had to write apologetic letters. That evening, I went to President Kirk's reception at the Faculty Club—a set event that supposedly had nothing to do with the Pulitzers —but an angry trustee grabbed me anyway and demanded to know why "Fiorello" was given the drama prize. I said quite honestly that the board members didn't like the Hellman play. But the trustee then wanted to know why the board didn't pick another play, 'The Miracle Worker,' and I said I didn't know. The trustee told me then quite seriously that the time will come when the trustees will overrule the board. When that happened, I said I hoped I wouldn't be around. [6]
>
> May 6—More protests. The Editorial Writing Jury squawked because its members had wanted to award no prize for 1960 and the Pulitzer board found an exhibit it liked. I also heard from a juror each in fiction and drama who were distressed, but so was I. That being Friday, Dorothy and I took off early for the old homestead on eastern Long Island and a beautiful spring week-end. I'd had all I could take.

There was more of this from time to time during the rest of the month, but I tried as best I could to be conciliatory. If Chairman Pulitzer and the other newspaper members of the board also received reproaches from victims of their day of jury reversals, they never did say. Mine came and went in spurts, as witness the following entries:

> May 12—A lot of protests. John Mason Brown's secretary called to say that he was distressed about the choice of "Fiorello" for a Pulitzer Prize. I expressed my regrets but could do nothing to help Mr. Brown.
>
> Next, Dean Barrett called to say that Jimmy Wechsler, then the editor of the New York Post, had charged that the J-school, the Pulitzer Prizes and Columbia University had discriminated against the Post. I again issued the identities of the five Journalism Jurors who had judged the 102 local reporting entries in which the Post was included and repeated that the paper hadn't been recommended.
>
> In the evening, to the annual dinner of the Society of Professional Journalists/Sigma Delta Chi where I was asked to announce that a former Columbia student, Woody Klein, had won an award for a housing inquiry for the New York World-Telegram. I'd guess I was asked mainly because I'd just published the first edition of my textbook, 'The

Professional Journalist,' which had drawn a complimentary column on the New York Times editorial page.

Also that day, the editor of a paper at Longview, Washington, phoned to say he was one member of a committee searching for a new dean for my old school, the University of Washington in Seattle, and was I interested? Recalling mainly the various unpleasant exchanges I'd had that year with Dean Barrett, I thanked the Longview editor but said I'd be staying on at Columbia. I was low on deans.[7]

May 16—My last two lectures of the school year—and I was delighted to survive this crisis year of 1959–60. I thought in my worst moments that I would never see the end.

After commencement, there were a few blessed weeks of rest for me on eastern Long Island. But, to help pay for necessary repairs that now were being conpleted on our old house in Aquebogue, I agreed to six weeks of summer school at Columbia that kept me in the city except for weekends. Fortunately, my courses included a series of discussions with high school journalism teachers that seemed to please both of us.

Even so, after the rough time I'd had at the J-school, I sometimes lapsed into regret for not having accepted the civilian Air Force executive post when it was offered to me. I remember one such experience that made a deep impression on me because of the thoughtfulness and respect with which I was treated by the military for a relatively small service I'd been willing to provide. The entry tells its own story:

> July 7—A little fun today. In place of the teachers' colloquium, a day off for them from summer school at Columbia, an Army staff car rushed me to the ferry at Fort Slocum in Westchester and an Army speed boat took me across to the Army Information School. I had an agreeable West Pointer for an escort all the way. My lecture and question period both seemed better than usual to me and Colonel Jackson, my host, was most gracious. A good day in every respect.

Still, when I came back to the lonely apartment on Morningside Heights (Dorothy remained on Long Island, supervising the repairs to the house), I realized that the Air Force option no longer was available to me. A new chief of information services had been appointed, a West Pointer and Harvard Law School graduate with a distinguished service record, Colonel Sydney G. Fisher, whom I'd liked as soon as I met him. Indeed, he and his wife were to become lifelong friends of ours at home and abroad in the years to come—a rich reward for my association with the Air Force while I remained at Columbia.[8]

When I returned to Aquebogue that weekend in July, I saw that there had been additional compensation for my labors. A new slate-gray shingled roof had been completed on the house. The chimneys had been painted white. The elms and the maples had been properly trimmed, and the lovely rose garden was in full bloom. Dorothy was waiting for me in the car when the Long Island Rail Road's express, "The Cannonball," chugged into the Riverhead station.

For dinner, there was another surprise. The ladies of The Steeple, our old Congregational church that served all of us regardless of our religious faith, had made a church supper for our tiny community—lobster thermidor and all the extras—and we brought ours home with us for a feast we didn't have to prepare. Gratefully, I took over the job of painting the old woodshed white next morning and finished with paint all over me—a good excuse for a mile-long swim in Long Island Sound off Iron Pier Beach nearby.

After that kind of weekend, I returned to the city Sunday night for the remainder of my summer school session and felt better about Columbia, the Pulitzer Prizes, and the world in general. I knew now what I would be doing for many years.

12 Presidential Politics

Of all my Pulitzer Prize experiences, there is a special place in memory for the 1960 Kennedy-Nixon presidential campaign.

From the outset, I had little doubt that the award of a Pulitzer Prize hinged on the manner and the method in which an unruly army of correspondents reported the outcome of the closest race in modern times. [1]

Having known many of the principals in the field of daily and weekly journalism, including the leaders of TV crews, it became an absorbing experience for both my students at Columbia and me to follow this unique rivalry from beginning to end. Then, we put together our own election-night extra on a tight deadline with student editors calling the apparent winner while the result was still in doubt.

The contest between such forceful candidates as Senator John Fitzgerald Kennedy and Vice-President Richard Milhous Nixon had aroused the American public from the beginning in early fall. At the time, feelings intensified when the bumbling Soviet premier, Nikita Sergeyevich Khrushchev, burst into the United Nations with tough talk and wild threats of retaliation after his gunners had shot down an American U-2 spy plane the previous May 1 over Soviet territory.

Until Khrushchev began warning of dire consequences in retaliation against American spying, there had been a fairly intensive anti-Catholic movement in the American heartland aimed at the Kennedy candidacy. While no one in the Republican Party or the Nixon entourage took responsibility for the attack, aimed as always at a bigoted audience, it could have had an effect on the campaign had it continued in force. But once the Soviet leader began slugging it out with the American delegation at the United Nations, little more was heard of the fundamentalist propaganda against the first Roman Catholic to seek the presidency since Governor Alfred E. Smith of New York in 1928.

What Khrushchev did unwittingly by putting himself in the midst of

American presidential politics that year of 1960 was to deflect the rise of anti-Catholic sentiment against the Kennedy candidacy. And since Khrushchev won no new friends for the Soviet Union with his outrageous conduct at the United Nations, the national polls toward the middle of the presidential campaign showed the two major parties locked in an exceedingly close contest.

Having had a substantial experience of my own as a political writer and a UN correspondent, I reflected in my diary:

> The State Department is trying to get TV and presumably the press to play down Khrushchev's anti-American campaign in the UN. This is like the old-fashioned longing for quiet diplomacy among the State department's senior officials at home and abroad. When will we learn that the Russians don't play the game by our rules? They aren't likely to keep quiet, especially Khrushchev and his people, and they know how to get into the world press and TV with their propaganda whether we like it or not.

Still, there was a negative benefit for the American position at the United Nations in all this. The net effect of Khrushchev's jaw-boning, it turned out, was to eliminate anti-Communism as an issue in the presidential campaign and blunt Nixon's usual claim to be the fiercest anti-Communist in the country by matching him against Kennedy's anti-Communist beliefs as a practicing Catholic. In that respect, if in no other, the candidates went into their series of debates equally matched.

But the situation at the United Nations still remained critical, as my diary entries in late September demonstrated directly before the beginning of the fall term at Columbia:

> Sept. 20—To the UN and found the atmosphere electric—the biggest meeting the UN has ever had—Ike, Khrushchev, Tito of Yugoslavia and Gamal Abdel Nasser, the Egyptian president. All of them have made their presence felt although I can't be sure what their effect will be on the American presidential race. Anyway, Vice President Nixon doesn't have to prove anything about being an anti-Communist but Kennedy had better show that he can stand up to Khrushchev if only to reassure his dubious conservative Democratic constituency.
>
> However you look at it, the scene at the UN is like a fever chart— and not only for the international organization. I stayed there until 7:30 p.m. and talked to many delegates, UN correspondents, UN and various national officials and so on, even a few former students who now are full-fledged correspondents here and all are impressed with the importance of the meeting.
>
> Sept. 21—Downtown to the UN again from Morningside Heights

and attended a United States news conference with my friend and former AP colleague, Frank Carpenter, now the American press officer. Only today, on instructions from on high with President Eisenhower still on the scene, Frank had to say "no comment" for an hour to 85 correspondents of all nationalities.

Sept. 22—Off to a fresh start on Columbia's new academic year with more than 80 graduate students, and downtown at the UN I was told that Ike did well in a conciliatory speech toward the Soviet Union although I don't believe that will change anything either there or in the Nixon-Kennedy race for president.

Sept. 23—At Aquebogue today, a Friday, I listened to Khrushchev at the UN via TV but got bored and turned him off, something I might have wanted to do when I was a working newsman but couldn't. The speech was repetitive as usual, all about his plan for moving the UN out of the U.S., etcetera. The big Russian won't get very far. Even his own delegates here are too comfortable in New York and not at all anxious to go home.[2]

This was the position when the first of the three Nixon-Kennedy debates on TV took place before a national audience on Monday night, September 26. I wish I could pretend that the speakers fascinated the nation with their ideas, their use of the language, and the inspiration they created for their tens of millions of auditors.

But in all honesty, this could scarcely have been considered something that would go down in history as so remarkable an encounter as the Lincoln-Douglas debates on the future of the Union in 1858 (Lincoln's famous observation; "A house divided cannot stand") or even the Webster-Hayne debates of 1830. Neither of the orators, given the problem of TV audiences in maintaining attention in the midst of comings-and-goings, telephone calls, and shrieks of children at play, could summon up the magnificence of language attributed to their predecessors.

The Nixon-Kennedy debate was wide-ranging, in which appearances counted for more than what was actually being said. Nixon, as always, seemed to be pale, somewhat perspiring, and not entirely sure of himself. Kennedy, the younger of the two by four years, acted as the forceful challenger of the Republican vice-president, but he didn't appear to carry much conviction with him before his TV audience. In any case, for whatever it may be worth as the verdict of a professional observer and by no means a fully committed Kennedy partisan, this was my reaction in my diary:

Sept. 26—Took up school details during the day and listened tonight, with many millions of others, to the first of the Kennedy-Nixon

TV debates. I thought Kennedy did a little better than Nixon, but neither one of the candidates was very impressive. They might have been running for alderman for all the conviction they showed.

For an equally cool assessment, I found the following that I'd set down in my diary two days later:

> Sept. 28—As a part of my work for Columbia, I attended a reception at the Carnegie Endowment for our international fellows and others at nearby universities and rode back with President Kirk and our director of news and information, Bob Harron. Dr. Kirk said that while he is probably voting for Nixon, he thought Kennedy had the better of the first TV debate last Monday and Nixon didn't look well. That," so I continued, "is the general impression but I know of no votes that were changed.

A second debate in mid-October, at the height of the presidential campaign, didn't seem to make much change in public attitudes either, although most of the veteran pollsters showed for the record that they believed Kennedy was slightly ahead. That, however, didn't seem too convincing to me, and I tried, as an entirely professional matter, to persuade my students to withhold judgment. The election, as the polls demonstrated, still was too close to call.

I offer a foreshortened report, taken from my diary for the crucial campaign month of October:

> Oct. 5—I had the students in my national reporting seminar covering Vice President Nixon today. But instead of coming in and writing their accounts for a late afternoon deadline, I asked them to report the story to the remainder of our students, then assigned everybody to do the account under pressure on a tight deadline. For young people of little or no experience in the field, I thought the experiment turned out well, particularly because nobody ventured to favor one candidate over the other because that truly was the position today.
>
> Oct. 12—I had my national affairs students cover Kennedy today, asked them to report to the rest of the class as they did the previous week and everybody then wrote the story. I hope I'm not kidding myself, but most of the people in the class of 1960 seemed to work well with a certain amount of professional assurance. Anyway, I'd say there is progress.
>
> Oct. 13—Tonight, I heard part of the third Nixon-Kennedy debate and again thought Nixon did poorly when he insisted we must defend the off-shore Asian islands of Quemoy and Matsu for Chiang Kai-shek, the nationalist China leader. Kennedy seemed to me to be making an impression, how much I can't say.

Oct. 14—Took students to the UN to view the confrontation of the United States and the Soviet Union. But by this time, as I was able to demonstrate to my charges in the Delegates' Lounge, any story about foreign opinion on the Presidential campaign had to be based on interviews, some on background (no identification of source), with foreign delegates in the lounge.

As Frank Carpenter explained to the students off the record, it was hopeless to expect any American official to talk about the election with Election Day only a little more than two weeks off. Later, I was able to get away to talk to the state session of the Associated Press Managing Editors at Albany and saw H. R. Ekins, with whom I began as a reporter in New York in 1924. Then home after midnight.

Oct. 19—Governor Averell Harriman of New York state came to Columbia and held a news conference for my national and international classes. As a Democrat, he was bound to plug Kennedy's chances but the test for the students was to keep their own opinion out of the story. Afterward, however, I went home, found my mail ballot and made it out for Kennedy although Dorothy was pretty sarcastic about my performance. Still, I couldn't bring myself to vote for Nixon although I had no illusions about Kennedy. Still very close.

Oct. 25—A slow, hard, punishing day of editing student copy about the election, 35 pieces in all ranging from 800–1,000 words each. I finished at 11:15 p.m. to make it possible to return the edited product to the authors tomorrow. The only pleasant moment I had was to see Dorothy off for a Women's Faculty party in a new purple dress, a big purple hat with a large brim and her mink jacket. I've seldom seen her look more lovely.

Oct. 26—My regular newswriting class for all our students, a three-hour operation on the election, and a Faculty lunch afterward. There was so much uproar over whether to continue the very hard work of making live news the basis for instruction, rather than the much easier canned newswriting examples, that I said I would get out as chairman of instruction and serve under somebody else. Only the dean said no, but that didn't seem to impress my academic critics.

Nov. 5—Tonight the Donoghues came over—Bill is the publicity director for the New York World's Fair and an old friend—and we sat in on the TV finale for Kennedy, Nixon and Ike. We all agreed that Kennedy, in his climactic night, had done poorly and Nixon and Ike had made votes for their party and themselves. Bill, who had directed Governor Harriman's winning campaign in New York state, said Kennedy may have a very close call and I think he is right. (A footnote: I was so interested in the roundup that I forgot to look at my own show on Channel 13, the non-commercial station.)

Nov. 7—The day before Election Day and two long classes left me little time to prepare the students for their election coverage and the production of their newspaper tomorrow night. They'll have to do a lot by themselves, I'm afraid. All the polls now point to Kennedy but cover themselves by predicting a close vote. [3]

. . .

The real problem of the election for all of us, professionals and students, began around midnight on Election Day. The student editor then decided on his own responsibility that Kennedy had been elected and ordered the "tight race" headlines on the first page changed accordingly. I didn't interfere but my charges were working on a 1.30 A.M. deadline—very close to the same deadline for the leading newspapers in the Eastern time zone. On radio and TV, the anchors also were declaring Kennedy elected, and so our students in effect went with the prevailing opinion of their elders at the time.

This was the kind of experience I wanted the students to have in their work for the school—to match themselves against the best professionals of their time and learn from experience whether their decisions had been right or wrong. What happened, I think, is best summarized in what I recorded in my diary for Election Day and early November 9, the day after the vote:

> The students made their Kennedy victory paper deadline of 1:30 a.m. Nov. 9 and I got home at 3 a.m. When I got up to go to class later that morning, I discovered that the New York Times, which apparently had also made the decision for Kennedy at about the same time and put out an early Kennedy election paper, had pulled back in its 7 a.m. edition.
>
> The head and the story were qualified to say that Kennedy 'apparently had won' the Presidency. The caution was justified.
>
> As we later learned from the official canvass, the final totals gave Kennedy an 84-point victory in the Electoral College, 303–219, but in the popular vote he received only 118,550 more votes than Nixon out of more than 68 million cast. At any rate, in my critique for the class, I mixed criticism with compliments because the students, like the professionals, had made the right decision on deadline but also had gone overboard on estimating the size of Kennedy's victory.[4]

However Dorothy voted in the election, she never did tell me; but it turned out on Friday, November 11, when we had dinner with Professor Ralph Halford and his wife, Marian, that Dorothy and Marian Halford had split the kitty on the faculty sweepstakes by coming closest to the Kennedy electoral vote. Anyway, on all counts, both the professionals and the students, the Kennedy victory climaxed a hard-fought election.

What, then, of the 1961 Pulitzer Prizes and the numerous candidates among the correspondents who had covered the 1960 presidential campaign? It is one of the peculiarities of the editorial mind that neither the journalism juries nor the Pulitzer board seriously discussed the chances of any newspaper, wire service, or free-lance correspondent for an award. Either there were no standouts among the professionals who followed the candidates night and day for the critical ten weeks leading up to Election Day or there were so many of high quality that it would have been an injustice to single out one or two for special honors. I never did find out why none of the regulars qualified for an award from the Pulitzer establishment in 1961.

But in 1962, in the first year of a new award for excellence in general nonfiction, a former reporter for weekly magazines, Theodore H. White, won this very special Pulitzer for his detailed account of the Kennedy-Nixon campaign in *The Making of the President, 1960*. He had completed the work in enormous detail in 1961, and Atheneum had published it the same year and then entered it in the 1962 competition for the newest Pulitzer Prize. [5]

White was forty-seven at the time, Boston-born and a *summa cum laude* graduate of Harvard, whose first work as a journalist had been for *Time* magazine as a correspondent in China from 1939 to 1945. After doing a book on Chinese affairs and working briefly as an editor in New York, he became a magazine correspondent in Europe for several years, published a few books, and then came home to establish his reputation as the author of the *Making of the President* series through 1972, together with several TV documentaries based on his published work. It is worth noting, as well, that his TV documentary for the 1960 campaign also won him numerous honors, including an Emmy award and another TV prize for the best program of the year.

White was invariably generous to his daily and weekly rivals who covered the 1960 and three other presidential campaigns in his series, crediting many of them publicly in each of his books with having given him assistance. But as one of my 1960 students observed after becoming a political analyst for a major newspaper, it was White who won the prizes beginning with 1960.

I can add only my own estimate of White's excellence as a journalist who didn't necessarily have to work against a fixed deadline. Under such circumstances, the race is not always to the swift.

13 Press versus Government

A Nobel Prize physicist at Columbia, Professor Isaac Isidor Rabi, had no trouble winning my respect early in my years at Columbia, although I had long since forgotten whatever physics I had been exposed to as a university student. I remember Professor Rabi in particular because he was the first at Columbia to draw me into a good-natured argument over the attitudes of a serious-minded press in America toward government actions of which it disapproved. [1]

My distinguished colleague, a pugnacious little man with a wiry shock of white hair, was convinced that the government was being unfairly stigmatized at the time by press attacks on its extensive funding of scientific experiments.

As far as I was concerned, my problem arose because nobody around the oblong table at our weekly faculty Peace Seminar seemed to want to challenge Professor Rabi on his own turf, even our chairman, Professor Phil Jessup. As one of the newest additions to the seminar, I'd been content to let others among my university associates handle discussions with visiting experts. But now, as the only journalist in the room at the Faculty Club, it did seem to me that there was something to be said for my centuries—old trade that still was struggling for recognition as a profession.

However, I had to summon up a lot of nerve to take on so renowned an authority as Professor Rabi before our colleagues, all of whom, I am sure, had done better than I at elementary pyysics in their bygone days as students. No matter. Professor Jessup had offered me up as the sacrificial object in this debate over press versus government, and I was committed whether I liked it or not.

I began mildly enough as a defender of the press by recalling very little criticism by the press or others in this country and abroad when the United States offered to yield our atomic bombs, and the atomic secret as well, to the United Nations in 1946, provided all other members would end their efforts to attain atomic parity. And this, as I recalled, was a challenge our government had addressed particularly to the Soviet Union.

My argument, at the outset, was that Professor Rabi surely was exaggerating when he accused the entire American press of being anti-government in the case of funding scientific experiments. I went on to say that I recalled no instance of press criticism of the Baruch offer in the United States, except possibly for the Chicago *Tribune*.

My opponent took me on, asking me skeptically if I had been refer-ring to the Baruch Plan[2] for atomic control, introduced at the United Nation in 1946, and I nodded. He then argued that this was no scientific experiment but a deliberate political effort by the American government to stop the Soviet Union's own experiments to create a nuclear device.

It was, he added, a political move of which he approved but—this with a fatherly air—it seemed to him to be outside the scope of the complaint he was making against the press.

Still, regardless of the purposes of the American government in offer-ing the Baruch Plan, I said that here was at least one instance in which not only the American but much of the world's independent press had applauded an American initiative in the most awesome scientific break-through of this century. And to that, my Nobel Prize opponent was bound to agree. That he did, with grace.

But almost immediately, there was an interruption that saved me from what I feared would have been a less respectable defense. The radiator in the room set up so tremendous a clatter and banging that the debate, if that is what it was, had to be called off. My distinguished colleague then rose to the occasion by advancing boldly to investigate the problem of the radiator. And, after judicious fiddling with the con-trols, he produced a sudden hissing noise and the disturbance halted.

Professor Rabi explained to us, as he resumed his place at the table, "It was just a little thing—the steam valve was stuck."

To which our chairman commented gravely, "How useful it is in a university to have a Nobel Prize-winning scientist who can also fix radia-tors while arguing the merits and demerits of the Baruch Plan for atomic control."

There was a ripple of laughter. Professor Rabi acknowledged the compliment with a wry smile and a shrug, and the discussion resumed until it was time to go home. Having been spared by the malfunctioning radiator from further intellectual sparring, I had sense enough then to hold my peace.

The encounter with Professor Rabi made an impression on me because it illustrated the vast difference between the world of the journalist, from which I had come, and the affairs of the academic community, into which I had been plunged with little preparation. What I had to do now was to come to terms with university life on a quite different level, both as a professor and as the administrator of the Pulitzer Prizes.

This was no mere technicality, such as the argument over the relations between press and government in which Professors Jessup and Rabi had led me into an intellectual gavotte. For on what I had thought was a quite ordinary spring evening at the Columbia Graduate School of Journalism in 1959, when some of us among the faculty were attending a meeting of our students, someone suddenly produced Premier Fidel Castro of Cuba, who had earlier that year overthrown the Batista government and now was creating a Communist state not far removed from the state of Florida, a matter of 90 miles.

To say that I was astounded by this strictly student enterprise is an understatement. But once Castro appeared, our problem—and that of the students—was to find space for all the gate-crashers who wanted to hear what this new Communist potentate in the Americas had to say. The entry in my diary continued:

> Altogether, as it turned out, the young people jammed our largest auditorium. As for Castro, he listened to questions from students and faculty, answered none of them, just made voluble speeches in Spanish with violent gestures. He seemed a grown-up child who played with his beard and threw kisses to the crowd. However, it is a sure thing that the Communists already were running him and his government, or vice versa. We were worried until he left safely. I thought the police did a magnificent job that night. [3]

What did all this have to do with the issue of press versus government as Professor Rabi had posed it as well as our students and the Pulitzer Prizes? I recalled the whole sequence of academic events in the spring of 1961 during the period between the decisions of the journalism juries in March and the meeting of the Pulitzer board the following month when the first rumors of the Bay of Pigs invasion began spreading throughout the land. And now neither President Kennedy, our first Pulitzer Prize-winning chief executive, who had just recently entered the White House, nor his supporters could halt a roar of protest from an outraged press asking: "Why?"

This time, there was neither a Nobel Prize-winning physicist nor a compliant steam valve that would halt the clanging and banging that shook an entire nation.

I have often asked myself ever since what could possibly have motivated this admirable young president, John Fitzgerald Kennedy, into supporting this mad CIA-sponsored adventure at the Bay of Pigs. The urge was there, certainly, to do something of major importance at the outset of his administration. Demonstrably, he aspired to greatness.

The night before Kennedy's inauguration, he had read Thomas Jefferson's first inaugural address, shook his head half in admiration and half in regret, saying, "Better than mine." What seemed to bother this young adventurer was his yearning for action and the bold cadences of eighteenth-and early nineteenth-century speech that animated the Revolutionary patriots—Jefferson's language in the Declaration of Independence, "We hold these truths to be self-evident, that all men are created equal, that they are endowed by their Creator with certain unalienable Rights, that among these are Life, Liberty and the pursuit of Happiness."

In his own inaugural, Kennedy caught that sequence in words that marched off the printed page into the minds of those who heard him, "Let every nation know, whether it wishes us well or ill, that we shall pay any price, bear any burden, meet any hardship, support any friend, oppose any foe in order to insure the survival of liberty."

Then, the almost breathless conclusion—-the trumpet-like summons to the struggle against tyranny, poverty, disease, and war itself. "And so, my fellow-Americans, ask not what your country can do for you. Ask what you can do for your country. My fellow-citizens of the world: Ask not what America will do for you, but what together we can do for the freedom of man." [4]

What a pity after so magnificent a beginning that this new president let himself be deflected from his noble goals into a poorly-planned, CIA-directed Cuban invasion by an ill-trained rabble of 1,200 refugees at the Bay of Pigs. Almost anything might have been expected from him after that classic inaugural—but surely not that.

Even after the CIA's adventure began on April 17, 1961, I was so heavily involved in preparations for the annual voting on Pulitzer Prizes that I had little time for much else. Of course, I had heard about a continual series of rumors about a Cuban attack by anti-Castro forces but had paid little attention to them.

When Adlai Stevenson discussed the Cuban situation next evening as our UN representative, I wrote in my diary:*

> April 18—I heard Adlai Stevenson say tonight that he didn't know who was being attacked in Cuba but he knew who was attacking. He went to a night UN meeting to give a statement for President Kennedy.

---

* Stevenson spoke at the Waldorf in New York before a fund-raising dinner for Robert College in Istanbul, Turkey, founded in 1863 and supported by private American philanthropy. Its name was changed in 1971 to the University of the Bosporus.

But nobody I know is at all concerned about the Cuban 'revolt' and there was more laughter about it at the Waldorf tonight after Stevenson spoke than there was handwringing.

The next night, April 19, the last of the three nights of the planned CIA invasion, I seemed to have thought so little of the Bay of Pigs incident that it wasn't even mentioned in that day's diary entry. "I attended the Bancroft dinner awards at Low Library, Columbia, and Max Schuster told me he was having Ely Jacques Kahn do a life of Herbert Bayard Swope."[5]

It became clear to me only by the night of April 20 that whatever else had happened at the Bay of Pigs, Fidel Castro and his Communist army still were very much in charge in Cuba as Nikita Khrushchev's man. I concluded my diary entry that day:

> The great invasion of Cuba is over and it is a terrible defeat, not so much for about a thousand bedraggled anti-Castro Cubans in the CIA-sponsored invasion as it is for President Kennedy and all the rest of us in the United States. Our Columbia president, Grayson Kirk, told me today, "The difference between the Russians in Budapest and us in Cuba is that they pulled off a bad job and got away with it in world opinion, but we didn't in Cuba."

To explain even at this late date the evident confusion of our UN ambassador, Stevenson, he had been given a phony CIA cover story and repeated it in good faith before the world organization. Evidently, the White House's idea was to give the impression that the United States was the victim, not the guiding force, behind the Bay of Pigs operation. It just didn't work. The CIA operation was a mess from beginning to end, a deception that was inexcusably presented to our own people but fooled nobody.

To me, like most other Americans, the proposition made no sense whatever, especially after it had been so well publicized in advance. Yet, such was President Kennedy's stubbornness in the face of an impossible situation he had taken over bodily from the outgoing Eisenhower administration that he later lectured the American press and electronic media privately on what he conceived to be their failure to do their patriotic duty by censoring themselves in a time of troubles.

It was only with great difficulty that he was persuaded eventually to drop that argument, although it still remains of a piece toward century's end among the extreme right-wingers of both major parties. They believe, despite the First Amendment's guarantee of press freedom, that the news media should take it on themselves to lie whenever necessary in defense of the national interest.

From my point of view, it was a position that never would have been recognized by any Pulitzer Prize juror or board member in national or international affairs. The concept of a government undertaking to lie to its own people was bad enough; to drag the press into the plot would have put the position in a criminal context.

As a citizen who voted for Kennedy and admired many of the other critical decisions he made under pressure in his brief time in high office, I have always been disturbed by reports of what he asked a private meeting of American editors to do after the Bay of Pigs debacle. I refer to reports of a private meeting at the White House between the President and the editors. To quote from my diary once again:

> May 10—I met Turner Catledge, executive editor of the New York Times, outside President Kirk's office at Columbia today. Catledge said President Kennedy had been pressed hard yesterday at his private talk with editors at the White House to disclose wherein the press had violated national security recently. He (Kennedy) said there had been instances but gave none. He put forward no proposals, although Catledge said he knew the president had wanted to set up a one-man editor "consultant" system which he apparently withheld at the editors' meeting for fear of their opposition.
>
> Later, from other sources, I learned that the president also had wanted the press to act as a 'cover' and print false information to throw the Communists off the track of our secrets. Anyway, that explains the Times's editorial of this morning, "The Right Not to Be Lied To."

I never again heard of the president's purported belief that the American press, in whole or in part, should act as a government agency in time of stress. What seemed to have happened, at a guess, was that Kennedy came into the president's office with some ideas that were grounded in surprising inexperience and had to dispose of them after he settled into the job. As Arthur Meier Schlesinger Jr. put the position, "He [Kennedy] set quietly to work to make sure that nothing like the Bay of Pigs could happen to him again."[6]

In terms of the encounter of the Nobel Prize physicist and the clanking radiator at Columbia, Professor Isaac Isidor Rabi had used the stuck steam valve as an alarm. By clearing it, he had caused the radiator to heat the room without undue commotion.

In terms of the CIA's mistaken notion that Castro's new Communist regime in Cuba could easily be overthrown, a free and uninhibited press acted as the stuck steam valve, but President Kennedy ignored it and the nation suffered an ignominious and unnecessary defeat. I suppose if life followed the style of dramatic art, the Pulitzer Prize for editorial writing in the next year of the competition, 1962, should have gone to the New York *Times*'s editorial, "The Right Not to Be Lied To."

But such pat solutions cannot be so simply created in an open competition for annual honors in a free society. It so happened that the 1962 award went to Thomas M. Storke, the eighty-five-year-old editor and publisher of the Santa Barbara (Calif.) *News-Press,* for his warning against a semisecret organization, the John Birch Society. In his editorial, he wrote:

> First, let there be no mistake about this: Communism must be opposed vigorously . . . But that does not lead logically to the conclusion that to fight Communism at home we must throw democratic principles and methods into the ashcan and adopt the techniques of the Communists themselves, as the John Birch Society would have us do.[7]

To state the case for the free press, as early as November 19, 1960, the New York weekly, the *Nation,* published the details of a CIA-supported camp in Guatemala, where about 1,200 Cuban refugees supposedly were undergoing secret training for an invasion of their homeland. To deal with that reality, Premier Castro reduced the American embassy's staff in Havana from 130 to 11 people. After that, less than two weeks before the Kennedy inaugural, President Eisenhower broke diplomatic relations with Cuba.

Instead of calling off the CIA's project, which Ike had mistakenly agreed to, Kennedy moved right ahead with a White Paper early in April denouncing Castro as a menace to peace. Castro then accused the United States of plotting an invasion, which Kennedy solemnly denied, saying there "would not be, under any conditions, an intervention in Cuba by United States armed force."

The truth, however, was so evident that Tad Szulc, long known as a first-rate combat reporter to his associates, including myself, reported to the New York *Times* that the CIA was masterminding an imminent invasion. But the always conservative *Times* used it on April 7 as a mere "report" on a Cuban refugee training program directed against Castro.

What President Kennedy did then was to deny the ragtag refugees air support, which canceled any chance they might have had to get a foothold at the Bay of Pigs. Within three days, once the invasion began on April 17, every member of the CIA's "army" was dead, captured, or missing. The *Guardian* in Manchester, England, commented, "Everyone knows that sort of invasion by proxy with which the United States has now been charged is morally indistinguishable from open aggression."

An angry Kennedy's first reaction was to blast the American Newspaper Publishers Association. "Every newspaper now asks itself with respect to every story, 'Is it news?' All I suggest is that you add the question, 'Is it in the interest of national security?' " The trouble was that Kennedy's invitation to self-censorship of the First Amendment couldn't be taken seriously. Once the president had a chance to think things over, he told Turner Catledge, the New York *Times*'s executive editor and a member of the Pulitzer board, "If you'd printed more about the [Bay of Pigs] operation, you'd have saved us from a colossal mistake." [8]

When it was all over, I couldn't help thinking of Professor Rabi and his argument against press opposition to government funding of too many scientific projects. At least, being a Nobel Prize winner, he hadn't suggested censorship.

14 The Soviet Challenge

The Pulitzer board should have had a relaxed session in the spring of 1961 for its annual prize selections but, once again, it was no go.

Although the Kennedy White House no longer was fussing about what a free press should or should not have to avert the Bay of Pigs disaster, the Communists were challenging the West in even greater strength. And this time, the foe was no annoying Cuban upstart.

The latest threat was renewed by the plump and earthy Soviet premier, Nikita Khrushchev. What he seemed to be preparing for was another tightening of the Soviet blockade about West Berlin, mainly because more than 2 million panicky East Germans had fled that impoverished Communist domain in a little more than a decade.

It was perfectly evident that most of them had boldly headed westward through the divided former German capital by night without being stopped by border guards.

Clearly, Khrushchev did have a problem. Since the failure of the 1948–1949 Soviet blockade of West Berlin, which had been smashed by an Allied airlift, the Soviets had done nothing to ease the plight of the East Germans. And now, by contrast, West Berlin was a glittering magnet—a lavishly prosperous showpiece set against the rags-and-breadcrust state of affairs in East Berlin and East Germany.

So the question that spring was whether the hard-pressed Soviet leader would threaten the West once more with another blockade and, if so, how the United States—as the leader of the Western coalition—would respond. [1]

There also was at the time a far less serious diversion from the board's regular business that was particularly annoying to the chairman, Joseph Pulitzer Jr., but President Kirk of Columbia had asked me to report on it to the 1961 session of the board, and I was prepared to do so. It was the prospect, this time more direct than usual, of an organized campaign for a TV Pulitzer Prize.

The reason for concern in the matter primarily was the identity of the latest petitioner, Robert Sarnoff, who then was the board chairman of the National Broadcasting Company. When I had interviewed him at his office earlier for a report to the board, he had suggested that TV news should be judged by the Pulitzer establishment on the same basis as that of daily newspapers and wire services because all would be competing for the same awards in journalism.

It was Sarnoff's notion that the TV news/newspaper rivalry for the prizes should first be established, after which meritorious TV works that fitted the various nonjournalism categories—drama, for example—also would be made eligible in due course.

My summary in my diary that year demonstrated how little possibility there was for an agreement between the TV people, a newspaper-dominated Pulitzer board, and the university:

> April 11—I had instructions from President Kirk, if Mr. Sarnoff seemed willing to negotiate, that I should propose a review committee for the prizes that would include representatives of the Pulitzer board, the university, and TV. But it did not seem to me, given the NBC board chairman's demands, that such a review committee could do much of anything. So I merely thanked him after the interview, said I would report to the board, and that was that. I could see no middle ground for negotiation at the time.[2]

I suppose I should have been pleased at the seeming unity within the Pulitzer establishment, but I sympathized with President Kirk's idea of a review committee. Realistically, the Pulitzers had changed only in a few details since the first prizes had been bestowed in 1917. Yet, despite that, vast new areas had opened in America in both public service and public communications, without any sign that the prizes might be affected.

Perhaps I was unduly influenced because students in my classes now were represented among the leaders in complex corporate communications structures that included such entities as book and magazine publishing, TV and radio, and even film now and then. Perhaps, too, I had been struck by the lack of enterprise among board members in bolstering new considerations in the nonjournalistic fields of letters, drama, and music.

Then also, as for art, the only semblance of recognition for excellence in that vast cultural domain had been a poorly funded art scholarship, but even that now was being abandoned. And yet, for our Columbia journalism students, we still could afford only three Pulitzer traveling scholarships that had only recently been increased from $1,000 to $2,000 each.

What bothered me most of all at the time, I believe, was the Pulitzer board's procedures that made no provision for review, except when there was a public outcry over a particular award. Otherwise, what had happened within the university itself was a growing impatience on the part of the Columbia trustees over their severely limited role in approving or disapproving of the board's prize selections within a few minutes before the formal public announcement.

But beyond my report on the Sarnoff proposal for a TV prize at the 1961 board meeting, no thought was given once again to change for the prizes. With a show of impatience, Chairman Pulitzer himself disposed of Sarnoff with the remark that TV "wasn't in my grandfather's will." Only Barry Bingham of the Louisville *Courier-Journal,* one of the most highly regarded members of the Pulitzer board, differed with the chairman—and that with an apologetic attitude.

As the board then turned to its regular business, I do not recall that anybody brought up the possibility of a major break between the Soviet Union and the United States over pending differences in Berlin that carried with them the ever-present threat of an atomic holocaust. What the members seemed to want to do that spring was to get over the voting on the awards as quickly as possible.

There were no differences around the board table that day with the nonjournalism prizes that had been recommended by their respective juries. For fiction, there was the bright little story, *To Kill a Mocking Bird,* that had made its author, Harper Lee, a best-seller almost overnight. There was what amounted to a double prize for drama, a play based or a previous prize novel, *All the Way Home,* by Tad Mosel. The history and biography awards were respectable—Herbert Feis's history of the Potsdam crisis and a first prize in David Herbert Donald's remarkable career as a biographer for his life of Charles Sumner. The poetry award deservedly went to Phyllis McGinley's engaging light verse.

Except for the prizes in local reporting that were won by two of my former students, Sanche de Gramont (Ted Morgan) of the New York *Herald Tribune* and Edgar May of the Buffalo *Evening News,* the Pulitzer journalism awards also attracted little public attention. Public service went to a small newspaper in Amarillo, Texas. National reporting was awarded to Ed Cony of the *Wall Street Journal,* but some of the Columbia trustees later kicked up a fuss because the writer hadn't been kind to a wealthy Columbia alumnus; nevertheless, the award went through without comment.

The rest included an international award to Lynn Heinzerling of the AP for his reporting in the Congo, to seventy-one-year-old Carey Orr of the Chicago *Tribune* for his cartoons, and to a Japanese photographer, Yasushi Nagao, for a gruesome picture of a stabbing in Tokyo that was distributed to the American press by UPI.[3]

If there was any concern by anybody in the Pulitzer establishment or the university for the perilous state of affairs that was developing in Berlin at the time, the 1961 awards didn't reflect it. The position amounted to business as usual, which had nothing to do with the widening crisis that increasingly matched the Kennedy administration against the ruthlessness of the new master of the Kremlin, Nikita Khrushchev. Within a little more than a month, on June 3, President Kennedy and Premier Khrushchev were trading warnings during a Vienna conference against miscalculating each other's designs and bringing on a nuclear catastrophe. That crisis suddenly came to a head in Berlin.

While I was teaching two courses and directing a teachers' colloquium at summer school in Columbia that year, the growing East-West tensions over Berlin distracted all of us. As we were continually reminded by correspondents from Europe and the early evening network news summaries, the Russians seemed willing to take the risk of nuclear war to drive the United States and the Western allies out of West Berlin. And we Americans, on our part, were frequently represented by the Communist side as re-arming to try to drive the Russians out of East Germany. In my diary for July 6, I wrote:

> James Reston in the New York Times wrote that Kennedy was bluffing in his talk of partial mobilization (of our armed forces) over Berlin. I do hope so but I think Kennedy means business. But he also is not a very stable character. We could be in trouble before this summer is over.

The talk became increasingly aggressive on both sides after that with neither willing either to back down or even show a willingness to negotiate. In his TV address to the nation on July 25, the president said:

> We cannot and will not permit the Communists to drive us out of Berlin either gradually or by force. . . . We do not intend to leave it to others to choose and monopolize the forum and the framework of discussion. We do not intend to abandon our duty to mankind to seek a peaceful solution.[4]

At such a juncture as this in international affairs, what I always hoped for was a cool, reasoned analysis of the position that would not needlessly alarm the public by accepting all the cold war rhetoric on both sides at face value. That late summer, however, I looked in vain for so unique an example of journalistic competence in a disorderly world that would be worthy of consideration by a Pulitzer jury.

Indeed, I don't believe my own estimate—made in my diary that same night—would have been any more reassuring than the published or broadcast work of some of my colleagues. I wrote:

> July 25—Listened to Kennedy's talk about Berlin to the nation tonight in ordering a big military buildup against the Soviets in central Europe. Actually, he talked a lot tougher than he acted. The country is ready for a lot worse and, in my judgment, is willing to follow him.
>
> July 27—There is a considerable amount of excitement among the young men at the university about the new military buildup over Berlin. But that is the only significant change I can see because of Kennedy's demand for action in the Berlin crisis. The people at least are not being panicked. But also, not many people really believe there will be a war.

As subsequent events demonstrated, Khrushchev meanwhile had devised his own minimal solution to the part of the Berlin crisis that meant the most to him—halting the continual departure of tens of thousands of East Germans for the West. Taking the White House completely by surprise, the Soviet premier on August 13 arranged for companies of East German border guards to close all the cross-over points to West Berlin. In place of the neatly paved streets, the East German guards saw to it that the paving was torn up after which roadblocks and barbed wire fences were installed. It would have taken a brave East German after that to try to use that route to escape to the West, particularly after the massive Berlin Wall went up beginning on August 17 and made further unauthorized connection impossible between East and West Berlin.

Perhaps I was overly optimistic when I wrote in my diary on August 18, "The big Berlin crisis appears to be over. The Russians have closed the border between East and West Berlin and nothing happened."

But instead of the violent reaction from the west that Mayor Willy Brandt of West Berlin had anticipated, all President Kennedy offered on his part was to condemn the border closing and the erection of the Wall as "brutal" but he quickly added that nobody was now proposing "that we should go to war on this point."

The only resultant troop deployment was a movement of a small detachment of the US Eighth Infantry to West Berlin.

That fall, there was an unexpected reaction to the Berlin crisis that was attributed to Premier Khrushchev by the former US High Commissioner for Germany, John J. McCloy. At a meeting in New York City, I heard McCloy relate a conversation he'd had with Khrushchev over the problem of stemming the flow of East Germans to the West. The Soviet leader began by relating a Pushkin story about an embarrassed army officer who had shot and killed himself because he'd farted at the Czarina's ball.

"You want *me* to kill myself over a fart?" Khrushchev is supposed to have demanded. To which McCloy said he replied, "Mr. Khrushchev, you let the fart."[5] To which I added in my diary: "Such are the diplomatic negotiations to save the world from war."

Late in the summer I also received an unexpected telephone call from Chairman Pulitzer in St. Louis, who wanted to know if I planned to leave Columbia and the Pulitzer Prizes for the State Department. It seems that a minor official in State had asked Joe to recommend me as a lecturer for the American Specialist program in State.

In my diary, I wrote, "I assured Pulitzer that I was unlikely to leave Columbia for the State Department—and if I ever did I'd consult him first."[6] That was the end of all the crises that summer, large and small, but the even more critical year of 1962 was just ahead for President Kennedy in the Cuban missile crisis.

15 Showdown

Toward the end of the 1961–1962 academic year, somewhat in advance of the Soviet missile buildup in Cuba, Columbia's trustees signaled that they'd had enough of the Pulitzer Prizes.

That was when they denied an award the Pulitzer board had voted that spring to W. A. Swanberg's *Citizen Hearst* in biography. The trustees acted because they didn't consider him an "eminent example" of the biographer's art as specified in the prize definition. To that, William Randolph Hearst Jr., his son, commented, "That's unfair. Everything my pop learned about journalism came from old man Pulitzer." [1]

I noted in my diary, "May 7—My assistants and I had to make corrections in the press packets in a hurry after the trustees approved the rest of the board's choices. So it was 4:30 p.m. before the press packets were given to the reporters, who then phoned that year's results to their offices."

Except for the veto of the Hearst prize, the rest of the awards weren't much of a surprise. They ranged from the musical, *How To Succeed in Business Without Really Trying,* to Theodore H. White for *The Making of the President, 1960* and Edwin O'Connor's novel *The Edge of Sadness.*

In journalism, we'd honored Walter Lippmann as well as the eighty-five-year-old publisher and critic of the right-wing John Birch Society, Tom Storke. As usual, several other newspapers and their people carried off awards that had seemed important at the moment.

Summing up the *Citizen Hearst* issue, I noted in my diary, "A Pulitzer board member, Ralph McGill, thought the whole thing was very funny. If I recover, I'll think so, too." But that fall, when the new class of 1962–1963 was trying to get its bearings at our school and the Cuban missile crisis was breaking wide open, I completely forgot about *Citizen Hearst,* the vengeful trustees, and the hurt feelings of the Pulitzer board and Bill Hearst Jr.

· · ·

To some like myself, who had followed the United Nations's failed efforts to control the uses of atomic energy, there seemed to be ground for morbid speculation on the ultimate problems of survival in the event of a nuclear disaster. But when I saw how jittery some of my students were as the crisis widened, I put aside my speculation for the future and tried as honestly as I could to face up to the concerns of the young people who now had to cope with a radically different world than their elders had known.[2]

I remembered then that Premier Khrushchev had given warning of the real crisis yet to come when he'd brushed aside President Kennedy's well-meant proposals for a nuclear test-ban treaty. The Russian's attitude reminded me very much of Andrei Gromyko's at the UN when the United States proposals for the control of atomic energy were put before the UN Atomic Energy Commission. "Nyet" was the one word Gromyko had been instructed by his home office to use and "Nyet" was Khrushchev's response to the nuclear test ban proposal as well.

At the same time, the persistent non-Communist foreign critics of American foreign policy also were calling the Baruch Plan for atomic control a "delusion" and Kennedy's nuclear test-ban treaty a "propaganda device." In the interim, Khrushchev had been tightening his line of attack from Laos to the Congo, from Berlin to Cuba.

It was, all in all, a difficult time for me to try to instruct graduate students in the twists and embarrassments of international affairs. Like my professional colleagues and some of the more perceptive graduate students in my classes, I already had begun to suspect that Soviet-American relations were headed toward a climax. But at our listening posts at the United Nations, there still was no hint of what Khrushchev was planning.

Unfortunately, we didn't pay much attention to articles by a little-known reporter, Hal Hendrix, who began his disclosures in 1962 in a small Florida newspaper, the Miami *News,* that the Russians were sending MIG 21 aircraft to Fidel Castro's forces in Cuba and installing missile launching pads there.* Instead, in bestowing one of our 1962 Pulitzer Prizes on the elderly Walter Lippmann, we'd honored him for an interview with Khrushchev that completely avoided the foggy but present danger.

The disclosure of what was going on in Cuba came eventually from a State Department briefer, Roger Hilsman, who told us about our secret U-2 overflights that revealed the Soviet missile buildup in Cuba.

Hilsman said at the time that as many as twenty Soviet cargo ships

---

* Hendrix and the Miami *News* were belatedly honored in 1963 for being the first to tip off everybody to the coming Cuban missile crisis.

had brought electronic and construction material to Cuba for about a month in the summer of 1962, beginning in July, and that the deliveries were continuing. He also speculated that SAMS (surface-to-air missiles) and their bases were being installed by Soviet technicians at selected Cuban sites with Castro's connivance.

That gave the nation as a whole the first news that the whole United States was being targeted for destruction. A New York Republican senator, Kenneth Keating, then turned into a reporter and kept filling in the public on what he'd picked up from Cuban emigrés about the missile base construction operation.

Still, as far as the public was concerned, neither President Kennedy nor the CIA was ready to challenge the Russians openly. A week before fall registration began on August 17, I'd been at the UN as an escort for our first Nigerian student, a new Dag Hammarskjold scholar, and heard a lot of discussion by delegates and reporters sub rosa about Russian activity in Cuba.*

However, it wasn't until weeks later that I heard Secretary of State Dean Rusk publicly expressing alarm about "rising trouble in Cuba." Even so, like his colleagues in the Kennedy administration, he seemed not to want to act against the Soviets and—like so many others in authority—contended that he didn't have enough proof to urge immediate counteraction. In any event, I couldn't blame him for being so cautious. To adopt a policy that might lead to nuclear war seemed impossible then. In my diary, I noted:

> Sept. 24—Had lunch with Dr. Liu, a Hong Kong editor. In the afternoon, to the Council on Foreign Relations where I heard Secretary of State Rusk expound on foreign policy in Cuba. Rusk saw no blue sky ahead on Berlin, rising trouble in Cuba but no intervention. He said, 'We'll have to call it something else if it happens.' He also looked for no cessation of atomic testing.

At around the same time, those of us familiar with the diplomatic reporting circuit also learned that the CIA chief, John A. McCone— "Uncle John" to insiders—had warned President Kennedy on August 22 that the Russian missiles being installed in Cuba were offensive in character and would be aimed directly at the United States. He also said he didn't have conclusive proof for public use. What he did have was a series of

---

* Secretary General Hammarskjold was accidently killed while on a flight to the Congo in 1961. After that, Premier Khrushchev pressed his campaign to abolish the secretary general's office with a three-member replacement—a Communist, a Westerner, and a neutral. But President Kennedy won a move in the UN to defeat the plan, calling for a "truce to terror." U Thant then became secretary general.

photos taken from a U-2 plane of what was then officially described as a Russian-constructed SAM operation that would soon be completed.[3]

To try to counter American suspicions, Khrushchev began floating a series of public denials that the United States was being threatened. The Russian disclaimers for the most part came through channels to the Soviet ambassador, Anatoly Dobrynin, with an occasional comment to the same general effect by the premier himself. A more sophisticated generation will wonder why the White House, the State Department, and the Pentagon stalled for lack of proof positive against such an open challenge by the Soviets and why Senator Keating took a public beating in the press as a sensation-monger for refusing to believe Soviet disclaimers.

As late as September that year, even a National Intelligence Estimate did not claim proof of Khrushchev's offensive intentions against the United States—and all the while the U-2s kept showing Russians working at a feverish pace to get the missiles in place as soon as the bases were completed. Finally, it took Kennedy's own resolve to go public—with Congressional approval—for the crucial American countermoves to put 100,000 to 150,000 troops in Florida, completely outfitted for an invasion of Cuba, and mobilization of air power in support of the army invasion buildup.

Still, the U-2s showed no slackening of the Russian drive to complete the missile bases. Finally, with the coming of autumn, photographs taken from U-2s over Cuba proved beyond doubt that the Soviets, within a very short time, would have the means to bring the major cities of North and South America within range of the nearly completed missile bases and their nuclear loads.

Beginning October 16, the White House was virtually forced to act. The options before the president and his advisers by that time had dwindled alarmingly either to an American invasion of Cuba, a blockade to halt further Soviet shipments, or both at once. However, regardless of his choice, the president also realized he would need support for the United States from NATO, the United Nations, and the Organization of American States.

The president then clamped an immediate blockade on Cuba. If the enemy chose to fight, he authorized nuclear air strikes and ordered American troops in Florida alerted as an invasion strike force if needed. On October 22, the president notified the American people in a televised address from the White House, as I recorded in my diary:

> President Kennedy has ordered a naval blockade of Cuba and told of it on TV tonight. My own reaction at home was mainly regret that the president had to take so drastic a position at the climax of a midterm Congressional election campaign, particularly when Senator Keating

had been warning us for at least a month that the Russians were building missile bases in Cuba.

Lord knows the threat is real and we should have acted against it
long ago. Both of us, Dorothy and I, believe the blockade may not be
enough and, despite possible Soviet retaliation in Berlin, we Americans
may have to do more. We are in for a long period of rising tension.[4]

The initial Soviet response to the American blockade of Cuba indicated both confusion and concern in Moscow. At sea, there were reports
that part of the Soviet fleet bound for Cuba had turned around and
headed for home. In any case, not a single vessel flying the red flag
attempted to run the blockade and take a chance on being cut down by
the American Navy's big guns and the carrier-based aircraft.

There also was no immediate answering blockade by the Soviets
either of West Berlin or an aggressive movement against American missile bases in Turkey, although Walter Lippmann already was proposing
an American missile withdrawal from Turkey, provided the Soviets
pulled out of Cuba. All that really happened immediately was a Soviet
statement attacking President Kennedy and assuring world opinion of
the purity of Soviet motives against "provocative" American acts that
could lead to thermonuclear war.[5]

However, the Soviets found out quickly enough that they had isolated themselves from the bulk of world opinion. On that critical Tuesday, the United States received unanimous support from its partners in
the Organization of American States and NATO. Also, in a speech before
the UN Security Council, Adlai Stevenson charged that Fidel Castro's
Cuba had given the Soviets "a bridgehead and a staging area in this
hemisphere." As for Castro himself, Stevenson added, "The day of for-
bearance is past."

But curiously, although I had thought President Kennedy would be
cheered and eulogized by an admiring public that October 23 following
his blockade speech over TV the night before, nothing of the kind happened. The young people in my classes displayed frozen attitudes for the
most part, some openly fearful of the prospect of a nuclear war. All
thought of the Pulitzer Prizes vanished from my diary entries for many
days from then on, starting with this entry for October 23:

> Strange that at our Columbia faculty meeting today nobody even
> thought to discuss the Cuban situation until I remarked on our attitude
> at the end of our meeting. It was as if we all thought it a fantasy, which
> it is not. People just don't seem to want to discuss it, including our
> students, probably because there isn't a damn thing we can do about it.
> Worked all evening preparing edited Associated Press copy to try to
> show my students how the story was handled nationally and interna-
> tionally minute by minute rather than as a part of history.

The next day was no different. There was no sign at the Soviet bases in Cuba that work on the missile bases had stopped or even slowed down. Indeed, even in the days yet to come, it seemed as if Moscow was determined to put the missiles in operation against us while playing for time by seeming to negotiate to close down the project. And yet, no Soviet vessel attempted to run the American blockade that formed in a sweeping arc 500 miles at sea from their island destination.

Internationally, the tension mounted steadily as the days passed without either side giving any indication of backing down. In Britain, Prime Minister Harold Macmillan commented wearily, "The week of the Cuban crisis . . . was the week of the most strain in my life. It then seemed to many of us . . . that the world might be coming to the brink of war."

At that juncture, UN Secretary General U Thant sent identical letters to the American and Soviet governments, urging suspension of both the blockade and further arms shipments to Cuba for two or three weeks. But neither power was in any mood to change its position. U Thant's score as a peacemaker was zero. I noted in my diary:

> Oct. 24—UN Day, the 17th birthday of the world organization and I had the students do a piece about it in the midst of the current crisis. The students were jittery, expecting the Russians to try to run the blockade outside Cuba and getting shot. No danger. The Russians won't take a chance if they can avoid it. But try and tell that to these kids right now!

The first break in the tension over the Cuban blockade came almost by accident on Thursday morning, October 25, when the Soviet tanker *Bucharest* was permitted to pass through the blockade bound for Cuba. The tanker's captain said his cargo was petroleum, which satisfied the navy, although the ship was trailed for some distance to be sure it was not an arms vessel in disguise.   However, before the Security Council that afternoon, there was a clash between Stevenson, the American representative, who challenged the Soviet ambassador, Valerian Zorin, to deny that his government was placing missiles and sites in Cuba. Zorin then demanded proof of the American accusation that offensive missiles were being placed in Cuba. Before Zorin could protest, Stevenson was ready with full-screen evidence of the purported offensive missiles at the ready.

It was, as I concluded in my diary entry, a "screwy, impossible day," when there was only momentary relief after the Soviet tanker was escorted through the American blockade on its voyage to a Cuban port.

The break came next day, Friday, October 26, in a strange manner.

A high-level Soviet diplomat, Aleksandr Fomin, who had masked his purported role as the chief of Soviet intelligence in the United States by calling himself a mere Soviet embassy counselor, arranged to have lunch with an American Broadcasting Company correspondent, John Scali, whom he knew. At their Washington rendezvous, Fomin proposed terms to be offered to the State Department for settling the crisis. Briefly put, what the KGB operative suggested was a Soviet offer to dismantle the Cuban bases in return for an American pledge not to invade Cuba.

Scali hustled to the State Department directly afterward, managed to see Secretary Rusk, and told him about the Fomin offer. Ready to grasp at even the slightest chance of averting an atomic catastrophe, the big, balding chief of State told Scali to inform Fomin the offer had "real possibilities." Without informing Fomin that his source was Rusk, that is what the correspondent did, and Fomin apparently signaled Moscow. [6]

Then, things began to happen. Later that day, in an unpublished letter that was long and rambling, Khrushchev suggested that if President Kennedy would call off the planned American invasion of Cuba, the reason for Soviet bases in Cuba "would vanish." But it didn't require any super statesmanship in Washington to determine that the Soviets in Cuba meanwhile were still working at top speed to make their missile bases operative. Moreover, there was no clear pledge in that unpublished letter of Khrushchev's agreement to pull his missiles out of Cuba.

The president, his White House conferees, and the State Department's experts stalled and decided to think things through overnight.

Next morning, Saturday, October 27, Khrushchev suddenly raised his price in a new letter, this one publicly released, in which he picked up Walter Lippmann's notion of swapping an American base pullout in Turkey for a Soviet cancellation of its Cuban bases. Worse still, it appeared that at least one Cuban missile base had become operative because an American pilot, Major Rudolph Anderson Jr., and his plane were shot down. It so happened that it had been Anderson, in a Cuban overflight, who had produced the clinching U-2 evidence that the bases were offensive in nature and nearly ready.

There was more bad luck for the United States that day. An American aircraft in Alaska had strayed off course and was flying over Soviet territory when Red fighter planes gave chase amid doubt about the outcome. So now, there was no more time for debating the issue. It was the president's brother, Attorney General Bobby Kennedy, who came up with the solution of the problem presented by Khrushchev's two letters by proposing to ignore the new one and concentrate on the implied offer in the first one.

That, finally, was what the president did, but first of all he demanded of Khrushchev that work on the missile bases in Cuba should be halted immediately before anything else happened. Next, Kennedy agreed to call off the invasion if the Soviets left Cuba with their missile bases. Finally, not knowing what the outcome was of the Soviet pursuit of the Alaska-based American aircraft, the president concluded gloomily that this American-Soviet confrontation now "could go either way," for or against the United States.

It was in this manner that the climax approached on the morning of Sunday, October 28. Just before 9:00 A.M., Washington time, Moscow radioed it would have a decision within the hour. And when it came, it was in the form of still another Khrushchev letter, this one right to the point:

> The Soviet government, in addition to earlier instructions on the discontinuation of further work on the Weapons construction sites, has given a new order to dismantle the arms which you described as offensive, and to crate and return them to the Soviet Union.

That was it. The American aircraft that had strayed over Soviet territory meanwhile had returned safely to its Alaskan base, but Major Anderson and his aircraft had to be given up for lost. To cap the climax, the Soviet ambassador, Dobrynin, hustled into Attorney General Kennedy's office at the Justice Department that Sunday morning, confirming the offer in the latest Khrushchev letter and giving assurances that the missile base closing offer was genuine. President Kennedy, toward noon, released the text of a reply to Moscow welcoming Khrushchev's "statesmanlike decision" while privately warning all hands not to proclaim American superiority over the Soviet leader's admission of defeat. The Chinese Communists in Beijing took care of that detail, crowing over Moscow's surrender to the Americans. [7]

The only disgruntled party to the operation was Fidel Castro, who sulked over the pullout of his Soviet partner and refused to return some over-age bombers Moscow had given him. President Kennedy commented, with reference to Abraham Lincoln's celebration of the North's Civil War victory, "Maybe this is the night I should go to Ford's Theater." He and his brother thought it was a big joke. In my diary, I concluded that Sunday:

> The big Cuban war is over. Nobody was hurt except one poor American airman whose plane was probably shot down. Khrushchev has said he would remove the missile bases, Kennedy has said he would call off the blockade and the invasion. The UN is being called into session. Castro has piped down and the status quo obtains. As in the Suez War which did not displace Nasser, it was a famous victory.

.   .   .

With the end of the crisis, everything returned to to normal for me, Columbia, and the Pulitzer Prizes. I did my class work, wrote nights on what turned out to be my best book, *Foreign Correspondence: The Great Reporters and Their Times,* and disposed of a well-intentioned proposal from the William Morris Agency about the Pulitzer Prizes in my diary, as follows:

> Nov. 2—I took a lawyer from the Morris Agency to lunch at the Faculty Club and discussed Pulitzer Prize business. I did not like his proposition about Pulitzer TV News Stories, to be produced by an organization called 4-Star, and wrote a memo to President Kirk of Columbia and Joseph Pulitzer Jr., chairman of the Pulitzer board, about my views. Then, phoned Pulitzer in St. Louis and got his agreement to revise the terms of the biography award to eliminate the phrase that caused all the trouble about the "Citizen Hearst" book, "as illustrated by eminent example." So ends still another famous victory.

PART THREE

The Prizes as History

16 The Greatest Sacrifice

In the summer of 1963, ushering in another sabbatical absence from Columbia, I accepted a commission from the State Department for a six-month speaking tour in Asia as part of its American Specialist program.

The trip was to be an effort in public diplomacy, as I called it, on behalf of the policies of the Kennedy administration in foreign affairs. Only, as I discovered too late for my troubled conscience, my itinerary from Japan to Pakistan carefully avoided Vietnam, where our youth already were being offered up as sacrifices in a mistaken war.

A still greater sacrifice, the worst in the nation's modern history, would compound that and many other problems along my route. For midway through my 250-odd meetings in 35 cities, I would be trying as best I could to explain to wondering Asian audiences the assassination of a president and the murder of his slayer in Dallas, Texas.[1]

However, even the thought of so great a tragedy yet to come never crossed my mind at the time I set out for Japan from San Francisco with Dorothy that summer on the SS *President Cleveland* bound for Yokohama, our first stop. I never would have taken so long a trip without her and insisted on paying her way.

I wrote in anticipation of that 12,000-mile tour through seven Asian lands:

> It is time to inquire with sympathy and care into the relationship between foreign correspondence and foreign policy, particularly as it exists in Asia in the latter part of the 20th century. In the 25 years since Pearl Harbor, the United States has waged war three times in Asia at enormous cost. During the four-year Pacific campaign in World War II, 41,000 Americans were killed in action; in the three years of the Korean War, another 33,000 were sacrificied in a drawn conflict. And in Vietnam today and the rest of Southeast Asia from which the French have now been ejected, the end of our effort to shoulder their burden cannot be predicted.[2]

121

The Pulitzer establishment at Columbia had not yet received any formal nominations that summer for prizes for correspondence from Vietnam. Indeed, the Kennedy administration at the time of my departure for Asia was making strenuous efforts to convince the nation that it would be only a matter of time before the rebellious Vietcong, the guerrilla allies of North Vietnam in the south, would be crushed.

Attorney General Robert F. Kennedy had said as much while on an inspection tour in Saigon during the winter of 1962, when the first American "advisers" were being sent to our latest war front. What the attorney general wanted us to believe was the promise of victory given by his brother, the president, in support of the South Vietnamese regime of President Ngo Dinh Diem right through to the destruction of the Communist North. [3]

Yet, what we did know in the Pulitzer office even before my departure was that this enormous American propaganda effort did not square with the facts. Some of the earliest dispatches from Vietnam included questions that were raised by the great veteran, Homer Bigart of the New York *Times*, who then was fifty-five, and the youthful Beverly Deepe, one of my students only a few years out of Columbia and the only woman combat correspondent in Vietnam, who was filing for the New York *Herald Tribune*.

Adding to the Kennedy administration's effort to try to make a bad situation look good, Secretary of Defense Robert S. McNamara had gone to Saigon in 1962 to try to bring the few complaining correspondents into line with administration beliefs. At a news conference, McNamara had opened up by asking correspondents if they'd had complaints, and Bigart led off. "Mr. Secretary, we're not getting enough news."

McNamara responded, still the loyal Kennedy adviser, "My impression in Washington is that you're getting a great deal of news, a very great deal."

Bigart had not won a Pulitzer Prize in war correspondence in Korea in 1951 by being bashful. "Yes, Mr. Secretary, but I'm having to work too hard for it."

That was the signal for younger correspondents to pile it on the administration, which is what happened from then on in Vietnam. Beverly Deepe once told me, "They don't like me at the American embassy because I won't say what they want me to say." [4]

Such observations as hers and Bigart's, however, turned out to be mild compared with what happened when more correspondents with fewer inhibitions arrived in Vietnam to cover the war and found that they were being regularly misled and even lied to by the South Vietnamese military command and, all to often, the less principled American "advisers."

I had already embarked on my Asian trip that skirted Vietnam when Bigart's replacement for the *Times,* a young and tough-minded David Halberstam, filed a story front-paged in the New York *Times* on August 15, 1963, under the headline:

VIETNAMESE REDS GAIN IN KEY AREA [5]

Secretary of State Rusk formally denied it in a press briefing. President Kennedy demanded and received other denials in quantity from his generals. But now, the panic was on. The truth was out, and a handful of young reporters matched themselves against the American generals in the field, the State Department, and the Kennedy White House. A few old-timers from the Korean War, among them the handsome Marguerite Higgins, a Pulitzer Prize winner, complained after a visit to Vietnam, "Reporters here would like to see us lose the war just to prove they are right."

But that didn't change the situation one bit. While I was on my Asian trip, the New York *Times* nominated Halberstam for a Pulitzer Prize in 1964. The Associated Press followed suit for its leading correspondent, Malcolm Browne. And while I was on the road in Asia that late summer and fall, I already knew that the Pulitzer establishment would have to choose between an outraged government and a few headstrong but brave young correspondents in determining who was telling the truth about the Vietnam War during the next Pulitzer Prizes upon my return in 1964.

The 1963 prizes, by contrast, had been fought out on the most divisive domestic issue of the latter half of the twentieth century next to race relations—the right of women to choose or reject birth control.

That year during the annual journalism juries' meetings in March, the recommended choice for the gold medal for public service had been the Chicago Daily *News* for its successful campaign to make birth control information available to families on Chicago's welfare rolls. At the Pulitzer board meeting the following month, I noted in my diary:

> April 25—We wrangled all day over giving the Pulitzer Prize for Public Service to the Chicago Daily News for its drive to make birth control data available to families on relief. The Daily News finally won but only after votes of 5–5 and 6–6. All members of the board at last agreed to honor the Daily News except Don Maxwell, the editor of the rival Chicago Tribune. [6]

I wish I could also report herein that the *Daily News* still celebrates this and many another triumph for the liberal ideal in the conduct of life in these United States. But like many another less fortunate paper in competition with the almighty tube toward century's end, the *Daily News* was unable to survive, and the principle it espoused remained under heavy conservative attack across the land.

The 1963 board meeting was memorable, too, for clashes of opinion among its members for jury recommendations in letters and drama. To revert to my diary record once again:

> April 25—The Pulitzer board rejected a prize for Edward Albee's drama, "Who's Afraid of Virginia Woolf?" and gave no theater award for the year.[7] The board also set aside a Fiction Jury recommendation for Katherine Ann Porter's "Ship of Fools" in favor of another William Faulkner novel, "The Rievers."
>
> However, Leon Edel was recognized for his Henry James biography and a posthumous award went to William Carlos Williams for poetry. But in all truth, the only popular prize of the year was for general non-fiction—Barbara Tuchman's best-selling "The Guns of August," an informal history of the coming of World War I.

As might have been expected with the announcement of the prizes on May 6, some of the Pulitzer jurors were mightily upset over the cavalier way in which their recommendations had been rejected by the Pulitzer board.

The drama jurors, John Mason Brown and John Gassner, announced they were quitting and denounced the board and all its works in the New York *Times*. Whether that had any effect on the board members, I do not know. But when it became known that two board members had voted against the Albee play without having seen it, President Kirk insisted thereafter that plays had to be seen and books had to be read before the honorable members voted on jury reports. It did seem like a basic element of literary justice and was voted into the record.

Over the objections of Chairman Pulitzer, the board also dropped a provision in the drama award requiring a prize contender in that category to demonstrate "educational value." The formula then read, "For a distinguished play by an American author, preferably original in its source and dealing with American life."

Once that Pulitzer season had ended on a discordant note, the early months of my Asian venture for the government went mainly according to plan. I had to make a major effort to keep up with a punishing schedule at the outset from Japan to South Korea, then to the Philippines and Taiwan. But before going on to Thailand, I had to arrange for a three-day break in Hong Kong because I needed rest for the even greater strain in India and Pakistan toward the latter part of my journey.

Although I had no engagements in Hong Kong because it still was British territory, the American correspondents stationed there could talk of nothing but the developing Vietnam War in Indochina to the south and the grim reality of North Vietnam's dependence on Communist China and the Soviet Union for support against the United States. Such views weren't based on guesswork. It was standing practice for correspondents going to or coming from Vietnam to brief or be briefed by their Hong Kong colleagues.

It was in this manner that I learned, for example, that President Kennedy had insisted on expanding the American role in the Vietnam War by adding still more "advisers" to the American military buildup there. It also was the talk of the Hong Kong correspondents that President Kennedy also had warned the publisher of the New York *Times,* Arthur Ochs Sulzberger Sr., that David Halberstam, still a *Times* correspondent there, had become "too involved in the conflict and maybe the Times might want to transfer him to another assignment." However, "Punch" Sulzberger had replied, no, the *Times* was satisfied with Halberstam's work in Vietnam and wasn't transferring him. [8]

As I observed at the time, even without going to Vietnam, too few news organizations so far had assumed the responsibility of maintaining reporters there because the American people on the whole still had very little knowledge of the risky position the government was taking in this growing conflict on the Asian mainland. One way or another, I determined on leaving Hong Kong that I would find a way within the coming year to get into Vietnam and view the conflict for myself if for no one else. [9]

I could not cast aside my increasing concern over the Vietnam conflict while on my way to India after leaving Thailand, especially when I learned that President Kennedy had sent a flight of US Air Force jets directly to Palam Airport outside New Delhi on November 6. I suppose the president had conceived of this gesture as a token of American friendship for India—the beginning of the first joint United States-India air exercises.

The trouble was, as I later learned from a despairing, American embassy headed by Chester Bowles, that the Indian government didn't think the visiting aircraft a suitable gesture of friendship. Prime Minister Jawaharlal Nehru didn't show up as the greeter-in-chief. As for the ranking Indian military commander at the scene, he walked away at once commenting in an aside, "I have my orders." [10]

It seemed to me that anybody with the slightest knowledge of Indian affairs would have known Nehru would take offense. What happened was predictable in view of his policy of "nonalignment" between China, the Soviet Union, and the United States—a position that was adopted by his successor, his daughter, Indira Gandhi. I refer to the scene here, even though it took place just before my arrival, to illustrate some of my problems as an American government representative while touring India during what turned out to be a tragic period in United States-India relations.

To be sure, I was well aware that India had cause to be critical of the United States. Its great enemy, Pakistan, had been armed in part with American help; moreover, the Paks were allied with the United States through SEATO, the Southeast Asia Treaty Organization, and two other smaller groupings. While such alliances may have been ineffective, Indians resented their existence.

But regardless of such prejudices, the United States still had given India considerable economic assistance, including many millions of bushels of wheat to make up for the failure of an Indian harvest. Still, in early appearances before Indian audiences, I felt sometimes as if none of this assistance had made a favorable impression on my more critical Indian opposition.

I remember one difficult experience in New Delhi, where I faced the most caustic criticism since the onset of my tour. If I didn't lose my temper under such pressure, I think it was mainly because I saw Dorothy in the front row gently nodding and smiling at me as if to say, "Take it as it comes." I finally had to remind my critics of the billions of dollars in economic assistance that the United States had bestowed on the Indian public and the $200 million a year that still came from the American treasury for military aid at the time.

After that, fortunately, the critics did let up and the dialogue continued on what I believed to be a milder and a more reasonable basis. Even so, as I headed south, where the majority of the people were far more used to Hindi than English and the criticism diminished, I had to continue to be very much on guard. That included places like Agra, the home of the Taj Mahal, where I spoke just before arriving in the great industrial city of Bombay, and in Bombay itself. However, at Poona, the next stop, I did have a break because the daily newspaper was owned and edited by one of my Indian students in the Columbia class of 1962, Claude-Lila Parulekar.

Then, as I continued south in the latter part of November toward a date in Mysore, the unbelievable, the incredible tragedy occurred. Over All-India radio, the news flashed of President Kennedy's assassination in Dallas on November 22 and the arrest of his killer, Lee Harvey Oswald. We were in a small hotel room, Dorothy and I, when we heard the news. I shall never forget her tears and her despairing cry, "What is happening to our country?" I was so distraught myself that I couldn't answer, just held her in my arms as if we, too, had been bereaved in that far-off land.

The American embassy people who accompanied us were as upset as we were—and as confused. And that night, when I had to go before an Indian audience at Mysore, all at once I was conscious, not of the raunchy, critical side of India, but of a sudden outburst of sympathy. From then on, through the end of the tour in India and on into Pakistan, the people who came to hear me reacted in an odd combination of curiosity mixed with sympathy.

Oswald himself had been shot and killed only two days after his arrest by the avenging night club owner, Jack Ruby, and Vice-President Lyndon Baines Johnson now was the president. What my audiences in the great Asian subcontinent wanted to know, however soft-voiced and sympathetic my interrogators seemed to be, was how such terrible things could happen in so rich and supposedly law-abiding a nation as the United States.

Being so far from home and out of touch with events, it wasn't easy to respond to such intimate inquiries no matter how sympathetic my audiences now seemed to be both here in India and later in Pakistan. Even when most of the details became known abroad, I still could only summarize the facts of the tragedy as I knew them and hope for the best. But Dorothy still was in tears at most of my meetings, and I'm afraid I wasn't of too much help.

It was in this discouraged manner that my Asian tour ended at last and we headed for London and home, leaving behind the image of Lee Harvey Oswald who had been promptly installed, as a commercial come-on, in the Chamber of Horrors in Mme. Tussaud's London gallery. When all was said and done, the Indian people had shown more understanding of the harm done to America than the British. I concluded the trip with this entry:

> Jan. 8, 1964—From London to New York, the last 3,473 miles of our global journey. We took off in a PAA Boeing 707 at 11 a.m. and landed in sunny weather at Idlewild, New York, at 11:30 p.m. (New York time) after a 7½-hour flight. The Morningside Drive apartment was warm and clean and, tired as we were, we tumbled into bed, grateful to be home.

We in America still did not even know what motivated the murder of the young president—the greatest sacrifice of all.

17 Asian Dilemma

When I returned to Columbia for the tenth year of my Pulitzer Prize administration, there already was no way in which the United States could have backed out of the Vietnam War.

President Johnson had committed himself to it as John Kennedy's successor. And his prospective Republican opponent in the 1964 presidential election, Barry Goldwater, even then was threatening to drop an atomic bomb on North Vietnam.

Moreover, merely by thumbing through the journalism entries for the 1964 prizes, I could tell how the war was dominating the news. To be sure, the angry young reporters and photographers in Saigon were well represented in the nominations, but so were others who approved of the conflict along with the chroniclers of the Kennedy tragedy.

True, the nation as a whole still did not realize what we were in for. But it didn't take me many talks with students in the class of 1964 to know how set these young people were against another conflict in Asia. Of course, no one yet had hollered, "Hell no, we won't go." That was yet to come.

And so, with foreboding and a heavy heart, I settled down to my routine once again, with these entries in my diary:

Jan. 28—I did an outline for the Council on Foreign Relations study group on my Asian book project, which took me well into the night after being busy all day at school with Pulitzer entries. It's an exaggeration, of course, but it almost seems as if the whole weight of American journalism falls on my little Pulitzer office at this time of year. But we must catalogue these 600 or more entries for journalism along with the hundreds of books, plays and musical compositions that also are to be judged.

Jan. 30—Still another day of cataloguing the Pulitzer journalism exhibits and the deadline isn't until tomorrow night. In the evening, I put away the foreign correspondence data and began rearranging my papers and library for the Asian study. . . . I shall be very busy.

Feb. 6—There seems to be no end to this. Another long day of Pulitzer cataloguing and checking. Dorothy, too, has her hands full.

Feb. 7—Most of the day at the office, still cataloguing Pulitzer journalism entries. I count 617 of them this year so far and many are about Kennedy but not as many as I had thought. Anyway, I'm near the end of the chore and we'll soon start teaching for the spring semester.

Feb. 17—My 58th birthday but we didn't do anything to celebrate, just considered it another day. Not even a birthday cake, but Dorothy got me some nice ties and hankies.

Feb. 18—Took an 8:30 a.m. flight to Washington and did the accounting chores at the State Department for my trip. Then, at 2 p.m. a debriefing before a half-dozen middle range executives. I talked for 40 minutes, was asked questions for another 30. Later, I had to talk again before various other people and didn't get out of State until 6.

Feb. 19—I had a nice time at the White House with Pierre Salinger, the Presidential press secretary; Chuck Daley, a former student, and some of the correspondents including old friends. The latter seem not at all friend to LBJ. In fact, in Salinger's office, most of the pictures still are of Kennedy. But the Kennedy influence, like the Kennedy memory, is fading fast. Took a 1:55 flight home without incident.

Feb. 20—A day of contrasts. In the morning, I took the New Haven RR to Darien, Ct., and spoke before the Women's Club at the Darien Community Center on 'The American Image in the Far East.' With time out for dinner, I talked between 5:30 and 10 p.m. on the same subject before my study group at the Council on Foreign Relations.

Feb. 24—My first foreign seminar at the start of the spring semester for the Class of 1964 and I thought it was fairly lively but not as engaging as the Asian experience. There is a difference in our student body that dampens one's enthusiasm.

With that sobering conclusion, I was on my way into the thick of a disturbing experience with students here and elsewhere across the land as the nation sank ever deeper into the Vietnam War. The president meanwhile seemed overcome by the enormous task of defending his high office from the encroachment of the Republican opposition. The conduct of his prospective opponent, Goldwater, known far and wide as "Mr. Conservative," had removed the last chance that the nation could escape from the Vietnamese pitfall.

In Wilton, New Hampshire, early in March, Goldwater had been quoted in a news conference as an advocate of "carrying the war to North Vietnam—ten years ago we should have bombed North Vietnam . . . with no risk to our own lives."[1] The notion was not new to him. The day before, talking to students in the state, he had been quoted as suggesting that ten years ago a low-yield atomic bomb might have been dropped on North Vietnam to defoliate the trees.

At any rate, not every battle over Vietnam was fought in the Asian war zone. In my judgment, what happened on the home front sometimes was even more crucial to the eventual cutting of our losses in the field and the final abandonment of Saigon (now Ho Chi Minh City).

I come now to the conclusion of my long struggle to finish and publish my book on foreign correspondence. Somehow, I had trouble ending the last chapter and sometimes had to be reminded that I'd contracted with Columbia University Press to publish the work in 1964.

If ever a book had been neglected in its final stages, this was it. I had a stroke of conscience on January 13, five days after arriving home, for I wrote in my diary, "I tried again to get started on my writing but with no success. It just wouldn't go." Then, on January 22, after having worked all day at the Pulitzer office cataloguing prize exhibits for journalism, I included this among other routine items, "All the rest of the day at home, grinding out the last chapter of the foreign book."

Apparently, I finished the chapter and sent it to Columbia University Press, for I came across this entry later on Feb. 12: "A routine day. I did a little more work on the last chapter of my foreign book and gave it back to the invaluable Joan McQuary, the nicest of editors—she doesn't cut my stuff very much except where she should."

More than a month elapsed after that, during which Ms. McQuary completed her editing. I wrote on March 15: "I finished going over the edited foreign correspondence book. It will be out in the fall but I don't like the title: 'The Story of Foreign Correspondence.' "

Finally, I had to give in to the logic of the argument that *Foreign Correspondence* correctly described the content of the book, but my editors permitted me to add the explanatory subtitle: *The Great Reporters and Their Times*, which seemed to me to be necessary. As for my concluding paragrphs, written late one night after returning from our global tour, there was nothing more I could do about it now. This was it:

> In the atomic age, when national survival may demand decisions that are reached within ten minutes or less, there is no time for popular government to function in a crisis. That was made tragically clear in the 'eyeball to eyeball' confrontation of the United States and the Soviet Union over the Cuban missile bases in 1962. The argument has been advanced, accordingly, that it is sufficient to inform an elite group of

foreign developments through the mass media. Aside from the impracticality of such a program, elite groups being in short supply as patrons of the mass media, the argument misses the point. While no one can say with certainty that the efforts of an informed public will be able to preserve the spirit as well as the form of democratic government in the years to come, an ignorant and craven public assuredly will kill it through indifference and neglect.

The work, therefore, goes on. There is no doubt that, while the mass media cannot and should not try to assume the burden of a whole society, their influence is vital in a campaign to persuade the public to accept broader information in foreign affairs. It is obvious that nothing can be accomplished without such pressures . . .

But whether his public is great or small, the foreign correspondent must persevere. In the years to come, he will face his greatest challenge. Whatever his influence may be, he will have need of it. For in every gathering crisis of the atomic era, it will be his highest duty to make himself heard and understood in a cruelly divided world.

In an age when the leaders of government will exercise frightening power in defense of national interests, it will be the role of the foreign correspondent to seek to create understanding between peoples by bringing them more meaningful news of each other. As such, he may very well be a decisive element. For it may fall to him in the future, as it has in the past, to represent the difference between war and peace.[2]

The next thing I had to do before resuming work on my classes for the coming semester and the Pulitzer Prizes was to complete arrangements with the Council on Foreign Relations for the remainder of my study of Asian-American relations. Fortunately for me, the council's authorities agreed on January 21 to send me to Asia for a second summer "to study the role of government in the use of news as an instrument of foreign policy." It was a fine, bravura statement of purpose, to be sure, but I had my doubts whether it ever could be achieved without access to classified records of our own government. I wrote in my diary on March 4:

> The Council on Foreign Relations' work has been bothering me. I don't want to do a small job of fact-finding that will duplicate what everybody already knows. My mind is turning to a study of public diplomacy, i.e., a study of the effect of the interaction of press on policy in our relations with Asia. In particular, the Vietnam War.

Even that at the time seemed a far-off goal; but the council, its directors, study group, and I went ahead with our preparations for a detailed examination of Asian-American communications involving hundreds of interviews and questionnaires. We authorized Pan Am to chart, ticket, and bill us for all the necessary journeys by air together with advance efforts to obtain the cooperation of American embassies and foreign governments along my route. I also made an outline of what I proposed to accomplish, which I submitted to both the council's management and my study group for comment.

Then, I prepared to tackle the State Department with results that might have been anticipated, as witness the following from my diary:

> "April 20—Got my Washington and Foreign Seminar started at Columbia and took the 11 a.m. shuttle for Washington. The meeting on Southeast Asia left a lot to be desired on the way the Vietnam War is going.
>
> "April 21—At the State Department, I heard Secretary of State Dean Rusk at top form explain why we weren't rushing into new foreign policy ventures. The current line, he said, is paying off too well in the light of Russian-Chinese quarrels. Next, to the White House and heard President Johnson speak with the fervor of an evangelist of his foreign aid program. Back to New York on the 2 p.m. shuttle.

And as I could tell by listening to TV, looking at the AP ticker, and reading the New York *Times,* the Vietnam War was still going downhill despite the onset of reinforcements. Nevertheless, even if I didn't have a great store of possibilities to offer, I met my study group with these conclusions:

> May 6—My big night at the Council on Foreign Relations, and my study group was docile. We had a peaceful time. I was given more orders than I can possibly carry out but everybody seemed satisfied. Thanks to Dorothy, we now have all our visas. I was at the Council from 5 to 10 p.m. Wow!

Finally, it was the Pulitzer Prizes that offered the clearest as well as the most difficult outlook for the future of the nation that year. The first sign that the nation's editors on the whole were in no mood to accept the government's bland optimism about the Vietnam War came as early as March 5–6 of that year, when forty-four of them, as members of our journalism juries, quietly accepted a recommendation for joint international awards to two of the major critics of the conflict.

The two who were selected by the international reporting jury, Malcolm Browne of the Associated Press and David Halberstam of the New York *Times,* were by no means the only correspondents who had concluded the war was being lost even in its earliest stages. In my own mind,

I already had determined that Browne's fellow AP correspondent Peter Arnett, and Neil Sheehan of United Press International also had been both accurate and influential in reporting the downward course of the war, but their honors would come later, together with others among their associates.[3]

I knew perfectly well that the argument already was being made among President Johnson's supporters that it was "unpatriotic" for any mere journalist to adopt so negative a view of American efforts to save all Vietnam from falling to Communist North Vietnam and its Vietcong allies.[4] That line, however, did not take account of what actually was happening in the field in Vietnam, despite all the brave pronouncements of the American military.

The issue, simply put, was whether the American public should have been told the truth about a war that already was being lost or if the two greatest among the nation's news organizations, the Associated Press and the New York *Times*, should have done the unthinkable—to instruct their correspondents to ignore the facts. I had no patience with that view, so informed my sponsors at the Council on Foreign Relations, and incorporated the recommendations for prizes for Browne and Halberstam with enthusiasm in my report to the Pulitzer board.

Of equal importance, it seemed to me, were the recommendations of others among the jurors for a prize for Merriman Smith of United Press International for his outstanding coverage of the assassination of President Kennedy and for the stunning photograph by Robert H. Jackson of the Dallas *Times-Herald* of the murder of Lee Harvey Oswald, the president's assassin, by Jack Ruby on November 24, 1963.

All four of these prize recommendations had vividly recorded American history in the making for the American people and for the world at large. There could be no higher recommendation for a journalist with the skill, perception, and courage than to be honored for such efforts in the line of duty.

The Pulitzer board wasted no time on debate over the Vietnam War on April 23 but voted, almost without discussion, the award of prizes to Messrs. Browne and Halberstam "for their individual reporting of the Vietnam War and the overthrow of the Diem regime." Of equal importance, Merriman Smith and Bob Jackson also won recognition for their coverage of the Kennedy assassination and the Oswald murder respectively.

It was a year when the journalists significantly overshadowed the accomplishments of American leaders in letters, drama, and music. In three major categories—fiction, drama, and music—there were no prizes and only one significant nonfiction book was honored, Richard Hofstadter's *Anti-Intellectualism in American Life.*

There was no discussion of the Vietnam War. The conclusions of the laureates were accepted without hesitation at the top of the long list of awards. Nor was any time spent in worries about the whys and wherefores of the many problems of the Johnson administration or the chances of the prospective Republican nominee, Barry Goldwater, to unseat him. As I summed up for the day in my diary, "It's over. We met at 9:40 a.m. and finished at 3:05 p.m., with an hour and 30 minutes out for lunch. The Pulitzer board was good this year—no juries overruled. . . . I'm glad it's over. Every year is more difficult."

In my preoccupation with so many more immediate matters of concern, I didn't have much cause to worry about *Foreign Correspondence: The Great Reporters and Their Times* for the rest of the year. Except for checking the proofs and consulting now and then with Columbia University Press on progress or lack of it, the book was often forgotten until late fall that year. Then one day, after a lecture at the school, the New York *Times*'s drama critic, Brooks Atkinson, stuck his head around my door and remarked, "I think you'll like what the Sunday Book Review is doing with your book about foreign correspondence."

Before I could get anything more out of him, he'd vanished with a cheerful wave of one hand.

It was hard for me to believe Brooks. Like his drama criticism, in which he always seemed to find something positive to write about even the least noteworthy of the season's stage shows, he liked to encourage his friends and admirers—and I had always considered myself one of them. As I puzzled over what the *Times* could possibly do to a very large book on a subject that was an unlikely best seller, I thought of how rushed I had been to wind up the work for publication earlier that year. I called Columbia University Press to find out if there'd been a leak about the *Times*'s forthcoming review. But—there wasn't a word of encouragement.

So what happened finally to this volume that had seemed to be completed almost by accident and issued by a university press that didn't, like most other scholarly undertakings in print, have money enough for advertising and promotion for a leading work, much less a history of foreign correspondence? Was it to be dismissed with a few sentences in a summary column in the back of the *Times*'s Sunday review in its issue of November 22, 1964?

Indeed, not! It received a glowing review all over its first page, with dramatic illustration and a jazzy headline:

DASHING MEN
SOMEWHERE OVERSEAS

Thereby, it became the most important work I'd ever published because it also drew praise from other major American newspaper book reviews and columns and even the august first page of The Times of London *Times Literary Supplement.*[5] All of which demonstrates how very fortunate or crazy, depending on your point of view, the literary life is likely to be even for a sometime university professor with a half-life of foreign correspondence behind him.

18 The Prizes and Vietnam

The Johnson administration sought to enlarge the Vietnam War by all conceivable means in 1964 despite the Pulitzer Prizes that were won by two of the conflict's chief critics. One of the president's supporters even proposed to put American troops in Thailand. For what purpose, no one could say.

Having witnessed the warm support Chairman Pulitzer and his board had given to Malcolm Browne of the Associated Press and David Halberstam of the New York *Times,* both of them unsparing critics of the conflict, I could understand how bitterly all concerned would have opposed carrying the war into Bangkok for no good reason.

Still, Roger Hilsman, who made the suggestion before the Council on Foreign Relations, didn't back off, even though he received no support of substance for his proposal. It was emblematic, in a sense, of the desperation of the administration in which he had served as a loyal supporter of Presidents Kennedy and Johnson.

Quite by chance, I'd come to the council the night Hilsman spoke there to discuss my plans for my second summer in Asia, this time in connection with my projected study the organization was sponsoring of Asian-American relations. Earlier during that same evening, I'd also attended the annual Joseph Pulitzer memorial lecture at Columbia. As I recorded both events in my Pulitzer diary:

"May 21—Joseph Pulitzer Jr., Mrs. Pulitzer and others in their family came to the World Room at Columbia tonight to hear Ben McKelway deliver the annual memorial lecture. Just as he had been at the Pulitzer Prize voting, Joe was in high spirits and all went well. Only the White House and the State Department seem put out by the New York Times's prize and the AP's for their Vietnam War coverage.

"Afterward, I ran into more Vietnam action. Roger Hilsman, who had been Kennedy's Assistant Secretary of State for Far Eastern Affairs, proposed to the Council on Foreign Relations that our troops should also be sent to Thailand because Southeast Asia, in his view, was collapsing. However, nobody seemed to agree with Hilsman even though he touched off a long discussion."

I'm afraid, in view of what actually happened, that all of us—both in the Pulitzer board and at the council—might have been more alert than we were to these and other moves in Washington and elsewhere to make a big war out of what now was just a little one in Southeast Asia.

For on August 2, 1964, President Johnson's Pentagon saw to it that two United States destroyers were on patrol in the Gulf of Tonkin, where they were sure to be attacked by North Vietnamese gunboats on patrol in these waters off the coast of Southeast Asia. Only five days later, the president's Democratic minority in the Senate whooped the Tonkin Gulf resolution through to passage for a wider war.

That, of course, was tantamount to a declaration of war, which gave the president the authority he needed to put hundreds of thousands of American troops in Vietnam. Now, we *really* had been shoved into the Vietnam War beyond recall. [1]

Neil Sheehan, who then worked for United Press International in Saigon and later for the New York *Times,* was to write many years later in his Pulitzer Prize-winning work, *A Bright and Shining Lie,* that President Johnson used the Tonkin Gulf incident "to trick the Senate into giving him an advance declaration of war for the far higher level of force he had decided by then he was probably going to have to employ." [2]

Trick or not, that was what happened. The government began using the draft to pull hundreds of thousands of young men out of civilian life to try to defeat a will-o'-the-wisp enemy in the Vietnamese jungles. And although I was at the time a fifty-eight-year-old World War II type, I had an unnerving time with a Vietcong bomb just after my arrival with Dorothy in Saigon toward the end of July.

With the council's approval, I had set out that summer of 1964 to travel the general Asian route I had followed in 1963 for my government lectures in the American Specialist program—an altogether vivid experience, except that I had not been able to see the Vietnam War at first hand. So while I put in my time and effort from Japan and the Philippines through Southeast Asia to India and Pakistan, including ever-sensitive Kashmir, it was South Vietnam that I wanted most to see.

But this time, instead of lecturing on Asian-American relations, what I had been asked to do was to conduct hundreds of interviews with Asian and American government leaders and their opposition and almost as many questionnaires for them and for the correspondents of the Asian-American news media, electronic and print. At the outset, I had worried about the questionnaires much more than the interviewing, but I needn't have been concerned. The on-the-record interviewing went well, even as far up the line as Secretary of State Dean Rusk and the American commander in Vietnam, General William C. Westmoreland. Nor did I have any trouble among those to whom I offered the questionnaires in Saigon and in the field.

Elsewhere, neither the interviewing nor the questionnaires posed any real problem for me. What I would do with them when it came time to draw my conclusions was something else to consider. However, as an experienced journalist with a decent background in American-Asian affairs, it seemed to me that my material and the judgments I drew from it would determine more clearly than anything else the direction in which my written work would have to go. [3]

In that state of mind, after beginning the latest Asian journey so close to the trip in 1963, I began work in Saigon with the Hotel Caravelle as my base of operations. Dorothy was with me as always—we had been married for thirty-six adventurous years—but she preferred staying in or near the hotel while I was away. "Don't you ever forget that this city is part of the war zone," she'd often warn me, so much so that it became a mild family joke.

For some peculiar reason, it had never occurred to me that the Vietcong could penetrate even the heart of South Vietnam's capital at that stage in the war. But I discovered all too soon how wrong I'd been to discount the range and adaptability of the enemy's operations.

One afternoon not long after our arrival, I'd spent part of a day flying with General Westmoreland on his up-front inspections of the enlarging American forces and their cooperation with the South Vietnamese army. I'd found the general to be both efficient and persuasive about his chances of forging a winning strategy for the war, something I hadn't believed possible before coming to Saigon. Now, riding back to the Hotel Caravelle by cab, I wanted very much to talk over my day's experiences with Dorothy and admit that perhaps I might have been overly influenced by the negative attitude of most of the small group of American correspondents toward the conflict.

But just outside the Caravelle, as I paid off the cab driver, a few Vietnamese police were trying to persuade a curious crowd of Saigonese to keep moving—a sure sign that there'd been trouble inside the hotel. And knowing that Dorothy had planned to stay in or near the hotel as usual during my absence, I pushed past the police in a hurry and saw that most of the lobby had been wrecked.

"What happened?" I asked a clerk who was directing a clean-up crew.

"The VC, it was a bomb," he said.

I asked about Dorothy.

He shrugged. "I don't know." He waved vaguely toward a corner of the lobby. "She was reading a book over there." Then he chattered away in Vietnamese to the workmen. Not knowing what else to do, I bolted for our room and found her there, looking out the window at the police who were still trying to disperse the crowd. She was unhurt.

"I was lucky, darling," she said. "About five minutes before the bomb went off, I was in the lobby reading a book and thought I'd come back to the room and wait for you."

It was the last time we ever joked about Saigon being in a war zone. I also underwent a rapid change of mind about General Westmoreland's chances of putting together a winning strategy for the Vietnam War. From then on, for the remainder of my stay in Saigon and elsewhere in South Vietnam, I spent more time with the correspondents than I did with the American and South Vietnamese military and never regretted it. I also never forgot the VC bomb that wrecked the Hotel Caravelle lobby and my heartfelt relief at finding Dorothy safe in our room. [4]

In my interviews with the relatively few correspondents and photographers for American news organizations in South Vietnam in the summer of 1964, I never came across one who had the slightest confidence either in the ability or the credibility of the native South Vietnamese army, its commanders, or their government. I would have expected, however, that there would be more trust in the small American military contingent and its command; but here, too, there often was hesitation or even outright disbelief sometimes among our correspondents.

What I tried at first to do, beyond circulating and collecting my questionnaires, was to try to determine what it was about the American military that had given rise to such mistrust—an attitude characteristic of the war in Vietnam almost from the outset. Although some correspondents traced it back to incidents as early as 1961 or 1962, nearly everybody agreed that disbelief was most marked in the claims for victory at the battle of Ap Bac in January 2, 1963.

Halberstam and Peter Arnett, who had covered Ap Bac, agreed that the South Vietnamese army had trapped a Vietcong battalion there but failed to attack in time to block their escape. Moreover, the best source the correspondents ever had, the then Lieutenant Colonel John Vann, an American military adviser, admitted disgustedly of the ARVNs, "A miserable damn performance like it always is." And Neil Sheehan, then filing for UPI, was told by Brigadier General Robert York, a senior American adviser, "What the hell's it look like happened, boy? They got away. That's what happened." [5]

However, the senior American military commander, Admiral Harry Felt, bawled out the assembled American correspondents two days later saying, "It was a Vietnamese victory, not a defeat as the papers say." And not long afterward he told the equally dubious Malcolm Browne, "You'd better get on the team, boy." To which his second in command, Major General Paul Harkins, added, "Yes, I consider it a victory, we took the objective."

Roger Hilsman, then still the State Department's top Far Eastern official under Secretary Rusk, also happened to be in Saigon and took part in beating up on the correspondents' accounts. Halberstam wrote of him, "Hilsman implied that the reporters were naive, that the important thing was not to be liked but to be tough and get things done. It was an acrimonious session."

Another visitor to Saigon that August, Claude Witze, a senior editor of *Air Force-Space Digest* magazine, summed up the position very much as I was just beginning to understand it when he wrote:

> A distressing amount of intellectual dishonesty is scattered through the record we have built up here in the 1960s. . . . When there will be any improvement is highly dubious. The same officials are still giving the orders and now they have put a single man in charge of dealing with the press in Saigon. The new and unified effort to tell the story has had as its real goal the correction of what is called erroneous information coming out of Saigon. The erroneous information, it is indicated, is critical of the South Vietnamese contribution and its willingness to fight. The same reports tend to ignore Vietcong terrorism, defections and losses. None of these criticisms of the reporting out of Saigon acknowledges that early 1964 was studded with Vietcong successes. [6]

This may have been unfair to the newly appointed American propaganda chief, Barry Zorthian, the director of the Joint US Public Affairs Office (JUSPAO), but it seemed to me to be an accurate statement of the position. And try as he might, being a devoted and conscientious part of the American Embassy staff, Zorthian could scarcely have changed the mistrustful attitudes of the most important among the small group of correspondents.

Newsweek summed up the position on September 4 to show that Zorthian had not been able to change a bad situation in this comment:

> In the nine months since the fall of Diem, harassment of reporters critical of South Vietnam policy has not abated. Yet the truth of what is really happening in the Southeast Asian nation seems just as illu-

sory. . . . Nevertheless, it was clear to any one within gunshot of Saigon that American policy and American interests were in serious trouble last week.

All this seemed not to have had any effect either on President Johnson, his State and Defense departments, or Congress, for UPI reported from Washington on September 9 along with others, "President Johnson said today that Maxwell D. Taylor, U.S. ambassador to South Vietnam, has reported 'continued progress' in the war against Communists there despite recent political turmoil. . . . The President said Mr. Taylor gave Congressional leaders a 'full and frank examination of the situation.' "

General Taylor, who then was responsible for the American performance in South Vietnam, did not impress *Newsweek* in its own account of the president's report, saying the ambassador had "fairly oozed optimism." And six days later the New York *Times* commented editorially:

> Less than a year ago high officials were proclaiming that the war against the Vietcong could be won by 1965. If illusions of that extreme nature have now been dropped, it is still true that the information given to the American people only last week has already proved to be too optimistic. . . . The American people deserve to know all the facts, regardless of how grim they can be.

Although it was obvious that the Johnson administration now was preparing for a major enlargement of the Vietnam War with the addition of hundreds of thousands more troops, it still was apparent during my stay in Saigon that there was no change in the guarded, even defensive attitude of most of the Vietnamese people in the countryside outside Saigon. It was no great secret, even at the American embassy, that it was difficult, often impossible, to persuade most Vietnamese to give accurate information to the authorities about the presence of the Vietcong even in their own hamlets.[7]

Despite the efforts of dedicated social scientists with Vietnamese interpreters to change this position, it was seldom that any of the farmers or artisans among the Vietnamese people would dare to cooperate. And if they were obdurate about helping the South Vietnamese government, they were downright fearful of the Vietcong, who were known to levy fees and collect taxes from people in territories under their control. It was a fair statement, I believe, to assume that the peasantry placed no trust in either side and cooperated with one or the other only when it became a life-or-death matter to do so.

Arnold Beichman, an AFL-CIO official who was in Saigon at about the same time as I was, later wrote of an expedition to the countryside:

I met peasants who had walked all night from their own little village 30 miles away to talk to my Vietnamese friends and me. They lived in an area that had been in Vietcong hands for five years. They paid taxes to the Vietcong, quartered their men and did their bidding— and fervently wished to be rid of them, for all the good reasons that peasants anywhere want to be rid of their landlord oppressors.

Between the Vietcong that already had overrun at least half of the enormous Vietnamese rice bowl, the noncooperation of the rest of the peasantry, and the dilatory tactics of the Vietnamese army, the outlook for an American victory in Southeast Asia was exceedingly dim while I was in Saigon. Even after the war was stepped up, the position did not materially change, despite all the optimistic propaganda that was issued in Washington to try to counteract the reasonably accurate reporting that usually bore a South Vietnamese dateline.

The refusal of the South Vietnamese army to stand and fight against the Vietcong most of the time was no mere journalistic illusion. A recognized military authority, Brigadier General S. L. A. Marshal, had written as early as 1962 of the conduct of the Twenty-second Vietnamese Division:

> The 22d tries to avoid waste motion. There is no deep patrolling just on the chance of ambushing or fighting engagements with roving Congs. Forces guide pretty much on intelligence data. When the information points to a Cong assembly anywhere in the neighborhood a battalion or so is mounted in Shawnee helicopters and flown to a spot marked X on the acetate [map]. Sometimes there is a blind payoff. Four times out of five at least, either the bird has flown or the information is wrong.

For a long time, both the South Vietnamese and American military commands maintained the fiction that the North Vietnamese army wasn't in action in the south, except perhaps for a few individuals, and that the Vietcong alone was the only active force on the Communist side. But within a short time after my visit, large units of the North Vietnamese 325th Division were identified with the Vietcong as the forces blockading a key route to the Cambodian border.

Nor was Saigon exempt from attack. At the time I was there, the South Vietnamese capital of nearly 2 million people could have been paralyzed at any time by the Vietcong, who seemed to move in and out with frequent disturbances of the nature of the bomb that had wrecked the Caravelle lobby. (I was aware that there was a strike of hotel workers against the hotel at the time, but that didn't change any opinions about the source of the attack in the lobby.) However, the guerrilla commanders apparently weren't ready then to risk a sizable force to turn the city's life upside down, for there never was a concerted attack on the capital until close to the end of the war.[8]

Just before I left Saigon with the completion of my interviews and questionnaires, a correspondent handed me the following to remind me that doubts about the reliability of most government sources hadn't softened the usually brutal competition among correspondents assigned to cover the Vietnam War:

> A correspondent coming in from the states who must work on his own is up against fantastic odds in information gathering, communications and every other aspect of assistance here. His only hope of survival against such competition is to join the USIS gang. That is, unless he has editors back home with vision enough to say, "To hell with the inclusive story. Leave that to others. What we want is your own probing, even if it is only a very small aspect of the big picture." But this attitude is very, very rare.
>
> An editor who has invested a substantial sum in sending someone to Vietnam expects "results." If the story of the day is about some complicated coup or counter coup, or if it is about the latest bombing of North Vietnam, that is what the editor wants to hear about in his man's copy, even if his man knows nothing about these subjects other than what he gleans from USIS. And that is why you are seeing an appalling likeness in much of the copy coming from here.*

The trouble with this oft-used defensive posture by the "play-it-safe" school of foreign correspondents is that it is self-defeating. Anybody on rewrite back home can do a slightly different version of a main wire service story any day just as easily as the special can do it from Saigon. And if that happens often enough, the special will soon find himself out of a job. Anyway, I never knew of a "play-it-safe" correspondent who ever won a Pulitzer Prize.

And so, in addition to that year's Pulitzer winners, Halberstam and Browne, I left Saigon with the liveliest admiration for such others as Peter Arnett of the AP and two of the photographers, Horst Faas of the AP and Kyoichi Sawada of UPI. It also struck me that all three were foreign nationals—Faas, a German; Sawada, a Japanese, and Arnett, a New Zealander.[9] There also were a number of others, including some ambitious youngsters and a few tough-minded veterans, whose stuff also would bear watching. It was my bad luck that I missed meeting one of

---

* I have withheld the name of the correspondent by request.

the best of all, Neil Sheehan, who had been pulled back temporarily to Tokyo by an overly cautious UPI executive.

Even so, when I left Saigon for Kashmir, India, and Pakistan before returning to Columbia for the fall semester, I was convinced that the Pulitzer Prizes would play a still larger role during the enlarged Vietnam War by rewarding the growth of a more aggressive brand of war correspondence in Vietnam.

19 Honors for the Duke

If there was one quality of the Pulitzer Prizes that merited public respect over the years, it was diversity. Like their founder, the interests of the awards were wide-ranging once the Pulitzer board broke from the domination of the Columbia president who obtained Joseph Pulitzer's $2 million deed of gift, Nicholas Murray Butler.

In journalism, from the earliest years of the Vietnam War, the Pulitzer board and its juries continually asserted their independence by awarding prizes to the venturesome young reporters and photographers who successfully disputed the government's false claims of victories in combat.

However, the record was by no means as clear in the cultural aspects of the awards. In fiction, there were long delays in recognizing Ernest Hemingway (in 1953) and William Faulkner (in 1955), but under President Butler's influence awards went to Booth Tarkington in 1919 and 1922.

In drama, too, a long-forgotten playwright won a prize as early as 1918 for an undistinguished show called *Why Marry?*, but the originality of the popular American musical theater, the nation's unique contribution to the art of the stage, went unhonored until 1932 with the opening of *Of Thee I Sing* on Broadway.

It was in music, however, that a real struggle developed about the Pulitzer Prizes because the definition specified that the award must apply to "music in its larger forms" as composed by an American. In the fifteen years from 1948 to 1963, three American composers were honored twice each, and the prize was passed twice. No one disputed the merits and the value of the winning composers—Walter Piston, Gian-Carlo Menotti, and Samuel Barber—and the two works each for which they had won awards. Nor was I aware of any complaints at the time. [1]

Nevertheless, President Kirk and Chairman Pulitzer of the board asked for the recruitment of an entirely new jury for the 1964–1965 academic year. They were three music critics—Winthrop Sargeant of the *New Yorker,* Ronald Eyer of *Newsday* on Long Island, and Thomas B. Sherman of the St. Louis *Post-Dispatch.* What everybody had hoped for was a new and highly original choice beyond the small circle of American composers who devoted themselves to opera, concertos, symphonies, and the like. All of us with an interest in music—and I was among them, having studied the piano for nine years and maintained a lifelong interest in it thereafter—expected a prodigious burst of novelty.

That, in effect, was what we received from the new jurors, but it wasn't in the form that we had expected. For the second straight year and the third since the beginning of the music prize in 1943, there was no award. Instead, all three of our new music jurors proposed a special citation for the great jazz composer, Edward Kennedy Ellington, universally known as the Duke. As Ronald Eyer stated the case for himself and his colleagues, it was both forthright and compelling:

> In lieu of a seasonal award, therefore, we respectfully suggest that an appropriate citation of some sort be given to Edward K. (Duke) Ellington, who has made many notable contributions to American music over a period of 30 years or more with compositions of high artistic quality couched mainly in the idiom of jazz. . . . Though its language is jazz, Ellington's work should not be confused with that of commercial, popular or show composers. It has true artistic quality, with roots in the traditional music of his race, and it has a strong influence on the music of a whole generation, both in this country and elsewhere.

Now it so happened that the Duke, in addition to the great volume of his previous works, had composed and performed a new work during that prize year, *Far Eastern Suite,* although it wasn't considered by his critics to be the best of his compositions. Even so, in the light of what happened subsequently, I believe the board might well have settled for a prize for *Far Eastern Suite* and given Ellington his well-deserved award. That, however, is only hindsight; and because the board refused a special award to Ellington, there never was a test vote on the latest Ellington composition.

Again, this is but hindsight, for nobody addressed the board on the length, the value, and the originality of Ellington's compositions over three decades. Perhaps Chairman Pulitzer or I should have suggested it; yet, there is no way of knowing whether it would have changed anybody's mind.

Nevertheless, any composer regardless of the idiom and method, could have been proud of Ellington's record. Beginning as just another jazz pianist in 1916 at the age of seventeen (he was born in 1899 in Washington, D.C.), the Duke formed his own band two years later and soon made his own music among the most popular in an America that was celebrating the jazz age of the 1920s. The current generation toward the end of the century still applauds his earlier pieces like *Mood Indigo, Sophisticated Lady,* and *Solitude,* although they were written many years ago. Then came *Creole Rhapsody* in 1932, *Liberian Suite* in 1947, *Harlem* in 1951, and *Night Creatures* in 1955.

It was with such compositions as these that Ellington established his reputation as a composer. There was an original quality about most of his work which, like George Gershwin's, won the admiration as well as the applause of their contemporaries. It was, truly, *American* music, for what Ellington did was to turn the mechanics of jazz into classical form. [2]

The Pulitzer board, however, did not take the Ellington nomination seriously because it did not conform to the terms of the music award at the time, which was for an original work of music in its larger forms by an American composer. I do not recall any debate or even a remark beyond Chairman Pulitzer's observation that he had hoped this new music jury would recommend a specific composition. The motion to skip the music prize for the second year in succession was approved unanimously in short order. [3]

Except for the prize to Horst Faas, the Associated Press's combat photographer in Vietnam, the first of two he was to win, I do not recall that the 1965 awards in themselves caused much of a stir, although they were thoroughly representative of the best of the year in American letters, drama, and journalism. But, as I noted in my diary for that April 22, "We passed music and cartoons and will hear from both."

I concluded, "Joe Pulitzer was deputized to see if LBJ will come to our dinner for the 50th anniversary of the Pulitzer Prizes next year. A long day, a long year—glad it's over."

I was an optimist on two counts. First, President Johnson was so angry about the continued Pulitzer Prizes to his Vietnam War critics that he wouldn't have anything to do with the celebration of our fiftieth anniversary. And we not only heard from the critics of our non-music award; they overwhelmed us and Columbia had to come to our rescue.

I had no advance warning of the row over the denial of a special award to Duke Ellington. In my diary for May 3, there are only a few lines of a hastily scribbled note, "The Pulitzer announcement came at 3:19 p.m. It was in the World Room and all went well."

For the moment, at least, I was able to view the proceedings with satisfaction. For the first 24 hours, most of the published and broadcast comment centered on the awards to Frank Gilroy for a mildly popular little play, *The Subject Was Roses,* to Editor Mel Ruder of a newspaper called the *Hungry Horse News* in Montana for the coverage of a local flood, and to Horst Faas for his Vietnam War pictures.

In letters, the awards went to Shirley Ann Grau for a novel, *The Keepers of the House,* to Ernest Samuels for his three-volume biography of Henry Adams, to Irwin Unger for his history of *The Greenback Era,* to Howard Mumford Jones for a nonfiction book, *O Strange New World,* and to John Berryman for a volume of his poetry.

The journalism prizes were equally respectable and noncontroversial —the Hutchinson (Kans.) *News* for leading a battle for legislative reapportionment; to Gene Goltz of the Houston *Post* for exposing government corruption in Pasadena, Texas; to Louis Kohlmeier of the *Wall Street Journal* for reporting on the fortune acquired by President Johnson; to J. A. Livingston of the Philadelphia *Bulletin* for a report on the growing independence of the east European satellites of the Soviet Union; and to John R. Harrison of the Gainesville (FLa.) *Sun* for his editorials on housing.

It was that kind of year, one in which the whole weight of public opinion would have been ranged against the Pulitzer board for an error in judgment such as the Ellington non-award. Only two days elapsed before the disappointed music jurors did what came to them naturally as journalists—they gave the story to the New York *Times.* In my diary for May 5, there is an entry to the general effect that the *Times* reported Ellington had been denied a music prize for his distinguished career in American music. I commented, "It was a mild uproar."

That was decidedly an understatement. On May 11, when I showed President Kirk my jury selections for 1966 preparatory to circulating them to the rest of the Pulitzer board, I noted in my diary, "The wailing over the music prize is long and loud." And indeed it was. As late as June 22, some of my colleagues in the Faculty of Journalism led a protest to President Kirk over the actions and nonactions of the Pulitzer board, and I had to listen to them. Dr. Kirk was good-natured through it all, for which I was grateful.

My colleagues were late getting into the act. William Schuman, a former winner of the Pulitzer Prize in music who had become president of the Lincoln Center for the Performing Arts, argued that the refusal to honor Ellington was "utterly preposterous." Other eminent former winners, Aaron Copland and Elliott Carter, agreed with him when he wrote:

"For the past two years, the Advisory Board has done harm to the cause of American music by its failure to make an award in either year. If there were no Pulitzer Prize in Music the world of music would be in a better state than it is in a year when no award is given. The negative effect of a no-prize discourages public acceptance of new music and is a black eye for our composers."[4]

The Pulitzer board's only defender turned out to be Irving Kolodin in the *Saturday Review,* who called attention to the limitations of the music prize to a composition in music's "larger forms" and added:

"I yield, to no one in my admiration for Ellingtom's distinctions . . . but larger forms are precisely what he is not distinguished for. The citation may be all wrong, muddle-headed and outmoded, but that is the rule of the road the jury members agreed to follow when they accepted appointment—had they bothered to read."

By that time, Eyer and Sergeant had resigned. Sherman, the remaining jury member, didn't resign but pointed out he hadn't been reappointed and that was that. The hero of the occasion, the Duke himself, acted with exemplary grace, saying, "Fate's being kind to me. Fate doesn't want me to be too famous too young." He was then in his sixty-seventh year.

Eventually, the trustees of Columbia University bailed everybody out of an embarrassing situation by voting to award the Duke an honorary doctorate for "his services to American music and his distinguished career." That was in 1972. He died two years later at age seventy-five.[5]

For the remainder of my administration of the Pulitzer Prizes, which ended in 1976, the Pulitzer board never interfered with a music jury's decision, nor did it ever again pass a music award. In fact, until the early 1990s, a decision not to award a music prize was taken only once—in 1981. And in Columbia's bicentennial year celebration in 1976, the board issued a special award to the ragtime pianist and composer, Scott Joplin (1868–1917), "for his contributions to American music."

It is worth noting, too, in examining the development of American music in its larger forms, that Aaron Copland forecast in 1962 that a musical revolution was gathering strength and eventually would have an effect on American music. Much sooner than the Pulitzer board's members or Copland believed possible, an innovative, thirty-two-year-old member of the Columbia Music Department, Charles Wuorinen, won a 1970 Pulitzer Prize in music for an electronic composition.

Wuorinen was honored for his electronic work, *Time's Encomium,* a two-part movement that was produced on an RCA Mark II Synthesizer and was given its first performance at the Berkshire Music Festival in Massachusetts in 1969. The piece and its electronic composer were nominated for the prize by a distinguished jury—Gunther Schuller, president of the New England Conservatory of Music; Professor Emeritus Otto C. Luening, of the Columbia Music Department, and Vincent Persichetti, of the Juilliard School, chairman. In their report, the jurors cited Wuorinen as follows:

> The jury considers it [*Time's Encomium*] to be a major statement in the purely electronic field in that it combines a perfect technical mastery of the medium with the imagination, inventiveness and musicality always associated with the highest standards of musical expression.

The problem was that Wuorinen's colleagues in the Columbia Music Department were not as enthusiastic about him as was the Pulitzer board and its music jury. Within a year after his computerized music award, the members of the Columbia Music Department faculty voted against giving him tenure. Directly after that, he resigned in a storm of charges and countercharges. [6]

There were other musical revolutionaries among Wuorinen's contemporaries who tried new methods and techniques without resorting to computerized music with better results. One was Professor George Crumb, of the University of Pennsylvania, who won a Pulitzer Music Prize in 1968 for his composition, *Echoes of Time and the River*. Robert W. Ward, the chairman of that jury, wrote that Crumb's piece "speaks in a musical language which has emerged only in the past decade and yet reflects a great sense of the classical tradition." This bow to the past, the jury chairman concluded, will "be applauded by those more sympathetic to avant-garde developments" despite the composer's respected status among musical conservatives. Evidently, Wuorinen hadn't been able to do both.

However, in 1971, still another electronic composer from Columbia, Mario Davidovsky, also won a Pulitzer for a work called *Synchronisms No. 6 for Piano and Electronic Sound*. Like Wuorinen's piece, Davidovsky's also had been first performed at the Berkshire Music Festival which, the jury found, "shows mastery of a new medium and its imaginative use in combination with the solo pianoforte."

At the Pulitzer board meeting, no questions were raised, and the computer helped still another composer attain Pulitzer honors. But an earlier Pulitzer winner, Virgil Thomson, who had won his prize for the movie music to a film called *Louisiana Story* in 1949, raised a key point about computerized music and other modern innovations when he asked pointedly, "Is it music or is it noise?"

He didn't really answer his own question, but he rambled on in a discussion of new kinds of sound that aspired to musical recognition:

Myself, I see no hindrance to the survival of both noise-art and music. Photography did not kill oil painting; on the contrary, it set off in landscape painting a development known as impressionistic which invigorated all painting. Similarly, the gramophone and the radio, far from killing off music, have contributed to their distribution, changed their sociology and corrected their aesthetics.

So I am not worried. Let the boys have fun. Let us all have fun. Let Europe survive. Let America exist. Indeed, I am convinced in music it already does exist. At least that.[7]

In the debate of music versus noise, there was one other aspect that obliquely came to the attention of the Pulitzer board, although it never was formally discussed in any session where I was charged with keeping a record. A few of the board members—and in my twenty-two years there was only one who could consider himself musically competent— suggested mildly to Chairman Pulitzer that the music prize could conveniently be dropped without creating too much of a fuss.

Ever faithful to his grandfather's will, the third Pulitzer refused to consider a proposal that might have turned out to be extremely embarrassing. So it never was openly discussed and certainly never came to a vote. Incidently, the one musician among the editors and publishers at the annual oblong table at Columbia was Vermont Connecticut Royster, editor of the *Wall Street Journal,* who never raised an objection to the music award. The most he ever attempted to do was to give his musical view, for the attention of the rest of the board, of a new noise-art style of composition. In any event, the two prizes for computerized music still stand in the Pulitzer records as the outposts of modern American music.

But as far as the Pulitzer board was concerned, there was more enthusiasm for the 1974 Pulitzer special award to the seventy-seven-year-old veteran Roger Sessions. To quote another veteran, Arthur Krock of the New York *Times,* at the conclusion of his farewell to his fellow-members of the Pulitzer board, "We're dealing with something very powerful here. Let's proceed with care."[8]

20 Fifty-Year Reckoning

The American cultural scene was changing rapidly during the first fifty years of the Pulitzer Prizes, but too many juries in some categories were refusing to make annual awards. The condition was often an unnecessary handicap, sometimes even an embarrassment.

The trend began early on when the novel prize was passed in 1917 and 1920, sometimes given to minor works in intervening years, and still was in evidence later in the century when short stories were honored for lack of what might have been an acceptable novel.

Similarly, the drama award was twice passed in 1917 and 1919 before being given to the first of Eugene O'Neill's great works in 1920, but there still were no awards for 1963, 1964, and 1966, when some younger or experimental playwright could have been encouraged.

The record was much better in history, biography, and journalism. In history, when this all-American award went to a French ambassador in 1917, a number of major works were honored leading up to the posthumous prize in 1966 for *The Life of the Mind in America* by Perry Miller. In biography, the progression was even more striking, going from an award in 1917 for a life of Julia Ward Howe to *A Thousand Days,* Arthur Meier Schlesinger Jr.'s chronicle of the Kennedy presidency in 1966.

Neither poetry nor music awards existed in 1917, and modest works were honored in 1966—Richard Eberhart's *Selected Poems* and Leslie Bassett's *Variations for Orchestra*—after the music award had been passed the two previous years.

By contrast, the interests of the newspaper proprietors and editors who dominated the Pulitzer board kept the journalism prizes abreast of the times. Instead of Herbert Bayard Swope's diplomatic reportage in "Inside the German Empire" that won the international award in 1917, the combat reporters in the Vietnam War were being given their due fifty years later, despite the protests from the White House.

In national reporting, too, the Pulitzers were not only timely but perhaps even ahead of their times in some respects. Whereas in 1917 the public service award had been withheld and in 1918 had gone to newspapers for publishing documents and teaching patriotism, the Chicago *Daily News* had won in 1964 for publicizing birth control services. In succeeding years other matters of timely public interest had won gold medals for the St. Petersburg (Fla.) *Times,* the Hutchinson (Kans.) *News,* and the Boston *Globe.*

The pious morality of the 1920s prohibition era, too, had long since vanished in the consideration of progress in national reportage. Fifty years or so later, the emphasis in the news was on covering the dangerously widening racial split in America, especially in the South. Here, the emphasis was on the crusade led by the Reverend Dr. Martin Luther King Jr. for racial equality, beginning in Selma, Alabama. The trouble was that very few reporters were winning prizes for that, and especially not black reporters.

There was a lot of room for progress here in the news business—a chance for the Pulitzer board once again to assert the kind of leadership it had shown in the case of the coverage of the Vietnam War.

To any broad-minded, concerned spectator of these annual proceedings, the conclusion was inevitable that there could be a vast improvement in the cultural aspects of the Pulitzer Prizes. And while the journalism awards to a greater extent had shown sensitivity to the public interest in Vietnam reportage and some major aspects of domestic policy, a stronger effort also could be made in encouraging greater coverage of the broadening racial and even religious controversies stimulated by the nation's swing to the Right. [1]

Such feelings as these lay behind the board's somewhat reluctant decision to hold a midwinter meeting at Columbia for the first time in 1966 as a manifest of good intentions at the start of the fiftieth year of the prizes. It was first of all a relief for me in my twelfth year as the administrator who had the initial responsibility of nominating jurors as well as scanning all entries. I also was increasingly conscious of pressures outside the board and Columbia for including TV news in the awards.

However, as I noted in my diary, I still managed to begin the year in good spirits and good health:

Jan. 1—Dorothy and I have spent New Year's Eve in many wonderful places—New York City, London and Paris among them—but never did we imagine that we would begin a year in a motel in Statesville, Ga. We drove there in our car from Fort Lauderdale in Florida after a lovely sunny Christmas vacation, had a skimpy dinner and so to bed. Nobody seemed to care if it was New Year's Eve in Statesville, Ga., a bend in the road on the route to New York City. Anyway, we resumed our drive north early on New Year's Day for nearly 500 miles to another motel at Petersburg, Va. It was a chore neither of us enjoyed but there was the midwinter Pulitzer board meeting to prepare for once I arrived back at Columbia and I had no choice.

Jan. 2—A rainy, miserable Sunday drive from Petersburg, Va., to New York, which had been paralyzed by a long transit strike. No buses, no subways were running, but it didn't affect us very much at Columbia because our apartment was just around the corner from the campus.

By January 6, after classes had resumed and I'd put the students to work covering the transit strike, I noted in my diary that "the strike's become a way of life here." Still, I did complete the arrangements for the board session well before we met on January 14, although I didn't have the slightest idea of what to expect.

The session apparently had been taken seriously by at least a few of the city's news organizations because the host of an NBC radio show interviewed me the day before.[2] It so happened that I'd generally described the functions of the prizes and the board in a new book published by Columbia University Press and I referred to it during the interview. But my host didn't seem to know about it; anyway, when I asked if he'd read it, he seemed shocked saying: "Why, we don't have time around here for things like that."

However, there were compensations for all of us at Columbia. Mercifully, the transit strike had ended that morning, so it was possible once again to move about the city without resorting to taxis (when one could be found) or walking fairly long distances for a quart of milk or a loaf of bread at a grocery store.

Chairman Pulitzer phoned me the previous afternoon from St. Louis, a practice he'd begun when he succeeded his father in 1955, to plan the midwinter meeting and find out what suggestions I had for keeping the discussion within reasonable bounds. I'd already been told by President Kirk that he'd have to leave for a conference in Washington except for a brief greeting at the opening, so the university had no particular interest in the proceedings.

Yet, from these and other conferences, I gained the impression that some of the board's members were disturbed by fairly recent attacks, mainly from faculty people at Columbia outside the Pulitzer Prize operation. This seemed to have to do principally with still more criticism of the board in withholding a special music award for Duke Ellington in 1965 after a jury of music critics had recommended it. Specifically, the objection appeared to have originated with the response of an anonymous board member to the jury's proposal. As published, the offending quote said, "The music jury was a craven goddam jury. They expressed contempt for contemporary composition and then threw in a special recommendation for Duke Ellington. If they thought Ellington was worth it, why didn't they give him the Pulitzer Prize itself?"

As had become known later, the outraged board member was Ralph McGill, the editor of the Atlanta *Constitution*, who wouldn't withdraw a word of his opinion of the jury and even added, "I will confess that the report of the jury did seem to me to be intellectually dishonest in that it recommended in the strongest terms that no prize be given and yet at the same time suggested that a citation be given to Ellington. It seems to me preposterous and sort of contradictory."[3]

Despite McGill's critics, he gained support from other members of the board, notably Sevellon Brown III of the Providence (R.I.) *Journal-Bulletin*, who called the jury's action "weak," and W. D. Maxwell of the Chicago *Tribune*, who argued, "The board couldn't decide on anything worth while to give the prize to so it seems outside limits to give a weaker prize to a citation."

In any event, what now was being suggested to the board's midwinter meeting, as I belatedly learned, was that its membership should refrain from creating a fuss over such matters as the Ellington dispute and entrust their comments instead to a spokesman who, so I was told, was likely to be me. I scarcely relished the honor, knowing perfectly well that it was tough enough for a journalist to please one editor or publisher, let alone the members of the board with their usually vigorous and widely differing political, social, economic, and cultural views.[4]

I envied President Kirk his previous appointment with the State Department's expert on cultural affairs, Charles Frankel, and wished mightily that he could have found an excuse to take me with him.

As I might have known, no editor or publisher worthy of the news business, in its struggle to be recognized as a profession, would under any circumstances yield the right of free speech, even more so than a free press, to anonymous academic critics. Following Chairman Pulitzer's example, I took no part in the midwinter meeting beyond announcing the agenda and recording the gist of any decisions that were taken. As far as limiting their right to discuss any part of the Pulitzer board's business without reservation, no matter when or where, all were completely against it. Nor was there any reference to me as a substitute spokesman; evidently, the members had been told beforehand that the idea was not mine. It was with relief, therefore, that I summed up the proceedings in my diary:

Jan. 14—The midwinter meeting of the Pulitzer board confirmed our plans for the 50th anniversary dinner. It also was decided to send me to the White House to ask President Johnson to be the principal speaker, an honor I did not relish. My peers also agreed once again to let me continue using three people each for our juries in letters, drama and music but increased the number of journalism jurors to five for each category in which we had prizes.

Everybody around the table in the World Room facing the Statue of Liberty Window listened politely to a report summing up criticism of the board and the awards from supposedly anonymous members of the Columbia faculty, then declined to muzzle themselves—a commentary on the uproar about the refusal in 1965 to honor Duke Ellington.

As expected, the members rededicated themselves to free speech, the Constitutional bill of rights and the inalienable principle of saying what they liked to whomever they pleased. So the internal Columbia war on the Pulitzers, which had begun last June with the Ellington controversy, ended with the rejection of the notion that only an official spokesman would thenceforth speak for the board.

Even if I couldn't show it, I was pleased with the outcome as the uncomfortable man in the middle, particularly when I was told once the meeting ended that my annual stipend would be substantially increased. So the midwinter exercise was not completely futile as far as I was concerned. Still, it also was evident from the comments of my colleagues at our midwinter lunch that it would be a long time before there was another session like the one we had just concluded. To which I added a heartfelt if private amen. [5]

The way was now cleared for the fiftieth annual Pulitzer Prize announcement on May 3 and the fiftieth anniversary dinner a week later, to which the ticket of admission would be a Pulitzer Prize or other eminent services in American public affairs or the arts as determined by Columbia University. Prior to that double anniversary, I'd already been authorized to query the White House and proceed as usual with the disposition of the various jury reports before the board's meeting later that year.

There also was a sharp reminder not long afterward of the baleful influence of the Vietnam War on American life in general. It happened on February 15 that the star of our school's annual Elmer Davis dinner was the CBS television director, Fred Friendly, who had just resigned in protest against the network's refusal to let him broadcast the Senate's hearings on the Vietnam conflict and had ordered him instead to use a rerun of the *I Love Lucy* show.

That, of course, was par for TV's attitude toward public service at the time, which caused our journalism faculty to invite Friendly to join us as our director of TV instruction. Fortunately for our students as well as ourselves, he accepted—a lucky break all around.

Two days later, I celebrated my sixtieth birthday with a defiant gesture in my diary against advancing age as follows:

Feb. 17—Sixty years old today and I don't feel any differently inside than when I was 30, 40 or 50. I slept well, was up in good time for breakfast with Dorothy, opened my birthday cards and presents and showed up on time for class on a sunny winter's day in New York. My secretary had made me a birthday cake with six candles, which I blew out, then sampled the cake with relish prior to taking the students to the UN with me for the assignment of the day—Secretary General U Thant being interviewed on his negative views toward the Vietnam War.

Next day I found myself saluted in the New York Times by a reviewer for my latest book who called me 'journalism's press agent'— a patronizing attitude that sent me into a state of low dudgeon. From the coverage of everything from murders to presidential elections and wars as well as the instruction of the next generation of journalists, I'd been anything but a press agent. But then, there was no accounting for book reviewers.

I also heard from Howard P. Jones at the East-West Center of the University of Hawaii who offered me a long-or short-term post there— whatever I wished. We'll see what comes of it. Next, I was asked if I wanted to be a candidate for director of the Ohio State School of Journalism, an honor I declined with thanks. And there still was a lot of work ahead for an Asian book topped off by the Vietnam War that I was preparing for the Council on Foreign Relations in following years. [6]

After six decades, a quarter century of them in a wide range of newspaper work, I was thankful that I still had more than enough to do. But I also realized that I, along with the rest of our older generations, would soon be caught up in the growing revolt of our youth against the Vietnam War. No matter how assuredly some of us had thought of it as a temporary phenomenon that would go away in time, it hadn't happened—and now it wasn't likely to happen.

At Columbia we'd already had a taste of the future. Our Navy ROTC, having scheduled a routine march locally, only recently had become the center of a campus brawl. [7] Not only that, but older and more important people now had come back from the UN to write about an interview in which Secretary General U Thant had said, as he had earlier before the Council on Foreign Relations, that our war in Vietnam already had been lost. Also, he still argued that we never would be able to establish and hold a neutral Vietnam.

The United States, in few words, faced a difficult future as the world's greatest military and economic power. And those of us among an older generation of Americans would have all we could do to hold the country together in the face of an unparalleled rebellion among our youth against military service in an unpopular war. With President Johnson's unyielding pro-war position in Washington, we could expect no help from the chief of our government.

I could not, in good conscience, suggest by word or deed that there should be any opposition in the fiftieth year of the Pulitzer Prizes to a jury's nomination of Peter Arnett of the Associated Press for an award as the year's outstanding combat correspondent in Vietnam and I did not do so. Like Malcolm Browne of the Associated Press and David Halberstam of the New York *Times* who had been similarly rewarded in 1964, Arnett—a stocky little New Zealander—had been in the field wherever Americans were fighting and had shared with them their risks, their hardships, and their sacrifices against an implacable jungle enemy. During my previous trip to Vietnam in connection with the new Asian book, I had seen the two earlier laureates and Arnett in action and would never have qualified my admiration for their work.

Like the rest of the fifty-year Pulitzer honor roll cited earlier in this chapter, Arnett's award went through unquestioned at the Pulitzer board's meeting prior to the fiftieth anniversary celebration and was announced with the approval of Columbia's trustees in advance of the festivities. I was confident at the time, moreover, that Arnett, like the others I had seen in the field, would win still more awards regardless of the antiwar attitude among the bulk of the nation's youth.

That, however, could scarcely dispose of the other and more persistent criticisms of the Pulitzer Prizes that antedated both the current board membership, President Kirk's administration at Columbia, and my part in the proceedings as the board's administrator. Prior to the celebration, it would scarcely have been politic to have dismissed these opposing views of the prizes as unworthy of consideration, and I did not do so.

Perhaps the most persistent attack on the prizes came from those who regarded them as a collection of largely middle-class prejudices that sought to avoid the unpleasant aspects of American life in order to stress conformity to the ways of our elders. I understood these views all too well because they were, in large part a product of the conservative chic of my generation and those of my elders. Sinclair Lewis had exploited it to his own advantage in rejecting the Pulitzer Prize that had been awarded to him in 1926 for *Arrowsmith,* a publicity pitch if there ever was one. The claim was that he was getting even because the board had denied him a prize for his best novel, *Main Street.*

It seemed to me that Ernest Hemingway had a much more valid complaint because his greatest works were passed over and he finally was given an award in 1953 for a minor work, *The Old Man and the Sea.* That, too, was the case with William Faulkner, who wasn't honored for his greatest work but received awards in 1955 for *A Fable* and eight years later, in 1963, for *The Reivers* posthumously. And what of Theodore Dreiser, Scott Fitzgerald, and Thomas Wolfe, who never did appear in the records of the Pulitzer winners? (Strangely, a Ketti Frings play about Thomas Wolfe won a prize.)

Regrettable as it is that these things had happened in the distribution of annual prizes, such injustices were not limited to the Pulitzers. You will not find in the records of the Nobel Prize the names of two of the greatest among the world's novelists, Leo Tolstoy and Thomas Hardy. But you also will not recognize the names of some of the Nobel winners —Frans Emil Sillanpaa and Johannes V. Jensen among them.

It follows that I cannot claim perfection for the Pulitzers any more than the executors of the Nobel estate can produce a perfect record for his enviably rich and prestigious international awards. And the Nobels would seem to be more resolutely the product of middle-class European mores than the Pulitzers conform to the conventions of middle-class morality in the United States.

It might have been more venturesome if the juries in letters and drama during the first fifty years had experimented now and then with newcomers. But the trend was, except in special circumstances, to play it safe, go with the best, and the result may be seen in the four Pulitzers each to Eugene O'Neill and Robert Frost, the poet; three each for Robert E. Sherwood, the dramatist; Edwin Arlington Robinson, the poet; Thornton Wilder, the dramatist and novelist; and Archibald MacLeish, the two-time winner, one in poetry and one in drama.

For most critics, it would be difficult to complain against such winners as these. There also is something to be said for some of the other winners who could not be pigeonholed by a captious critic.

Carl Sandburg, for example, was no slave to convention either in his poetry or in his life of Lincoln. Nor was Tennessee Williams merely a sedate middle-class dramatist. There also was good reason to honor such eminent figures as Richard Hofstadter, Margaret Leech, Edith Wharton, Gian-Carlo Menotti, Samuel Eliot Morison, Allan Nevins, and Walter Piston, all of them double winners.

In the great advance in the American musical theater that the Pulitzers helped stimulate, it is true that modest figures in American literature like James Michener were cast in a heroic role. And why not? From one of his award-winning *Tales of the South Pacific* in 1948 came the glittering musical, *South Pacific,* which won a prize in 1950 for Richard Rodgers, Oscar Hammerstein II, and Joshua Logan.

As for journalists, their work in the Pulitzer Prizes alone would dispose of the notion of extremists that there is little of significance for American life in the Pulitzer Prizes for the first fifty years. To be sure, as has already been pointed out earlier in this chapter, the multiple refusal of juries to award prizes in letters and drama cannot be justified when there is so much that is new and worth testing in American culture. But, with a few major exceptions, the great ones in drama and letters have been recognized, encouraged, and honored. And that is even more true of the advances in American journalism, as witness the major tests the Pulitzer Prizes met in the awards for the disclosures in the Pentagon Papers and Watergate cases among others.

Understandably, it will never be a simple matter for a panel of prize-givers to keep up with the times in American letters, drama, music, and journalism. But the fifty-year record of the Pulitzer Prizes in large part is solid and offers a safe base for the broadening of the awards when the time comes.[8]

21   The Grand Show

The fiftieth anniversary celebration of the Pulitzer Prizes opened on a sour note.

When I was sent to the White House early in 1966 to invite President Johnson to address the multitude of laureates at a testimonial dinner later that year, he refused to see me. His press secretary, Bill Moyers, was properly sympathetic, but there was no disguising the president's anger because Pulitzer Prizes had been awarded in 1964 and 1965 to correspondents critical of the conduct of the Vietnam War and more were likely for 1966.

The White House's fears were realized. After the Pulitzer journalism juries had come and gone, the candidacy of the Associated Press's Peter Arnett was among the highest on their list of nominees for an award because of his courageous reporting under fire in Vietnam—a war that already seemed irretrievably lost. I noted in my diary:

> March 18—Furious activity on the Pulitzer anniversary dinner. The first 700 invitations went out after a meeting with President Kirk at his Columbia office. He decided after consulting Chairman Pulitzer not to invite a single speaker to substitute for President Johnson. Instead, I am to invite five Pulitzer winners to speak at the grand show for five minutes each."[1]

Fortunately for me, I had been corresponding with a number of laureates at the time about the impact of the awards on their careers so I was not at a loss for suggestions although not all the opinions I received were laudatory.

The dramatist Edward Albee thought of the awards as a "declining honor" because he believed his best play, *Who's Afraid of Virginia Woolf?* had been slighted. Another in the theater, Arthur Miller, was also discouraging, saying that the award usually "comes to those who don't need it." And Bernard Malamud preferred the National Book Award.

But for the majority, the thrill seemed never to have worn off. The historian Arthur Meier Schlesinger Jr. remembered a friend had told him it was "the best label anybody could have." And the soldier-poet Archibald MacLeish recalled his surprise and delight when he bought the old Paris *Herald* on the Rue Jacob one day and saw himself plastered on page 1 as the winner of a Pulitzer. As for Virgil Thomson, he did even better—a congratulatory letter from President Truman.

There were picturesque ways, too, in which a Pulitzer award made an impression. John Strohmeyer, the journalist, liked to dream about the fair lady who sent him a rose a day for twelve days after he received the good news. And another journalist, Roland Kenneth Towery, found out about his prize when he was staring right into the cameras of CBS-TV for a news show. What pleased Jean Stafford, the novelist, was Walter Cronkite's announcement of her prize. And as for Al Friendly of the Washington *Post,* he was crowned with laurel leaves in a remote Turkish village when the townspeople learned he had won an honor from his native land.

The most practical reaction, however, was the tripling of Professor Ernest Samuels's salary at Northwestern after he received his Pulitzer. And John Toland won anew the love and admiration of his Japanese wife when the literary editor of *Mainichi Shimbun* in Tokyo phoned her with formal congratulations for her husband, *"Omedeto gozaimasu."*

For the diplomat, George F. Kennan, his prize money went at once for a new Swedish guitar on which he could strum music—*classical* music, he emphasized sternly. And in southern India, Professor David Brion Davis was besieged by a local reporter for an Indian daily for an interview, only the reporter didn't know what it was Davis had won. It might just as well have been a bet on a horse race.

Then there were the skeptics who couldn't believe their good fortune at first. One of them, Professor David Herbert Donald, was so reserved when his publisher's wife called with word of his first Pulitzer that she threatened to have her husband on the telephone to reassure the historian that she wasn't lying. The professor, incidentally, was still around almost thirty years later when he published a new Lincoln biography in 1995. And then there was the even more difficult case of the novelist Shirley Ann Grau who responded when told of her prize, "Don't be silly." She believed it only after confirmation.

Two future New York *Times* executive editors had quite different experiences after winning their prizes. Max Frankel's was announced by his publisher, Arthur Ochs Sulzberger Sr., while A. M. Rosenthal's failed to win him recognition from a tourist in Geneva who congratulated his luncheon companion instead. But all Peter Kann could do as another future editor when he received word of his prize from the *Wall Street Journal* at 5:00 A.M. in Hong Kong was to celebrate by smoking a stale cigar in bed.

John S. Knight, one of the oldest Pulitzer winners at seventy, worried unnecessarily about maintaining the quality of his work, while Sanche de Gramont, one of the youngest, wondered, when his boss called him by trans-Atlantic phone in Paris, how to explain a presumed *faux pas* only to learn instead that he'd won a Pulitzer. Paul Conrad, the Los Angeles *Times* cartoonist, also was puzzled when a little girl on his block wanted to know all about the "pullet" he'd won. When he told her a "pullet" was a chicken and he hadn't won one, she burst out, "Well, you know, the *surprise* you won."

So it went for many others who detailed their gratitude, their disappointment, their skepticism, their pride, and their reservations to me about the manner in which the Pulitzer Prizes had affected them. And from the lot, and others I knew whose responses were not as immediate or as colorful, I managed to produce the nominations for the five distinguished speakers at the fiftieth anniversary dinner who marked the occasion at the Plaza Hotel in New York City on the evening of May 10, 1966.[2]

Among those who attended were almost two hundred other laureates including the latest to be honored, the 1966 winners including the Vietnam correspondent Peter Arnett, all of whom received their awards before the evening was over.[3] As President Kirk said in greeting Columbia's guests, it was the university's intention "now as in the past half-century, to do our very best to carry out the mandate of Mr. Pulitzer's will."

In the pursuit of excellence in the specialized fields Joseph Pulitzer favored, President Kirk went on, "the existence of these prizes, and the national prestige they have achieved, is one more demonstration of the fact that man does not live by technology alone. No matter how great our devotion to machines, which now perform our daily menial tasks and which have opened up a glimpse, however banal, of the world's horizons to the humblest citizen, we know that in the inexorable judgment of time, a nation will be remembered not by its technical artifacts but by its cultural achievements. If recognition is not extended to those worthy of it, how shall these achievements be known?"

The answer came promptly from the poet Archibald MacLeish. With an all-embracing gesture toward his fellow-laureates, he spun a poetic hyperbole: "We are Mr. Pulitzer's dream made flesh." It was a cherished

moment in an evening devoted to vivid memories, during which MacLeish in particular seemed to try to draw his brilliant audience with him
in self-examination.

Again turning to his fellow-winners of Pulitzer Prizes, he continued,
"We need, most of us, a sign of recognition. Not recognition of our
ultimate worth as poets—only poetry itself can give that—but recognition that we exist. That we are there. Among those who went before and
those who will come after."

To which he added, as if in concern that he might seem too mindful
of his distinction:

> No one believes, least of all the perceptive president of the univer-
> sity whose guests we are, that the Pulitzer Prizes will change the art of
> letters in America; art is not impressed by awards. But there are men
> and women in this room—among the most intelligent of the time—
> who will testify that these prizes have warmed the world in which the
> art of letters must be preserved.[4]

The position seemed far more complex to the novelist Robert Penn
Warren, who wondered whether the age of Gutenberg had really ended,
then quoted D. H. Lawrence in seeming despair. "It becomes harder and
harder to read the *whole* of any modern novel. One reads a bit and
knows the rest; or else one doesn't want to know any more."

And so he wondered vaguely before this exclusive public before him,
"Is the trend of the novel toward extinction?" He tried seemingly to seek
a less drastic future for the world's printed storybooks as if to perish the
thought of such works as Tolstoy's *War and Peace* and Thackeray's
Vanity Fair on the scrap heap of time immortal. He argued:

> Certainly the novel will change as it discovers new insights and
> encounters new materials. But this is only to say that it will be renewed
> by the continuing challenge of life. The novel may even leave the printed
> page—if the age of Gutenberg is really over—but it still could be a
> novel; if, that is, the medium remains an image of human life recorded
> in language, in language because the deepest reality of the novel is in a
> story sustained by the interplay between what psychologists call the
> primary language of imagery and the ordinary verbal language of narra-
> tion and comment.

Despite this dismal speculative assessment of the future of the novel,
Warren tried—in the hopeful spirit of the evening—to conclude on a
positive note, but he was too much of a realist to let his laggard spell of
optimism carry him very far:

The uninspected life is, we know, not worth living, and the novel is one way which we have developed for inspecting life in its inwardness. The discovery of inwardness can be made by—and only by—the act of artistic imagination which is radical, central and to be distinguished from the historical imagination. There is no substitute for it, and as long as it can, in proper humility, be cultivated, the novel will not die. It will not even get very, very sick.

As D. H. Lawrence put it some forty years ago, if there is trouble, it is not with the novel. It is with the novelists. If they listen hard enough they will catch what James called "the very note and tick, the strange irregular rhythms of life." What they make of what they hear will be known only, as it has always been known, after the fact.[5]

But after the fact, it had to be said—as many in this accomplished and extremely critical audience realized—that the novel in America had, through the crudest mass influences on too many millions of uninspected lives, descended to the threadbare mockery of its earliest masters in America, from Hawthorne to James. It remained a good question whether it ever could recover.·

The trends in serious music, as Aaron Copland described them for this distinguished audience, seemed even more discouraging for even the trained listener that evening. For as one of the foremost laureates in serious American music explained, "We are living in the midst of an unprecedented musical revolution. The art I practice is in the process of being dismantled, broken down into its component parts, and put together in ways we never dreamed of." What Copland referred to, of course, was the mechanization of serious music in America by electronic means which can be recorded on magnetic tape "and tampered with so as to produce every possible sound combination from the most shattering noise to the most delicate tonal mixture."[6]

Whether that had anything to do with the failure of juries to recommend music prizes in 1964 and 1965, Copland didn't say, but I happened to know that the Music Department at Columbia, in particular, had been torn by dissension over the introduction of specialists in mechanical music into the course of instruction and had not yet decided on tenure for any such newcomers. This, however, had had nothing to do with the Pulitzer Prize for 1966 to Leslie Bassett for his *Variations for Orchestra,* first performed by the respected Eugene Ormandy and the Philadelphia Orchestra in 1965.

But make no mistake, musical mechanics had a long way to go before the sophisticated audiences for orchestral and operatic music in the United States accepted it. Copland, too, expressed his doubts, especially when he remarked that "IBM has gotten into the act," namely with Computer 7090, which "if fed the necessary information, can write out its own music *and* perform it." Still, he added seriously, probably with the situation of Columbia's music faculty in mind.

> Isn't it astonishing how quickly all of us have become accustomed to the idea that we can have a new kind of music: music without instruments, without performers, and even without composers? Under such circumstances, is it too much to expect that so-called normal music will remain just as it was in the past?

As for the younger generation of serious musicians that seems interested in the mechanics of music rather than its soul, Copland wasn't quite sure how to describe this section of the avant-garde but he warned prospective audiences for musical jacknifing, "You're on your own. . . . People are slower to swim upstream with the aural art."

I would have suggested, as well, being a lifelong part of the great American musical audience, that we are likely to be even slower to neglect the music of Bach, Beethoven, Brahms, Mozart and all the other historic masters who established our Western musical culture. Nor would it seem possible for the distinctive American musical theater to turn from Rodgers and Hammerstein and their lively contemporaries to the descendants of Computer 7090 to grind out show-stoppers as the last curtain slams down on the last chorus line.

Like the novelists and the musicians, James Reston saw little' that remained of Joseph Pulitzer's world of journalists, although he found a vast difference in the stand-pat reaction of his fellow-professionals. Out of his own experience with the New York *Times* as a Washington correspondent and later executive editor, he told his bemused audience of Pulitzer Prize winners:

> The biggest story of the last 50 years has been revolutionary change, which we have urged everybody to embrace, but we have changed less than any other business in America, done less research and development than any other industry and established a system of labor relations that makes Jimmy Hoffa [an old-time labor racketeer] look like a statesman.

As a life-long newspaperman, Reston was quite naturally influenced by that branch of the vast communications industry rather than the electronic media and computer science. He pictured himself and his newspaper colleagues as sticking "in our furrow in the floodlit electronic age."

He added in seeming resignation:

"The new age is good for us. It is forcing us to use our minds as well as our legs. It is making us think about the causes of violence, rebellion and war rather than merely reporting the struggle in the streets. And this in turn is giving us the opportunity to attract—although I'm not sure we are taking advantage of it—a much more intelligent, sensitive company of reporters than we have ever had before."[7]

The newspaper problem in the electronic age, however, was that the number of dailies in the United States already had been cut in half, and some of the greatest and most influential journals in the land—including some of those with numerous Pulitzer Prizes—had been put out of business by a public more geared to less news and more TV entertainment. Apparently, Reston took it for granted that his audience recognized the difficulties of the surviving printed press, for he went on:

Some of the old newspaper traditions, of course, we maintain. Our self-righteousness, I can assure you, is undiminished. Our capacity to criticize everybody and our imperviousness to criticism ourselves, are still, I believe, unmatched by novelists, poets or anybody else.

Although there was a great degree of truth in all this, Reston still thought enough of the news business to call it a profession and express his belief once again in its operations. But what he held up as an example for all of us in journalism was the opening issue of the eighteenth century *Spectator* of London, which sought "to correct the vices, ridicule the follies and dissipate the ignorance which too generally prevails at the commencement of the 18th century."

He might well have added Joseph Pulitzer's own statement of principle in his newspapers:

Always fight for progress and reform, never tolerate injustice or corruption, always fight demagogues of all parties, never belong to any party, always oppose privileged classes and public plunderers, never lack sympathy for the poor, always remain devoted to the public welfare, never be satisfied with merely printing the news, always be drastically independent, never be afraid to attack wrong either by predatory plutocracy or predatory poverty."[8]

Quite properly, it was the historian Arthur Meier Schlesinger Jr. who summed up the evening's discussion with the broadest view of a great and powerful nation and its problems. Although he began mildly enough with the observation that the modern revolution in historical studies has also affected biography and autobiography, he stressed the importance of the contemporary historical revival "for reasons other than the vanity of the historians." He explained:

> For history should be much more than simply a technical exercise or a literary flourish. I do not mean to suggest that history offers sure answers to the conundrums of public policy or infallible insights into the future. But I do believe that history is a moral necessity in a society marked by power. It is man's best antidote to his illusion of omnipotence and omniscience.
>
> It should forever remind us of the limitation of our passing perspective; it should strengthen us to resist the pressure to convert momentary interests into moral absolutes; it should lead us to a profound and humbling sense of our frailty as human beings—to a recognition of the fact, so often and so sadly demonstrated that the future will outwit all our certitudes and that the possibilities of history are far richer and more various than the human intellect is likely to conceive.
>
> A nation informed by a vivid understanding of the ironies of history is, I believe, best equipped to live with the temptations and tragedy of power; and, since we are condemned as a nation to this role of power, let a growing sense of history temper and civilize its use.

So the celebration of the fiftieth year of the Pulitzer Prizes ended on a sober and thoughtful note. The poet's view was by all means the most human, the journalist's the most practical, the novelist's the most visionary, the musician's the most reproachful. But it was, finally, the historian's quiet reflection on the future of a nation "condemned to power" that lingers on in memory.

For the missing president, Lyndon Johnson, history also enveloped him only a few weeks later on July 1, 1966, not through the terrible ordeal of fighting and dying he had ordained in a losing war, but in the creation of a blessing for the many millions of America's older citizens with the birth of Medicare. It was for this, rather than the tragedy of Vietnam, that he would be more likely to be remembered at the celebration of the Pulitzer centennial.

22 Losing a Prize

There was a sense of anticipation across the land at the outset of 1967 because a break, however brief, seemed likely in the Vietnam War.

It was one of those spasms of hope that were wrenched out of a people trapped in an apparently endless conflict, a feeling that was fated to disappear as the vision of a slight move toward peace flickered out as quickly as it had appeared.

As nearly as I could tell at the time, what had happened toward the beginning of the year was that the Chinese Communists, whose help was so important to our enemy, North Vietnam, had been sending conflicting signals from Beijing regarding the war. To some who tried to read the Chinese tea leaves, the regime founded by Mao Zedong had so many mounting problems at home that it seemed to be encouraging a move toward ending the conflict. [1]

Only Hanoi wasn't listening. And in Washington, the hard liners still vowed there was no way we were about to give in and let the Communists claim victory. So a campaign known in some quarters as "bombing the Reds to the conference table" was stepped up. More US troops kept pouring into South Vietnam, as did American funds and hopes; but it took an uprising of youth to show that the heart of the nation wasn't in this "dirty little war" [2] that showed no sign of ending. And yet, to a visionary and perhaps idealistic few, there still was dispassionate talk of doing something, anything to search for an opening in the war clouds that might let in just a tiny bit of sunlight. But to those who cried peace, there was inevitably a conservative sneer: "You're helping the Communists."

It was out of this Babel's Tower of confusion and hatred that a sandy-haired New York *Times* reporter in his fifty-ninth year, Harrison Salisbury, decided to try to make it to Hanoi over the 1966–1967 year-end holidays for a story behind enemy lines. And the story he had in mind was a quest for peace—something no diplomat in his right mind would have attempted. Nor would just any reporter have embarked on such a 100–1 shot in a losing war.

But then, Salisbury was no garden-variety reporter. He'd come up the hard way as an ambitious kid from Minneapolis. Then he'd transferred to United Press, in the era when the UP was a first-rate news service and a respected rival to the AP, where he fought his way to the top by asking for and getting the toughest assignments. Upon transferring to the New York *Times* in mid-career, he'd been posted in Moscow for six years and, at the end, with a series called *Russia Re-Viewed*, he'd won a Pulitzer Prize in 1955 when he was forty-eight.[3]

The question he had to ask himself now, before going hell-bent for Hanoi, was whether the New York *Times* would approve. He needn't have worried. The paper was solidly in his corner as always and wanted his dispatches from Hanoi. Nobody so much as lifted a cautioning little finger. As he made his plans and considered his route to Hanoi, he received encouragement from the executive editor, Turner Catledge, who was then a member of the Advisory Board on the Pulitzer Prizes; Clifton Daniel, the managing editor, and Seymour Topping, the foreign editor. All signs at the *Times* were set on "go," but it remained for Salisbury himself to find a way to get to Hanoi and back all in one piece with an account that might, by a miracle, bring about negotiations for peace.

In his own diary as he set out for the Far East from Paris in the week before Christmas 1966, he wrote:

> I think my trip is supposed to convey an image of confidence, of hardihood, in the face of U.S. bombing; of horror at what we have done; a positive image of North Vietnam but at the same time it is designed to bring peace or a truce or talks nearer, in part by assuring the U. S. and U. S. opinion that the present policy is not winning; in part by showing a reasonableness on the part of North Vietnam."[4]

That was the intent. But the accomplishment was, as any rival reporter would have said at the time, a great gamble if there ever was one. And for the *Times,* it was a tremendous risk in what the editors truly believed was the best interests of the United States and its people who seemed in part to support the revolt among its youth against an unwinnable war.

At the outset, I was not aware of either Salisbury's plans or the *Times*'s support based on his integrity and previous accomplishments as a reporter. Like everybody else in the news business, and that still was a major part of my work at Columbia, all I knew was that the Vietnam

War was being steadily enlarged by the Johnson administration, that South Vietnam still was an undependable ally, and that the North Vietnamese, with their Chinese and Soviet support, seemed to be capable of holding out indefinitely. General Westmoreland, our commander in Vietnam, had tried by every device known to American arms since 1963 to defeat the Vietcong guerrillas in South Vietnam and batter the North Vietnamese army and their military bases. But now both our enemies were stronger than ever.

President Johnson's heavy bombing campaign in the north, begun on February 9, 1965, also had failed to obtain results; but the supporters of the bombing spree in the Pentagon were still confident they could make the enemy quit. The only weapon we hadn't used was the atomic bomb; but that would have been the sheerest madness, for the Soviet Union and the Chinese Communists could drop a few of those on our cities, too, if it came to nuclear war.

And so, my life as a university professor at sixty was quite the opposite of Salisbury's, whom I had known for many years and considered one of the standouts in the news business. In my preparations for the new year of 1967, my greatest concern was very far, indeed, from matters of war and peace.[5] I offer these lines from my diary for New Year's Day:

> A quiet, grey New Year's Day with a breath of rain; last night, a celebration with music at Douglas Moore's in New Suffolk, L.I.; tonight, in Riverhead without music at Clyde and Amy Tooker's. It has been an uneventful holiday season at the old homestead in Aquebogue —just a little work on a new edition of my textbook, 'The Professional Journalist.'
>
> What a difference from 1966! Then I finished revising 'Between Two Worlds,' a book for the Council on Foreign Relations; wrote a new critical book on the news media for Holt and in November I left Dorothy in Paris while I went on to India to speak before the International Press Institute in New Delhi. On the way back I met Dorothy in Paris and we flew home together for the holidays. Regardless of what 1967 brings, it is going to be different!"[6]

Just how different, I could not possibly have imagined, for the highlights of the coming Pulitzer Prize season even then were taking shape without my knowledge. I learned only long afterward that while Dorothy and I were enjoying Paris that Christmas season, Salisbury was worrying the Hanoi consulate in Paris about obtaining his visa for North Vietnam. And while we were happy in our homecoming, he was en route to Hanoi via Phnom Penh and Vientiane.

By contrast with Salisbury's adventure in North Vietnam, the worst that happened to us in New York after he arrived home from his Far Eastern journey from December 23 to January 7 was described in these entries from my diary:

> Jan. 17—A 23-year-old black man with a police record as a thief entered the Columbia University Gift Shop in Dodge Hall about 1:40 p.m. today and pointed a sharp wooden spear a foot from Dorothy's face. Dorothy was in charge of the shop that day (and she was 62 years old at the time). Anyway, she yelled to another woman, Janine Kryzanowski, to call Campus Security and rushed out the door, brushing the spear aside, to get help.
>
> There was no guard in sight, but some of the college boys tried to catch the man who had made off with Janine's pocketbook but he get away. Patrolman Francis Fallon of the West 126th St. station picked the man up on suspicion an hour later at W. 139th St. after chasing him seven blocks on foot and then fighting him hand to hand. Dorothy and Janine identified the man at the West 126th St. Station in a lineup and Janine recovered her watch and pocketbook, which the police found on him.
>
> The spear was picked up, too. At night, we (Dorothy and I) went to 100 Centre St. by cab at the request of Police Capt. DiNisco of the University Security Police. Dorothy met Janine there and they swore out a complaint against the prisoner. A Night Court Judge then held him in $5,000 bail for the grand jury and trial on Feb. 1.

The accused was indicted, convicted, and sentenced to prison; but Dorothy never gave up her day at the Gift Shop, something she liked doing along with other university women. In fact, they elected her as their director and she loved it for as long as her health permitted her to work there with all proceeds going to university charitable causes.

The next day after the incident of the spear-carrying thief, I made this entry:

> Jan. 18—Harrison Salisbury came to my newswriting class and made an eloquent defense of his reporting from Hanoi for the New York Times but conceded that it could have been called treason had Congress formally declared war on North Vietnam. (The Tonkin Gulf Resolution passed by Congress was not a formal declaration of war although it was certainly a commitment to fight.) Our students gave Salisbury a very cold reception.[7]
>
> In the evening, we saw old friends, Col. Syd Fisher of the U. S. Air Force and his wife, Sug, and took them to dinner at the Overseas Press Club. It was good to see them again but sad because he is leaving the Air Force. We talked about the Salisbury articles and concluded that they weren't helpful.

Despite that, I couldn't help admiring Salisbury's resourcefulness and courage, his willingness to expose himself to danger in checking on the bombing runs of American military aircraft in and around the Hanoi area and elsewhere, and his efforts in interviews with enemy leaders to raise the prospect of talks headed toward negotiations and peace.

Eventually, when the *Times* submitted Salisbury's articles for a Pulitzer Prize, I took the time to reread them carefully before sending them along to the jury in international reporting, which would make the first judgment on his bid for a second award.

That, however, would then lead to another vote in the Pulitzer board with only eleven members participating, the twelfth being Catledge, the *Times*'s executive editor, who would be out of the room until a decision was reached. But finally, Salisbury would have to pass muster among the Columbia trustees, who still had the final decision over all awards.

Any way the position was considered, it seemed likely to me that each of the three decisions on Salisbury's experiences behind enemy lines would be reached by an exceedinly close vote. This, after all, was no business of our students, who had shown so much prejudice against Salisbury's presence as a guest speaker (and it was even worse when the South Vietnamese ambassador, Vu Van Thi, came for a separate lecture at my request).

But then, there was no student interest, either, on February 21, when Bernard Fall, who had predicted both French and American failures in Southeast Asia, was killed in action while a reporter in South Vietnam.

The student position, as I saw it, amounted to a complete lack of interest in the war regardless of how it was presented to them. Professor Philip Mosely, certainly one of the most respected scholars in the field, had given a series of lectures on the background of the war and the way it was being conducted both by the United States and the opposing Vietnamese armies. I had tried as best I could to summarize the position of the war's opponents. And both Salisbury and others had tried to do their share of reporting all the failed moves for peace.

What I also attempted to do was to make the point that, as the position now stood, the war was likely to be with us for years and some in the class without doubt would be involved in it sooner or later either as combatants, correspondents, or editors.

For my efforts, what I received once the student strikes began in earnest in succeeding years, was a friendly request to meet my foreign correspondence class outside the Journalism Building so its members wouldn't seem to be strikebreakers. The student mind sometimes was wondrous to behold in the depths of the Vietnam War, when Salisbury's reporting offered a lamentably brief gleam of hope for peace negotiations.

·   ·   ·

Regardless of the Pentagon's denunciations of Salisbury's venture behind enemy lines, his series in the New York *Times* established beyond doubt that the immensely costly American bombing campaign had failed to break North Vietnam's will to fight. This country of 18 million people, crowded into an area a bit smaller than Wisconsin, had survived the relentless American bombing attacks, and after almost two years still was able to resist President Johnson's air offensive. Even worse, as Salisbury reported, at least 1,600 American aircraft had been either shot down or accidentally wrecked—something the *Times*'s Hanson Baldwin verified in Washington while the Pentagon was claiming a loss of only 400 planes. At an estimated cost of $1.9 to $3 million a plane, that in itself was quite an expense; and it already was known that several hundred American airmen were Hanoi's prisoners.

As for the other part of the conflict—that in South Vietnam with about 15 million people in an area the size of Florida—the Vietcong guerrillas already occupied most of it and were collecting taxes from the peasants. I'd known that in my earlier visit to the war fronts when the VC were strong enough to bomb the lobby of my hotel in Saigon and get away without being caught. What Salisbury wrote about the VC already was widely known—and getting worse. The truth is that *our* Vietnamese weren't doing much fighting.

To be sure, Salisbury's reports demonstrated that the North still was taking a terrific pounding from the air; but the effect there and elsewhere, as he emphasized, only intensified the will of a tortured people to resist. It seemed to me no exaggeration when he compared Hanoi's reaction under mass air attack to that of London, Moscow, and even Berlin in World War II.

Naturally, many of Salisbury's readers couldn't help being puzzled over the ability of so primitive a state to survive the worst that a great world power could do to them from the air, despite increasing civilian casualties after every bombing run over the area. As the reporter explained the position, the answer to Vietnamese resistance to bombing was self-evident. In a country with an economy that was at best only about 10 to 15 percent industrialized, a determined people under veteran leadership could continue to operate with what amounted to a cottage industry, a huge annual import of Chinese rice, enough rails to repair bomb damage to rail transport quickly, and an efficient system of road repairs to keep supply trucks moving.

Antiaircraft batteries and aircraft in large numbers for both combat and transport still were being supplied from the Soviet Union either by sea through the port of Haiphong or by road through China. And the Chinese supplied all the rest for their ally.

Still, the Pentagon's argument against the Salisbury series was based on his on-the-spot reports that discredited American claims at the time of "pin-point accuracy" in the bombing of military targets in North Vietnam. It was a position that had been widely praised in some of the most respectable of American publications and applauded in news broadcasts. Yet, in his two-week stay during which he visited many parts of North Vietnam in addition to Hanoi, the reporter noted and even photographed some of the widespread damage to schools, hospitals, homes, a few churches, and even a cemetery.

The result demonstrated that, at the very least, American claims of bombing accuracy with regard to military targets were vastly exaggerated and that civilian casualties were substantial. Toward the end of his visit, Salisbury even huddled in a primitive air raid shelter with frightened native civilians. What his eyewitness account verified once again is that there is no such thing as a "humane" bombing attack, despite virtuous Pentagon claims.

Still, Salisbury's four-hour interview with Premier Pham Van Dong did raise hopes for eventual peace talks—but only through a misinterpretation of the Vietnamese leader's position.

These were the premier's four points which he called the basis for a Vietnam War settlement:

1. End of the bombing, withdrawal of US troops, and recognition of the peace, independence, sovereignty, unity, and territorial integrity of Vietnam.

2. The two zones of Vietnam should be free of interference by other nations.

3. South Vietnam's questions should be settled through the National Liberation Front's program and without foreign interference.

4. The peoples of North and South Vietnam would then settle the peaceful reunification of the nation.

Pham Van Dong stressed that these were not preconditions for negotiations but "conditions for a valid settlement." However, when the *Times* published Salisbury's account with what seemed like a slight change in Hanoi's position, the removal of the word *preconditions,* the reaction in the United States and the West was such that the Foreign Ministry cautioned against faulty interpretations abroad but did not blame the reporter for it.

Salisbury concluded the premier had made "a distinction without a real difference" in reviewing the North Vietnamese position. It also became clear, as the excitement over the so-called peace feeler died down, that Hanoi still insisted on a first move by Washington for peace. But when reminded of President Johnson's willingness to go anywhere for peace talks, the premier was plainly mistrustful and said masses of Chinese "volunteers" were ready to join his cause if needed.

The reporter concluded:

> There was a great deal in what the premier had told me, and not all of it was designed for public consumption. I only hoped that the talk would have the positive effect on negotiations which, I was certain, it was intended to have. But the answer to that, of course, lay in Washington.

The response came promptly. More bombing. And if indeed there really had been the slightest chance for peace in 1967, it was irretrievably lost.[8]

All the emphasis later that spring at the Pulitzer board meeting was on the New York *Times*'s proposal of Salisbury's file from Hanoi for a Pulitzer Prize in international reporting. The five-member jury in that category, all of them competent and experienced newspaper editors, had voted by 4–1 in favor of Salisbury's series for his second Pulitzer Prize. But almost immediately, in the required absence of the *Times*'s board member, the executive editor, Turner Catledge, a violent debate began over the pertinence and usefulness of Salisbury's exploit.

Chairman Pulitzer, led the fight for the Salisbury award, but opponents favored R. John Hughes of the *Christian Science Monitor* for his reporting of a failed Communist coup in Indonesia in 1965 and a purge that followed in 1966. No one could criticize Hughes's credentials as a first-rate professional, nor could anybody attack Salisbury's good faith in taking extreme risks in North Vietnam to try to move Hanoi toward peace negotiations.

So the debate continued for some time without a sign that any of those siding either with Hughes or Salisbury would change their minds. When the vote finally was taken, I counted 6 votes for Hughes, 5 for Salisbury. Upon Catledge's return to the room, I notified him of the outcome at the request of a disappointed Chairman Pulitzer.

The *Times*'s executive editor was livid. He angrily denounced Salisbury's opponents at the meeting, accusing them of "playing politics" instead of deciding the issue on its professional merits, but that didn't change the outcome. The 6–5 vote of the Pulitzer board for Hughes went to the Columbia trustees for final approval along with the rest of the board's recommendations for the 1967 prizes.[9]

The balance of the session was mild by comparison. In letters, drama, and music, the outcome seemed foreordained. Bernard Malamud's novel *The Fixer* won the fiction award and Edward Albee's play *A Delicate Balance* won for drama. The history prize went to William H. Goetzmann's *Explorations and Empire*, biography to Justin Kaplan's *Mr. Clemens and Mark Twain*, poetry to Anne Sexton's *Live or Die*, and nonfiction to David Brion Davis's study of slavery in Western culture. Leon Kirchner's *Quartet No. 3* received the music award.

Among the journalism prizes, domestic investigative reporters distinguished themselves in the same manner as Hughes and Salisbury had done abroad.

The Milwaukee *Journal* and the Louisville *Courier-Journal* each won a Pulitzer gold medal for public service for campaigns to conserve natural resources. Gene Miller's feat in helping free two people wrongfully convicted of murder brought a reporting prize to the Miami *Herald;* and two reporters for the *Wall Street Journal,* Monroe Karmin and Stanley Penn, each won a Pulitzer for proving that American criminals had extended their sway to the Bahamas as gamblers. Even in photography, there was outstanding achievement—a prize-winning photograph by the AP's Jack Thornell of the murderous shooting of James Meredith in Mississippi.

Although I did not receive a verbatim report of the trustees' final vote on the Pulitzer Prizes of 1967, I was told that virtually the same intense argument occurred at their session over the issues posed by Salisbury's reporting from North Vietnam. But here again, the voting still was close with Hughes winning by a narrow margin, so I learned, while all the rest of the Pulitzer board's choices were routinely adopted.

This was a contest that I would remember with deep regret, not so much because Hughes of the *Christian Science Monitor* won the prize in international reporting rather than Salisbury. That was not the point. Hughes was always a first-rate reporter, and his paper was principled and well-edited; so no one with knowledge of the news business could reasonably object to their victory. But Salisbury and the New York *Times* should also have been listened to for the implicit warning to the American people that was conveyed in his dispatches from North Vietnam.

So, yes, congratulations were due to Hughes and the *Monitor* for the correspondent's work. But Salisbury and the *Times* still merited the gratitude as well as the respect of the nation for their 1967 effort in North Vietnam to seek what amounted to a negotiated peace that might have averted a stunning defeat for American arms within less than a year.[10]

PART FOUR

Surviving the War

23   The Oldest Rebel

John Shively Knight hated war with the passion of an old soldier. Of all the rebels against the ever-enlarging conflict in Vietnam, he was probably the oldest at seventy-two in 1967.

As the owner of a powerful chain of American newspapers with a twelve-year record of previous service with the Advisory Board on the Pulitzer Prizes, he also was among the most influential opponents of the war. Nor could he be accused of partisanship. He was equally vehement in his condemnation of President Johnson's policies and the delay of the president's Republican opposition in challenging him.

At a danger point in the rioting that swept the nation's college campuses in 1967, Knight wrote in his Editor's Notebook in the Akron (Ohio) *Beacon-Journal* and other newspapers:

> It is not dissent at home that is prolonging the war.
>
> Rather, it is the determination of the man in the White House—entrapped by pride and circumstances—to bring about a victory or at least an accommodation with honor prior to the 1968 [presidential] elections.
>
> As history is being written, the possibilities of a wider struggle cannot be discounted.
>
> Nor will our involvement in Vietnam be depicted as one of the glorious eras of American statesmanship. [1]

Unlike most of the youthful antiwar rioters of the 1960s, Knight had fought for his country. In World War I, he had served in the front lines in France as an infantry volunteer, even though his father, Charles L. Knight, had opposed that conflict. During World War II, John S. Knight's oldest son had been killed in action and his youngest was in a military academy when the war ended.

There can be no doubt, therefore, that Knight knew war, hated it, and was bound to do whatever he could to try to keep the United States from being involved in still another conflict.[2] As early as 1954, when he saw that the French were about to lose their overseas empire in Indochina, he wrote in the Akron *Beacon-Journal*:

> It is almost certain that at some stage France will pull out of Indochina. Are we prepared to cope with such a contingency? The plain answer seems to be no.
>
> Our government lacks a coherent policy. It does not know the answer to a problem as large as Indochina.[3]

Now Knight was no expert on Indochina any more than was Dwight David Eisenhower, the president at the time. And Ike had more important concerns with the end of the Korean War although a US Military Assistance Advisory Group (MAAG) had been helping the French in Vietnam since July 1950, with a $23.5 million fund for the 1951–1952 fiscal year.[4]

However, not everybody in Washington was as detached about the French problem in Indochina as Ike had been at first. As a young congressman from Massachusetts in 1951, John F. Kennedy paused briefly in Saigon while on a round-the-world trip with his brother Bobby and his sister Pat. An AP correspondent, Seymour Topping, (later an executive editor of the New York *Times*) briefed the Kennedy party on all the mistakes the French then were making in Indochina under the general known as *le roi Jean,* General Jean de Lattre de Tassigny. Even that early, Kennedy saw enough of France's hopeless position to have taken warning.[5]

But then, in July, 1953, France sent a new leader, General Henri Navarre, to take over from *le roi Jean,* upon which no less a figure than Secretary of State John Foster Dulles proclaimed, "Navarre will break the organized body of Communist aggression"[6] in Indochina by 1955. But around Christmas time in 1953, Joseph Alsop reported in the New York *Herald Tribune* after an interview with French Foreign Minister Georges Bidault that France might well lose Indochina (including Vietnam) unless the United States joined in the war there.

That kicked up a real fuss. Bidault denied saying so, blamed the confusion on Alsop's less than perfect French, and in effect set the stage in the Far East for the French collapse at Dien Bien Phu not long afterward. The denial carried no weight in Washington, however. For the CIA chief, Allen Dulles, let it be known on January 14, 1954, that the French garrison at the Dien Bien Phu fortress on the Vietnam-Laos border was down to a six-day supply of food.[7]

Even so, General Navarre at the time was proposing to give battle to the Vietminh, as the Vietnamese opposition then was known, Ho Chi

Minh being their commander. To a French diplomat in Washington, President Eisenhower cautioned, "You *cannot* do this!" Still, Navarre's supporters in Washington argued combat would bring Ho Chi Minh's forces "into the open" instead of maintaining a guerrilla action.

Eisenhower concluded privately, a position that became known later publicly, "The French know military history. They are smart enough to know the outcome of becoming firmly entrenched and then besieged in an exposed position with poor means of supply and reinforcement."[8]

By this time, the American investment in the French position in Indochina had reached more than 1 billion dollars, and the leading political figures in Washington, including John Kennedy, now a senator, and another senator, Lyndon B. Johnson, were warning that America must stay out of this mess.[9] Johnson in particular was quoted as saying that no American soldier should be a part of a "blood-letting spree to perpetuate colonialism and white man's exploitation in Asia."

To conclude the tragedy, Dien Bien Phu fell on May 7, 1954, when 40,000 Vietminh ended their siege of the fortress's 10,000 defenders in triumph.[10] In the St. Louis *Post-Dispatch,* there was a cartoon by D. R. Fitzpatrick showing a morass with a gun-bearing Uncle Sam confronting it under the caption, "French mistakes in Indochina" and the overall heading, "How Would Another Mistake Help?" It won the Pulitzer Prize for cartoons for 1954.[11]

And yet, after President Kennedy's assassination, President Johnson had reinforced the contingent of 15,000 American "advisers" in Vietnam with 400,000 American troops—a fateful commitment because by 1967 Ho Chi Minh and *his* advisers in Hanoi already were planning another Dien Bien Phu knockout blow, this time against the United States.

But President Johnson was either too blind or too stubborn, in view of the oncoming 1968 election, to pull back from the brink of another disaster. He even gave in to General Westmoreland's continuing clamor for still more soldiers. It was like an echo of the French military formula for defeat, as the few American combat correspondents then in Saigon accurately reported.[12]

John Mecklin, the American embassy's public affairs officer in Saigon, wrote at the time:

> In its dealings with newsmen, the U.S. Mission . . . was often wrong about the facts, in a situation of the utmost importance to the U.S. national interest in support of a controversial policy that was costing the lives of U.S. servicemen. Even if conditions had otherwise been normal, this was incompatible with the inquisitive, skeptical nature of American journalism, and trouble would have been inevitable. Unhappily, conditions were not otherwise normal.[13]

On April 4, 1954, only a little more than a month before the French collapse at Dien Bien Phu, John S. Knight had written in his Editor's Notebook for all his newspapers:

> Haven't we learned from Korea that united action in Asia would be little more than a phrase; that we could expect only token assistance from other nations?
> Can't we recognize the dangers of gradual involvement? That they inevitably lead to war? Members of Congress . . . must be made to see the folly of engaging our land forces in the jungles of Indochina. [14]

But that warning, like Eisenhower's after Korea against again putting American ground forces in Asia, was completely forgotten in President Johnson's lamentable decision to show himself a bold anti-Communist who wasn't afraid of Ho Chi Minh's formidable Vietcong guerrillas, even though they already had overrun most of South Vietnam with the help of their "volunteer" cadres from the North Vietnamese armed forces.

This was the position on February 5, 1967, when Editor Knight resumed his campaign against a continued and even more dangerous American enlargement of the Vietnam War by quoting still another warning, this one from Edwin O. Reischauer, former American ambassador to Japan. Like most diplomats familiar with the problems in Indochina, Reischauer had repeated the seemingly endless warnings to the Johnson administration against making "new commitments" [15] in the Vietnam War. To these, Knight added his own comment, "Is anybody listening?"

Only the youths of military age on the nation's college campuses would have taken the time to acknowledge all the warnings against a wider war if they'd stopped their antiwar demonstrations long enough to read what some of their elders were saying. Always the realist, Knight wrote editorially that early February day:

> At that time, some 13 years ago [when Dien Bien Phu fell] these warnings went unheeded. They were dismissed by the Secretary of Defense, Charles E. Wilson, who said he saw no possibility that American troops would be involved and that "no such plan is under study."
> "Mr. Wilson, as has been the case with our present Secretary of Defense, proved to be a poor prophet."

Just then, dissatisfied with in excess of 400,000 American soldiers, Westmoreland was demanding at least 500,000 and maybe more as circumstances warranted. Yet, as his deteriorating position demonstrated, he didn't know how to make effective use of either his American forces or the relatively few but capable combat-ready South Vietnamese out of a much larger army that had been handicapped for years by too many corrupt or incompetent commanders (sometimes both).

The result was a frightening casualty figure in a relatively small encounter with the enemy on March 12, 1967. After the fighting ended, the US command in Saigon announced 232 had been killed in action, 1,381 wounded, and four were missing.[16] Now Knight roared impatiently in his Editor's Notebook through all his newspapers:

> This "dirty little war" is now assuming the proportions of a major conflict. General Westmoreland reminds us that American forces in Vietnam total 417,400 and will continue to increase. The end of the war and its outcome defy prediction.
>
> To those of us who have long opposed U.S. intervention in Vietnam, there is no solace to be found in our past warnings that "little wars" have a way of erupting into big ones.
>
> The blood, the tears, the sacrifices of our gallant men in the field leave us sick at heart. We are saddened by this cruel slaughter, depressed over our inability to make the slightest contribution to our young men who are but the instruments of what we believe to be irrational foreign policy."[17]

The oldest rebel was reaching the end of his patience. A note of despair, strange to so strong and competent a military critic, was creeping into his commentary. Like so many millions of others, young and old, both in and out of uniform, this conflict in Vietnam was assuming monstrous form for Knight and the worst shock was yet to be felt.

In an extensive commentary on August 6, 1967, Knight demonstrated how depressed he was about the likely outcome of this longest of all wars in American history, when he wrote to a reader who asked if he knew of a solution to "this tragic conflict":

> In reply, I must be brutally frank in saying there can be no "good solution." If there were, I feel sure that President Johnson would have thought of it long ago.
>
> The war as presently conducted could drag on for years. We are not winning despite President Johnson's statement on July 13 of this year that he was "generally pleased with the progress that we have made militarily."
>
> On the other hand if we go all out to win by bombing Hanoi and

Haiphong into rubble—as many people have suggested—the risk of bringing Red China or Russia into the war is indeed very real.

The civilized world could not survive a third world war fought with nuclear weapons.

By that time, the Senate Republican Policy Committee had issued a study that Knight credited with noting the mistakes of the Kennedy and Johnson administrations in Vietnam. But he added, while acknowledging the truth of the criticisms,

> Where were the dissenting Republicans several years ago when they could have questioned the wisdom of policies they now deplore?
>
> Strangely silent, I submit. Did they fear being tarred as unpatriotic? Or were they coolly calculating that it was politically expedient to support the war while being critical of President Johnson's "mismanagement"?
>
> Whatever the reasons for past GOP strategy, the Republican leadership stands indicted for failing to challenge the successive steps which have brought us to our present dilemma.
>
> Only a handful of courageous Democrats rose in the Senate to pose the searching questions which might better have been advanced by a responsible minority party. [18]

If Knight was deeply disturbed over the depths to which Johnson's regime had descended in his Vietnam strategy that deceived only his own people, there was also another inside the president's cabinet who was just as disillusioned in the summer of 1967. He was Secretary of Defense Robert S. McNamara. For almost a year, this architect of the American military buildup in Vietnam had been worried about lack of American progress in the conflict. And on October 14, 1966, he had gone so far as to warn the president in a private memorandum:

> I see no reasonable way to bring the war to an end soon. Enemy morale has not been broken—he apparently has adjusted to our stopping his drive for military victory and has adopted a strategy of attriting our national will. He knows that we have not been, and he believes we probably will not be able to translate our military successes into the "end products"—broken enemy morale and political achievements by the GVN. [19]

What McNamara recommended then, without any real hope of achieving his aim against a still tough and valiant foe, was a negotiated settlement to end the war. For that reason, he refused to honor General Westmoreland's almost frantic demands for more and more American troops—a recommended total of 670,000 that included an immediate added force of 200,000.

There followed an intense debate within the White House about the weakened view the secretary of defense had taken of the Vietnam War, something neither an alarmed public nor a discouraged John Knight suspected at the time. The result, following a break between McNamara and the Joint Chiefs of Staff, was that the president stuck with the Joint Chiefs and ordered an increase of Westmoreland's troop strength in Vietnam to 550,000 during 1968.[20] Probably out of concern for his own future even more than the interests of history, McNamara then ordered the preparation by the Defense Department of the Pentagon Papers' secret chronicle of the war on June 17, 1967.

It was originally labeled "Top Secret"—something the American public supposedly should never have known about—and from that time in 1967 onward the lamentable record of the Johnson administration in Vietnam began mounting in the Pentagon's files, its authors sworn to secrecy.

A little more than six weeks later, John Knight ended his long August 6 editorial as follows:

> We cannot conquer the North Vietnamese or the Vietcong. Even if North Vietnam is totally bombed and a victory of sorts is achieved, the U.S. would have to garrison the country for a long period of years.
>
> So there is no solution in a permanent sense. Unless, of course, a new Vietnam government in Saigon to be elected should decide the Americans should go home.
>
> This is not beyond the realm of possibility. In the long run the Asians will shape their own destiny and the white man's military presence will no longer be tolerated.

Having been a member of the Pulitzer board from 1944 to 1956, it was natural enough for both Knight's associates and those who had faith in his judgment to make certain he was nominated for a Pulitzer Prize in the following year. But with it to the very end went his gloomiest fears for the nation, together with the Pulitzer Prize he received at age seventy-three:

"The nation is over-committed, our resources strained, the treasury bare, inflation out of hand, and each of us must be prepared for am uncertain future of war, higher taxes and personal sacrifices for an indeterminate period."[21]

To that gloomy outlook, I had little I could add for the young people in my charge at Columbia, and especially the young men of military age, for nothing about the Vietnam War that I brought to their attention from American government sources, the United Nations, or the literature of the day gave them any promise of a secure future. In my diary for my sixty-first birthday, February 17, 1967, I find this typical notation, "My birthday—and I spent much of it with my class of eight students at the U.S. Mission to the UN where all they heard was aimless discussion of the Vietnam War from our press officers."

All too soon, the war would break wide open—and not in our favor.

24 Turnabout

When mobs of angry students take to instructing the professors and administrative officials at a great American university, the consequences for higher education are likely to be serious.

So it turned out in the illusory bright spring of 1969 after the success of the enemy's Tet offensive in Vietnam the previous year had blasted all hope of victory at the Pentagon. Antiwar student rioting erupted across the land at this turnabout, with thousands of young people taking to the streets chanting:

"Hey, hey, LBJ, / How many kids have you killed today?" [1]

It meant the end for President Johnson, who was succeeded in 1969 by President Nixon—third in the line of American chief executives who had ignored General Eisenhower's warning against committing American forces to a war on the Asian mainland. At Columbia, the campus uproar was massive, as it had been at universities elsewhere.

When five more Pulitzer Prizes were granted for heroic American performances in Vietnam to the four that already had been voted from 1964 on—a total of nineteen awards would be granted over all—the resentment in the arena of public opinion seemed to mount rather than diminish. As the more militant students put it, "We want out of Vietnam, no prizes, no glory."

Among faculty people at Columbia, we had hoped that campus quiet would be restored with the appointment of President Andrew W. Cordier, the dean of the School of International Affairs, as President Kirk's replacement, but Cordier's UN experience hadn't prepared him for such unruly conduct. At the world organization's headquarters in Rockefeller Center, during the six years I'd served there on and off as a correspondent, he had been a trusted friend and a first-rate news source.

Still, I wrote in my diary in 1969 for April 23:

189

Andy Cordier and Columbia have been lucky so far this year. Harvard has gone up in student rioting. Students have taken guns into university buildings at Cornell and there are disorders at most other universities. The kids have no program. They're just anxious to kick older people around.

That season, not by any means to appease the rioters, Pulitzer juries, the Pulitzer board, and the university trustees had voted three Vietnam War prizes respectively to William Tuohy, a combat correspondent for the Los Angeles *Times;* John Fetterman of the Louisville *Times and Courier-Journal,* also for reporting; and a photographer, Edward T. Adams of the Associated Press.

These had followed the two that were voted in 1968, the year that the enemy had wrecked General Westmoreland's defenses in South Vietnam. [2]

But it was only a week after the 1969 awards were announced that the Students for a Democratic Society suddenly struck at President Cordier, the Columbia trustees, and all the rest of us in the faculty. These entries tell the story as I set it to paper that year:

April 30—SDS students took over Math and Fayerweather Halls on the Columbia campus today and Andy Cordier's luck ran out. He called two meetings of deans, directors and advisers at Low Library and we gave him a unanimous vote to go ahead with a move for court injunctions to get the kids out of our buildings.

One lawyer got so excited that he wanted to lead a faculty charge on the barricades to prove we were red-blooded men but nothing came of it. The same old weasel university crowd let a bunch of kids tie us up in the same old way. Anyway, I distributed my Pulitzer press releases for the 1969 awards to make sure they'd get out Monday if the trustees and Andy remember to act.

That, however, was just a prelude to what turned out to be temporary relief when Andy obtained a court order and served it on the kids at Fayerweather, Math and—believe it or not—our Journalism Building, where there seemed to be a mischievous notion that the protesters would halt the announcement of the Pulitzer Prizes. This was my record:

May 1—Our radical students, about 150 of them, celebrated May Day by evacuating the two buildings they had seized and laid off an attempt to close down Journalism after the university had them cited for contempt of court for defying an injunction. They seemed a sorry lot, later, keeping hankies over their faces as they left the buildings they had occupied. We gave Andy two big rounds of applause at our meeting with him this afternoon. The UN was never quite like this.

In a spirit that often seemed like a sardonic comment on togetherness in academe, all of us at Columbia managed somehow to finish the school year at an anxious commencement that spring. There was more to come, for the tragedy at My Lai—the worst of that losing war—had occurred on March 20, 1968, but it would be twenty months before a free-lance journalist would reveal the massacre to the nation. The anitwar movement meanwhile continued in the fall of 1969 with the beginning of what was called a series of "War Moratorium Days" at universities across the land. This was my report of one that happened at Columbia:

Oct. 15—War Moratorium Day and Columbia closed shop because the students demanded it. I was summoned to appear in the World Room of the Journalism building and account for the press's coverage of the war in Vietnam. I suppose I'd been expected to accuse my colleagues, including some distinguished alumni, of lying to cover up the government's mistakes when the facts indicated quite the opposite was true.

Anyway, Professor Phil Davison and I were lucky that a recent alumnus, Kim Willenson of the Class of 1962, one of the younger correspondents in Vietnam, showed up with a colorful account of the real situation in Saigon—and the Pulitzer Prizes that were being won by reporters who successfully opposed the Pentagon's version of events in the field. [3]

Anyway, it was a lively and realistic session and none of us compromised our beliefs. The young people who had come to hear tales of villainy at the front seemed to be disappointed that we thought the correspondents and photographers under fire in Vietnam had given a good account of themselves.

Nevertheless, despite the quietness and good manners of our own students that were very largely duplicated in similar meetings at universities across the country, there was no doubt in my mind that the younger generation still was committed to anti-war protests.

At year's end, just before Christmas, Andy Cordier was inducted as Columbia's fifteenth president, but his choice for Journalism dean, Elie Abel, a 1942 graduate of the school, suffered a rough start with a critical account of his appointment by two of our faculty members in the *Spectator*, the Columbia College newspaper. It was only to be expected from a faculty as divided as our own.

Knowing how difficult the job would be, both Dick Baker and I had asked the new president not to consider us. At age sixty-three, I had more than enough to do as a teacher and prize administrator in any event.

. . .

The worst of our military position in Vietnam, as I recorded in my diary at the time, was that General Westmoreland knew well in advance of the enemy's plans for a Tet offensive and completely miscalculated its strength and its objectives. He left intact a 36-hour holiday and cease-fire so the South Vietnamese could celebrate their religious holiday. On the evening of January 29, 1968, he helped celebrate Tet with an embassy lawn party for our new ambassador, Ellsworth Bunker. However, it turned out not to be a lively party. There was too much anxiety at the embassy for that. The realists in the American military command and the highly placed civilians who worked with them and the Vietnamese realized this might be the climactic effort of Ho Chi Minh to shatter the enemy with one massive blow, the American Dien Bien Phu.

But General Westmoreland kept dreaming. He had his own pet scheme, a snare he had set for the foe at a point called Khe Sanh, which he hoped to induce Ho Chi Minh to attack. Then, the plan was to overwhelm the enemy with an enormous but concealed American force. Moreover, Westmoreland centered his main strength of ground forces and bombers within easy reach of Bien Hoa to meet, deflect, and rout the enemy at what he suspected would be the main point of their attack.

Alas, the American commander turned out to be mistaken on every one of his main assumptions. From the night of January 20 onward, there had been distractions in the early hours before dawn at various points throughout South Vietnam. All manner of rumors were planted by the enemy affecting various strong points heavily guarded by the American forces. Some nights, there was relative calm in the field, appar-ently an enemy ruse to indicate a change of plan, a retreat. On others, there were vigorous thrusts and threats at some of General Westmore-land's targets—more of the foe's byplay.

The real offensive began before dawn on January 30 with severe assaults by major Vietcong forces at a half-dozen or more strong points held by combined American/South Vietnamese forces. Although some were initially repulsed by the defenders, the offensives at these widely separated objectives continued.

At 3:00 A.M. on the next night, January 31, the entire weight of Ho Chi Minh's offensive smashed into the unlikeliest target of all, Saigon itself, and more than half the forty-four provincial capitals as well. Now there was no doubt whatever that Ho Chi Minh was taking a desperate gamble against a formidable enemy by risking the entire strength of his veteran Vietcong cadres and some of his best North Vietnamese troops on a single, brilliantly planned offensive. [4]

The first to become aware of the enormity of the foe's objectives was

Ambassador Bunker, who was hustled out of bed at 3:00 A.M. by his Marine guards and hurried to a safer spot in an armored vehicle. The Marines tarried in the embassy long enough to burn some papers, then fled only minutes before the place was seized by the enemy in triumph.

Nobody could have been more surprised, and more sobered by his shocking experience, than the ambassador, who saw at first hand how General Westmoreland had been tricked. But American TV audiences weren't far behind in noting for themselves how poorly their huge Vietnam force had been outmaneuvered by a capable and determined enemy. Right in the center of Saigon, in brilliant TV color, the enemy was shown storming some of the city's strong points with a force estimated at 15,000 well-trained guerrilla fighters.

Such scenes at home as these provided final proof, if proof were needed, that this poisonous war was irretrievably lost as far as the public was concerned. In the field in South Vietnam, except for a few feints at Bien Hoa, General Westmoreland was left holding an empty bag. As for his own well-prepared trap at Khe Sanh, this was one of the few places the enemy didn't touch in its continuing offensive. But in Saigon, the foe hoisted its flag over City Hall as a sign of victory that January 31, and it was three weeks before the American defenders could rally sufficiently to put the American flag back in its rightful place. At a tactical American operations center, Long Binh, the Vietcong blew up an ammunition dump with a tremendous concussion and even worse damage. It took a fleet of tanks, helicopter gunships, and part of an American divisional force to save Tan Son Nhut Air Base outside Saigon.

All told, the Tet assault by a well-prepared enemy had killed 20,000 and wounded at least 50,000 more, some of them so seriously that they eventually died. It was difficult to estimate the national toll, but figures issued later by the South Vietnamese government put the casualties at 14,300 civilians killed, 24,000 wounded; 72,000 houses destroyed; 627,000 people rendered homeless. For Saigon alone the official estimates were 6,000 civilians killed, twice that many seriously wounded, and nearly 20,000 homes destroyed.

It was two to three weeks before the American forces were able to rally sufficiently to break the enemy's hold on both Saigon and key points elsewhere. From eyewitness accounts, the Vietcong invaders in Saigon and elsewhere fought to the last man in a number of spots rather than surrender.

Now, even to the bitter-enders in the White House, there could be no doubt that not even the ability of the American forces in Vietnam to rally would avert defeat in this ill-starred conflict. President Johnson finally had to give up. He ordered General Westmoreland home on March 22 and, to save face, gave him a promotion to Chief of Staff of the Army but put his second in command, General Creighton Abrams, in charge in Vietnam. At the same time, Secretary McNamara vanished from the Defense Department and turned up as president of the World Bank after Clark Clifford took over the Defense Department.

On March 31, in a televised address to the nation, President Johnson announced he was limiting the air war in the north, proposed to suspend it altogether on October 31, and officially bowed out as a candidate for reelection in the 1968 presidential race.[5] Not long afterward Secretary Rusk belatedly accepted a North Vietnamese proposal, broadcast just before the Tet attack, to begin negotiations to end the war once the American bombing ceased. As a result, on May 10, delegates from the United States, North and South Vietnam, and the Vietcong met in Paris to arrange for an end to the fighting and an agreed program for peace.

At about the same time, the Pulitzer board honored John S. Knight with a prize for editorial writing in 1968 for his long and resolute campaign against the Vietnam War. In a salute to a more rebellious younger generation than his own, he had written:

> If the young people of today are different from those of us who accepted the gauntlet without question, it is because they dare investigate the causes of war and examine its immorality. . . . So let our patriots on the home front—who have been called upon for no visible sacrifice—understand the feelings and emotions of our youth when they are less than enthusiastic over our professed goals. For theirs is a new generation which rightly challenges what their elders have done in the past.[6]

At seventy-four years of age when he won his prize, Knight had no illusions that a truce in the American bombing campaign in the north and the opening of peace talks in Paris would bring about a quick halt in the fighting. On the contrary, the war continued as preparations for the 1968 presidential campaign intensified at home and the Republican nominee, Richard Nixon, announced he did not intend to be the first president of the United States to lose a war. Nor was his Democratic opponent, Vice-President Hubert Humphrey, raising the white flag.

Black rioters already had disrupted Nixon's drive for the presidency before it even began. They closed down temporarily the proceedings of the Republican National Convention in Miami and managed thereby to delay the nominating process. At the Democratic National Convention in Chicago, the position was worse as rioters and police fought in Grant and Lincoln Parks and protestors decorated General Grant's statue with a Vietcong flag. The police responded with shots of tear gas that drifted into the auditorium where the Democrats were meeting.

From then on, both Nixon and Humphrey had to contend with antiwar riots that often disrupted their respective campaigns. Neither could gain much of an advantage under such circumstances, especially when it became known nationally that the conflict in Vietnam had become America's longest war that summer. What Nixon proposed eventually was the "Vietnamising" of the war—meaning that fewer American troops would be engaged in the conflict—but that didn't give him as much of an advantage as he had hoped.

At a Republican rally at the University of Tennessee in Knoxville, a disruptive group of antiwar demonstrators created such a fuss that the Dr. Billy Graham, who was in the Nixon party, had to come forward to pacify the angry crowd. But nobody quite like Dr. Graham turned up on the Democratic side, so Humphrey often had to take his lumps without any merciful intervention. [7]

On election day, Nixon received only 576,000 more votes than Humphrey—fewer than 1 percent out of a total of almost 65 million cast. But in the Electoral College, the difference was substantial—301 to 191—because of the third party candidacy of Governor George C. Wallace of Alabama, who drew almost 10 million votes and a total of 46 in the Electoral College, mainly from the Democratic total. [8]

If the American public took President Nixon's "Vietnamization" program seriously, millions of his partisans were bound to be disappointed. For in his first year in office, the total American forces in Vietnam reached a high of 543,000, more than had been engaged in the Korean War. So Nixon, too, had to take his lumps as president when 250,000 antiwar demonstrators staged a mammoth peace march in Washington before he and his administration had effectively taken over the government.

To be sure, with the exception of a small proportion of effectives, the Vietcong had been sacrificed as a fighting force during the Tet offensive and the American bombing of the north had been halted in line with Johnson's proposals before he left office. In 1969, too, Ho Chi Minh had died—the architect of the enemy strategy that had forced the French from Vietnam and now had enveloped the Americans. But under Nixon, the conflict entered still another phase in its long and difficult history.

Like the Prophet Jeremiah, "They cried peace, peace, but there was no peace."

25   The War at Home

There is a note in my diary early in the discouraging winter of 1969 that captures the mood of the times:

> Ralph McGill died last night in Atlanta. A great man and my wonderful friend. I'll never forget how he would roar at me over the phone when I wanted to quit Columbia and the Pulitzers, "Hang on, boy! Hang on!" He did for as long as he lived and I have so far. Still, it's tough to lose Ralph McGill.

The student uproar over the Vietnam War already had cost Columbia dearly. One of the best presidents in the university's history of more than two centuries, Grayson Kirk, had resigned, and his temporary replacement, Dean Andrew Cordier of the School of International Affairs, soon had become a storm center. Dean Edward Barrett of our Graduate School of Journalism also had quit in protest over the standpat policies of the university's trustees and we were in trouble trying to find a successor.

As I wrote in my diary at the time of both resignations: "Saw Grayson Kirk and he seemed in good spirits but lonely. . . . We are as far as ever from a new Columbia president on a permanent basis and no one is in sight for dean of our school."[1]

Despite the inauguration of President Nixon on January 20, 1968, and his seemingly sincere plea for peace abroad and an end to division at home, it was clear enough to any concerned citizen that the youthful revolutionaries among us were determined in this year of 1969 to put an end to the fighting in Vietnam before any more of them were drafted into uniform. Call it wrong-headed, shameful, even unpatriotic if you will, as many among us did at the time, but this was the position with which all of us in the nation's universities had to contend that winter.

When I saw former President Kirk again toward spring, he summed

196

up our unhappy situation with merciless logic as the following entry demonstrates:

> March 24—When I saw Grayson Kirk today, he said Andy Cordier was only kidding himself if he thought he could keep order on the campus this spring against SDS [Students for a Democratic Society]. Kirk thought I should move the Pulitzer board meeting off campus. But when I phoned Scotty Reston and Spike Canham, two board members, both said no—it would look like the Pulitzer Prize Board was running away. So—we will stay but I have the Columbia University Club downtown as a fallback if all hell breaks loose again. [2]

As might have been expected, I felt immensely put upon in trying to conduct the Pulitzer Prize operation as well as my classes in so difficult and trying a position with the campus often in chaos and a red flag flying from the Mathematics building. At this distance from events (and this is being written toward century's end), both my feelings and my reasoning may seem intemperate but I find this entry in my diary for the day after I worried about the disruption of the prize announcement:

> March 25—We saw "1776" tonight—a tremendous show with a walloping finale, the signing of the Declaration of Independence. After rubbing shoulders with the scruffy gang who riot over Vietnam, it was sheer relief to be able to cheer for John Adams, Ben Franklin and Thomas Jefferson and the rest. Brooks Atkinson [the New York *Times* critic] asked me outside how I liked the show and I said, "Great!" And he said, "I thought so, too." . . . I have rarely felt so moved in the theater.

Still, regardless of my feelings, the drama jury didn't see it my way that strange year of 1969. Less than two weeks later, the jury's verdict came in and I recorded it in honest disappointment:

> Walter Kerr [the New York *Herald Tribune*'s critic and drama jury chairman] phoned this morning with the jury's verdict. It is for "The Great White Hope" by Howard Sackler. Kerr said it was a compromise —that he and Richard Watts wanted "1776" but Brendan Gill held out. At first, Watts didn't want "Hope" but finally gave in. The alternative might have been the homosexual play, "The Boys in the Band." I sent the news to the Pulitzer board and didn't like it. I'd wanted "1776." [3]

Such philosophical difficulties as these, to a greater or lesser degree, also were typical of this era of often violent change.

.   .   .

Under the wary leadership of President Nixon, who feared a Communist-imposed peace more than more war in Southeast Asia, what he opted for was an initial moderate reduction in American forces in Vietnam and gradual resumption of the burden of the conflict by the South Vietbamese.[4] However, this new Nixon doctrine brought no comfort, much less relief, to those of us in the embattled universities. We still had to fend off agitated groups of radical students who sometimes occupied our buildings; conducted student strikes to halt those who sought to attend classes; and marched, carried banners of protest, and screamed epithets at all who differed with them night and day.

At Columbia, the campus disorders were fomented mainly by Columbia College undergraduates, but I noted very few in our professional schools—law, business, medicine, and our own journalism people among them—who participated in the rioting. This was not merely a matter of being of draft age for service in Vietnam or having family and other deferments to delay the inevitable. The older graduate students who were studying for doctorates or masters' degrees either had jobs to go back to or other career opportunities that influenced their conduct.

In the J-school, at first, we seldom had to worry about being shut down by strikers or facing sudden interruptions in classes. Sometimes, during the most critical years, I did have to be concerned about threats to halt the Pulitzer Prize announcements or break up meetings of the Pulitzer juries and the Pulitzer board. But with a certain amount of planning, caution, and good luck, I didn't have too much to worry about for the time being. At most during the worst of the student demonstrations when some of our people were reluctant to come to class, I did oblige them by doing my class work either at the UN, City Hall, the U.S. Mission to the UN, or out of doors on the campus.[5]

During the winter and early spring, most of the other colleges and universities in the New York area suffered worse than Columbia did. Elsewhere there were reports that students had been using guns and manhandling faculty. Just about the only place in higher education where normal conditions seemed to prevail was in Cambridge, Mass., where our faculty associates predicted loftily, "It will never happen at Harvard." Or so it seemed during the intense cold of winter. The Nixon doctrine for Vietnam was stalled.

Toward spring, former President Eisenhower fell ill and died within a short time, which reminded those of us among his generation of a quite different time in America. As I noted in my diary:

March 28—Eisenhower died today at 79 in Walter Reed Hospital and both of us, Dorothy and I, felt sad. I'm not sure why. He was closer to us physically as president of Columbia than FDR or Truman had been but Ike never meant as much to us even though I often worked for his administration in the Pentagon and traveled to Europe and Asia for his Air Force. Maybe it was that his presidency was tranquil and he was a symbol of a more secure and a happier time between the Korean and Vietnam Wars.

But three days later, there was a shock during the Eisenhower funeral when it had to be closely guarded to prevent demonstrators among others from interrupting a public tribute to a victorious American general and a well-intentioned peacetime president. This is how I recorded the event:

> March 31—We saw Ike's funeral on TV and it was very impressive. Still, I thought it odd that so few people outside the official mourners were permitted anywhere near the Cathedral where the service was held or even the funeral route—a reflection on the kind of country we live in today. It isn't Ike's America right now. [6]

Out of concern for a radical student attempt at interrupting the decisive meeting of the Pulitzer board that year, we moved it to early April rather than the end of the month as usual and made no public announcement of the change. Consequently, we had a relatively quiet session in the World Room of the Journalism Building, of which not even our students took notice. But at Harvard, the tradition of gentility was torn apart by that university's first SDS riot. Even there, students mistrusted Nixon's plans for Vietnam.

When I noted Harvard's lapse from serenity, I added without any other sign of regret, "Too bad they didn't clobber the creeps." The Pulitzer board, however, in no way reacted either against the continued reporting of doubt about Vietnam or of prejudice against supporters of radical movements at home.

Norman Mailer, from his earliest days an irreverent critic of American life, was awarded a Pulitzer nonfiction prize for *The Armies of the Night,* an account of the 1967 peace march on Washington, D.C. And in addition to the Vietnam war reporting prize to the Los Angeles *Times*'s Bill Tuohy, the paper itself—a determined critic of the Vietnam War—was given the public service award for its exposé of wrong-doing in the Los Angeles city government.

I thought it praiseworthy of Ben Bradlee of the Washington *Post,* a member of the board, to lead the fight for a Mailer prize, especially when I am sure the *Post* had made every effort to give major coverage to the same peace march for which Mailer won his award. It also impressed me that the board honored a local report of a GI funeral, *Pfc. Gibson Comes*

Home, in which the body of a soldier killed in Vietnam was returned to his home in Louisville, Kentucky, for burial. The prize went to a local reporter, John Fetterman of the Louisville *Times and Courier-Journal.* The photography award, too, was a graphic reminder of the suffering in Vietnam, a picture entitled *Saigon Execution,* taken by Edward T. Adams of the Associated Press.

As for my own favorite for a prize, *1776,* the play that Brooks Atkinson and I had liked so much, the drama prize went as scheduled to the jury's compromise choice, *The Great White Hope,* and it was so recorded. The rest of the awards were for less controversial performances in letters, music, and journalism, but it did seem to me that the board on the whole had given a good account of itself in that difficult year of 1969. I concluded my record of the proceedings:

> April 10—After staying up until after midnight doing telegrams and letters of notification, I decided to do the publicity, order the checks, certificates and other details of the Pulitzer announcement even though the trustees of Columbia won't take final action until Monday, May 5, when all details will be released. We must get the whole thing done before the university explodes again.

I added a sour footnote, "There was much comment in the papers about the Harvard men who said, 'It couldn't happen at Harvard.' Well, it did."

Even in such distressed times, Dorothy and I enjoyed a break when we were invited to a White House reception by President and Mrs. Nixon together with members of the American Society of Newspaper Editors and their wives in mid-April. First of all, after arriving in Washington and putting up at the Shoreham, we attended an ASNE reception for its own members, then finished the evening with an early dinner and so to bed. The next four days are summarized in my diary notes mainly because it was as glamorous a visit as any I can remember at a series of functions arranged by the White House to sell Nixon's Vietnam program.

> April 16—At lunch we heard the Secretary of State, William P. Rogers, who indicated in labored diplomatese that nothing would happen as a result of the recent loss of 31 American airmen over North Korea. We sat with Elie Abel, Marvin Kalb, Peter Grose and other reporters and enjoyed talking with them.
> April 17—We heard the Secretary of Defense, Melvin Laird, at lunch but he said little of consequence about Vietnam or Cambodia.

After a long day, we had dinner by ourselves and later talked briefly about the Pulitzer Prize announcement on the first Monday in May with Joe Pulitzer Jr. Then, bedtime.

April 18—We were among the ASNE's guests and President Nixon's at the White House reception. Dorothy wore her new green gown and looked beautiful, I was in black tie and dinner jacket. We were received in the Gold Room, then President and Mrs. Nixon greeted us in the Blue Room, a fancy sales pitch for Nixon's Doctrine.

Nixon seemed better looking than his pictures, Dorothy said and I thought Mrs. Nixon was attractive in pink. In the Red Room, we saw two of the tables made by one of Dorothy's distant French ancestors, Charles Honoré Lannuier, after which we were ushered into the white and gold State Dining Room for drinks and a layout of hors d'oeuvres. The White House grounds were in blossom and the South Portico was grand-looking—military uniforms, a band performance, etc. Among others, we passed the time with Defense Secretary Laird, who told us he hadn't really wanted his job, and the Secretary of Commerce, George Romney.[7]

After that impressive show, the annual ASNE dinner at the Shoreham for several hundred editors and their guests was lively but just a bit of a comedown. Still, it was an evening to remember.

April 19—We left the Shoreham around 9 a.m. on a lovely spring morning and boarded a train to New York because the Eastern Air shuttle wasn't running due to bad weather. After dinner at Butler Hall, we folded up for the evening at the Morningside Drive apartment.

April 20—A Sunday afternoon reception at the New York Times and I told a Columbia trustee, Arthur Ochs (Punch) Sulzberger Sr., that I'd find him a journalism dean if he'd come up with a Columbia president. After almost a year without a president (Andy Cordier was still serving temporarily), Sulzberger said it still would be tough to replace Grayson Kirk. We met so many people we knew including Dolly Schiff, for whom I'd once worked at the New York Post and who seemed genuinely glad to see us.[8]

I had a particular reason for welcoming the annual Pulitzer announcement that year. The Knight Foundation had engaged me to do a study called *Free Press/Free People: The Best Cause.* It had been John Knight's reaction to the receipt of his Pulitzer Prize, for which I was most thankful. He also had encouraged me to include a section contrasting conditions in the United States and the Western world with the deteriorating position of the peoples behind the iron curtain.

It had been many years since I had been in Moscow and Leningrad (more recently restored to its former identity, St. Petersburg), so I wasn't at all certain how I would be received and whom I would be able to find to speak out against repression. Still, the very uncertainty of the project was what increased its interest for me.[9]

Fortunately, except for the details that ended the academic year after the Pulitzer announcement, my time was my own for the four summer months. The arrangements for the trip had been completed and the passports and visas approved. Dorothy was determined this time to keep the luggage down to essentials. And so, as the days dragged by, the tension mounted.

Although I wouldn't have admitted it at the time, there was a certain amount of suspense for all of us in the Pulitzer office and elsewhere among university officials while waiting for the climactic meeting of the Columbia trustees on May 5 and the prize announcement. I was able to occupy myself mostly with my regular class schedules, appearances by leading figures in the news before student groups at the university and elsewhere, especially at the UN, and an almost overwhelming number of student conferences on job prospects with the approaching end of the academic year. In midweek after the White House gala, I noted in my diary.

Ordinarily, it would be risky to issue a hold-for-release announcement five days ahead of time, particularly when it had to do with Pulitzer Prize winners, but the possibility of a trustees' reversal or refusal to act apparently saved me from still greater embarrassment. All I had to do Monday, therefore, was to await Cordier's appearance before the trustees in mid-afternoon and his telephoned instructions to release the news without change.[10]

It happened at 3:25 P.M., much to my relief, after which the reportorial crew phoned their offices and the news initially was carried by the TV networks, radio stations, and the wire services. As expected, the Mailer prize was featured above the rest, not only because of his reputation but also because he was making a publicity pitch through an independent effort in New York's mayoralty election.[11] The rest of the awards attracted comparatively little attention and nobody, not even Brooks Atkinson, protested over the failure of 1776 to win the drama prize.

In this manner, following our final examinations, we approached commencement for the class of 1969 and still had no president for Columbia and no dean for our school. But somehow, it didn't seem to matter. We knew the trustees always had the option of making permanent Andy Cordier's acting presidency of the university and also elevating Dick Baker from acting dean of our school. Why they didn't do it is beyond me, but I suppose quarrelsome faculties in both instances had something to do with paralysis at the top. Whatever the reason for the trustees' inaction, no decision requiring my presence was likely during the four summer months, so I was free at last to take a long-planned trip with Dorothy behind the iron curtain. [12]

In the end, therefore, I was grateful once again to the spirit of Ralph McGill, my treasured old friend, and the memory of that hoarse-voiced plea of his, "Hang on, boy! Hang on!" But even as I left for a summer's inspection of the mood in Moscow and Prague, I was well aware that the doctrine Nixon had been trying to sell to the American people about a limited reduction in the Vietnam War had aroused only doubt and even suspicion among our draft-age generation.

It seemed to me that it would take a lot more than Nixon's so-called disengagement program to settle the Vietnam War. Despite the four-sided talks in Paris, peace in Southeast Asia still seemed frighteningly distant.

26 Another World

Behind the iron curtain in the late 1960s, I came upon a sick society. [1]

The expression is not mine. It was in a protest written by the Russian novelist, Aleksandr Solzhenitsyn, against what he called the "hate vigilance" of those who had forced his expulsion from the Soviet Writers' Union—an act that eventually led to his temporary exile in Cavendish, Vermont.

In one of my notebooks for that Moscow visit, I have preserved this quotation from his letter:

> It is time to remember that the first thing we belong to is humanity. And humanity is separated from the animal world by thought and speech and they should naturally be free. If they are fettered, we go back to being animals. Publicity and openness—honest and complete—that is the prime condition for the health of every society and ours, too. [2]

Whenever I think of such brave defiance as this of Solzhenitsyn's Communist overlords, I also recall a quite different scenario—an old Czech journalist in Prague who told me of the shocking end of the "Czech Spring"—his government's attempt to return to a system of free speech and free press.

> For 25 years we journalists told our young people that our future lay with the Soviet Union, that they could trust the Russians, that our hope was for the development of a truly beautiful Communist society. And what happened? The Russians invaded us because we insisted on free discussion, on a free press, on Alexander Dubcek's socialism with a human face.

The old journalist stirred his coffee and sighed. "At one stroke," he concluded, "we have lost a whole generation of young people. They will never again believe anything we older people tell them. [3]

The tragic event he referred to was the Red Army invasion of Czechoslovakia on August 20–21, 1968—a force of 500,000 with added satellite divisions of Poles, East Germans, Hungarians, and Bulgarians. The Czechs couldn't resist so formidable a force, as the Prague radio admitted at 4:30 A.M. on the twenty-first: "The defense of our state frontiers is now impossible."

In protest later, a twenty-one-year-old Charles University student in Prague, Jan Palach, poured gasoline over himself and set himself aflame. With his death, an occupied nation of 14 million people—including those in Holici, my father's Moravian village—mourned. And a year later, I saw little children placing flowers on Palach's grave.

The masters of the Kremlin had forgotten Solzhenitsyn's protest, "The first thing we belong to is humanity." For this, they and those who followed them in the Kremlin would be condemned by their fellow-countrymen.

As I was about to leave for my trip behind the iron curtain on July 1, 1969, I wrote in my diary, "It is chilling to think of what suffering people have gone through for even a whisper of free expression. I know I shall not have a moment's peace or happiness all the time I am in their country."

During the previous summer, it had been quite different because I had been working in Britain and Western Europe on a study called *Free Press/Free People: The Best Cause*, of which the iron curtain report was to be a contrasting part. John Knight had suggested the inquiry after winning his Pulitzer Prize; and I had been asked to conduct it under Columbia's management and sponsorship, something I was glad to do.

Having witnessed the events in Czechoslovakia from the safer precincts of Switzerland, France, and Italy in 1968, I had planned—with my university's agreement—to make a closer examination of the Red Army's takeover in the following summer. However, neither I nor anybody else in America so far as I know had the slightest suspicion at the time that the end of the "Czech Spring" would foreshadow the collapse of the Soviet Union itself less than a quarter century hence.

Such an assumption, which seems so credible now in the wan light of recent history, would have aroused only doubt and incredulous laughter in the West had I dared suggest it at the time. In my 1968 tour of Britain and Western Europe during my summer's leave, the principal concern wherever I went had been the survival of some of the weaker daily newspapers against the drain of their advertising revenue and circulation by the mighty tube. If there were problems of undue government influence over the news, as occurred in the United States during the early Vietnam War years, they were secondary. [4]

You may be sure, however, that the editors of Pravda and Izvestia in Moscow took advantage of the struggle by the American correspondents in Vietnam for the truth about our failures in the war, especially after the Tet offensive. It was the Soviet rejoinder to my own sharp questions about what had been published and broadcast in the Soviet Union after the Red Army's takeover in Czechoslovakia. Their excuse was "security." As a Kremlin spokesman put it, "We do not fear the United States because maybe after the Vietnam War is over, our relationship will improve. But we must watch the Chinese." [5]

I often heard references to Beijing's rise to atomic power, but the Kremlin's apologists nearly always continued to counter my questions about the Red Army's occupation of Czechoslovakia with the American role in Vietnam. As I pointed out, however, there was a profound difference. In the Vietnam War, we had been awarding Pulitzer Prizes for accurate reporting and photography as well as soundly based editorial dissent whereas the Soviet reaction to criticism in Czechoslovakia had been punitive.

The best the Soviets then could do was to refer to what they called "the spirit of Hollybush," a puzzle to me until I was reminded that this reflected on the meeting of President Johnson and Soviet Premier Alexey Kosygin in such a place in New Jersey on June 23, 1967.

The Moscow regime also agreed to a few limited treaties while the Czechs were being held down and other East European satellites watched in silence. One was a nuclear test ban treaty, which didn't amount to much because both the French and Chinese wouldn't comply. The other was even more fanciful—a pact by the two super powers to bar atomic arms from outer space—a threat that wasn't likely to exist for years yet to come.

But as for some practical contribution toward future peace such as an agreement to reduce arms and missiles on earth, Moscow's answer was still "nyet." So in practical terms, the United States and the Soviet Union were still as far apart as ever. And for as long as the Vietnam War continued, it was an embarrassment to the United States as well as a continued threat.

As for the Soviet's internal affairs, I was fed the usual quota of unbelievable statistics testifying to Soviet might and high hopes for the future. But what I saw in public places was a continued tableau of a people bereft of hope for the future and even some of the fundamentals of life. I was often told surreptitiously of the circulation of an underground press through a system called *Samisdat* (self-publication), but it didn't seem to be effective enough at the time to impress some of the foreign correspondents I knew.[6] Because of the severe limitation of my movements and the relatively short time at my disposal, I was given no access to the leading writers and intellectuals who had spoken out against Soviet repression.

I did receive a copy of a paper from *Samisdat* in which a historian, Andrei Alexevitch Amalrik, forecast a Soviet collapse in the 1980s following a war with China and added, "The [Soviet] regime is getting old, it's as simple as that." But I also was told that Amalrik was caught and punished for his daring.

Seven protestors against the Czech invasion who led a demonstration in Red Square also were arrested, beaten, and sent to prison. Their leader was Pavel Litvinov, the son of a former ambassador, and the wife of another writer, Yuli Daniel, who already was in prison. One of the few who escaped that fate was a seventy-five-year-old scientist, Pyotr Leonidovich Kapitsa, who warned in 1969 in the journal of the Soviet Academy of Sciences, "Our ideologists will lose the privileges they have in our country, where there are no competing views."

When he later was able to go to the United States, he accepted an honorary degree that was conferred on him at Columbia, but such leave for dissenters was rare, as was illustrated by the punishment given to two of the most illustrious rebels against Soviet conformity—Boris Pasternak and Aleksandr Solzhenitsyn.

For his challenge to the very basis of the Soviet state toward the end of the Stalinist period in 1954 in his novel *Dr. Zhivago,* a best-seller in the United States and Western Europe, Pasternak was bitterly attacked at home and in 1958 was forced to refuse the Nobel Prize that was awarded to him four years later. In the year when *Dr. Zhivago* was published, a more dedicated Communist, Ilya Ehrenburg, had issued a more acceptable work called *The Thaw,* which the Kremlin seized upon as the slogan for the post-Stalinist era. But a young poet, Yevgeny Yevtuchenko, wrote more realistically of the period.

> They tell me, Man, you're bold!
> But that is not true. Courage was never my strong point
> I simply considered it beneath my dignity
> To fall to the level of my colleagues' cowardice. . .
> One day posterity will remember
> This strange era, these strange times, when
> Ordinary common honesty was called courage.

Of all these and their fellow-rebels who had survived Soviet persecution, the one I wanted most to see during my Soviet visit, Solzhenitsyn, was unavailable to me or, for that matter, to anybody else from the West

who came to Moscow to talk to him. For here was the most dedicated of
Russian writers in his lifelong opposition to Soviet terrorism, imprisonment, and threats of even worse yet to come. After being humbled by the
Soviet Writers' Union, it was a foregone conclusion during the year of
my trip behind the iron curtain that he would be banished from his
homeland. It was, so I was told upon my arrival, only a question of time
despite his eminence in the outside world because his will to resist could
not be broken.

Solzhenitsyn was then fifty-one and at the height of his career as a
novelist, extensively published abroad for his critical views of the Soviet
system, and more closely watched by the Kremlin than any other writer
of prominence. The regime had good cause for concern. Solthenitsyn had
endured savage punishment, including eight years in prison labor camps
as a young man for criticizing Stalin in a letter to a friend. And this
despite a heroic record in World War II in the Red Army as a captain of
artillery who won decorations for bravery. Thereafter he was exiled to
Khazakstan until after Stalin's death.

It was then, in Nikita Khrushchev's opening burst of criticism of
Stalinist excesses, that Solzhenitsyn achieved his first great triumph in
1962 with the publication of his caustic prison camp novel *One Day in
the Life of Ivan Denisovitch*. By chance, Premier Khrushchev seized on
the book as an attack on Stalinism, which it was, and honored the
struggling author.

Then in succession came the writer's other major novels—*The First
Circle*, about the treatment of scientists in the Soviet in 1964 and *The
Cancer Ward*, about the plight of cancer patients in Soviet hospitals in
1966. His greatest project, a re-telling of the history of the Russian
struggle against Germany beginning in 1914, was interrupted at the time
I tried and failed to see him in 1969, when the regime already had
cracked down on him.

Already famous in the West, where he was widely translated and
read in both the United States and Europe and being considered for a
Nobel Prize, Solzhenitsyn was confined to his home in the ancient city of
Rostov. It was evident at the time of my visit, which preceded his award
of the Nobel Prize that he had to refuse and his expulsion to the United
States, that the Kremlin considered him a danger to successive Communist dictators. Yet, for all the threats to himself and to his family, the
writer never backed down.

After being branded an "anti-social slanderer" by the regime, he
retorted to the Soviet Writers' Union after expulsion from membership
by seeking a hearing about the "now intolerable oppression in the form
of censorship, which our literature has endured for decades and which
the Union of Writers no longer can accept." He didn't get it and was in

the process of being forced out of his country to a hospitable New England village in the United States at the time I had to move on to Czechoslovakia later that summer.[7]

I was closer to the beleaguered people of Czechoslovakia than I ever could have been to the Russians. I had spent considerable time in Prague, Bratislava, and the tiny Moravian village of Holici with my uncle, Simon Hohenberg, during the year of my Pulitzer Traveling Scholarship at the University of Vienna in 1927–28.[8] However, it had been forty-odd years since those carefree student years with the intervening Hitler Holocaust, during which my uncle had died, and the Nazi occupation of World War II. Now I was faced with the equally rigid Soviet control of the land.

Right off, I learned a Russian "editor" was sitting in the offices of each of the thirty Czech dailies either as a censor for the party press or a dictator for the non-party papers. To those news people who were barred from work because of their unconcealed opposition to the occupation, the problem was how they and their families would survive, even though the occupation force had been cut to 70,000.

When I asked one desperate journalist what he proposed to do about the reduced occupation force, he responded angrily, "Whether it is 7, 700 or 70,000 makes no difference. This is an occupied country and we will not rest until they are gone. The Soviet Union has forfeited the respect of every citizen of this country."

To another, an editor of a leading daily, who now had to work under a new Russian editor-in-chief, the occupation seemed likely to last for years. As he explained, "These Russians have seen what we can do if we have a chance. We won't have such opportunities again very soon."

Another editor, a Czech Communist, argued in despair that the Russians had lied when, as he put it, "They invaded us because they claimed they had to prevent us from overthrowing the Communist Party. The Rumanians did it better than we did because they dissented from the Russians but didn't advertise it in their press."

For the young people, Jan Palach's fellow-students at Charles University, the first anniversary of the Soviet occupation was the signal for a silent gathering about the base of the statue of Good King Wenceslas in the center of Prague. In tin cans, cracked vases and pots, many brought with them flowers that they placed about their patron saint in a gesture partly of mourning, partly of defiance.

But the urge toward freedom still had not been beaten out of them, for I heard one young man muttering to me in English, "We are willing to wait for 20 years if necessary. But we can tell you this: We will not always live this way."

Many seemed much like American youngsters—the boys with long hair and skin-tight costumes, the girls in miniskirts. Many to whom I talked professed to be unafraid, although their future under the Russian occupation was admittedly cloudy. Others were defiant. A few sought to emigrate and asked me about their chances in America or Britain or France. None, however, wanted to trust the Germans; the shame of and the revulsion for the Nazi occupation still was too recent among their families to have been forgotten.

What interested me in particular was the somewhat despairing argument of some of their elders that the growth of Czech Communism was different somehow from the Soviet brand, that the Communist leader Dubcek's proposed "Socialism with a human face" still was possible if, by some miracle the Russian occupation could be dispersed and the Czech brand installed in its place. It bothered me, too, that the young Czechs somehow believed they could survive successive occupations by the German Nazis and Soviet Communists because they were, as some put it, stronger than other peoples in their country. I didn't have the time to test this separatist theory in Bratislava or the village of Holici, but I knew, despite the post-World War I union of Czechs, Slovaks, and others, it always had been a shaky position.

The other argument was that Dubcek's "Socialism with a human face" somehow could create a land of milk and honey if only the Russians would move out. This theory was advanced by a former Washington correspondent of the Communist daily in Prague, *Rude Pravo,* Jiri Hochman, who wrote from Prague to the Washington *Post* during the 1968 occupation year. But he conceded as a realist, "If decisions on Czechoslovakia's future are left principally to foreign judgment, the human and moral interests of a small country will carry little weight." [9]

Not long after I came home and began writing *Free Press/Free People: The Best Cause,* I scribbled a note in my diary after a long day at Columbia:

> Sept. 30—A visiting delegation of French journalists came to the school today and were very emphatic, in talking to me, about their determination to have a say over what goes into their newspapers through invoking the strength of their editorial association. I wished them luck.

Somehow, it made me think back to that strange time during the Red Army's occupation of Czechoslovakia when, as Yevtuchenko put it in another context, "ordinary honesty was called courage." And I also thought of *Rude Pravo*'s Washington correspondent, now fighting the good fight against the Russians in Prague and the old Czech journalist who mourned the loss of the trust of a whole generation of young people.

The contrast with the assurance of the visiting French journalists was striking. Whether they won or lost in their bid for a share in deciding the editorial policies of their newspapers, the French still acted in the spirit of *Liberté! Egalité! Fraternité!* which they considered to be their birthright. And this after three occupations by German armies in fewer than a hundred years, which their forebears had survived with unbroken vitality. [10]

True enough, but as my sympathetic inner self was quick to remind me, the French remained a great power in the Western world with the closest of allies, headed by America and Britain. The much smaller Czechoslovaks, a polyglot nation so often in conflict within itself, lay at the mercy of its often oppressive and much stronger neighbors, Germany and the Soviet Union, each of which had successively occupied their land over only a little more than a quarter-century. And where were the allies of the Czechs, the Slovaks, the Moravians, and the splinter groups when the first two became separate countries?

The only recourse for such small and isolated nations in the post-World War II division of Europe was a lamentably weak United Nations, in which the Soviet veto in the Security Council barred any possibility of armed action in defense of helpless peoples. While we in the United States were closing out our own ill-starred war in Vietnam, it was time for us also to remember, as Solzhenitsyn had said to his leaders, that the first thing we belong to is humanity.

27 The Peace Riots

During the first nine months of President Nixon's regime, there was a vague though unrealized hope across the land that he might accelerate the search for peace in Vietnam. Even the most dedicated peace rioters seemed willing, for a while at least, to give him a chance.

However, when he announced what appeared to be a policy of disengagement of July 25, 1969, it made no difference in the way the conflict was being fought while the four-sided peace talks droned on in Paris. Nor did his first 60,000 cut in troop strength, doled out in two announcements five months apart, slow the fighting to any appreciable extent. [1]

As might have been expected, with 485,000 GIs still engaged in combat, peace seemed far off in Vietnam—the longest and worst-fought war in American history. And so, thousands of radical students resumed their riotous conduct on the home front from time to time but the White House seemed unimpressed.

The war dragged on, this time with a difference. The North Vietnamese Army now made its presence known in a more effective way along with the Vietcong that had occupied almost three-quarters of South Vietnam outside Saigon.

In response, the American armed forces began a pacification strategy that consisted mainly of terrorizing unarmed civilians in native villages in the Quang Ngai district because they were called "totally hostile" to the Saigon regime. As Neil Sheehan wrote years later in his account of the war, *A Bright and Shining Lie*, the burning of villages began as early as 1966 and continued with heightened tension through 1967 and 1968. One of the first to document the carnage, Jonathan Schell of the *New Yorker* magazine, was quoted as follows in Sheehan's authoritative work:

> Whereas I had learned that at least ten other hamlets had been
> flattened as thoroughly as the five along the coast and a further twenty-

212

five heavily damaged, Schell discovered that fully 70 per cent of the 450 hamlets in Quang Ngai had been destroyed. Except for a narrow strip of hamlets along Route 1, which was patrolled after a fashion, the destruction was proceeding apace.

Day after day from the back of the spotter plane, Schell watched the latest smashing and burning in bombings and shellings and rocket runs by the helicopter gunships and in the meandering progress of flames and smoke from houses set afire by the American infantry. He tallied the previous destruction from the traces of the houses and, going to the military maps, carefully checked his estimates with the L-19 pilots, officers of Task Force Oregon, members of the CORDS team in Quang Ngai, and several local Saigon officials.

Sheehan, then a United Press war correspondent who later shifted to the New York *Times,* commended Schell's account of this "scorched earth" policy in the *New Yorker* in January 1967 but added that a much longer account by the same reporter, while certified by army investigators as substantially correct, ended up with General Westmoreland and never saw print. There was much worse yet to come—a massacre of native villagers that was uncovered by a young free-lance correspondent in 1968, which intensified the antiwar demonstrations to hysterical pitch and eventually involved the Pulitzer prizes.[1]

The nationwide student demonstrations did have the effect, in large part, of convincing the White House that the president would have to try harder to sell his supposed disengagement policy to the public and particularly to the students. So on November 3, he tried again in a TV appearance, which he summed up in this manner:

> The United States will keep its treaty commitments.
>
> We shall provide a shield if a nuclear power threatens the freedom of a nation allied with us, or of a nation whose survival we consider vital to our security and the security of the region as a whole.
>
> In cases involving other types of aggression we shall furnish military and economic assistance when requested and as appropriate. But we shall look to the nation directly threatened to assume the primary responsibility of providing the manpower for its defense.[2]

If this was intended to appease the concern of the home front that we were forever to support this seemingly endless war, the effect was dubious at best. And as for the nations in Southeast Asia that were threatened either by China, North Vietnam, or the Vietcong and their allies in Laos and Cambodia, the result bordered on panic. But nowhere was there any clear realization of Nixon's meaning.

On my part, after listening to Nixon that night, I wrote, "Nov. 3—

In the evening, we heard Nixon defend his Vietnam war policy over TV
and thought he did a very poor job. The first reaction will come in the
universities and it is not likely to be pleasant."

Ten days later, the massacre of more than a hundred Vietnamese
civilians by supposedly disciplined American army combat troops was
reported by the St. Louis *Post-Dispatch,* Joseph Pulitzer's paper, and
thirty-five others in the first of several syndicated articles by a free-lance
journalist and an upstart syndicate. It was hard to believe. Yet, this
tragedy and others soon would outrage the public across the land and
force President Nixon, however unwilling he may have been, into a
massive American troop reduction in Vietnam within a year. Now it
wasn't the usual patriotic broadside against the forces of Communism
that had become the main issue in the public mind. It was, rather, a cry
wrenched from all manner of antiwar protesters—a cry for human decency and an end to aimless slaughter for no good end.

Had it not been for the thirty-two-year-old free-lance journalist, Seymour M. Hersh, the nation might never have heard of the massacre at
My Lai on March 16, 1968. Even so, it was almost twenty months before
he was able to break the story that disgraced the army, shocked the
nation and started President Nixon's long slide downward in public
opinion.

Hersh was Chicago-born, a history major who was graduated from
the University of Chicago in 1958 and worked his way to a modest
Associated Press job nine years later. Then, leaving the Pentagon beat
he'd covered for the AP, he tried politics briefly in working for Senator
Eugene McCarthy's losing presidential primary campaign in New Hampshire during 1968. That, as he said, "drove me crazy," and he knew he'd
never be a politician. [3]

What to do at a loose end with no job at thirty-one? Hersh himself
wasn't sure as he pondered his future. Then, he had a break. Somebody
he knew in the Pentagon tipped him to a ghastly tale that had been
whispered about for months at the highest levels of the military along
with the backlash over the enemy's Tet offensive in 1968.

Hersh's source early in 1969 told him that a regular army unit under
a lieutenant's command had wiped out a village the Americans called
"Pinkville" in South Vietnam with scores of civilian deaths—a senseless
slaughter because "Pinkville" happened to be in an area of South Vietnam that was under Vietcong control.

It was a monumental job of investigative journalism that Hersh un-
dertook. He had no help, no funds, but had to travel tens of thousands
of miles to try to find witnesses to this tale of mass murder, identify the

commander and the unit, and bring the perpetrators of the crime to military justice. Through a friend, he was able to obtain a grant of $2,000 for his inquiry from a small foundation, the Philip Stern Family Fund of Washington, D.C.

Then he set out to locate soldiers who belonged to a specific army unit that may have been involved—a platoon of the Eleventh Brigade of the Americal Division. If ever there was a 100–1 chance, this was it; but his luck held out. First of all, he was able to locate "Pinkville," a village called My Lai near the larger town of Quang Ngai. He also verified the date of the crime and, at last, the identity of the alleged leader of the unit involved, Lieutenant William L. Calley Jr.

It turned out that Lieutenant Calley already was in custody at Fort Benning, Gabon, as a result of a year-long undercover army inquiry and was facing court martial proceedings, which finally gave Hersh enough to go on. Having no news organization himself, he confided in a neighbor, twenty-four-year-old David Obst, who circulated the first article on the My Lai case through his Dispatch News Service and placed it in the St. Louis *Post-Dispatch* and thirty-five other American newspapers.

Under a copyright by Dispatch News Service, Hersh's first article in the *Post-Dispatch* began:

> FORT BENNING, GA., Nov. 13—Lt. William L. Calley Jr., 26 years old, is a mild-mannered, boyish-looking Vietnam combat veteran with the nickname "Rusty." The Army is completing an investigation of charges that he deliberately murdered at least 109 Vietnamese civilians in a search-and-destroy mission in March, 1968, in a Vietcong stronghold known as "Pinkville." [Its real name: My Lai.]
>
> Calley has formally been charged with six specifications of mass murder. Each specification cites a number of dead, adding up to the 109 total, and charges that Calley did "with premeditation murder . . . Oriental human beings, whose names and sex are unknown, by shooting them with a rifle."
>
> The Army calls it murder; Calley, his counsel and others associated with the incident describe it as a case of carrying out orders.[4]

Two eyewitnesses in a later article Hersh contributed to the *Post-Dispatch* and other newspapers gave such incriminating details as these: From Michael Terry of Urem, Utah, as quoted by Hersh:

> "They [Calley's unit] just marched through, shooting everybody. . . . One officer ordered a kid to machine gun everybody down but the kid just couldn't do it. He threw the machine gun down and the officer picked it up . . .

"Seems like nobody said anything. . . . They just started pulling people out and shooting them."

In another scene Terry described, twenty villagers in a line were shot in front of a ditch—"just like a Nazi-type thing."

From Sergeant Michael Bernhardt of Franklin Square, New York, whom Hersh interviewed at Fort Dix, New Jersey, and who had been in another platoon while viewing Calley's men in action at My Lai, "They were setting fire to the hootches and huts and waiting for people to come out and then shooting them. . . . They were going into the hootches and shooting them. They were gathering people in groups and shooting them."

There was further corroboration in a three-page letter, Hersh reported, that had been sent to the army and public officials by an ex-GI, Ronald Ridenhour, then a student at Claremont College in California. [5]

Obst's Dispatch News Service didn't wait long to send Hersh's articles to the Pulitzer office toward the end of 1969 with his nomination for a Pulitzer Prize in international reporting. Nor was there any doubt, when I forwarded the series with other nominees to the international reporting jury, about the ultimate outcome. The students' reaction to My Lai, even more so than the general, public's, was frantic to the point sometimes of hysteria.

Toward year's end, when Andrew Wellington Cordier was formally inducted as the fifteenth president of Columbia University, he took notice of the nation's problems in this manner:

> Great civil rights issues are far from resolved. Both our social order and our economy are being subjected to buffeting storms making the outcome totally unpredictable. Changes—important changes—in all these areas must come, but there is genuine doubt whether we have the spiritual, moral and intellectual resources to attain them in a creative and just manner. War is still on our doorstep and the specter of new conflict of world-wide proportions and great destructive impact cannot be discounted.

Soon after the beginning of the new year, President Nixon tried once again to soothe public opinion with one of his temperate but inconclusive speeches. This one was his State of the World message to Congress on February 18, 1970, in which he offered this formula for further action in Southeast Asia to a deeply disturbed public and a national university student body that once again was on the verge of open revolt:

> While we will maintain our interests in Asia and the commitments that flow from them, the changes taking place in the region enable us

to change the character of our involvement. The responsibilities once borne by the United States at such great cost can now be shared. America can be effective in helping the peoples of Asia harness the forces of change to peaceful progress, and in supporting them as they defend themselves from those who would subvert this process and fling Asia again into conflict.[6]

But only a month later, Nixon's good faith once again was put to the test when the Vietcong's protector in Cambodia, Prince Norodom Sihanouk, was barred from office while he was out of his country and a pro-United States general, Lon Nol, took over. This may not have attracted much public notice in the United States, but at the Pentagon and the White House there was enormous activity. For with the Prince out of the way, the privileged sanctuary of the Vietcong and North Vietnamese forces just across their border with Cambodia was wide open for an American attack.

Nixon couldn't resist the temptation. For all his fine words about American disengagement and more fighting for the South Vietnamese against the Communists, the president secretly ordered 30,000 American soldiers to prepare for an invasion of the Cambodian sanctuary of the enemy. D-Day was set for April 30.

At the meeting of the Pulitzer board that voted the prizes for 1970 on April 9, the international reporting jury recommended Seymour Hersh's exposé of the My Lai tragedy for its top award with unanimity and enthusiasm as follows:

> In the face of disbelief and disinterest on the part of many newspapers and operating with limited resources, Hersh showed initiative, enterprise and perseverance to break the My Lai story—a story that shook the nation and had vast international repercussions.
>
> In pursuing his story to the point that the topmost officials in the United States, South Vietnam, Great Britain and other countries became publicly and directly involved, Hersh's performance met the highest journalistic standards for which Pulitzer recognition is traditionally granted.

Unanimously and without debate, the Pulitzer board approved Hersh's prize. But the formal announcement to the news media and the public was withheld until May 4, the usual first Monday in May when the university trustees were to meet for their expected approval of the proceedings, which included all the rest of the awards as well as Hersh's.

A week after the Pulitzer board vote, the students on campus reminded me that their own personal domestic conflict was still on. As I recorded the incident in my diary, "April 16—After a window-breaking rampage on campus last night by radical students, I entered the Journalism Building this morning and was overpowered by a stink bomb in an elevator."

Such unpleasant details had become a part of academic life by that time, so I met my classes as usual and tried to carry on, decided I couldn't very well penalize those who refused to show up under the circumstances, and did the best I could for the regulars who stuck with me. I had the usual warnings meanwhile that the May 4 Pulitzer announcement might very well be halted in some undetermined fashion by a student insurrection. But that, too, had become a part of my life, and I made my plans accordingly.

Although the nation still was in ignorance of President Nixon's planned invasion of Cambodia . . . at the end of the month, he appeared on TV the night of April 20 with a speech that, in the light of what transpired later, was intended to make the public more sympathetic to his program in Indochina. To quote my diary:

> April 20—We heard President Nixon on TV tonight proclaim victory in Vietnam and announce the withdrawal of another 150,000 troops in the next year. The victory claim is sheer *chutzpah*. The troop withdrawal is a long-deferred step, necessary if Nixon is to have a chance of support in the midyear Congressional elections this November. As Dorothy said, the whole business means "trouble" in Southeast Asia.[7]

Then, emblematic of the feeling throughout the land at the time, I had this entry in my diary eight days later:

> April 28—Suddenly, some are crying that 1970 is 1929 and intimating that Nixon is another Herbert Hoover. The Wall Street Journal, no radical sheet, used on its lead story about the stock market today a headline that read "Street of Despair." It quoted an unnamed source, a New York Stock Market official, as saying the nation is in a depression with auto and steel sales off 30 per cent. The New York Times lead editorial said Nixon's financial policies have failed. . . . But no brokers are jumping out of windows and the apple sellers are not on the streets. The affluent college kids are still rioting. So I suppose it's a *new* kind of depression.[8]

No matter. It was neither the fear of an economic downturn nor the *Wall Street Journal*'s "Street of Despair" that stirred the nation two days later. Nor did the Pulitzer Prize for the revelations about the My Lai massacre do more than add to the public's fury once it was announced. There was just a brief note in my diary that said it all. "April 30— Nixon's order to U.S. troops to attack in Cambodia was a terrible shock tonight."

Overnight, turmoil erupted at more than 2,000 of the nation's colleges and universities as the antiwar protest movement burst all bounds. The mammoth reaction doomed any hope President Nixon may have had of averting an American defeat and total disaster in Indochina during his administration.

28 Tragedy at Kent State

Long after the Vietnam War, it still was difficult to account for the difference between the American public's attitudes toward the military killings in South Vietnam and Kent State University in Ohio.

Although Lieutenant William L. Calley Jr. had been court-martialed and sentenced to life imprisonment for directing his army unit's massacre of more than a hundred Vietnamese civilians at My Lai, there was no public protest of consequence when he was released after a comparatively short imprisonment with President Nixon's approval.

What a difference there was, however, when panicky National Guardsmen at Kent State opened fire on rock-throwing antiwar protesters at Kent, Ohio, and killed four students. The Akron *Beacon Journal* was unfairly stigmatized by a censorious public—a treatment that sometimes had been given by ancient peoples to the messenger who bore evil tidings. The usual year's delay in the paper's consideration for a Pulitzer Prize didn't help matters any.

Bob Giles, who was managing editor at the time, recalled, "There were those who felt that the student demonstrators had received exactly what they deserved and those who were quite ready to charge the National Guardsmen with murder. We believed it was vital for the Beacon Journal to be deeply involved." [1]

Why was it that the American public seemed to accept Lieutenant Calley's minimal punishment for his responsibility for the Vietnamese victims of a riotous army attack but registered at best a divided opinion about the responsibility of the National Guardsmen in Ohio for the four students who were shot to death and eleven others who were wounded? On the basis of the *Beacon Journal*'s original account of the events of Monday, May 4, 1970, when the killings occurred, the only recorded casualties among the Guardsmen that day were two who were treated for shock at a hospital.

It would seem, therefore, that the blame attached to the students who protested against the war was based primarily on an older public's support of the military, an attitude that had led President Johnson to send more than a half-million troops to Vietnam. Admittedly, the patience of the Guardsmen was tried by a weekend of antiwar demonstrations, including rock-throwing. But surely, the frequent use of tear gas by the troops, as ordered by their commander, should have been sufficient to maintain order instead of permitting their guns to be used to end the demonstrations against the war.

A famous photo snapped by twenty-one-year-old Paul Filo—that of a weeping fourteen-year-old girl kneeling beside the body of a slain student—should have helped restore the militant portion of the public to its senses once the rioting ended in disaster. But evidently, as Giles concluded, it didn't.

That May 4, the Akron *Beacon Journal* had 27 reporters and four photographers on the Kent State campus, 12 miles from Akron, when the shooting began. This is what the paper published in listing the dead:

> Sandra Scheuer, 20, a sophomore from Youngstown, Ohio. She was walking to class when a bullet went through her windpipe.
>
> Allison Krause, 19, a freshman from Pittsburgh, Pa. The day before, she had placed a flower in the barrel of a National Guardsman's rifle. She was running across a parking lot with her boyfriend when the Guard began to fire.
>
> Jeffery Miller, 20, a sophomore from Plainview, N.J. Moments before he was shot, he was among a group of students who were taunting the Guard. A bullet hit him in the face. It was his body before which the 14-year-old girl knelt in Filo's picture.
>
> William Schroeder, 20, a freshman from Lorain, Ohio. He was attending Kent State on an ROTC scholarship and was watching the demonstration when he was shot.[2]

Eleven others, all students, were injured when the shooting began and two Guardsmen were later treated for shock.

The *Beacon Journal*'s account of the tragedy began when the Guardsmen sprayed tear gas on about 500 people on the Commons behind the university's administration office at about noon. Some in the crowd threw rocks and tear gas grenades toward the troops in response. Others tried to get away because the soldiers were carrying loaded rifles. The students had been told not to assemble.

At about 12:30 P.M., according to an eyewitness, "One section of the Guard turned around and fired and then all the Guardsmen turned around and fired." But not all aimed at the crowd, for some were seen firing into the air. [3]

When an officer told the students to disperse, pleading it was "for your own good," some laughed and mocked him. After that, more rocks and sticks were thrown, and some Guardsmen began firing without orders.

The melee climaxed with three days and nights of rioting and other disorders, including smashed store windows in downtown Kent and a burned university ROTC building. The demonstrations began with President Nixon's order sending 30,000 American troops into Cambodia. There were 1,300 National Guardsmen confronting a shifting crowd of anywhere from 500 to 1,000 students on the Kent State campus over that May Day weekend. An FBI report later concluded the shooting had been unnecessary, but that was long after the four victims had been buried.

The weekend of rioting, climaxed by the four shooting deaths, left their mark on a distressed nation. As the Carnegie Commission on Higher Education determined after months of research, more than 500 of the nation's 2,550 colleges and universities were closed during the rioting over the Cambodian invasion, and more than half the rest had to battle against disorders of varying degrees of violence. About 100, the study found, had to summon police to restore order. (So far as is known, only the mayor of Kent called out the National Guard.)

Clark Kerr, director of the Carnegie Fund Study for the Future of Higher Education, concluded after the inquiry was completed, "No episode or series of episodes had a higher impact in all of our history than the events of April and May, 1970." [4]

Judged by my diary entries for the same approximate period at the beginning of May 1970, the reaction at Columbia University may have been noisy and troublesome for some but it never seemed to be dangerous to life and limb. There were no shootings on Morningside Heights or any other college or university in New York City that could be attributed to dissent from President Nixon's order.

As usual at Pulitzer Prize time, some of our students apparently decided to try to disrupt the scheduled announcement for May 4, as it turned out. My colleague Dick Baker had located me that weekend at our home in Aquebogue on eastern Long Island with Dorothy. I noted in my diary:

> May 3—Dick Baker warned me by phone in Aquebogue that our students were on strike against Nixon's extension of the war to Cambo-

dia and also intended to force cancellation of the Pulitzer Prize announcement. I asked why and later got a response from Elie Abel,
who'd just been named as our new dean. He said the students told him
they had to strike against something so they picked the Pulitzers.[5]

Anyway, President Cordier told me by phone to announce the
prizes wherever I wished.

Our May 4 was decidedly more peaceful than the violent anti-Nixon
outbursts elsewhere. When the Columbia trustees approved the Pulitzer
board's slate of awards, I noted the results as usual in my diary:

> "The great student revolt at Columbia didn't come off although
> we'd made all preparations for it. My office was in the Women's Faculty
> Club building (on the theory that our opponents, if any, would be male)
> and I forwarded the results to the Men's Faculty Club through our
> respective rear entrances. The bulk of the reporters were waiting for the
> announcement in the larger building.
>
> The go-ahead from the trustees came by phone at 3:50 p.m. and
> my people were ready with phone lines and the usual thick stack of pre-
> printed announcements for the reporters in the Women's and Men's
> Faculty Clubs. Only four students showed up outside to protest and we
> gave them coffee and cake.
>
> Seymour Hersh's prize for uncovering the My Lai massacre in 1969
> was the big news for the 1970 awards as far as the anti-war people
> were concerned. I was more interested in the drama award to Charles
> Gordone, the first black dramatist to win with "No Place to Be Some-
> body." Newsday's two prizes for public service and cartoons were bit-
> ter-sweet because the Los Angeles Times had just bought the paper.
> Nobody protested Jean Stafford's short stories for the Fiction prize (the
> jury was over-ruled) and all the rest were accepted without fuss. We
> start for 1971 with a nomination for reporting—the Akron Beacon
> Journal staff for public service for the coverage of the Kent State
> tragedy.

It should not be assumed, however, that the student strike was ineffective at Columbia for the rest of the academic year. On the contrary,
most colleges, schools, and departments at both graduate and undergraduate levels operated with difficulty if at all on the evidence of the following diary entries;

> May 6—Our school is almost paralyzed and the university itself is
> a shambles. Like the UN, Columbia's triumph is that it still exists.
>
> May 7—I told my secretary at the Pulitzer office, Rose Valenstein,
> to stay home and I read and graded my last student honors project

papers at home and turned them in. My year is now over. I could just as well take off right now for the Far East with Dorothy (on my summer and fall Sabbatical leave) but I won't. It would look like running away.

May 8—A miserable day with pickets trying to block us out of the Journalism Building. I kept things going as best I could (Pulitzer jury appointments for 1971 among them) and took off in the afternoon, then went on to Aquebogue for the weekend. I thought Nixon made a good impression in his TV interview tonight but I could have been drummed off the campus if I said so. No dissent permitted by the dissenters as usual.

May 9—The big Washington anti-war rally went off peacefully but it will not change Nixon's policies, I'm afraid.

May 11—A long Faculty-student meeting at which we agreed to cancel points for the May project (this was a special reporting job for extra credit) and they agreed to turn in their Honors projects (a requirement for the M. S. degree) as the last work of the year. Also, they promised to provide unimpeded access to the building. Meanwhile, Rose came in and reported she had to talk her way past pickets at the door. As for the building itself, it's a pig pen.

May 12—A quiet day at school for a change. The so-called strikers began coming in for advice and a few jobs, the latter being very scarce this year.

May 13—Only Columbia College is now blockaded and they deserve what they're getting.

June 1—I attended Andy Cordier's presidential dinner for the prospective recipients of Columbia's Honorary Degrees (I was the chairman of the Honors Committee) and heard Professor Arthur Burns lecturing us on economics and the saintliness of Richard Nixon. Also delivered the proofs of 'Free Press/Free People' to Columbia University Press, the publisher.

June 2—A shaky Commencement—hot, humid and sparsely attended because about half the male graduates didn't show up as a protest against the Vietnam War. They'll show up when the Army calls them. Had a lousy dinner with Dorothy at Butler Hall, then collapsed in bed at 11 p.m. But tomorrow: Shoo-Shoo, Baby: We're off once again for Vietnam and the rest of the Far East.[6]

My sabbatical leave project, as it turned out, was directly related to the wrenching antiwar experience through which the nation was passing—a 40,000-mile journey during eight months in the Indo-Pacific—my sixth sojourn in Asia since 1950. The Ford Foundation was financing the trip with a generous travel-study grant (I paid for my wife's expenses separately), but I had others to thank as well. One was the East-West Center at the University of Hawaii, where I had taught and worked mainly with Asian students in the summer of 1967. Another was the Chinese University of Hong Kong, where I proposed to teach in the fall of 1970 before returning to Columbia for the spring semester of 1971 and the Pulitzer Prize selections for that year.

What I sought to do this time with the help of past and potential Pulitzer Prize winners in Vietnam and elsewhere in the Indo-Pacific was to study and report on the interaction of peoples and their governments for war or peace with the United States. Based on such researches as these, the title of the book I expected to write was *New Era in the Pacific: A Study in Public Diplomacy.*

But even before my departure, I knew perfectly well that a large part of my findings would be influenced by the winding down of the Vietnam War and the eventual outcome of the long press/government conflict there over the reporting of such Pulitzer Prize winners as Peter Arnett, Harrison Salisbury, Seymour Hersh, and others. Then, too, there was one of the most important, Carlos Peña Romulo, still the foreign minister of the Philippines, who had won his Pulitzer in 1942 as an American citizen and the author of a survey in the *Philippines Herald* early in 1941 that forecast Japan's war for control of the Pacific.

With such sources as these to begin with, and the probability that still others would be forthcoming, I stated the position as follows at the outset of my long journey:

> The wars in Indochina and the nature of American policies in the Pacific that flowed from them have left a bitter heritage that will haunt the United States in Asia for years yet to come.
>
> The effect is particularly noticeable on the young America and the young Asia that are emerging today. To approach the situation realistically, it might better be said that there are several young Americas, going by political interests and regional and social groupings, and numerous young Asias, accepting the old standards of nationalities, castes, tribes, religions and political and economic groups.
>
> But whether the forces are two, several or many on the rim of the Pacific and Indian Oceans, the home of one-third of humankind, the dominant issue is still the same. How are these giant continents to live together in peace in the remaining years of this century and the long and desperate uncertainties of the next? The animosities born of three Asian wars over the last three decades will not easily be laid to rest among the generations that had to fight. [7]

What the Pulitzer Prizes helped stimulate in all three of these conflicts was a record, more often than not filed from a battlefield, but only a few correspondents each year were given recognition for their efforts. There were only five in the World War II, six in Korea, and six more between 1964 and 1970 in Vietnam. Indeed, what I was trying to do in Asia now, among othet things, was to assess the chances of averting more such calamities.

For the first two conflicts, the price in American combat deaths alone had been very high—and now, two years after the enemy's Tet offensive, the toll in Vietnam was approaching 50,000. It was scant comfort to realize that the foe's losses had been even greater, that Japan also had paid dearly at the end with two atom bombings for the 1941 sneak attack on Pearl Harbor, and that our UN forces had been able to save South Korea from being overrun. Now, the defeat in Vietnam and the rest of Indochina loomed ever larger as the end approached.

For those of us who grew up in the Pacific Northwest early in this century with Asian children as our schoolmates, the wonder was not that we Americans had found ourselves so closely associated with the peoples of Asia but that it had taken three wars over only a little more than three decades to awaken us to both the enormous risks as well as the importance of our global position.

The failure of three American presidents in Vietnam—Kennedy, Johnson, and now Nixon—had impressed on us in the United States more forcibly than ever before the most urgent necessity of an open society—a close and trustful relationship between government and people. That had not existed for us since the four-term service in the White House of Franklin Roosevelt and, to a lesser degree, the Truman and Eisenhower years. By contrast in North Vietnam, we also had seen how Ho Chi Minh even after his death still inspired his army and his people to resist more than half a million American troops using the most modern military armaments and the even larger but less disciplined South Vietnamese army.

For the rest of this century and well into the next one, the sharp divisions in American society and its effect on our leadership would be closely watched by our neighbors across the Pacific—the Japanese and Chinese, the Russians, Indians, Pakistani, and the many less numerous Asian peoples.

Of that much I was certain as I set out in the summer of 1970 on my latest Asian journey. As to what we elders could do to start healing the rift between our embattled youth across two continents, that was beyond my capacity to forecast. What I did know was that the twin tragedies of My Lai in Vietnam and Kent State in America had burned themselves into the conscience of the nation so that we would never again forget that we are, and will forever remain, a Pacific as well as an Atlantic power in our strategic position high in the North American continent.

29 Rommy

Of all the Pulitzer Prize winners in Asia's wars in this benighted century, the one I wanted most to see on my latest tour was the forceful little Filipino with a thunderous voice—my friend, Carlos Peña Romulo.

Now at seventy-one, Rommy was serving his last term as foreign minister of the Philippines, but he still seemed to me to be more an observant reporter than a diplomat when Dorothy and I dropped in on him at the Padre Faura on July 9, 1970. Having come from a resurgent Japan, a fearfully divided Korea, and a somewhat panicky Hong Kong, I brought up the matter of Filipino security first of all.

Rommy referred to the presence of the Seventh Fleet and American air power based in Guam and Okinawa which, he said, would help the Filipinos to defend themselves if it became necessary. Then, characteristically, he remarked that Philippine-Japanese relations currently were excellent but he had to "look to the long tomorrow," which he illustrated with a vivid incident.

Four Japanese warships, he began, had paid a visit recently to Manila harbor while on a route, his words, "that exactly paralleled Baron Tanaka's old Japanese Co-Prosperity Sphere."[1]

He went on, "The Japanese are a strong, highly disciplined people with an enormous potential."

Aboard the warships, he recalled seeing a large, well-drilled corps of Japanese cadets in spotless white uniforms, white gloves, and showing disciplined mannerism. They deeply impressed him by rejecting drinks and refusing to be fed at lunch before their officers. It was, he observed, a chilling demonstration for those with long memories, then abruptly concluded that the American public badly needed to be better informed about Asian affairs—a belief he linked to the public protest in the United States against the Vietnam War.

With that kind of a preface, Rommy asked us to call on him for a longer talk at 8:30 next morning. Seeing how anxious he was to get at the papers on his desk, we left him to his work and went on with our business elsewhere along Roxas Boulevard.

There may be some who would have criticized Foreign Minister Romulo at the time as predisposed to be suspicious of the Japanese even with their "no war" constitution, their severely limited armed forces, and their much-publicized lack of a nuclear weapon.

To be sure, while still an American citizen early in 1941, Rommy had concluded a Pacific tour for his *Philippines Herald* with the articles that forecast a Japanese attempt to wage a successful war in the Pacific. Even more dramatic, his Pulitzer Prize had been voted to him in 1942 while he was a brigadier general on General MacArthur's staff during the last days of their heroic band's resistance to the Japanese at Corregidor just before both were flown to safety at FDR's orders.

But since the end of World War II, from the time I first knew Rommy in 1946 at the United Nations, his record as an internationalist and a leading citizen of his own independent nation had been equally impressive. He had been the third president of the United Nations General Assembly, the Philippine ambassador to the United States, the president of the University of the Philippines, the secretary of education, serving for a previous term as foreign minister, and the author of five books on Asian affairs as well as his autobiography. With such a record, what he had to say about Asia deserved a decent hearing.

I suppose I was more the partisan than the aloof student of international affairs when Dorothy and I returned to Rommy's office at the Padre Faura for our appointment next day. At 8:30 A.M., when we arrived, he already had been at his desk for two hours—an early routine that also was typical of the way he liked to work.

Speaking as the Filipino foreign minister, he was as blunt about his pro-American position as Prime Minister Eisaku Sato of Japan had been careful in picking his way through a verbal minefield of reservations. Rommy began:

> I can't imagine a United States withdrawal in the Pacific. That would leave it to others to divide the hegemony of many more than a billion people and their markets in Asia. No, the United States is a Pacific power and it will remain a Pacific power. To withdraw to any great extent would mean America's reduction to a third-rate power with a vastly lower standard of living for its people.

After some discussion, in which he strengthened his point of view, he concluded, "As for the Asians, do they really want to have the United

States withdraw and be forced to choose between Russia and China?" Out of deference to Japanese sensibilities, I suppose, he omitted a reference here to his volatile neighbor, then wound up, "Can the United States give up its power in the Pacific by default? I don't think so."

As for the widespread conclusion in the United States that Americans cannot be the world's policeman, he observed with a grin, "You Americans have never been the world's policeman. You've been more like a samaritan toward Europe, India, even Japan and China. And samaritans are taken advantage of, but not policemen."

After brief reflection, he added:

> I think it's a mistake to believe that the American type of democracy can be exported, the good life, the undisciplined life. [He sighed.] In this part of the world, outside Japan, we can't possibly be industrialized for 50 years or more—maybe China in a little less.

The inference was clear enough. For the long tomorrow, most of the Asian peoples were likely to continue to be customers for the industrialized powers, principally the United States and Japan, with an outside chance of China—-all fighting to maintain leadership in the balance of trade. The Soviet Union seemed not to figure very largely in Rommy's calculations, as I recalled, but I never thought to ask him why.

Still, on balance, it was heartening to visit once more with an old and trusted friend. Probably Dorothy was bored stiff, but he and I sat and yarned together as old newspapermen will the world over. I remember one last story of his—a lonely dinner for John Foster Dulles as the "ex-secretary of state" in 1948 after Thomas E. Dewey's loss to President Truman. But four years later, when Eisenhower became president and named Dulles as his secretary of state, the delighted diplomat voluntarily became Rommy's guest at a lavish celebration dinner. "Cost me $8,000 and worth it," said the foreign minister of the Philippines happily. It was the last time I ever saw him, but the memory of the only Filipino winner of a Pulitzer Prize lingers on—as does his influence in Asian affairs. Unfortunately, he couldn't control his boss, President Ferdinand Marcos, but that is another story.[2]

I had already seen Senator Emanuel Pelaez, an attractive and articulate opponent of President Marcos, who had blamed the Filipino leader for creating what he called "an atmosphere of violence" that had seriously affected the country's future. However, toward the end of our discussion at his law office, Senator Pelaez hazarded the guess that the country and its people had the vitality to survive the Marcos regime. Romulo, as the foreign minister, wasn't mentioned in our discussion.

It was under these circumstances that Dorothy and I called at the Malacanang after leaving the Padre Faura and were ushered into Marcos's office by his armed guards. I wasn't sure what to expect because I had heard the president had been quoted as expecting that Japanese power eventually would replace American power in the Pacific. However, he volunteered none of this to me but burst out a few minutes into our interview, "You Americans couldn't withdraw from the Pacific even if you wanted to. You are a Pacific power."[3]

The rest was a less articulate presentation of the foreign policies in which Marcos's foreign minister believed, after which we smiled and bowed ourselves out of the palace, as Marcos's guards called it. Much the same view was given to me in a different way later in the week at the University of the Philippines, where the president, Salvador P. Lopez, another friend from the earliest days of the United Nations, said, "No great power has ever voluntarily given up its power. I don't believe the United States will do so in the Pacific, either. It isn't in Nixon's nature to do it in any case."

Lopez pointed to a parallel with Britain's supposed retreat from the Pacific during and after World War II, saying:

> Britain will come back to Singapore and this is what Singapore, Malaysia, Australia and New Zealand all want. I think the United States and Britain already have decided to stick it out—and this in spite of an adverse public opinion in the United States.
>
> Anyway, [this with emphasis] I can't believe that the United States will give up its power to Japan or yield it by default to either Russia or China.

It was clear enough to me then, during my visit to the Philippines, that Foreign Minister Romulo's concept of Filipino-American relations had prevailed at the two other most influential offices in Manila besides the Padre Faura. If I had had the time and the inclination, of course, I knew I'd have found some opposition, especially those who sympathized with the Hukbalahops, the radical students and country people who had taken to the hills in Luzon in opposition to the Marcos regime. But there would be time enough for that.

However much Rommy's beliefs may have been shaped by his experiences as an American army officer in combat against the Japanese and as an American Pulitzer Prize-winning journalist, he had given me a few moments of optimism about the new role of the United States in the Pacific. And for that I was grateful.

. . .

It was the overly confident Japanese attitude that had bothered me at the outset of my journey in the Asian Pacific, something that I had expected but scarcely to as large a degree as I had witnessed.

During my interview on June 19 with Eisaku Sato, then the three-time prime minister, he had cast aside the niceties of diplomatic discourse from the outset with his summation of Japanese-American trade rivalries. The objective, he began mildly enough, had been from the outset to conduct trade problems in such a manner as not to impede relations between the two countries. "And there," he said, "is where the difficulty lies."

Textiles and electrical goods, at that point, were the problems that required negotiation with Washington, the prime minister continued, but he appeared concerned over what he believed to be a rise in American sentiment for greater protectionism for American goods sold abroad. However, instead of being willing to listen to a reduction in the large balance of trade for Japan and against the United States, he argued that import restrictions were not the only way to resolve so intricate a problem.

Everything else we discussed at considerable length appeared to be secondary, at that particular time, to the Japanese interest in maintaining their huge favorable trade balance. To justify his position, the prime minister recalled everything from Japanese dissatisfaction with the Treaty of Portsmouth of 1905 (Theodore Roosevelt's fault, of course) to American boycotts of Japanese goods and various immigration restrictions.

That spirit of resistance, Sato said, seemed once again to be rising in Japan today, and it was a matter of concern to him and to his government. But as to Japan's national security, he took refuge in a frequently expressed belief that the United States would continue to honor its commitments in the Pacific. However, he said he didn't believe the American invasion of Cambodia was "a good thing" and he hoped for an eventual settlement of the Vietnam War. But in concluding the interview, he also expressed fear that it would take greater effort and patience to maintain peace in a world that has grown "smaller and more dangerous." It was his conclusion, as well, that Japan believed the actions of the United States, the Soviet Union, and China would be crucial to the question of war or peace.

At the Japanese version of the Pentagon in Rappongi on June 22, the director general of the Japanese Defense Agency, Yasuhiro Nakasone, briefly outlined the country's security program—the development of enough sea power and air power, together with a small but hard-hitting army, "to make the Sea of Japan the Lake of Japan," as he put it. Nakasone also had concluded that, with the renewal of the Mutual Security Treaty, the Japanese and American forces should be linked in a joint use of bases and other measures "more appropriate to powers of equal rank."

Nakasone, an ex-Navy commander, wanted no NATO base arrangements under Japan's "no war" constitution but, as he put it, "Something more appropriate to Japan's needs." When I asked what would happen if there were an American pullback in the Pacific, he said it would be a very grave matter for Korea and Taiwan, but he believed Japan would be able to defend itself by conventional means. For a nuclear deterrent, in the absence of a Japanese nuclear device, he conceded his people still would have to depend on the United States.

His final remark, a tough one, was that the United States now was having more trouble with textiles than its base on Okinawa. Like Prime Minister Sato, the director of the Japanese Defense Agency seemed more concerned with maintaining the country's trade advantage than anything else. Nor did the possibility of an American military pullback in the Pacific overly concern him. [4]

Other than that, my conversations with others, including more Japanese officials, close friends, and former students, demonstrated without doubt that the good life had come to Japan's middle class. The satisfaction of the mainstream public across the land was clearly evident wherever we traveled either in Tokyo or at the World's Fair in Osaka, in Kyoto, and smaller cities. Particularly at the World's Fair, it seemed to be a part of the scene that Japanese people not previously known to us wanted to pose with us for pictures. However, in my visits to various universities, invariably I came across the bitterest kind of anti-American prejudice that sometimes verged on violence.

When we stopped off at Seoul at the end of the month and remained there in the first week of July, the Japanese influence was also evident in trade and finance. Two-thirds of foreign funds in South Korea then, so we were told, were Japanese, and wartime security in large part still prevailed. With North Korea still dependent on Russian support, American forces in the south exceeded 60,000—twice as many as President Nixon had sent into Cambodia and almost as quickly withdrawn after the peace riots.

It did not surprise me when I heard unofficial speculation in American circles that in the long run Japan might assume at least part of the responsibility for the security of South Korea, however unpalatable it might be to the Korean people. After a helicopter trip to the still fortified demilitarized zone at Panmunjom almost a decade after the end of the shooting in Korea, a peaceful flight without seeing an enemy rifleman, I concluded that there might be a basis for more South Korean nervousness over a resurgent Dai Nippon than the waning threat from the Communist North.

I learned, too, that the worry over the Japanese economic colossus was felt as far south as Hong Kong. On a flight from Seoul during the first weekend in July, we had stopped off in Hong Kong to make sure we'd have a place to rest our heads while I taught in the fall semester at the Chinese University of Hong Kong.

The suggestion had come from my ever-practical wife, who reminded me en route that she supposed we could move into the Hong Kong Hilton for four months if all else failed but it might be a trifle expensive. However, we found that the university people had an apartment for us at Inter-University Hall in Shatin and an office for me at 545 Nathan Road. We also had time during the Hong Kong stopover to cancel a trip to Cambodia via Pan Am in order to extend our visit in Saigon, which still seemed more important to me.

In the light of my Manila experience, however, what impressed me at our Hong Kong stopover in particular was a morning's discussion arranged by university administrators with some of Hong Kong's academics, business people, and journalists. I was by no means a complete stranger to the group, for one member was my Columbia colleague Professor Frederick T. C. Yu and another was a former student, Robert Ho, the editor of a local paper, *Kung Sheung*.

As I had expected, Hong Kong was bound to be panicky over an eventual Chinese Communist takeover from Britain. What surprised me was the growing concern in Hong Kong over the Japanese threat to its status as an Asian bellwether in business and finance. It seemed to me that the Crown Colony's influential citizenry were not at all certain what their position was likely to be in a prolonged economic struggle against the Japanese colossus.

That, I believe, explains the dour mood in which I arrived in Manila with Dorothy via Cathay Pacific from Hong Kong. And despite the optimistic outlook of Foreign Minister Romulo, President Lopez of the University of the Philippines, and my other friends and former students in Manila, it was difficult for me to maintain even the semblance of a cheerful outlook when we left for Saigon and the dregs of the Vietnam War.[5]

Looking over my notebooks for the opening weeks of that sixth long adventure in Asia while enroute to Saigon, I was struck by the unanimity with which some of the leaders of Asian opinion criticized the American press. I couldn't be sure sometimes whether they objected to the reporting, which was admittedly confined to a few leading publications and occasional brief segments on the TV newscasts, or the indifference of most of our news media to all save the biggest breaks in foreign news.

Even Romulo, our best friend among Asian journalists, had his critical moments in our conversations. Once he burst out with a reproach, "You don't care what Filipinos think." And another time he protested against an image of the "gun-toting Filipino" in the American press rather than the more pervasive figure of the farmer laboring from dawn to dusk in the rice paddies.

But when I asked what he'd suggest to change the use of images of the worst sides of Filipino and American life in our news media, he shook his head and muttered, "It's very difficult," then changed the subject. Maximo Soliven at the Manila *Times* was far more critical of the United States and his own government, as well, for he put the numbers of the rebellious Huks at 25,000 rather than a much smaller figure in the Marcos government's estimates. And J. P. (Chino) Roces of the Manila *Times* concluded that he couldn't tell from one minute to the next what the United States intended to do to repair its shattered Asian policies. Just about the only even-handed editor was a former student, Tony Escoda, managing editor of the Philippines *Herald,* and he was unhappy about the Marcos regime's attempts at news management. [6]

With so critical a press in the usually friendly Philippines, it was to be expected that the Nixon administration would get its lumps in the Japanese press and the American public image would suffer accordingly. Almost immediately after our arrival in Tokyo toward mid-June, we frequently ran into huge demonstrations of young people against the rerewal of Japan's Mutual Security Treaty with the United States. At one point, we saw an estimated 35,000 youngsters marching in the rain against the treaty's extension. Of course, it was all for outward show; the treaty was renewed as a matter of course.

I had a much more serious impression of the hostility of a cabinet minister, Kiichi Miyazawa, the head of MITI, the Ministry of International Trade and Industry, who began our talk by saying the course of American-Japanese relations was "downward." He was, at the time, the Japanese point man in the textile dispute with the United States. He had made a great to-do about American hostility toward Japan's mounting trade advantage, contending at one time that the United States was "going into isolation." He also accused the American press of reviving fear of the "yellow peril," but seemed just a bit abashed when I didn't take him seriously. Still, he complained about references in the American press to "the Ugly Japanese." So it went throughout the interview with the Japanese trade minister apparently content to press for "shock value" against the visiting American.[7]

I heard other violent criticism, too, particularly during university visits, but there was little I could do about it. What did give me a few moments of pleasure was the sight of so many younger Japanese who seemed to enjoy the attractions of the American movies, rock music, dancing, and generally youthful defiant behavior. Often, such attitudes seemed to go over better with foreign audiences than they do at home. So much for the theories about American conduct abroad.

On that note, we took off Sunday, July 12, for Saigon aboard Air Vietnam, no. 751 and almost immediately ran into reality. A former Columbia student of mine, George Watson of ABC-TV, had been badly beaten by Vietnam police while watching an antiwar rally in Saigon and still bore nasty infected bruises.

When I complained to an American civilian official that George hadn't even been given a booster shot against tetanus, I was told coolly that with the increase in American military withdrawals from Saigon more such incidents could be expected. And the Nixon administration wondered why it had inherited a bad press in the Indo-Pacific when even worse was ahead.[8]

30 Saigon Revisited

The end of the Vietnam War was in sight when I began looking around in Saigon once again in mid-July 1970, but the American government's press agents still were operating in force.

There were 101 civilians in the press office and an additional 108 public relations military in MAC-V, the Military Assistance Command —Vietnam.[1]

This staff was supposed to "inform" 474 accredited correspondents —197 United States, 89 Vietnamese, and 188 fron other countries in addition to unexpected wanderers like me. While on another sabbatical leave from Columbia and the Pulitzer Prizes, I was there to gather information for my latest book project—a Ford Foundation study called *New Era in the Pacific*.

Even so, despite the ratio of one civilian press agent per American correspondent, I still couldn't get George Watson a booster shot against tentanus, despite the now infected wounds he had suffered in an unprovoked assault by Vietnamese police.[2] I could imagine how much hell David Halberstam would have raised in 1964 if that had happened to him while he was working for the New York *Times*.

But now, with the American presence in the war winding down, the last person an Army press agent was likely to help in a bind, clearly, was an American journalist. And so, as I soon learned, for the correspondents this was still the same no-holds-barred war in which they apparently were considered by some to be more dangerous than the Vietcong.

In place of the young rebels of 1963–1964 who won the first Pulitzer Prizes for telling the truth about this miserable conflict, I noticed on closer acquaintance with the current breed that they seemed to have a more sophisticated view of the war. Of course, by this time, the government's public affairs battalions from the American embassy down realized the futility of trying to make a bad situation look good. But the only two press briefings I attended were singularly uninformative.

236

The dominance of TV people over the old newspaper and wire service crowd from the United States, too, changed the outlook in a curious manner. At lunch with George Watson and Frank Mariano of ABC-TV early in my visit, we fell to debating whether the TV coverage actually was serving to prolong the war by persuading the American public that the fight was worth continuing.

In my view, although I didn't make much of a to-do about it, the picture story seldom was on the home screen long enough to make much of an impression.

Another time at dinner with some other TV people, the discussion turned to the reason for the relatively good press for Ambassador Ellsworth Bunker at this increasingly hopeless stage of the war. Sometimes there even were a few kind words for General Westmoreland, now the army's chief of staff. And as I listened, I thought of how Neil Sheehan, Malcolm Browne, David Halberstam, and company would have cried out in disbelief at such agreeable attitudes.

To be sure, Saigon and the Delta areas now were relatively safe at this stage of the war; and Dorothy, who again was with me and staying at the Caravelle, did not have to fear another Vietcong bomb that blew up the lobby a few minutes after her departure in 1964. But I took more stock in the prevailing opinion of the older news people I knew who suggested that Saigon was safer now mainly due to President Nixon's threat to Cambodia.

Anyway, it was in the I Corps area around Hué in the north that North Vietnam then was attacking in an evident attempt to pinch off the northern provinces of South Vietnam. Of course there was talk of compromise, of negotiations for peace; but any realist who had seen Vietnam before knew by this time that North Vietnam and the Vietcong, backed by China and the Soviet Union, would settle for nothing short of complete victory, especially after the American pullout.

Whatever else I did while I was in Saigon on this visit, which undoubtedly would be my last under current circumstances, I could not leave without seeing the most durable war correspondent of all, the Pulitzer Prize-winning New Zealander, Peter Arnett. At the end of eight years of ducking shot and shell and unashamed lying on our side about what had begun as just a "dirty little war," Peter—so I'd heard—was signing off at the Associated Press for a rest, reflection, and, no doubt, more interesting action elsewhere.

When I caught up with him in Saigon on July 15 while I was leaving an American embassy briefing, he was heading for coffee with Robert Shaplen of the *New Yorker,* another veteran whose presence in Vietnam

dated to 1962. Since both were in an accommodating mood for an assessment of the "downsizing" of the American part in the war, I joined them
in a cafe where we could hear each other above the persistent roar of the
motor bikes.[3]

Arnett led off with a blast, which I have taken verbatim from my
notebook:

> The Vietnamese have butchered each other for 2,000 years and I
> see no prospect that the fighting will end soon. The ARVN [South
> Vietnamese] are stronger now so they can take over as the U.S. pulls
> out. But the North Vietnamese are even stronger, so this kind of war
> could go on for quite a while with the U.S. supplying one side and the
> Chinese and the Soviets the other.

Shaplen's view was just as hopeless, but he wasn't as sure about the
length of the war because he thought the South Vietnamese government
could collapse eventually. "There are too many factions, too little chance
of union," he said. "The state of the economy also is crucial now. The
land reform program is being sabotaged. The *montagnards* in the countryside are being denied aid."

Arnett agreed the current ARVN government couldn't last much
longer but he was, quite frankly, relieved to be getting out while he was
in good health, mobile, and still all in one piece. As the two durable war
correspondents elaborated on the woes of the American high command
and its tricky native allies, I had to reflect on the dismal familiarity of
their opinions with what I had heard from Arnett and his colleagues in
my previous visit in 1963–1964. Then, Columbia was awarding Pulitzer
Prizes for truthful reporting in this maze of deceit to Malcolm Browne
and David Halberstam.

Later that day I wrote in my notebook:

> Really, we know so little more even now of where we are going
> than we did in 1963–64. Defeat so far has been averted, but not chaos.
> Our American government people, with few exceptions, are even more
> defensive now than they were in 1964. And as for the correspondents,
> I find the same attitudes, the same doubts, the same suspicious—things
> do not seem to change in Vietnam . . .[4]

The difference in feelings about this war had developed mainly at
home. And with the Tet offensive of 1968, the protests against sending
ever larger hastily-trained conscripts to this deadly front had increased
frequently to fighting pitch. And there would be still worse to come.

. . .

On our flight from Manila to Saigon the previous Sunday, July 12, one of our fellow-passengers, an American community development officer at Pleiku, had given us a disheartening account of conditions up-country in South Vietnam, despite the weakening of years of Vietcong occupation and forcible tax-collecting after Tet. It was not that the Vietcong had become more merciful. Rather, many of the guerrillas had been ruthlessly sacrificed by their North Vietnamese allies in this last-ditch offensive to force the American troops out of Vietnam.

As a result, our fellow-passenger said, the mountain people around Pleiku—the *montagnards*—still had no loyalty to anybody except their own small tribe, even if they had been obliged for years to do the bidding of the Vietcong. As for land reform, on which the United States had pinned so much faith to attract support from country people in Vietnam, it was perceived to be too undermanned to be effective.

In sum, our fellow-passenger was so discouraged about his work that he believed Vietnam now to be just about where the Philippines were in 1910, and he doubted that much progress could be made toward nation-building for another twenty years or more. And as for industrializing this run-down part of Asia, he was inclined to put off hope for such a possibility until well into the next century. [5]

With that kind of hard-headed reintroduction on our return to Saigon, it was no surprise to me to be dumped off unceremoniously at Tan Son Nhut Airport—a difficult landing at the spot where so many American lives had been lost outside Saigon. We were crowded into the same old crummy airport building, saw the fleets of military aircraft parked harmlessly outside as usual, the well-worn military uniforms of all kinds, and heard the racing engines of so many vehicles coming to and going from the airport.

Then we were herded with other civilians into a line for passport inspection, had to fight a bunch of Vietnamese waiting for tips before we could reclaim our baggage, then had to exchange our dollars for Vietnamese currency at 118 to the dollar (the going rate on the street by the black market operators ran as high as 400 and 500 to the dollar with no questions asked).

Finally, we were turned loose with our baggage and had to wait in line for what could have been the same miserable Air Vietnam bus that came lurching along with standees already in the aisle and every seat taken. But we had no choice—not a taxi was in sight. So up went our baggage, tied atop the bus with a lot of others, but we still didn't move.

Why?

This being Saigon in wartime, I might have expected that there was a racket attached. And so it turned out. Everybody who wanted to reach Saigon had to fork over 200 piastres to the driver before he'd move. Illegal? Sure, but what would you do? We were helpless and so was everybody else, so we paid.

Even so, all of us were deposited on a lot outside town; but now I spotted a cab, grabbed it, and had the driver take us to the Caravelle for another 200 piastres—our reintroduction to the scene.

It was far from a heroic arrival. Except for the masses of uniformed men wandering the streets on a Sunday and the inevitable prostitutes some so pathetically young, plus the mass of spluttering Japanese motorbikes (the locals rode bicycles in 1963–1964), Saigon was much the same as I remembered it. Only, it appeared to be even more beaten. The National Assembly building was rusty. TuDo and LeLoi, the main streets, were so ripped up that it was difficult to cross, and the sidewalk was little better. (Arnett guessed the sidewalks hadn't been repaired for eight years and nobody knew why.)

The little blue bullets—the old French taxis—were six years older than when I'd last seen them and even more decrepit, but the native drivers were just as reckless and demanding as ever. It was a town and a society that were completely unregulated—everybody for themselves, and devil take the guy next door.

The sidewalk shops were loaded with contraband from cigarettes to cameras and watches and even more expensive things. In the plainest restaurants, the food was very high. In the bars along TuDo, the street boys peddled everything from black market piastres to women; and the Vietnam police were seldom seen, except to take their cut now and then. Nor did they seem to have very much authority beyond that. The other Vietnamese on the streets appeared to be unfriendly to the bored, wandering American troops of a Sunday afternoon.

Outside one of the military offices off LeLoi, there were bales of rolled-up barbed wire and rows of heavy cement castings, 3 feet in circumference and almost 4 feet high—a buffer zone for riot control. Inside, a bored GI was shining his shoes for want of anything better to do. In 1964, when the Vietcong were a daily threat in Saigon, I doubted if the GI would have been that relaxed.

As another barometer of the pace of the war in Saigon, we saw that the aperitif, tea, and coke drinkers were out in force on the terrace of the Continental Hotel—something they wouldn't have dared attempt when the VC were a daily threat before so many were sacrificed in the Tet offensive.

However, when we called at the AP office and passed the time of day with the bureau chief, Dave Mason, he assured us his forty news people including some in Cambodia were well aware that the war was still on.

Only the day before, he said, a French TV girl and an Agence France-Presse correspondent had been shot and captured by the enemy, which raised the number of correspondents in enemy hands to twenty-three. Like Arnett and Shaplen, Mason also saw no end to the war, even though he doubted much was likely to happen in either Laos or Cambodia once the enemy sanctuaries along the Vietnam border had been cleaned out.

By dinner time that Sunday, I had picked up enough bits and pieces of information to make me realize that, regardless of President Nixon's posturings in Washington, the diversion in Cambodia, and the fiery campus protests at home, the war still was being lost in the Vietnamese uplands outside Saigon. With the prospect of a drastic pullout of American forces, our troop strength would be cut nearly in half by next spring. Scant wonder I was now so nervous.[6]

However, once we were settled at the Caravelle, where the CBS-TV and the ABC-TV crews had offices, I felt more comfortable because I was among friends. Now and then during my visit, I enjoyed down-to-earth sessions with three former students—Dave Miller, the CBS bureau chief; Bruce Dunning, one of his reporters; and George Watson of ABC, who by this time had recovered both his good health and his spirits after his encounter with the Vietnamese police. It also helped that another student, Bill Beecher, turned up on an assignment for the New York *Times* on a tour that was just the opposite of mine, which gave me at least an idea of what lay ahead for Dorothy and me.

Merely because I was curious one afternoon soon after my arrival, I attended the 4:15 Follies, as the daily official American news briefing was known to the correspondents and some of the more disillusioned government press agents. There, nothing had changed in six years. The scene still was in the patched-up briefing hall at the corner of TuDo opposite the Caravelle, and that day it was over in less than a minute, par for the course.

The briefer reported as expected that he had no news. The predictably small turnout of correspondents didn't bother to ask questions because they knew the answers would be either "No comment," "I'll see about it," or "I don't know." Anyway, everybody was glad to duck out for a drink at the nearest bar or, for us nonalcoholics, the terrace of the Continental Hotel and tea or a coke.[7]

That, with very few exceptions, was the way it was for official sourcing on the Vietnam War now except when Ambassador Bunker or the military had something to say. Regardless of the fury of the nationwide protest at home, the news people in Saigon seemed to feel themselves relatively isolated from the war. Even in Pnom Penh, the Cambodian capital, the AP's Hugh Mulligan reported relative quiet when he returned from the front after President Nixon's abortive move in that direction.

When I saw Ambassador Bunker on July 16, he readily conceded that the United States was near the end of its military involvement in Vietnam but cautioned that the cost of supporting the residual South Vietnamese army would be rising sharply within the foreseeable future. There was no pretense about this lean, silver-haired, seventy-six-year-old New Englander, our fourth envoy to Saigon since my last visit, which was a welcome change in policy. But no matter how much we paid the Thieu government to keep fighting, it still seemed to me to be a fair question how long the new dollar war would last when the American presence shrank to fewer than 100,000 troops within a little more than a year.

The ambassador didn't contest my doubts, but suggested calmly that he believed the American defense in Asia would hold along the "Big Island" line—Japan, the Philippines, and Taiwan. Japan, he predicted, would be "our strongest reliance in the Pacific" for some time to come. Japanese trade with the Saigon government, he said, already was three times that of the United States at the outset of the decade of the 1970s. However, he admitted that he had received no satisfaction from the Sato government when he asked for more Japanese funds for the South Vietnamese.

Like President Nixon, Bunker seemed all for backing out of further American involvement in Cambodia or Laos. And as for China's growing pressure on Hong Kong and its continued threat to Taiwan, the ambassador limited himself to the observation that China couldn't be counted out in a final settlement of the Vietnam War. As to when that was likely to be, he shook his head and couldn't say—a glum if honest outlook on the American prospects in Pacific Asia. [8]

When I saw Prime Minister Tran Thiem Khiem three days later, all he sought was more Anerican money, and he cried for much more from the United States than Ambassador Bunker expected the U.S. Treasury to yield. As for Japan's willingness to pick up a larger part of the tab with the decline in the American military presence, Khiem expected very little from Tokyo. So if the Saigon government was to put its own house in order to handle the bulk of the war effort, as both President Nixon and Ambassador Bunker now proposed, it was clear enough even in 1970 that the expectations of a larger Japanese financial contribution to bail out the United States were bound to be disappointed.

That left me with the final interview of my stay in Saigon at MACV, the Military Assistance Command Vietnam. In the absence of General Westmoreland's replacement, General Creighton Abrams, his deputy, General W.B. Rosson, had agreed to see me directly after I left Khiem.

General Rosson put the position bluntly. With the sharp cuts in the American military presence in the ensuing year, the general said South Vietnam could be held only if a successful pacification program could be put together for the countryside. This was a reference to CORDS, Ambassador William Colby's Civil Operation and Revolutionary Development Support, which I knew was lagging because Colby had told me village chiefs still were being knocked off by Vietcong remnants.

"If South Vietnam can't build a pacification program," General Rosson said, "the whole effort will go down the drain. The problem of the economy, therefore, is more critical right now than the military position."

As for North Vietnam's forces, the general believed they were currently overextended. But, he went on, the enemy apparently had decided on a program of protracted warfare that could go on for two generations or more. It will take a great deal of strength in South Vietnam, given the sharp cut in American armed forces, to resist the renewed drive from the north, he predicted. And on that discouraging note, my return tour of duty in Saigon ended. Like a loyal but tough-minded old West Pointer, General Rosson had shown that he disapproved of President Nixon's decision in favor of the "Vietnamization" of the war. But as the general said, given the enormity of public disapproval of the American participation in the conflict, the president had no choice.

It may have been scant comfort, but when Dorothy and I left Saigon for Bangkok the following Sunday, July 19, there seemed to me to be little difference between Peter Arnett and General Rosson in their outlook for the Vietnam War—a belief that Ambassador Bunker and most of the correspondents shared in varying degree. As the years passed and the American presence faded, it turned out that the fairly unified view of the military and the correspondents at last was dismally correct.[9]

On April 29, 1975, Saigon fell to North Vietnam, the last Americans fled, and the country became unified under Communist control from Hanoi with the name of Saigon symbolically changed to Ho Chi Minh City. Two decades later, when another American president calmly concluded, "It's time," the United States meekly recognized its tiny conqueror in the heart of the Asian mainland.

The United States had paid a terrible price in lives, treasure, and even prestige for disunion at home and abroad toward century's end.

This was the historic record of the war that had been compiled by the nineteen winners of Pulitzer Prizes during the long conflict, its extensions and its divisive effects at home and abroad:

1964. Malcolm Browne, Associated Press, and David Halberstam, New York *Times,* for their combat reporting.

1965. Horst Faas, AP, for combat photography.

1966. Peter Arnett, AP, for combat reporting.

1966. Kyoichi Sawada, United Press International, for combat photography.

1968. Toshio Sakai, UPI, for combat photography.

1968. John S. Knight, Knight newspapers, for his editorials that were critical of the war.

1969. William Tuohy, Los Angeles *Times,* for his combat reporting.

1969. John Fetterman, Louisville *Times and Courier-Journal,* for his account of the return home of the body of an American Vietnam veteran for burial.

1969. Edward T. Adams, AP for his combat photography.

1970. Seymour Hersh, Dispatch News Service, for his reporting of the tragedy of My Lai.

1971. John Paul Filo, *Valley Daily News,* Tarentum, Pa., for his report of the antiwar riots at Kent State in 1970.

1971. Staff of the Akron *Beacon-Journal* for their report of the Kent State riots.

1972. The New York *Times* for obtaining and publishing the Pentagon Papers, produced by Neil Sheehan.

1972. Dave Kennerly, UPI for his combat photography.

1974. Slava Veder, AP, for his combat photograohy.

1976. Syd Schanberg, the New York *Times,* for covering the fall of Phom Penh.

For Books on Vietnam

1973. Frances FitzGerald, *Fire in the Lake: The Vietnamese and the Americans in Vietnam.*

1989. Neil Sheehan, *A Bright and Shining Lie: John Paul Vann and America in Vietnam.*

PART FIVE

The Trials of Peace

31 Life after Vietnam

After my last sabbatical leave, my homecoming to Columbia and the Pulitzer Prizes was both leisurely and pleasant.

Reopening the Morningside Drive apartment and the old homestead on eastern Long Island required the better part of a week each with a certain amount of delay for the Long Island trip until the new Pontiac LeMans was delivered. My faculty colleagues told me meanwhile that the students in the class of 1971 were a serious lot, not much interested in riotous conduct for at least the first semester.

In any event, with the exception of an occasional antiwar demonstration on campus or in Washington, even the Nixon administration had been spared greater damage in the public opinion polls with the coming of the new year. [1]

Although the winter semester still had not concluded and I would have no classes until February 8 at the opening of the spring semester, the students had discovered me, knew about my Asian trip and my international seminar, and were coming to my office rather shyly in ones and twos for interviews about the seminar mainly.

But unlike the mob scenes on campus and in our Journalism building directly after Nixon's order to invade Cambodia the previous year, these students appeared more like those who had given our school so much of its reputation over the years. I observed in my diary from time to time:

> Jan. 14—This year's students do not seem like the bold, dashing revolutionaries of song, story, TV and print but impress me instead as fine-looking, well-spoken young people with a serious outlook on life and a great yearning to begin their careers. I had thought they'd be disenchanted with foreign affairs after all that has happened in Vietnam, but it now seems to be a matter of major interest to them. And can they talk! An interesting group of people.

247

Jan. 20—A little Chinese girl came to see me today about my
seminar. The procession has been very steady. I was told that 27 students had given my seminar their first choice, a response such as I
haven't had in a dozen years.

Jan. 27—My seminar is finally stabilized at 18, four more than the
largest I've ever had. My first assignment, as might be expected, was on
the major continuing foreign issue of the day—the removal of Taiwan
from China's seat in the UN Security Council that bears the veto and
Communist China's admission as a replacement. I've already heard that
the Secretary General, U Thant, is predicting the change will take place
next year. Anyway, the situation in Vietnam being what it is, I doubt if
President Nixon will want to veto this long overdue change. [2]

From then on, with hundreds of Pulitzer exhibits piling in on my
assistants and me in the Pulitzer office as the February 1 deadline approached, my precious last month of leisure vanished. All we could do
was to expedite the cataloguing, our annual chore, and take note as we
did of potential contestants for high honors—first among them the
Akron *Beacon Journal* exhibits for coverage of the Kent State riots and
John Paul Filo's picture of the weeping girl on her knees before the body
of one of the National Guard's victims.

As for the rest, since I had been out of the country for the better part
of eight months, I expected there would be enough exhibits to give the
1971 journalism jurors some worthy choices. In the interim, between the
time I finished the cataloguing chore and met my first class, I forwarded
my Ford Foundation's report on my sabbatical year in Asia, did one of
my regular articles for the *Saturday Review,* and tried to moderate ambitious plans for the observance of my sixty-fifth birthday.

My international seminar meanwhile had a firsthand experience in
the influence of domestic politics on foreign affairs. In my first visit with
students to the United Nations, I recorded the incident in my diary for
February 11:

My 18 students and I met Ambassador Yost, chairman of the
American delegation, at the United Nation today for a discourse on
U.S. policy toward the admission of Communist China, something his
public affairs officer had suggested. But after two minutes of mumbling,
Yost suddenly left and others had to take over for him. The fear of
President Nixon's unchanged anti-Communist policies is almost pa-
thetic among his subordinates and testifies to the inflexibility of the U.S.
position on the China issue.

However, on the strength of my sabbatical leave in the Far East, the
students were at me again the following day when I conducted a sympo-

sium in the World Room for an hour and a half, with Dean Abel presiding, and about 50 students in attendance. This turned out to be no mere lecture but a serious discussion of US alternatives in maintaining an advanced position in the Pacific after the end of the Vietnam War.

As I summarized the position in my diary:

> Feb. 15—Strangely enough, it was the students who raised the economic argument against the possibility of a U.S. departure from the far Pacific. They even talked about a no-no, the possibility of the use of tactical atomic weapons. However, we came to no conclusion over the question with which I began: "Where does the government draw the U. S. defense line in the Pacific after we leave Vietnam?" I don't think Nixon knows, either, but the question is worth asking at the next White House news conference.

Two days later, I observed my sixty-fifth birthday with a private office party to which the ever-valuable Rose Valenstein made sure that Dorothy was invited but no one else. As I observed in my diary, "The hardest part of being 65 is getting there but once it arrives it's not so bad." After which Dorothy lied gallantly and said I still looked like a boy.

The unexpected gifts began coming in March 2, just before the Pulitzer journalism juries met, when John Barkham gave *Free Press/Free People* a first-rate review and was followed by a four-page excerpt from the book in the *Bulletin of the American Society of Newspaper Editors*, plus other favorable reviews in the *Quill* of the Society of Professional Journalists and in *Variety*, the theatrical weekly, of all places.

It made me think of finishing the Asian book, on which I'd worked while teaching at the Chinese University of Hong Kong but had neglected since arriving home. By coincidence, shortly afterward, a letter arrived from Simon & Schuster expressing interest in the book, probably through the good offices of the Ford Foundation. In any event, it put me in a good mood to complete the book as soon as I found the time and the strength to do so. But I still had to ask myself regretfully, "Why couldn't all this have happened to me when Dorothy and I were so much younger and begging publishers for a hearing?" Somehow, it didn't seem fair to load some of what I conceived to be the best things in life on a writer at age sixty-five.

Regardless of my moodiness on my homecoming, I soon realized quite clearly as a teacher of this post-Vietnam generation of journalists that some, based on the records of their predecessors, would find themselves reporting from critical centers in Asia within relatively few years. Whether it was Tokyo or New Delhi, Beijing or Karachi, and the always sensitive Middle East beyond, their first lessons in international correspondence quite possibly would begin in a Columbia classroom or in my weekly trips to the United Nations.

This was to be my work, at least in part; and although I looked forward to it with the coming of the new semester, I was mightily puzzled over how and where to begin.

After all, in the closing stages of the Vietnam War, the United States now was very much on the defensive in its relations with the great Asian powers, except for the restless peoples under Soviet rule in the Asian Pacific. Wherever Dorothy and I had traveled after leaving Saigon on our way to the Indian subcontinent, I'd found no support and even less sympathy for the weakened American position in Vietnam.

Instead, among most of the Asian leaders who had received us during some 300 interviews in a dozen countries along our route, there seemed to be a certain amount of satisfaction over the victorious stand of a small native Asian army, backed by the great Communist powers, against what we in America conceived ourselves to be—the strongest military power on earth.

President Nixon's last-gasp attempt to rally Asian anti-Communist opinion against the Chinese and Russian backers of North Vietnam seemed in fact to have added to the alienation of a certain amount of influential neutral Asian opinion (true especially in India and Indonesia). And in Hong Kong, where I spent the fall and early winter teaching at the Chinese University of Hong Kong (my textbook, *The Professional Journalist,* had been printed in Chinese), the ominous presence of an ever-powerful Beijing regime was a still more discouraging factor for American interests in the Pacific.

To report on so complex an American position to the home front, as I realized, would require a great deal more background and sophistication than could be expected of all but a handful of graduate students who already knew something of the nation's problems in the Pacific. And even so, the places where they would find employment were bound to be limited to the greatest newspapers and networks or, with a bit of luck, a beginning spot on a major wire service. Nevertheless, a beginning would have to be made on Morningside Drive, and I was one of those who would have to present a meaningful introduction.

The thought that my auditors might possibly include a future Pulitzer Prize winner or two served to cheer me up temporarily, but that is before I got down to spelling out the ABCs of correspondence from Asia. What I had to think of for my young people was how they would have to deal with the rise of anti-American sentiment that I already had encountered from Nepal in the high Himalayas to Bali off eastern Indonesia. In varying degree ranging from disappointment to anger, such veteran foreign ministers as Thanat Khoman in Thailand and Adam Malik in Indonesia were voluble in their concern for the future of their respective relations with the United States. Like so many others among leading Asian diplomats who unburdened themselves to me, the prospect of lessened American foreign aid in the face of continued Japanese expansion was even more worrisome than American military disengagement on the continent.

For such Chinese neighbors as India and Indonesia and the smaller countries such as Taiwan, Nepal, and Ceylon (soon to be renamed Sri Lanka), the anticipated growth of Beijing as a global military and economic power, too, was likely to become critical if the American retreat from Asia turned into a rout.

In my last meeting with Indira Gandhi at Parliament House in New Delhi, her eloquent summary of her country's position in relation to those of the United States, China, and Russia also applied to some extent to those of her smaller neighbors who were similarly affected. The prime minister did not seem to have changed very much since I last had seen her six years before. She was tired after a day-long series of parliamentary conferences; her eyes had dark shadows under them, but she wasn't as tense as I remembered and nowhere near as nervous or as irritable.

She welcomed Dorothy and me with a charming smile—a small, engaging and slender woman in an expensive violet-figured sari, a small white vest and a necklace of dark beads. Dorothy told me later that her dark hair with its colorful white streak had been newly set. She was still very much "The Lady," as friend and foe in India always had called her.

Seated at her desk in her large and rather dark office, she fingered papers momentarily while she looked at me expectantly to start the questioning. Instead, I just wanted to hear her express in her own way what she thought of India's relationships with the United States, China, and the Soviet Union.

She began, familiarly enough with the observation that India still was a poor country and needed aid for development on somewhat different terms, the nature of which she didn't specify. I guessed that what she referred to was the usual American specification for the payment of India's debts in terms of dollars rather than Indian rupees, understandable from our point of view.

She observed then that yes, India paid in dollars for her very limited trade with the United States but eastern European countries were glad to accept Indian rupees, as did the Soviet Union and some of the African developing countries. I suggested that it would be tough if India tried to compete with Japan for trade in developing countries, to which she agreed.

It was time then, and I sighed inwardly, to ask the usual question about India's close ties militarily and economically with the Soviets, to which she replied as usual that the position was "grossly exaggerated." She added, "In trade as in weapons," a reference to large Soviet armaments for the Indian armed forces against Pakistan, "India pays for what it gets. Our effort as always is to treat the U.S. and the U.S.S.R. equally and I think it is being achieved."

I could see I wasn't getting anywhere in the merry-go-round of diplomatic talk and tried to turn to current conditions, specifically, "After Vietnam, will an American military presence in the Pacific still be welcome?"

It didn't bother her. One military presence, she said, created another military presence, and this sort of thing could go on indefinitely. I suggested that India might soon be independent of the Soviet Union militarily, to which she responded with just a touch of impatience that India's defense requirements were always increasing in one way or another so it was difficult to say what constituted self-sufficiency. In her own way, she was being painfully honest—she still needed Moscow's military equipment.

There was a little chatter toward the end about the introduction of TV in India—there were now 15,000 sets in the New Delhi area, and the service was soon to be expanded to Bombay and elsewhere. She told also of going to a village near New Delhi to listen to a program on rural development. But, she concluded with regret, it would take a long time and a great deal of money before TV had the kind of political impact in India that it already had achieved in the United States.

So, "The Lady" politely ushered us out of her office with a smile and her best wishes for a safe journey home. I never saw her again. And Dorothy, who had been a particular guest of Mrs. Gandhi's (having been excluded from Sato, Marcos, and other male chauvinist interviews), observed that her hostess was very charming but didn't like the United States very much, although she seemed to have liked us.

Next day, August 8, the thirty-eight-year-old home minister in the Gandhi cabinet, Krishna Chandra Pant, readily admitted—as Mrs. Gandhi had not—that the balance of the great powers' relationship in India had shifted to the Soviet side mainly because the United States had furnished arms to Pakistan and not to India. However, it didn't seem to help the Paks very much in the third Indo-Pakistan War late in 1971. [3]

But that Indian military victory didn't resolve the nation's more pressing problems, beginning with the basic necessity of caring for the well-being of nearly a billion deeply divided Indian people. Nor would the United States disengagement in Vietnam materially alter in a significant way such fundamental needs among the other developing peoples of the Indo-Pacific.

It was on this discouraging note that my travels and my teaching experience in Asia concluded at year's end when I returned to New York with Dorothy by way of Hawaii.

At just about the time I was becoming deeply interested in the reactions, the questions, and the analytical problems of the eighteen students in my International Seminar after a little less than five weeks of the spring semester, the forty-eight journalism jurors finished their Pulitzer Prize recommendations for the Pulitzer board on March 5, and the prizes of necessity preoccupied me.

The jurors seemed somehow to have tried to de-emphasize public reactions to Vietnam (as if that were possible!). Instead of the unanimous vote I'd expected for the Akron *Beacon Journal*'s coverage of the Kent State tragedy, the jurors twinned Akron with a UPI reporter's work on an entirely different subject. And for international reporting, the recommendation was for South African coverage by a Washington *Post* reporter. The photography jury alone supported the most dramatic exhibit of all, the picture of the weeping girl beside the slain student at the Kent State riots.

The letters and music prizes that year were no help, either. There was no fiction award, and for drama the nominee was a peculiar show called *The Effect of Gamma Rays on Man-in-the-Moon Marigolds,* which was quite a mouthful. The history prize was recommended for a book about a "good war"—J. M. Burns's *Roosevelt: Soldier of Freedom,* with a companion nomination in nonfiction for *The Rising Sun* by John Toland. But there was nothing very remarkable about the choices for poetry and biography, and a music award was proposed for a piece for piano and electronic sound. When the Pulitzer board met on April 8, what bothered me more than anything else was the continued absence of a president of Columbia University from the proceedings, which made me directly responsible for the university's role. As I noted in my diary that day:

> President McGill did not attend any of the sessions of the Pulitzer board in the World Room any more than Andy Cordier did last year. So for the time being, everything is left to me and I have no instructions and no vote. It is not an enviable position.

However, I should not have been concerned. The letters and music awards followed the juries' recommendations as did the journalism prizes, except that the Akron *Beacon Journal* won the reporting prize as did the Filo picture. With the exception of the international award to the

Washington *Post*'s South Africa series, the rest of the prizes were for worthy domestic reporting and comment. I didn't make a great point about the jurors' warning about excessive nominations by the large newspapers, but notified the appropriate representatives.

To conclude the week's proceedings, I spent most of Easter Sunday, April 11, at the typewriter doing the text of the prize announcements for release on the first Monday in May, which was May 3. Once again, there were no questions and no supervision from the president's office. I was entirely on my own—a vote of confidence in a way, I suppose, but it still left me uncomfortable.

After completing my Pulitzer chores and meeting my classes as usual, Dorothy and I had a pleasant weekend break at the annual convention of the American Society of Newspaper Editors in Washington, D.C., and once again attended a White House dinner for the editors on April 16. I noted in my diary, "I thought President Nixon handled himself well under questioning by six panelists. He emphasized our new relationship with China. He will take a lot of beating in 1972, even if I don't intend to vote for him." [4]

The only querulous note in the long period before the Pulitzer Prize announcement came not from students this year but from the Faculty Honors Committee as I recorded it a few days before the announcement:

> April 27—In the afternoon, John Hastings and Nancy Carmody of the university's Department of Public Information and I locked up the Pulitzer publicity and discussed the Faculty Honors Committee's demand for prior knowledge of the winners. They won't get it this year.

The weekend was quiet at the university, and I had a peaceful time over the May Day weekend in Aquebogue. On Monday morning, the campus was calm, my classes were conducted as usual, and all the apprehension about another student attempt at a blockade of the Pulitzer announcement vanished that sunny afternoon. [5] This was my summation:

> May 3—The Pulitzer Prize announcement—No. 55—was made today without incident. In Washington, 6,000 war protesters were arrested for trying to disrupt the government, so precious little attention was paid to us. We were careful, anyway, and sent word to the news people that their press packets would be available at the Faculty Club as soon as the trustees voted. That news came to me at 3:40 p.m., but this time there was no excitement, no argument, no demonstrations. The only question to me was about the reason for no fiction award. It was no great secret. The judges had disagreed.

For the long tomorrow, to use Carlos Peña Romulo's expression, it did seem to me then that my involvement in the national trauma over the Vietnam War had ended—a quiet farewell to the troubles of Asia. For a little more than five weeks in the sunny quiet of eastern Long Island, I enjoyed the illusion. Then the unexpected, the inconceivable came crashing down on me.

On June 13, 1971, the New York *Times* began the exclusive publication of the Pentagon Papers, revealing top secret government documents on how the Johnson administration maneuvered us into the Vietnam War. In his opening paragraphs, the Times's reporter, Neil Sheehan, wrote:

> The Pentagon Papers disclose that in the six months before the Tonkin Gulf incident in August 1964 the United States had been mounting clandestine military attacks against North Vietnam and planning to obtain a Congressional resolution that the Johnson administration regarded as the equivalent of a declaration of war.
> The Papers make it clear that these far-reaching measures were not improvised in the heat of the Tonkin crisis . . .

Two days later, I recorded in my diary, "June 15—The Attorney General of the United States went to court today for an injunction to stop the *Times* from publishing the Vietnam War documents it obtained from the Defense Department. It's censorship of the worst sort and it can't last."

Once the New York *Times* was enjoined, as the history of the Pentagon Papers long since has established, a member of the top secret study group, Daniel Ellsberg, saw to it that the Washington *Post* was able to continue publishing the disclosures. The public uproar rocked the capital until the Supreme Court settled the legal issue. As I noted then in my diary:

> July 1—So the Supreme Court supports the New York Times and the Washington Post by holding the government had not proved the Vietnam papers were vital to national security. It isn't a very clear-cut victory, for the court obviously would have upheld an injunction if it had felt national security was imperiled. It makes me very uneasy but the issue is now drawn and there is no help for it.

I remember that I feared the coming of a struggle between the Pulitzer board, the Columbia presidency, and the university trustees if the New York *Times* and the Washington *Post,* among others, sought a Pulitzer Prize for public service because of their publication of the Pentagon Papers.

For a quarter-century since then, all major parties to the issue have given their views and described in some detail their part in the proceedings. I have not until now, even though I was Columbia University's administrator of the prizes and the secretary of the prize board. However, through changed circumstances and the passage of time I shall do so in the next chapter and thereby complete the cycle.[6]

It should be emphasized that the Pulitzer board's decisions on prizes in the late 1960s and early 1970s for Vietnam War reporting and attendant domestic turmoil came at a time of immense change at Columbia. In fairness to Presidents Kirk, Cordier, and McGill, therefore, emergencies at the university often obliged them to leave the administration's views on the Pulitzer board to me. The J-school dean was then not a board member.

As a fact-finding commission reported on Columbia's riots in 1968, President Kirk was deeply involved in combating building seizures and student strikes partly attributed to the Vietnam War and the radical Students for a Democratic Society. With his resignation in 1968, President Kirk concluded a sixteen-year career as Columbia's president and an additional two years as acting president in General Eisenhower's absences from Morningside Heights until he entered the White House in 1953.

Dean Cordier, who succeeded President Kirk, served only a little more than a year as university president until 1970, mainly struggling against more student strikes and building closures before being succeeded by William James McGill Sr., who had been chancellor of the University of California at San Diego. President McGill, as will be shown in the following pages, then had to shoulder the responsibility both to keep Columbia functioning and to oppose the trustees of the university who tried to block well-merited Pulitzer Prizes for the publication of the Pentagon Papers. Dean Cordier, meanwhile, returned to the School of International Affairs until 1972.

32 Turmoil at Columbia

The New York *Times*'s 1972 bid for a Pulitzer Prize for its Pentagon Papers disclosures touched off the most violent reaction in my twenty-six years at Columbia.

The infighting reached such a low point that the Columbia president, William J. McGill, publicly guaranteed the Pulitzer board that he would not permit the university trustees to block their decision in the *Times* case. And he kept his word, although he couldn't resist a last-minute jibe at "those who steal papers." [1]

But even within the Pulitzer board, the divisions were deep, although the members tried to avoid personal brawling in the required absence of the *Times*'s representative, James Reston, as a party to the issue. In the end, however, the trustees objected so strenuously to the *Times*'s award and collateral prizes at other periods that they yielded control over the awards to the Pulitzer board three years later.

To separate this divisive university conflict from the larger struggle between press and government posed by the Pentagon Papers, I am presenting the record I compiled at the time in my diaries. It has been withheld until now out of respect for the feelings of my colleagues, some of whom since have died.

Unlike the Pentagon Papers, commissioned June 17, 1967 by a disillusioned Defense Secretary McNamara and prepared by a Pentagon Study Group [2] to trace the origins and conduct of the Vietnam War, my diaries' entries were written during the heated debate at closed meetings at the university. Whatever my work may lack in clarity, it is at least as honest and as representative of the clashing arguments as a professional journalist could produce at the time. I have omitted only the unnecessary and often meaningless personal remarks of the combatants.

The *Times*'s exhibits of the Pentagon Papers, being the most complete, were the only ones entered for the Pulitzers that year. [3] The largest, consisting of more than fifty full-size printed pages, was for the newspaper itself in the public service category; the lesser entry, mainly to reward Neil Sheehan for his efforts to obtain the secret papers, was in national reporting. This was the first passage in the Pulitzer record I kept:

> March 8—The chairmen of the public service and four reporting juries met today on policy and jurisdictional matters and at once argued the case of the New York Times and the Pentagon Papers. At first, they leaned toward not judging them at all and asking the Pulitzer board instead to issue a special award to each of the newspapers that had played a role in the Pentagon Papers release.
>
> By afternoon, they swung around to accepting the Times's exhibits in public service and national reporting with a suggestion that the board should vote only one prize if the Times comes out on top in both juries. The important thing, in my judgment, is that the Times's exhibits are to go before the two juries. Other matters were more easily adjusted.

When the complete journalism juries assembled next day, another government-press conflict turned up that attracted attention—Columnist Jack Anderson's account in national reporting that exposed another failure of American policy making, this one in the third Indo-Pakistan War of 1971, in which the United States backed the loser, Pakistan. At stake once again was the question of honoring a classified government disclosure in the public interest which, even though it was not as important a matter as the government's secret maneuvers at the outset of the Vietnam War, nevertheless bore on the same principle. An entirely separate entry, that of Peter R. Kann of the *Wall Street Journal,* dealt with the reporting of the Indo-Pakistan conflict itself and had nothing to do with the press-government issue.

In the *Times*-Anderson cases, this was what happened in my record of the two-day jury session:

> March 9—The 46 Pulitzer Journalism Jurors went to work at 9:30 a.m. on almost 700 entries in all categories. All went well until we broke for lunch when Bill McGill, with the Pentagon and Anderson Papers in mind, assured the jurors that he and his associates would not permit (his phrasing) the trustees of the university to interfere with the juries' verdicts. Everybody then went back to work until 5:30 p.m.
>
> March 10—The Pulitzer Journalism Juries unanimously voted for the New York Times for public service in the disclosure of the Pentagon Papers and for Jack Anderson's revelation of mistaken government policy in the Indo-Pak War for national reporting. The issue is now drawn between the Pulitzer board, which acts on both matters next month,

and the university trustees, who have the final say. I took pleasure in phoning the results to President McGill, particularly after he had asked me that morning "to guarantee the impartiality of the juries." The people in both juries concerned are all conservatives and mostly from small papers.

Other jury choices were also approved without dissent and sent to the Pulitzer board, including the unanimous verdict for Peter R. Kann of the *Wall Street Journal* in the Indo-Pakistan War reporting for the international prize. There was another Indo-Pakistan War recommended award, too, a second photography prize for one of the nation's outstanding combat photographers, the German-born Horst Faas of the AP, which he shared with Michel Laurent.

Between the juries' deliberations and the decisive meeting of the Pulitzer board on April 13, I prepared the documents and briefing papers for the board's members, met my classes, approved Simon & Schuster's decision to send bound galley proofs of my Asia book to fifteen critics and others, and even had a little time for relaxation as the following entries indicate:

March 14—We saw the best show of the season tonight—Joan Sutherland and Luciano Pavarotti in "Daughter of the Regiment" at the Metropolitan Opera. The house was packed and the singers did all the old tricks with Donizetti's music—and everybody loved it. The living theater is comatose in the U.S. today but the dance and opera are very much alive. This, anyway, was my reward for working all day on the Pulitzer materials and sending them to the printers' for the use of the Pulitzer board.

March 16—To the UN with my international class for a Mideast briefing and it was pleasant to see all my old friends once again.

March 19—I am about halfway through the writing of the third edition of my textbook, "The Professional Journalist," and think I can finish it before June 1, given a few long week-ends.

March 21—I finished picking my Pulitzer jury panels for 1973 and we celebrated in the evening by seeing Clifford Odets's "The Country Girl" at the Billy Rose Theater. It is no great shakes as a play but it was wonderful to see Jason Robards, Maureen Stapleton and George Grizzard acting as if their lives depended on it. A fine evening in the theater. [4]

April 5—Bill Petersen, chairman of the Columbia trustees, phoned to say that Joe Papp had charged in a letter that Walter Kerr (a leading critic and a Pulitzer juror) was prejudiced against "Sticks and Bones" for a Pulitzer Prize. I learned only later that the Drama Jury Report had just come in and there will be no award this year. "Sticks and Bones" —an anti-war play—didn't get one vote. [5]

April 10—Eight out of ten of my term paper first drafts have come in and I read them tonight, criticized them and decided to give them back tomorrow. Dean Abel told me today that the main opponent to the New York Times award among the trustees is Arthur Krim of United Artists. Dean Abel said he told McGill that the trustees simply could not vote down a Times award even if it means a resignation from the trustees.

April 12—First, came my McGill briefing on the Pulitzers before the board meeting tomorrow and he made little comment, gave few instructions. When I asked him if I could go to the meeting of the American Society of Newspaper Editors in Washington as usual, he said yes. Then he suddenly laughed and said if he were I, he wouldn't come back. In the afternoon, to the Carlyle to brief Joseph Pulitzer Jr. and he also laughed when I warned him of the trustees' opposition to the New York Times and Jack Anderson awards.

It was in this atmosphere that the Pulitzer board meeting took place in the World Room next day. The discussion lasted for more than an hour, with Chairman Pulitzer leading the fight for the *Times* and Vermont Royster of the *Wall Street Journal* opposing the award with help from several other members. But finally, somebody—and I'm not sure who it was in the tangle of voices at the moment—asked, "Vermont, if the Wall Street Journal had had the Pentagon Papers, would you have published them?"

Without hesitation, Royster replied, "Yes."

That ended the debate. The board voted unanimously for the combined *Times* exhibits as the recipient of the 1972 public service gold medal for the publication of the Pentagon Papers, and that was that. The Anderson prize also was approved by a split decision in national reporting, and the Kann war reporting in the Indo-Pakistan War carried off the international award. I concluded:

Barbara Tuchman's Stilwell book won in non-fiction, knocking out a book by Gay Talese that had been the jury's choice, and there'll be a row about that.[6] All else went through with little debate. At lunch Bill McGill grumped about rewarding people for stealing papers but nobody argued with him. He didn't go to the board meeting, morning or afternoon, and just shrugged when asked why he didn't attend as a member. He said he had a standing offer to go back to San Diego, California and Stanford.

So it was off to Aquebogue for Dorothy and me after I did the minutes and filled in the publicity office. Then, I began the long business of doing all the press releases, the orders for checks and the engraving on the gold medal, the engraved prize citations the formal letters and telegrams of notification to the winners. I was up until 1 a.m. and I can't do that very often now. There must be an easier way for a 66-year-old professor to earn a living.

In mid-April, Dorothy and I had a lovely time at the annual ASNE meeting in Washington and the usual White House reception by President and Mrs. Nixon. The president ducked the pending issue of the Pulitzer gold medal for the *Times*'s Pentagon Papers exposé, on which the trustees had yet to vote, and remarked instead on the importance of the Columbia journalism school. Unblushingly, I followed his lead and briefly held up the receiving line while I introduced Dorothy as a descendant of the White House furniture maker, Charles Honoré Lannuier. For my brashness, Mrs. Nixon rewarded both of us later with a personally conducted tour of the upstairs White House—the Lincoln and Queen's bedrooms and two sitting rooms, charming places all. In my diary for April 20, I concluded, "The State dining room was crammed and everybody had a fine time. But Wally Carroll expressed what some of us thought, saying, 'It's wonderful but dammit, I'm still not voting for him.' We were there for more than two hours."[7]

Now the real struggle began at Columbia with a sudden revival of the antiwar demonstrations on campus. That it happened at the university in the week before the trustees' meeting seemed to me to be a coincidence, but perhaps I was wrong. The Pulitzers always had been a target for the college mob, and it was general knowledge that the prizes were to be announced at the time on the first Monday in May. Whatever the part or lack of it that the *Times*'s gold medal played, this is what I recorded in my diary:

> April 24—The anti-war demonstrators closed down four buildings at Columbia today and President McGill went around serving court orders to open them up. By the end of the day, he had them open temporarily—how long, nobody knows. Rose Valenstein worked on some Pulitzer material at home, although our office in the Journalism building turned out to be peaceful. At day's end, Dean Abel looked at a small demonstration outside and said grimly, "This is no longer fun." It never was.
>
> April 25—McGill called in the cops and there was a real bust on campus but Hamilton Hall and the other buildings were temporarily cleared. Rose had to bring in the Pulitzer publicity stencil to be mimeographed but I took everything else home with me.
>
> Dorothy and I heard "La Boheme" at the State theater in the evening and enjoyed it. When we came home, we learned that Hamilton Hall had been reoccupied and the students had fought with the cops

again. The police center is right on our corner—looks like a rough May Day.

April 26—Although five buildings including Hamilton Hall are still held by student strikers, the Columbia campus itself is fairly calm and we aren't affected so far in the Journalism building. Anyway, we are surviving.

April 27—Now that I have all the Pulitzer stuff for Monday, May 1, out of the Journalism building, we are beset with rumors that our students will take over the Journalism building as part of the anti-war campus protest. We had a well-attended faculty meeting with a number of students and only two or three sounded militant including an Indian Indian and a Frenchman. Not much of a threat there, or so it seemed to me.

I had my regular class, which was well-attended, and also was assured that the students' political tabloid for the 1972 presidential election would be put out on schedule before the end of the academic year.

April 28—There was another phone call from President McGill today warning that our students would try to take over the Journalism building, and a request to have a faculty member sleep in the building. [8] However, there were no takers for sleeping in when we closed shop for the week-end, this being Friday, with the executive committee of the trustees and the main body of the trustees meeting soon on approving or disapproving the Times and Anderson prizes in advance of the scheduled announcement on Monday, May 1. If the trustees vote down the two awards I'll have to make the announcement verbally and issue a corrected set of press releases when the publicity office is able to do it.

Just before I left for the week-end in Aquebogue, I was told two of our campus buildings had been taken back by non-striking students, which was an unexpectedly pleasant change in the usual routine. Anyway, the Journalism building went untouched for the time being.

Over the weekend at our home on eastern Long Island, I was able to relax and was reluctant to leave on Sunday afternoon—a gloriously sunny spring day—for the Monday showdown with the trustees, the striking students, and the annual alarm about the threat to blockade the Pulitzer announcement.

All I knew after our arrival at our Morningisde Heights apartment was that the executive committee of the trustees had met for three and one-half hours and twice voted down the Times and Anderson prizes over President McGill's protests. It didn't look too good for the fifty-sixth announcement of the Pulitzer Prizes, but there was nothing I could do about it. I slept soundly with Dorothy in our own bed and ventured out early to meet my regular morning class, which went off as scheduled. The day's proceedings were summarized in my diary:

May 1—There was no student threat this year to disrupt or halt the Pulitzer Prize announcement but I still took no chances. The last of the anti-war strikers were routed from Hamilton Hall at 5:45 a.m. today by campus police. However, it was uncertain what the students would do next so I waited with my press packets at home and covered the trustees' meeting by phone as it developed.

First, I learned that all the trustees at a four-hour meeting last night had twice voted down the awards to the New York Times and Jack Anderson but had agreed to let them go through only after Bill McGill threatened to resign as Columbia's president. After that, much of the rest of the day was spent in drafting a legal statement of the trustees' position which was to the general effect that the Times and Anderson awards would not have been approved if the trustees had been solely responsible. The statement concluded that the trustees had given their approval out of respect for the position of the Pulitzer board. [9]

McGill then phoned me to let me know the prizes had been adopted as the Pulitzer board had recommended and chuckled over the 'compromise' he had worked out with the trustees. After that, Joe Pulitzer said he'd make no comment on the affair, so I was ready with the press packets at the Faculty Club and authorized releasing the details of the trustees' agreement. When it was all over, the only regret I had was that Neil Sheehan, the reporter who had made the whole thing possible, lost out on his individual Pulitzer as he had in 1964 in Vietnam while working for United Press.

It was eighteen years before Sheehan won his Pulitzer in 1989 for his major account of the Vietnam War, *A Bright and Shining Lie,* on which he had worked for sixteen years. It was a monument to devotion and integrity in a profession that needs much more of both.

There was an epilogue to the Pentagon Papers case. At a meeting on June 20, Joseph Pulitzer Jr. and I talked from 10:15 A.M. to 11:30 A.M. at my Columbia office about our projected conference on the Pulitzer Prizes later that afternoon with President McGill and Dean Abel. In preparation, at the chairman's request, I had drafted a statement of the legal position as I interpreted it but, not being a lawyer, I was understandably nervous about any action that was based on my views. This was my diary entry:

June 20—To my surprise and pleasure, all of us at our Pulitzer Prize reform conference—President McGill, Dean Abel, Joseph Pulitzer Jr. and I agreed that the trustees of Columbia University should be persuaded to yield the granting of Pulitzer Prizes exclusively to what then would no longer be an advisory body but would rightly be called

the Pulitzer Prize Board. President McGill agreed to undertake the negotiations with the trustees, also consented to remain on the Pulitzer board
as an active member and formally announce the prizes each year when
the trustees bowed out.

There were a number of other parts to the agreement, as well, which
I summarized as follows:

> The juries for letters, drama and music would be broadened to five
> members each, drawn from non-conformist as well as conformist critics
> and scholars. These new juries and the board itself would be pledged to
> try to be as adventurous in letters, drama and music as we had been in
> journalism. Also, all juries would be made known to the public with
> the annual prize announcement. As a final informal agreement, I was
> asked to remain as administrator of the prizes beyond my normal retire-
> ment year, 1974, at age 68, and would continue to serve until 1976 at
> age 70. When I agreed, JP Jr. said he'd let me know soon enough if I
> were losing my buttons.

All this except for my status took time, patience, and President
McGill's best efforts until 1975 as an academic diplomat, but it all turned
out well. The trustees, with unusual grace, quietly accepted the 1972
Pulitzer Prizes, and the student strikes faded away for the summer.

There was one more development later that year when James Reston,
as a Pulitzer board member, suggested that I should be authorized to do
a history of the prizes for the sixtieth anniversary year of 1976. With the
board's permission to explore the university's records, consult the Pulitzer family, and "pull no punches" for this authorized record, I agreed to
do the work and hoped for the best. [10]

But three days before our Pulitzer Prize reform meeting on June 17,
1972, there was a peculiar incident of which none of us took much
account at first. A night watchman, while making his rounds at a large
building in Washington, D.C., noticed a door there had been kept open
with a piece of surgical tape across the lock.

When the watchman called the police, five men were arrested for
breaking into the offices of the Democratic National Committee in the
Watergate office building. It marked the beginning of an inquiry that was
to shake the American government to its roots and destroy the career
of the thirty-seventh president of the United States, Richard Milhous
Nixon.

33 Watergate in Retrospect

When Howard Simons died at sixty on June 13, 1989, the Washington *Post* acknowledged that he had played an "important part" in its rise to national prominence.

Howie, as he was known to his staff, did better than that. He literally broke the Watergate scandal wide open through sheer persistence by leading the *Post*'s day-to-day crusade for justice that ended at last with President Nixon's resignation.

This is taking nothing away from Bob Woodward and Carl Bernstein,[1] the reporters who helped Howie win the Pulitzer Prize gold medal for public service for the *Post* or his superiors, Katharine Graham, chairman of the Washington Post Co., and the executive editor, Benjamin C. Bradlee. They also had a lot riding on the outcome.

But as Woodward wrote after Howie's death, he was "the one who ran around the newsroom inspiring, shouting, directing, insisting that we not abandon our inquiry, whatever the level of denials or denunciations." And in the end, as the *Post*'s managing editor, he was content when justice triumphed after a lot of close calls.[2]

If so gallant an adventure in good government is to mean anything for the American future, however, every new generation should have its own view of Watergate in retrospect and decide for itself, as Howie did, what should be done to hold its highest public officials to their oath of office. And that is particularly urgent for the newest generation that will come of age early in the next century with the ebbing of the current high tide of public disillusionment in our federal establishment.

That is the reason for this account of Watergate which, unlike the usual and well-deserved repetition of how two cub reporters won their Pulitzers, emphasizes the dedicated leadership of an unselfish veteran journalist in a cause that so many already had abandoned as hopeless.

No matter how many marvelous new gadgets the journalists of tomorrow will have to learn to use instead of their well-bitten pencils and

265

wadded copy paper and their busted Underwoods and Remingtons, it should never be forgotten that no computer or fancy announcer forced President Nixon to plead in his last extremity before resignation, "I am not a crook." Somebody is still going to have to lead, to inspire, to urge the diggers after truth to persevere. You'll never find a chip to do that.

Howie Simons's beginnings are familiar in this broad land of ours which, despite all its grievous shortcomings and violent prejudices in matters of race and religion, still offers opportunities to a few of humble birth who are willing to read, work, hope, and eventually seize the main chance whatever it is.

He was born in Albany, New York, to loving Jewish immigrant parents who lost all they had during the year of his birth, 1929, the onset of the Great Depression. By the time he was in the sixth grade, he was sweeping a grocery store's floors to bring home a few dollars for food, but he never felt sorry for himself. These were the conditions that confronted other less than affluent newcomers to the American way of life early in this century. So he accepted it, did the best he could, and doggedly forced his way through grade and high school and, finally, a fine small institution in Schenectady, New York, Union College.

The record shows that he did almost anything honest that came to hand to pay his way—washing dishes, selling ice cream, cleaning floors, working in the school library and the like. This wasn't a matter of pride with him or others who had to do much the same thing to pay their way. It was a means of survival—and Howie was a survivor to begin with.

I first met him when he was twenty-three years old as a student at Columbia's Graduate School of Journalism in the fall of 1951. Just how or why he decided to become a newspaperman, I do not know. There is one story that he and two friends put out a little one-page newspaper when he was only seven or eight and somewhere found a printing kit, but any number of kids could have done that.

Anyway, whatever his beginnings, Howie may not have been the greatest student in that truly remarkable class of 1952, the second I'd helped offer to instruct in news writing and so on, but he also was far from the worst. Although I didn't start my Pulitzer diaries that year—all I had for the 1952s was a small black notebook for the spring semester —I do remember Howie as a small, doggedly persistent young man who made his deadlines, demonstrated a talent for investigative journalism, and seemed to be well-liked by his classmates.

To the doubters who would smile at the clarity of such recollections, I would offer the ultimate defense of any teacher worthy of the profession that some in this class became lifelong friends with whom I still correspond now in my ninetieth year. Together with my first night class in General Studies in 1948 and the first class in the J-school, 1951, the 1952s from Father (later Professor) John Bremner to Kevin Delany, Sam McKeel, Stan Asimov, and Howie Simons helped make a teacher out of me. So I have the best of reasons to remember them in what turned out to be a more crucial year for me than for most of them.

But to get on with Howie's story, he attracted notice in Washington first as a science writer in 1954, doing regular pieces for an agency, Science Service. Two years later, he was doing a series from Moscow on Soviet progress in science that happened to anticipate the launching of Sputnik in 1957 into the stratosphere. Having married upon his return, he settled down in 1958 with a year at Harvard as a Nieman Fellow, then made do with free-lancing until he became a Washington *Post* reporter in 1961 as age thirty-three.

Howie did a lot of science pieces for the *Post* that won him the Raymond Clapper award for reporting from Washington when he was first with the news that an unarmed hydrogen bomb, dropped accidently from an aircraft off the Spanish coast, had been found in the Mediterranean after an eighty-day search. After that, his course at the *Post* was straight up—assistant, deputy, and finally managing editor in 1971.[3]

Just a year later, early on a quiet Saturday morning, June 17, 1972, Howie had a call from a friend, Joseph A. Califano Jr., the general counsel of the Democratic National Committee, who tipped him off to what at first seemed to the uninformed like an attempted robbery at the Watergate offices of the committee before dawn.

Howie and his city desk pounced on that one right away. Next day came the first *Post* story that began, "Five men, one of whom said he was a former employee of the Central Intelligence Agency, were arrested at 2:30 a.m. yesterday in what authorities describe as an elaborate plot to bug the offices of the Democratic National Committee here."

Even before the *Post* hit the street that day, Howie had insisted on a special investigation. Call it a hunch, a nose for news, a happy accident, whatever you like, the paper was on the job before anybody else that otherwise quiet weekend in Washington. And in the news business, that's all-important: Go get the jump on the opposition.

But the investigators who won Howie's approval didn't seem to impress the lordly Washington correspondents when they found out what was going on at the *Post*. Even as far off as the Pulitzer Prize office in New York, I heard from friends that the *Post* was going with two kids as investigators, one with only a year's experience (that was Woodward) and the other who had made so little impression that he'd nearly been fired but was kept on for luck. (Bernstein, of course).

Well! The mighty ones of the capital's journalists might have damned Woodward and Bernstein up and down, but within twenty-four hours they delivered the first big break that began June 19 on page 1:

> One of the five men arrested early Saturday morning in the attempt to bug the Democratic national headquarters here is the salaried security co-ordinator for President Nixon's re-election committee.
>
> The suspect, former CIA employee James W. McCord Jr., 53, also holds a separate contract to provide security services to the Republican National Committee, GOP National Chairman Bob Dole said yesterday.

With a lofty air, a White House spokesman, Ron Zeigler, dismissed the whole business as a "third-rate burglary." But this same McCord eventually was to involve President Nixon fatally in this "third-rate burglary" and—in the bargain—embarrass another eminent Republican, Bob Dole.

I heard from one of the wiseacres among the Washington press corps by telephone next day in New York. "The Post is crazy to be going against the President with two green kids. Before this is over, he'll take the presses out of the Post building."

So much for expert forecasts of the course of the *Post*'s investigation led by a managing editor with only a year's experience in his office and two cub reporters. But for a long time, Howie and the kids didn't seem to be making much headway, even when they discovered a secret informant, promptly named "Deep Throat" by Howie because the man seemed to know the inside of goings-on at the White House. [4]

President Nixon, well into what seemed likely to be a successful reelection campaign in the fall of 1972, gave no appearance of concern. No comparable paper of the *Post*'s size and position in American journalism was following its inquiry into Watergate. Indeed, some already were challenging the *Post*'s judgment and defending President Nixon.

By election day that November, the *Post*'s case against a reelected president appeared hopeless. Howie, the cubs, and "Deep Throat" hadn't made a dent in Nixon's popularity with the voters. Among some of the Pulitzer board members with whom I kept in touch, Watergate already had become an "in" joke.

I remember on December 2, at the Columbia president's ball on campus, Bill McGill saw me dancing with Dorothy and, as I noted in my diary, "President McGill danced over to us, introduced us to his wife and said he hoped I'd never put him through so difficult a Pulitzer situation as I did last May. Without much conviction, I promised I wouldn't and he and his wife danced off laughing."

. . .

It took little perception then to determine that differences between the White House and the Washington *Post* were not negotiable as Howie virtually forced the paper to continue its lonely effort to disclose wrong-doing by a reelected president.

Even Mrs. Graham now was weakening on the Watergate inquiry, for she was heard to mourn, "Are we never going to know about all this?" Still, Howie Simons and his city desk, the two cubs, and "Deep Throat" kept up the fight but without being able to link the White House to the Watergate conspiracy—the crux of the *Post*'s problem.

Still, in 1972, the Post had developed enough information to uphold the indictments of two White House staffers, G. Gordon Liddy and E. Howard Hunt, as well as others naming McCord and the four arrested with him in the Watergate break-in. That had happened on September 15, 1972.

Two weeks later, on Sept. 29, former US Attorney General John N. Mitchell was accused by the *Post* of being in control of a secret intelligence fund used by Republicans to gather secret information about the Democrats. Next, in another story, the *Post* also linked H. R. Haldeman, Nixon's chief of staff, to the fund.

With the beginning of the new year, all seven of the indicted figures were tried and found guilty. A jury also convicted McCord and Liddy—so Howie and his crew finally were showing real progress after seven months. As a result, the Democratic-controlled Congress set up a Select Committee to investigate Watergate on February 7, 1973.

By that time, I had received and catalogued two big blue folders of Washington *Post* exhibits for Woodward and Bernstein as entries for a Pulitzer Prize in public service and local reporting. However, it didn't do the *Post* any good. In my diary, I concluded, "March 9—The Washington Post's Watergate entries for public service in the Watergate expose and local reporting were ignored in favor of lesser stories in my opinion."

What the journalism juries involved had done was to put a Chicago *Tribune* vote fraud exposé and a New York *Times* municipal corruption inquiry ahead of the Washington *Post* and Watergate. The simplest and most earthy explanation of that decision was given by a member of the jury to me: "Watergate is just a pimple on the elephant's ass."

But that explanation didn't last very long, for on March 23, 1973 when Federal Judge John J. Sirica was about to pronounce sentence on President Nixon's security coordinator, James W. McCord Jr., as one of the original Watergate five, the jurist suddenly received the defendant's celebrated letter confessing to the Watergate cover-up.

That was it for the *Post,* Howie, his cubs, and "Deep Throat." In his letter, McCord confessed that he and others in the failed Watergate break-in had been under pressure to keep quiet about higher ups in the conspiracy who had arranged for the break-in and that there had been perjury at his trial with his associates. That was enough to crack the Watergate scandal at last. And now everybody was pushing and shoving to get on Howie Simons's bandwagon at the *Post* for the biggest story of the year.

Judge Sirica meanwhile promised leniency to any of the jailed conspirators who would talk, and McCord was the first to oblige.[5] On April 5, a week before the Pulitzer board meeting, he told the judge about the conspiratorial roles of former Attorney General Mitchell; John W. Dean III, counsel to the president; and Nixon's former deputy campaign manager, Jeb Stuart Magruder.

Dean took over then by accusing Nixon's two stalwarts, H. R. Haldeman and John D. Ehrlichman, of complicity in the cover-up. After that, Senator Sam Ervin Jr. of North Carolina, the chairman of the Senate's investigating committee, had all the witnesses he needed for a direct attack on the presidency.

A shaken Nixon had no alternative. He gave all his remaining operatives the protection of executive privilege rather than let them be forced to talk, then said everybody in the White House was willing to cooperate with the Ervin committee. It was a typical Nixon ploy; but this time it didn't work, even though he went on national TV to seek the sympathy of the public. Still, the public wasn't moved to support him now.

The Washington *Post* had become the paper to watch, and Woodward and Bernstein no longer were mere cub reporters. They were variously identified by the papers that either picked up or rewrote their articles as investigative reporters, specialists with sources inside the White House (meaning "Deep Throat," whom they never identified), and even political experts.

Regardless of what they were called, they produced results; and Howard Simons, as their managing editor, expressed his pride in their work, even before the anticipated award of the Pulitzer Prize gold medal to his newspaper.

When the Pulitzer board met on April 12 at Columbia, the outcome was foreordained with Chairman Pulitzer leading the membership in the award of the cherished Pulitzer Prize gold medal for public service to the Washington *Post* for "its investigation of the Watergate case." Knowing something of the magnificent effort Howie had made that ultimately had benefited the nation as well as his newspaper, I had hoped that somebody might have put in a few words for him. But nobody did. I noted in my diary:

April 12—The Pulitzer board meeting went well. In two hours and 46 minutes, the board approved 19 Prizes prizes with a lot of discussion of the main one. The Washington Post's Watergate expose now won unanimously for the public service gold medal. The Chicago Tribune was given instead the prize for general local reporting.

As a board member, James Reston of the New York *Times* made a valiant effort to gain recognition for Woodward and Bernstein; but the rest of the board's membership, including those who had denied Neil Sheehan a part in the *Times*'s prize for the Pentagon Papers a year earlier, ruled that the *Post* alone deserved the gold medal. It was a position with which I disagreed in both the *Times* and *Post* cases, but I couldn't change the board's opinion. However, a third member of the *Post*'s staff, the political columnist, David Broder, won a separate prize for commentary.

Now, the issue went before the university's trustees, who still retained veto power over any prize they disliked and I knew perfectly well that President Nixon still commanded the loyalty of some of his supporters there. It didn't surprise me, therefore, when Nixon began cleaning house on April 30, a week before the scheduled trustees' vote in advance of the prize announcement.

Among others, the president announced the resignations of Haldeman, Ehrlichman, and Dean, shifted Defense Secretary Elliot L. Richardson in place of Attorney General Richard Kleindienst, and then shamelessly pleaded his case before the public on national TV. To cap the climax, it became known at about the same time that the two top convicted Watergate burglars had previously broken into the office of the psychiatrist for Daniel Ellsberg, the source for the Pentagon Papers.

Thereby, for all Nixon's maneuverings, the White House once again was humiliated because the news wiped out the possibility of an Ellsberg conviction at his trial in Los Angeles.

Such developments as these, in which the Washington *Post,* Howie and his reporters, and "Deep Throat" had no hand, cooled off the ardor of Nixon's remaining defenders among the Columbia trustees when they met on May 7 for the decisive up-or-down vote on the Pulitzer board's prize decisions. Now it didn't take long.

Instead of fruitless argument, the trustees approved all the prizes but issued this disclaimer:

> The trustees have acted on the recommendation of the Advisory Board on the Pulitzer Prizes. Under the terms of the Pulitzer bequest the trustees of the university do not have the authority to substitute their judgment for the judgment of the Advisory Board. They can act to

accept or reject the recommendations of the Advisory Board on the Pulitzer Prizes. In this instance, all recommendations have been accepted.[6]

However, the trustees also did not interfere with the university's award of an honorary degree to Katharine Graham as the owner of the *Post,* and they clung to their right to accept or reject for two more years. So whatever it was that Howard Simons had fought for, he won where the elite of the Washington press corps had predicted the most dismal failure for his paper and himself. Like all his former classmates and other friends at Columbia, Union College, and Washington, I rejoiced in his victory and its cleansing effect on the nation.

Never one to run away from a fight, Howie stuck it out at the Washington *Post* through the final despairing struggle that Nixon and his people waged to try to save his doomed presidency and during the nation's long effort thereafter to heal itself and seek renewal through more trustworthy leadership. But there came a time eventually when the academic life he once had known with the Niemans at Harvard once again had a powerful appeal for him.

It was then in 1984 that he found honor and solace once again in academic surroundings, this time as the curator of the Nieman Foundation for Journalism. And there, five years later, he died of cancer, being survived by his wife and five daughters. To the end, his faith in and love for journalism showed through, for his living family carried out his last wish—the creation of a substantial fund to help native American journalists.

For Richard Nixon, the end was entirely different—a sordid battle to retain his high office, in which the Pulitzer Prizes once again played a significant role. And that, too, remains a part of Watergate in retrospect.

34 The Awards under Fire

As President Nixon faced still more charges of misconduct that were being considered for Pulitzer Prizes in 1974, he struck back bitterly at his tormentors saying, "People don't win Pulitzer Prizes by being for, they usually win them by being against."[1]

The newest accusations had come from Jack White of the Providence, R.I., *Journal and Evening Bulletin,* with a disclosure of the president's minimal income tax returns in 1970 and 1971, and James R. Polk of the Washington *Star-News,* who had revealed irregularities in the financing of the president's 1972 reelection campaign.

All the president was able to do by aiming his fire against the awards before the National Association of Broadcasters was to insure the adoption of Pulitzer Prizes for both reporters at the next meeting of the Pulitzer board on April 11, 1974. Both already had won recommendations from the national reporting jury.

After the jury recommendation, I had noted in my diary:

> March 19—President Nixon's cheap crack against the Pulitzers before the NAB cheering section tonight was intended to embarrass us for the Watergate and Pentagon Papers prizes. However, the Pulitzer Prizes have survived criticism by Vice President Spiro Agnew, now resigned. They will survive criticism by President Nixon, too.

The reference to Agnew had to do with his own attack against the prizes in 1970 while still vice-president when he said, "Pulitzer Prizes are not won for exposing the evils of Communism as readily as discrediting American elective officials. Tons and tons of innuendoes designed to smear officials are printed every day."[2]

Three years later, it was not through any prize initiative but rather through Agnew's confession of fault that he was forced to resign as vice-president on October 10, 1973. He had pleaded no contest to filing fraudulent income tax returns. To replace him, President Nixon on October 12 selected Gerald R. Ford of Michigan, the Republican leader of the House of Representatives. "So now," I wrote in my diary, "we have an almost totally discredited presidential administration."

As for Agnew's charges that the Pulitzers had been inactive against Communist activities, a glance at the record by any fair-minded person would show at least a score of awards had been won for attacks on Communist initiatives at home and abroad. Nor did Vice-President Ford, realizing how close he was to replacing a fallen president, waste any time on such nonsense. [3]

Still, President Nixon wasn't giving up. Vice-President Ford had been in his new office only a little more than a week before the celebrated White House "Saturday Night Massacre" occurred on October 19. This was my diary record:

> Nixon has fired Archibald Cox as the Watergate prosecutor, forced Elliot Richardson to resign as Attorney General and also fired William D. Ruckelshaus as his deputy because they wouldn't discharge Cox. All this because Nixon won't give up the Watergate tapes. It looks like a showdown.

Even so, the showdown was delayed because President Nixon wouldn't yield the tapes that had been demanded by Judge Sirica on August 29, 1993, following the disclosure by a White House official, Alexander Butterfield, that all White House telephone conversations had been recorded since 1971. Nor did Nixon name a new special prosecutor immediately to replace Cox; it wasn't until April 1974 that the replacement, Leon Jaworski, was appointed.

But all save Nixon's most devoted associates now were giving up on him, as witness the following from my diary toward the end of 1973:

> Nov. 4—So now Time magazine has called on Nixon to resign. It is like Osservatore Romano calling on the Pope to step down. The New York Times, Detroit News and others are joining in this extraordinary demonstration. It is almost as if somebody had given a signal. But Nixon is at Key Biscayne and says nothing.

Then, there was this summary on the night of the election:

> Nov. 6—We [Dorothy and I] heard "Rigoletto" at the City Opera and thoroughly enjoyed it. On the way home, we stopped at the school

and saw the students working on the election night extra. But I wasn't needed so we left. It was a Democratic sweep as expected with Abe Beame as New York City's new mayor.

At year's end, Nixon was still clinging desperately to the presidency, refusing to give up the tapes, trying to carry on, although his closest associates, Haldeman and Ehrlichman and others, now were under indictment. For myself, I summarized the position on New Year's Eve:

> Dec. 31—We made it to the end of this most difficult and trying year of our lives, Dorothy and I. I seemed to have kept in touch with my students. And in the Pulitzer office, things went well enough to insure, barring accidents, that I will stay on for two more years after I become an emeritus professor next June 30. If not, I have other offers.
>
> Anyway, I finished the Pulitzer history[4] a whole year ahead of schedule, a miracle in a small way, and it now must be approved by President McGill, Joe Pulitzer and others before it is published next year. Dorothy had her troubles which I have described elsewhere [Alzheimer's disease], but she still remembered me now and then and in our best moments we were still devoted to each other after 45 years. Whatever 1974 may bring, I shall not be afraid now.

Moving ahead directly to the 1974 Pulitzer board meeting, there was unanimous agreement for two national reporting prizes for Polk of the Washington *Star-News* and White of the Providence *Journal and Evening Bulletin*, despite President Nixon's objections. The rest of the journalism awards constituted a respectable summary of the other achievements of newspapers and wire services for the previous year. But I saw almost as much trouble ahead for the prizes because of the board's refusal to award either a fiction or a drama prize for 1974. As a summary, I wrote:

> April 11—No fiction prize and the jury is going to blow up—they recommended Pynchon's "Gravity's Rainbow." And the drama jury wanted no award but Newbold Noyes of the Washington Star-News asked the other board members to consider "Raisin," a black musical, only there were no takers. Anyway, Bill McGill had a fine lunch for us.

However, it wasn't the lack of either a fiction or drama prize that upset the Columbia trustees on May 6, the usual first Monday in May when the news media expected the Pulitzer Prize announcement. Nor were there any campus riots, for the Vietnam War at last was simmering down and even the Pentagon now was conceding that most of our troops were being withdrawn. This was, instead, the last stand of President Nixon's loyal supporters among the trustees against two more prizes for the reporters who were helping bring about his downfall. As I wrote in my diary after the meeting, which I did not attend:

> President McGill, so I was told, stood up against the Columbia trustees today for an hour and 15 minutes when they wanted to vote down two Pulitzer Prizes for reporters who got the goods on President Nixon—James Polk of the Washington Star-News and Jack White of the Providence Journal and Evening Bulletin.
>
> The trustees who opposed these prizes are conservatives who believe quite sincerely that they are doing Nixon a favor but who are actually doing a disservice to Columbia University. Fortunately, McGill was able to face them down by a vote of about 16–5, according to those who told me what happened at the meeting.[5] The fiction denial to the Pynchon book, which the trustees upheld hadn't broken at the time, but even when it did it would not be much of a story. I didn't see much chance of an uproar over no drama prize, either.

My forecast was accurate. Two more anti-Nixon Pulitzers made little impression on TV, which long since had taken over the first telling of the news. And I doubted there would be much excitement in the press about the latest anti-Nixon awards except possibly in their own papers, the Washington *Post* and the New York *Times*. What everybody expected, of course, was Nixon's resignation; but he still clung to the tapes as his insurance against leaving the White House. And an able and experienced Gerald Ford was ready to replace him, which seemed just a matter of time.

The day after the Pulitzer announcement, I had to face up to a serious problem when I learned belatedly that the trustees had tried to dissolve the Pulitzer board at their meeting. This is what happened, as I recorded it:

> May 7—Dean Abel told me this afternoon that President McGill had told him that the trustees had "refused to reappoint the Advisory board" at their meeting yesterday. I did not raise the question of whether the trustees had the authority to do anything at all to the board but asked Dean Abel instead to find out from President McGill whether I was to appoint juries for 1975.[6] I explained to the dean that the year was one-third over, my jury invitations for 1975 were ready and dated for today's mail amd we either would or would not have Pulitzer Prizes in 1975.
>
> Dean Abel, once an old friend, now was so obsessed with the notion that he should be on the Pulitzer board that he began a tirade

against Joe Pulitzer Jr. for blocking his appointment, which didn't answer the question of the moment. But finally, I did manage to get his attention long enough to ask him to phone McGill about my instructions. The president then told me to go ahead. He also laughed when he talked about the trustees' refusal to reappoint the Pulitzer board and predicted they'd reverse themselves at their next meeting.

Later, a more subdued Abel told me McGill intended to "confront" Joe Pulitzer in St. Louis and "demand" enlargement of the board to include non-journalists such as critics of the arts, writers, people from other universities, etc. As for the trustees' vote on the board, once I had a chance to see McGill later, he attributed their anger to the two reporters who won the latest anti-Nixon prizes. I also heard from someone else at the trustees' meeting that somebody had said quite seriously that the board, if voted out of office at Columbia, might take the Pulitzer Prizes to Harvard. One response to that was, "Harvard wouldn't want them." Anyway, that meeting is now history. [7]

There was a pleasant interlude two nights later when Howard Simons of the Washington *Post* and Peter Kihss of the New York *Times* were given special awards at a Columbia alumni celebration, and I received the usual honors as a professor about to assume emeritus status. In addition, there was a scrapbook of reminiscences from former students about their experiences in my classrooms and an announcement from Dean Abel that I was staying on "for years to come" as the administrator of the Pulitzer Prizes. It was that kind of a night. Everybody was generous, and I was relieved when it was over.

With the onset of summer 1974, President Nixon still remained under siege in the White House, despite the pleas of his strongest supporters, the Chicago *Tribune* and Senator Barry Goldwater among them, to resign in favor of Vice-President Ford. This entry in my diary was typical of the news of the presidency at the time:

> June 28—The impeachment proceedings before the House Judiciary Committee drag on with Nixon's people still trying to put the press, the Pulitzer Prizes and even Congress on trial. Apparently, the president believes that he still can command the loyalty of 34 senators, one-third of the upper house plus one, to block his removal even if the House votes impeachment proceedings. Nobody else of importance believes that's possible.
>
> Still, Nixon tries to pretend to be conducting business as usual. After a show tour of the Middle East, he is now in Moscow for a chummy series of pictures with Leonid Brezhnev and little else. Somehow, I think both these people are in trouble right now.

When the Supreme Court took part in the proceedings early in July in a special prosecutor's move to obtain the White House tapes, the harsh winds of realism finally blew apart the president's dream world, as the following entry in my diary demonstrated. "July 8—The big day of argument in the case of the U.S. vs. Richard Nixon before the Supreme Court. From the sharpness of the judges' questions, I think the president soon will be told to give up the tapes."

Then, after Nixon's number 2 deputy, John Ehrlichman, was found guilty by a federal jury of ordering the raid on the offices of Daniel Ellsberg's psychiatrist in the Pentagon Papers case on July 8, I added, "Nixon maintains a phony air of calm. How horrible these people are who have such power and misuse it. What strange creatures the American political system can produce!"

Then, toward the last of July, the climax to the long struggle approached with these entries:

July 24—As the House Judiciary Committee was preparing for its TV hearings tonight, the Supreme Court finally voted 8–0 to oblige President Nixon to turn over 64 tapes of conversations in the White House on criminal matters to the Watergate special prosecutor, Leon Jaworski.

It was a demonstration by one branch of our government that the president is not above the law. Will he comply? Senator Goldwater says he'd better and that is warning enough. At last someone has spoken out for common decency and stopped the lying and delays and the miserable legal trickery.

July 25—I worked a little on the proofs of the Pulitzer history now that President McGill, Joe Pulitzer and Elie Abel have approved it for publication, but kept turning on TV now and then to see what the House Judiciary Committee was doing about impeaching President Nixon. Evidently, nothing for today. The high-flown speech-making was hard to take—sounded like a UN debate on Israel where almost everybody talks in code words for fear of offending one of the parties.

July 26—The House Judiciary Committee just before midnight voted 27–11 against killing the Watergate impeachment charges against President Nixon. And that's close to what the final vote will be on Nixon's last chance to save himself. It is now almost certain that the House committee and the House itself will vote to impeach, but Nixon apparently still thinks he has the votes to escape conviction by the Senate.

July 27—We watched TV with friends in Aquebogue at 7 tonight as the House Judiciary Committee voted 27–11 to impeach President Nixon for obstruction of justice in the Watergate burglary. There were three articles of impeachment, all of which carried by the same margin.

It was a sober and impressive scene that was spread before the nation at long last—face after face, concerned and tense, speaking out in measured tones that guilt in the highest place in the nation must be punished. There can be little doubt now that the entire House will vote to impeach and the Senate will vote to convict upon trial if Nixon decides to go that far.

July 30—The House Judiciary Committee completed its work tonight and the full membership of the House now will take over for the decisive vote that will precede the first Senate trial of a sitting president in the history of the United States unless Nixon resigns forthwith and leaves the White House—and high time, too.

The last acts in the Watergate conspiracy as it affected the American presidency were played out before a public that was confused at times, apathetic at others, and unavoidably cynical throughout of the motives of its highest elective officeholder. Never before in the history of this democracy had a president faced the sudden loss of his leadership as the head of state and commander-in-chief either through resignation or summary judgment upon conviction of the crime of impeding justice.

That he and his coconspirators and their powerful allies had sought to blame Congress, the press, and the Pulitzer Prizes for their plight did not matter now. The country and its people somehow would have to try to renew faith in the democratic system and the integrity of the executive, legislative, and judicial processes. There wasn't a thoughtful person across this broad land, regardless of political or social status, who believed that the necessary healing and renewal could come about overnight.

Only a wooden-headed economist who centered his ideals on money could pretend under these strange circumstances that business as usual would settle everything. To view once again the way a sordid act in American history ended through the hastily scribbled notes of an academic diarist serves to demonstrate how far down the presidency had been dragged by Watergate and how long it would take to restore confidence in the system. The finale began early in August:

August 5—President Nixon admitted tonight the Watergate cover-up and withholding evidence of the commission of a crime, both impeachable offenses for a chief executive of the nation. How he now expects to remain in the White House I do not know. If he concedes he may be impeached by the House, as I understand his position, how can he hope to avoid being found guilty by the Senate?

I believe, therefore, that Gerald Ford soon will take over the White

House by arrangement under the 25th Amendment—and soon. The Republicans in and out of Congress now are desperate in their demands upon the president to resign.

August 6—It seems as if the Republican Party itself has run out on Nixon. Almost every major leader has asked him, even pleaded with him to resign. The jig is up.

August 7—The TV people and the newspaper reporters are saying that Nixon will resign tomorrow. There is considerable substance to this. I thought the process would drag out for a week or so but that doesn't seem possible now.

Today Nixon received the bad news from a committee of three Republican senators headed by Barry Goldwater[8] that the Senate would vote to convict the president if the House impeached him. There aren't 34 votes in the Senate, which has a Democratic majority, to block conviction so that's that. Either way, Nixon has disgraced both the presidency and the country and will have to pay for it.

August 8—Richard Milhous Nixon resigned as president at 9:05 tonight.[9] In a brief TV addresss during which he announced his decision, he posed as a noble, much-maligned statesman who was leaving the White House only because his Congressional support had vanished.

True, Nixon once again admitted to mistakes of judgment in the Watergate scandal but that was all. And yet, despite his noble posture, I doubt that anybody had any respect for him. He was too plainly at fault.[10]

Gerald Rudolph Ford, who will become president tomorrow, made a stumbling, extemporaneous TV speech later outside his home in Virginia, calling for a closing of ranks and announcing that Henry Kissinger had agreed to stay on as secretary of state. Ford is certainly no orator, no FDR, no JFK, not even a Harry Truman. He reminds me more of Ike—and maybe for two years that won't be bad.

August 9—We watched Gerald Rudolph Ford of Grand Rapids, Michigan, our Vice President, take the oath today as the 38th president of the U.S. This noon, I was impressed with his speech—brief and crammed with cliches—but cliches it was time we heard again from the occupant of the highest office in the land—openness, candor, honesty is the best policy.

Whoever wrote it for him—and it sounded as if he'd done a lot of it himself—hit exactly the right note of plainness and decency that reflects this country at its best.

August 10—With Nixon's resignation and Ford's accession in the White House, a great calm seems to have descended on the country. The new president and his wife made news on TV today by not making news, much to everybody's relief.

August 11—Nationally, judging by TV and the papers, it is just as if Nixon and Watergate were a bad dream. As Ford said, "The nightmare has ended."

Well, not quite. The ascent of President Ford after Nixon's pose as a noble political martyr in yielding the White House to him seemed too incredibly perfect as a fitting conclusion to a chapter in the somewhat scary modern history of American politics beginning with the assassination of John Fitzgerald Kennedy on November 22, 1963.

I had a sense that something about the transfer of power just didn't fit, that neither Nixon nor Ford had acted completely in character in their respective roles. And yet, I couldn't decide on what bothered me, told myself I had fallen victim to the cynical curse of old journalists, and was persuaded to settle down to the routine business of preparing for the publication of my Pulitzer Prize history. Then, the political storm clouds gathered over the nation once again after President Ford's announcement that former Governor Nelson Rockefeller of New York would be his vice-president when confirmed. This was how the news affected me:

> Sept. 8—President Ford pardoned former President Nixon today for any and all crimes he might have committed in connection with the Watergate burglary and coverup. [10] The president acted before Nixon had even been indicted and denied any deal. However, Jerry Ter Horst immediately resigned as press secretary. So the Republicans are back in the soup and this is how they're starting to campaign for the mid-year Congressional elections.
>
> Sept. 16—In the evening, I heard President Ford conduct a TV news conference in which he said nothing we didn't already know about the Nixon pardon-in-advance. He refused to tell what he knew of Nixon's health and again denied any deal.

Of course, the Republicans had to suffer for all this misgovernment and nongovernment as the polls almost immediately indicated. The anti-Republican mood across the country became apparent very quickly at the midterm elections, as I noted in the following:

> Nov. 5—CBS was reporting a major Democratic sweep of the mid-term elections tonight. By 9 p.m., in the eastern time zone, Republican governors, Congressional representatives and senators were being bowled over like tenpins. It was, I believe, not because the public suddenly loved the Democrats but they hated the Republicans who put over Watergate and all its consequences beginning with Richard Nixon's forced resignation as president and President Ford's pardon-in-advance for any crimes his predecessor may have committed.

As for the critics of the Pulitzer Prizes, including the friends of Richard Nixon among the university trustees, President McGill and Joe Pulitzer agreed during a fall meeting to maintain the awards under current procedures until the next Pulitzer board meeting in April 1975.

It was, in effect, a truce between the warring factions, something I appreciated. After all the infighting over the 1974 awards, I had been sorely tempted to accept one of several teaching offers from other universities instead of staying on to administer the prizes for two more years. But, I had agreed to President McGill's proposal, with Pulitzer's endorsement, and that was that.

All I could hope for now was the prompt appointment of a successor, but even that was unaccountably delayed.

35 A Prize Solution

To nobody's surprise, neither the truce in the struggle for control of the Pulitzer Prizes nor my retirement from teaching at Columbia lasted very long.

While I was attempting to catalogue a record 908 entries for the 1975 journalism awards a week after the February 1 deadline, Chairman Pulitzer suddenly decided to accept President McGill's plan for separating the Columbia trustees from the annual festivities.[1] By that time, I already was back in the classroom supervising, with added faculty help, the preparation of a weekly 16-page tabloid newspaper by 64 students.

All that happened just before my sixty-ninth birthday on February 17, which I celebrated—if that is the proper word—with a critique of the first issue of the tabloid followed by a long afternoon of individual student conferences in my office. To legalize my teaching at the same university that had granted me emeritus status, the authorities who worry about such things informed me that I had been designated as a special lecturer in Journalism for the 1975 spring semester.

But that scarcely resolved the continuing problem of the conflict between the Pulitzer board and the university trustees over which one should have the final word in the annual announcement of the prizes at Columbia. Even as the board secretary as well as the administrator, I sometimes didn't have the faintest idea of how all this would turn out on the first Monday in May, when the prize announcement usually is made, so I took refuge in silence when curious jurors asked me what they could expect. It was, of course, still entirely out of my hands.

I could understand the puzzlement of President McGill and Chairman Pulitzer as they tried quite sincerely to reach a solution of what had sometimes been a troublesome problem during the almost sixty-year history of the awards. But I was also increasingly conscious of the criticism of those most vitally concerned—the people and the organizations that competed for the prizes in letters, drama, music, and journalism.

The complaints, which usually had centered more on the arts, now were increasingly concentrated on journalism. And it did make a difference because all the voting members of the board still represented newspapers or the Associated Press, with the exception of the presidents of Columbia University, who had been absent during recent meetings. But until now, President McGill had made no progress in converting Chairman Pulitzer to his additional proposal that the board's membership should be broadened.

One of the most voluble protests aimed at the prize-giving machinery in recent years had come from Herbert Brucker, the president of the American Society of Newspaper Editors at the time, who had advocated the abolition of the Pulitzer board. In the lead article of the ASNE Bulletin, headlined "The Pulitzer Prizes No Longer Need An Advisory Board," Brucker had written:

> It comes down to the ancient fact that if any enterprise is to avoid trouble, authority and responsibility must be exactly co-equal and must be in the same hands.
>
> "Therefore, why not give the juries, which already have the responsibility—sort of—the authority as well? . . . And while you are at it, why not put a few of those "most distinguished persons" in arts and letters on this new Advisory Board as a leavening force?" [2]

What Brucker proposed to do in effect was that these jury decisions should go directly to the Columbia trustees, something that seemed so likely at the time that I even asked Barbara Tuchman, the historian and double prize-winner, if she would serve as a combined juror/board member. And although she agreed, among others, Brucker's complaint and his proposal were brushed aside.

This is the way I recorded the step-by-step negotiations between Pulitzer and McGill beginning with the period just before I became an emeritus professor in 1974 but agreed to stay two more years to run the prizes:

> Dec. 11—Pulitzer phoned from St. Louis and told me he had changed his mind about the McGill plan for a removal of the trustees from a final "yes" or "no" vote over the prizes. Joe explained that the trustees previously had vetoed only one prize in 59 years, Swanberg's book about W. R. Hearst Sr., and protested only two others, that the complicated legal arrangements for changes were too great and that he wanted things left as they were.
>
> Pulitzer also doesn't want Dean Abel on the board as a voting member, says McGill should stay away from board meetings if he

wishes, tells me I am to retire as planned on June 30, 1976 and says the whole thing should be threshed out at the annual April board meeting.

However, over the winter, Pulitzer had another idea and after I saw him in February I recorded this new decision. "Feb. 10—Joe Pulitzer and I had a two-hour luncheon conference at the Carlyle. He decided to accept separation of the trustees from the prizes if it could be done without court action, but to reject separation of the president of Columbia from the board in favor of the journalism dean."

Once Pulitzer returned to St. Louis and had further discussion with other board members, he added this:

> Feb. 19—Joe Pulitzer wrote that two board members favored his approach to the Pulitzer Prize changes proposed by President McGill— to go slow and investigate. He also will reply to McGill this time by phone in the apparent hope of persuading the president not to circulate a letter he has drafted to board members, together with a response from Joe. I am also to circulate a board-approved list of five newspaper candidates for three vacancies—still no change in broadening the field. [3]

I could, as these notes indicated, expect a great deal of unpleasantness ahead, in which I would doubtless be involved. And with almost as heavy a teaching load as I bore while a tenured professor along with my wife's deteriorating condition that required a nurse in daily attendance at home, it seemed to me that I was all too soon likely to be involved in far more difficulties than I'd bargained for.

It was in this extremity that I received an invitation to deliver two lectures at the University of Tennessee in May, which would be followed by my appointment, effective in the fall of 1976, as the Meeman Distinguished Professor of Journalism for 1976–1977 at that university if all went well. Since the first occupant of the chair, honoring a Scripps-Howard newspaper editor, had been the former executive editor of the New York *Times,* Turner Catledge, I was so impressed that I accepted the offer without consulting anybody. [4]

I thought it would be wise, under the circumstances, to make public my decision to leave Columbia at the end of the following academic year to try to speed up the appointment of my successor, who would probably need extensive briefing before my departure. In a sense too, I did want my superiors to know that all good things must end and I was insisting on my date for departure. [5]

I spoke my piece at the annual luncheon of the Pulitzer journalism jurors at Columbia on March 6, 1975, in the absence of President McGill. After reviewing the request to me to remain as the Pulitzer administrator for two more years upon reaching emeritus status in 1974 and my acceptance, I continued:

> It seemed to me to be important to have a successor chosen by the time of the 60th anniversary of the prizes in 1976. But here it is 1975, with spring approaching, and I think it appropriate to tell you, my friends, that I shall be leaving the Pulitzer Prize office after the 60th prize awards, my deadline being June 30, 1976.
>
> You will note that I do not say I am retiring. After what has happened to me as an emeritus professor who suddenly inherited 64 students and four assistant instructors, I have become a bit discouraged about announcing my retirement from anything.
>
> I promise you that I shall not drop my successor, whenever he or she is appointed, into the maw of the Advisory Board without a word of counsel.
>
> Let me, finally, thank you for this long association with you and let me thank Columbia, both the school and the university, for standing by me so handsomely through many difficult periods.

Having given notice as politely as I could that I wanted to have my successor appointed, I felt much better about my situation both at Columbia and at home. I did not know then who had proposed me as the occupant of a distinguished professor's chair at the University of Tennessee, nor did I worry about the May visit to Knoxville when it seemed all but certain that the details of the appointment could be agreed upon without too much trouble. Through the clarification of my position, I could face the future now with equanimity whether or not the principals in this Pulitzer dispute reached agreement.

However, the arguments between the principals—Messrs. McGill, Pulitzer and Abel—seemed interminable during my last two years. These had to do not only with the control of the awards and the continual confrontation between the Pulitzer board and the trustees but also the dissatisfaction of expert jurors whose choices were overruled from time to time in the arts as well as journalism. Usually, it was left to me to try to satisfy disgruntled jurors and I did the best I could, but eventually I had to cope with long delays or rejections from some of those whom I invited to serve.

There was one other area involving the trustees, the board, and the presidency, the use of the Pulitzer Prize fund, in which I had no authority to intervene and it was the most critical of all. Usually, all I knew was the limit on my expenditures from year to year; but in hard times, for understandable reasons, the university authorities had to economize.

How that could be done was left to my discretion, so that in my earlier years as administrator, I had to make do with one assistant and whatever part-time help I could induce to accept substandard wages.

Still, without any complaint on my part toward the end of my service, Chairman Pulitzer told me that he would oppose any proposal by the Columbia authorities to launch a fund-raising drive for the Pulitzer Prizes. He said he didn't believe it was necessary and concluded, therefore, that the university would have to make do. What he did propose was a wiser investment policy for the fund under Columbia's continued control, but as far as I knew the suggestion brought about no immediate changes in the way the fund operated.[6]

What Pulitzer's objection to fund-raising did do was to intensify his dispute with the Columbia authorities headed by the president and the trustees during the remainder of my tenure. The exchanges between the parties, those at least of which I had knowledge, became increasingly tense until agreement was reached as the following extracts from my diaries demonstrate in early 1975:

> March 9—Joe Pulitzer sent me a copy of a letter he had sent to McGill Feb. 21 opposing any court action to separate the trustees from the Pulitzer board and the Pulitzer Prizes. What he did do was to agree to separate the trustees from the board through the consent of both parties while retaining President McGill's membership in the board.
>
> March 12—Dean Abel asked me by phone if I had arranged for President McGill to order a two-day meeting of the Pulitzer board in April. I told him the president had approved the usual board meeting for Friday, April 11. The dean insisted he'd heard there was to be a two-day meeting and I tried to assure him it was not so. For some strange reason, this seemed to infuriate the dean, for he told me then that he was through with the Pulitzers and that I could run them as long as I wished. I reminded him as gently as I could that I had announced my departure as of June 30, 1976. A miserable exchange.
>
> March 20—President McGill evidently gave up on Dean Abel and phoned me this morning to read me a letter to Joe Pulitzer, in effect agreeing to Joe's simple method of separating the trustees from the Pulitzer board without court action. McGill also agreed to remain on the board instead of being replaced by Dean Abel, as previously proposed. He also wrote that he wanted me to have some kind of honor on retiring in 1976. We set up a briefing on the prize session of the board for April 7, in advance of the annual meeting, and I was asked to circulate the McGill-Pulitzer correspondence to the board members.
>
> March 21—John Wheeler, the university's counsel, phoned me today to read me the proposed resolution of divorcement between the trustees and the Advisory Board. It seemed clear enough, if acceptable to both parties, and would avoid a court session that nobody wants.

The Pulitzer Advisory Board then would become the Pulitzer Prize Board because there would be no trustees to advise.

March 27—At least, we seem to be moving toward agreement. Today I sent the McGill-Pulitzer correspondence to the other board members. When McGill phoned me, I urged him to summarize before the board on April 11 and he agreed. I also sent out all jury reports a full two weeks before the board meeting.

Ralph McGill always said, "Hang on, John," and I will to the end, which is not far off now.

April 11—The trustees were separated from the prizes without a struggle at the Pulitzer board meeting today with the joint adoption of the draft resolution McGill and Pulitzer had approved. As for the prizes, just so-so this year. There were awards for the reporting of a school desegregation crisis in Boston, a tornado in Ohio, a police crime exposé in Indiana, an attack on the IRS and so on but nothing approaching the high drama of the Pentagon Papers and Watergate topped by the resignation of President Nixon with President Ford as his successor.

The only prize that stood out for me was one to Mary McGrory, a columnist for the Washington *Star-News,* who wrote about the effect of Watergate on the English language at the fall of Richard Nixon:

> That was a war in which words were almost wiped out. Through systematic abuse, they lost their meaning. "Protective reaction raid," one of the baser coinages, meant creating an alibi to bomb the enemy. When our former first citizen said, "I am not a crook," what he meant was, "You can't prove it." When he said, "One year of Watergate is enough," he meant the fire was getting hot. When he said he was "trying to get to the bottom of it," he meant he was trying to get out of it.
>
> It may be a while before the country stops reading "down" for "up" and "white" for "black." But a noble beginning was made in the House Judiciary Committee.
>
> Thanks partly to these men and women and their words, we now have a new president. On being sworn, he promised "just a little straight talk among friends." It is long overdue. The country will survive. So may the English language.

Sometimes, as McGrory observed, it does help when the country can trust its president. Anyway, it was worth a Pulitzer Prize.[7]

The severance of relations between the trustees of Columbia University and the Pulitzer Prizes occurred on Monday, May 5, 1975, without further ado. Having been presented with a resolution of divorcement that already had been agreed to by the Pulitzer board, the trustees added their unanimous approval without discussion just before the announce-ment of the fifty-ninth annual prizes later that day.

Fred Knubel, the university's publicity director who had been wait-ing with President McGill for the outcome, notified me of the trustees' action by phone shortly after 3:00 P.M. After that, we made public the Pulitzer Prize packets, in which the decision had been anticipated along with the trustees' approval of the board's list of prizes.

Even at the end, there was just a touch of the chaotic relationship that had been so characteristic of disagreements between the two organi-zations. As I noted in my diary once the trustees had voted, this hap-pened: "President McGill told Knubel, "Fred, do your work," meaning to release the press packets on the prizes, and the university's counsel John Wheeler, rushed after Fred to say everything was legal. And the rest is minor history." [8]

I emphasize "minor history" because the first TV and radio bulletins omitted mention of the end of the long battle over control of the Pulitzer Prizes. Even in the late afternoon and morning newspapers, the creation of the Pulitzer Prize Board through the trustees' abdication of their au-thority received very little notice. In my diary next day, I concluded:

> The Pulitzer Prizes are, more and more, a newspaper show because newspapers have become so important a factor in government, a tempo-rary advantage I fear. Dean Abel told me he'd nominated former Dean Richard T. Baker to replace me, an excellent choice, and I hope he will be quickly approved by Chairman Pulitzer and the new board.

36 Beyond Defeat

Pulitzer Prizes have been won for eyewitness accounts of American victories in foreign wars, for disclosures of corruption in high places, even for revelations of a president's criminal conduct.

But what of those other brave ones who risked their lives to stay behind the lines to report on American defeats, particularly those who covered the final disasters in Vietnam and Cambodia? Were they to be ignored because the news displeased those of us safely at home?

The issue arose suddenly in the spring of 1975 while we still were celebrating the latest Pulitzer awards at Columbia when enemy forces threatened Saigon in South Vietnam and Phnom Penh in Cambodia. [1]

On the home front, we hadn't expected that kind of ending to a conflict that had cost the nation more than 50,000 dead, 150,000 wounded, and at least $150 billion.

Ever since the signing of the four-power peace treaty for the Vietnam War in Paris in 1973, most of the American public had assumed that the conflict was simmering down or ending. After all, the United States and South Vietnam representatives had signed for our side as had the delegates of the enemy on the other, North Vietnam and their Communist allies in the south, the Vietcong.

To us, as a formality, that was good enough, but not for the enemy. Its troops continued to fight, especially after the last American forces were pulled out of the conflict and sent home on March 30, 1973. And in Cambodia, the Communist Khmer Rouge didn't give up, either, but bided their time until the last Americans left. Then, the enemy offensive began there, too.

However, the American public paid little attention to sporadic news of more fighting in Vietnam and Cambodia. The struggle no longer was being covered in depth. And the war correspondents, who at the height of the struggle had numbered more than 2,000 for TV, radio, wire services, and newspapers, now were sharply reduced because so few back home seemed to care.

And so on April 17, the Khmer Rouge occupied Phnom Penh but the world at large didn't hear the full story until an American correspondent in the city took refuge and escaped three weeks later. The conquest of Saigon was completed April 29. [2]

That day I wrote in my diary:

> It's over—the 30-year war in Asia.
>
> The last Americans were flown out of Saigon in a panicky rush today because the army of a 4th class power, North Vietnam, had taken the measure of the greatest and most important military power on earth, the United States.
>
> President Ford and Secretary of State Kissinger have appealed for unity among Americans, apparently expecting to be blamed and forgetting how a militant member of their Republican party, Senator Joseph R. McCarthy Jr., charged the Democrats with "20 years of treason" for the loss of China to the Communists and the drawn Korean War against the Communist North.
>
> We never could have won this time without a World War against the great powers of the Communist world which we were unwilling to risk. And so we lost, crying all the time that we could have won. Our foreign policy in Asia is now bankrupt.

It was not a part of my business then or later to counsel the White House, the Pentagon, and those responsible for the fighting on the Asian mainland on the measures through which such disasters could have been avoided. However, it *was* my job to learn who it was and under what circumstances they were able to report on this terrible last act in a losing war, the longest conflict in American history; to obtain copies of their reports; and to suggest their nomination for Pulitzer Prizes for 1976. The juries then would take over.

In most cases, that kind of research by a Pulitzer Prize administrator had never been necessary because the news organizations involved were usually alert to their quest for honors and did not have to be prompted to enter exhibits.

But now, in a losing war where the details of a military action sometimes could not be quickly announced to the home front by our military authorities, I had to be sure that extraordinary work by correspondents would not be overlooked. And in both Saigon and Phnom Penh, I suspected that the correspondents who filed the news of the defeats had stayed behind, not because they were ordered by their employers to do so, but because they *wanted* to be witnesses to history.

The reporters who covered the loss of Saigon were easier to identify than those who were not permitted to file directly from Phnom Penh. I knew right off that George Esper of the Associated Press had remained on duty in Saigon, even though he should have left for safety when he was able to do so. It was he who filed the last bulletin from the beleaguered city. "Saigon, April 29 (AP)—South Vietnam has declared unconditional surrender to the Vietcong, ending 30 years of warfare."

Two other reporters, Keyes Beech and Robert Tamarkin, both working for the Chicago *Daily News,* escaped just before the Vietcong, the rebel South Vietnamese arm of North Vietnam, battled their way into Saigon. The correspondents joined the last Americans who left the embassy in the city on a panicky flight to the USS *Hancock,* which had anchored offshore.

While on the aircraft, Beech radioed his newspaper, "My last view of Saigon was through the tail door of the helicopter. Tan Son Nhut [Saigon's airport] was burning. So was Bien Hoa. Then the door closed—closed on the most humiliating chapter in American history."

It seemed to me that these three—Esper, Beech, and Tamarkin—and any others like them who turned up later as correspondents who had witnessed the conquest of Saigon and Phnom Penh—were almost automatically candidates whose complete file should go before the international jury the following spring. Beech was the veteran in the group, having won a Pulitzer Prize for his correspondence in the Korean War.[3]

What the jurors would decide to do about such candidacies as these in judgments to be made in the spring of 1976 was beyond speculation at that juncture. But it seemed to me to be a part of the Pulitzer function to reward heroism and fidelity to duty, whether a correspondent was covering an American victory or a defeat. And in this, my colleagues on the new Pulitzer Prize Board agreed with me when I proposed exhibits for the correspondents from their respective employers, the Associated Press and the Chicago *Daily News.*

The situation in Phnom Penh was entirely different, as I discovered long afterward. There, the last American correspondent on the job as the enemy stormed the city's battered defenses was Syd Schanberg, a forty-one-year-old New York *Times* veteran, married and the father of two small daughters.

The foreign desk in New York City had told him to get out of Phnom Penh while he still could and file elsewhere on the fate of the city. Both he and his superiors knew perfectly well that there'd be no way for an American to send messages to his paper once the Communists took over and rounded up all foreigners.

Still, unaccountably, Schanberg stayed on. It wasn't sheer bravado. Having served my time in New York as a reporter, I'd known a few like Schanberg who often shrugged off risks as part of the news business and followed the story because they were too stubborn to quit. From Mike Berger to Ernie Pyle, these were the greatest.

People like that, from the veterans on the police beat to the crustiest old editors, had always been the heart of the business; instinctively, I accounted Schanberg to be one of them. But once the city fell to its Communist conquerors, the *Times*'s foreign desk lost contact with him and guessed he'd been captured, which is exactly what happened to him.

But there was a twist, as there is sometimes when a reporter follows a big story because he figures it's the thing to do. When Schanberg saw his chance, he took off with others for the French embassy in Phnom Penh, which had recognized the invaders. He and other foreigners were given asylum there but were able to leave 13 days later on a foreign refugee truck bound for Bangkok in Thailand.

There at last, he had a chance to file—to put together what he hoped might be the first account of the terror that had seized the Cambodian capital from the fatal moment the Communist conquerors took over. With rare presence of mind, he had filled his notebook with the details of the fall of Phnom Penh and now he had a chance to put the whole thing together in what turned out to be one of the epics of foreign correspondence of our time.

These were some of his observations:

Just before the end at Phnom Penh, "The city is falling. White flags sprouted from the housetops. Some soldiers were taking the clips out of their rifles; others were changing to civilian clothes."

And this at the American embassy, "The embassy is burning some of its files in order to 'thin itself down,' to prepare for the possibility of evacuation—and the ashes drift slowly to the embassy courtyard."

A vignette of a soldier carrying his child, with an apparently fatal wound, from a bomb shelter, "He picks up his daughter in his shaking arms: his face, bathed in cold sweat, contorts as he tries to hold back the tears that come anyway. 'I love all my children' is all that he says as he walks away with the dying child."

And then, at 9:00 A.M. on April 17, the Khmer Rouge hordes swarmed in and took over a city of 2 million horrified people as the correspondent observed, "A once-throbbing city became an echo chamber of silent streets lined with abandoned cars and gaping, empty shops. Street lights burned eerily for a population that was no longer there."

And the people? What of them? The refugees by the tens of thousands began the frantic exodus to nowhere. As the correspondent noted, they covered the roads "like a human carpet." There followed all the unanswered, even tragic questions that the correspondent put down in his notebook as they occurred to him:

> Was this just cold brutality, a cruel and sadistic imposition of the law of the jungle, in which only the fittest will survive? Or is it possible that, seen through the eyes of the peasant soldiers and revolutionaries, the forced evacuation of the cities is a harsh necessity? . . . Or was the policy both cruel and ideological?

But now in the safety and even the comfort of Bangkok, once Schanberg had reached the Thai capital in his refugee truck, the first thing on his mind was to put the whole thing together. And so it turned out, for he wrote 8,000 words of history-on-the-run that the New York *Times* published on May 9, 1975—the first full account of the fall of Phnom Penh and a certain candidate for a Pulitzer Prize.

I had not waited for Schanberg's piece to begin the preparations for the 1976 Pulitzer Prizes, which were to be the last under my administration. Three days before the appearance of his *magnum opus*, I had noted, "May 6—The invitation to the 1975–76 Pulitzer Prize Juries went out today on schedule and soon we'll be set up for the new season."

Still, even with the settlement of the argument for control of the prizes with the agreement of the university trustees to give up their right of final approval or rejection, so many other basic problems remained that I recorded both my doubts and my distress later in the year as follows:

> June 29—I can't help wondering what is to become of the Pulitzer Prize organization I have helped to develop. JP Jr. still wants the Columbia Graduate School of Journalism and its dean separated from the prizes, won't have any outside contributions to the Pulitzer Prize Fund, asks to have the Fund put in bonds temporarily for a higher return of income and offers to put in $500,000 more himself over three years if and when he can do so. All this is a very large order.

To that, Pulitzer had recently added the observation that the Pulitzer Prizes were "entering a period of turbulence" at Columbia, a forecast with which I hesitantly agreed even though I could do nothing about it with my scheduled departure to the University of Tennessee in the fall of 1976.[4]

Earlier that spring, I had visited Knoxville with agreeable results as the Edward Meeman Visiting Lecturer in Journalism at the University of Tennessee's College of Communications. What happened was summed up in my diary:

May 12—I made final arrangements for the end of the academic year at Columbia, presumably the end of my teaching career on Morningside Heights, and took off via United at 6:20 p.m. for Knoxville, arriving at 8:15 p.m. I was met and driven to the Hyatt Regency, an imposing hotel for a relatively small community.

May 13—Up early at the hotel and conducted three classes on the Tennessee campus in the morning, attended a faculty lunch, another class in the afternoon, then was taken to a faculty dinner. After that came my Meeman lecture, apparently an annual affair, before a full house of faculty and students at UT. Then there was a party at a faculty member's home and back to the hotel where I fell into bed exhausted but didn't sleep too well.

For the first time in five years, I was alone at night and wondering about Dorothy. Naturally, I phoned her nurse, Miss Parker, who said all was well. UT sure is scouting me hard!

May 14—Up at 6 and Dean Hileman drove me to the local CBS affiliate for an 8 a.m. TV interview. Then, three more classes back on campus, a lunch and at 1:30 I flew out on Delta for New York, arriving at 5:30. Dean Hileman had said he wanted me for 1975–76 and promised agreeable arrangements for housing, pay, classes and so on but I told him I was committed to Columbia for a final year. He then said he'd like to have me for 1976–77, the original proposal, to which I again agreed but we each left the other with a small out—in case of ill health or a major change in circumstances, all bets were off.

There was one other circumstance for which I was grateful to the University of Tennessee during that and succeeding years. The Gannett Foundation had asked me to consider researching and writing about current changes in public attitudes toward threats to freedom of the press in the United States in the wake of the Watergate conspiracy that led to President Nixon's resignation. What held me back from immediate acceptance was my shift of base from Columbia to Tennessee in the 1976–1977 academic year.

I knew perfectly well, as did my proposed sponsor, that I couldn't have done the research based on new circumstances, let alone the writing, during my last year at Columbia ending June 30, 1976. And of course the University of Tennessee contract, regardless of the firmness of my agreement with Dean Hileman, still couldn't be initialed by either of us so far in advance.

To settle the matter, Dean Hileman cheerfully agreed to accept the Gannett Foundation grant for my exclusive use, meaning that Tennessee wouldn't take the usual administrative cut for handling the transaction. The presumption was that I would start work on the research with my succession to the Meeman chair in the fall of 1976. All parties, including myself, agreed to the suggestion without signing anything—a fairly unique example of academic trustfulness. [5]

I also suggested a title for the book, *A Crisis for the American Press,* and my academic publisher at the time, the Columbia University Press, agreed to give it first consideration, so the work wasn't likely to languish on the back burner for very long. What I deeply believed then in the wake of the Pulitzer Prizes for the Pentagon Papers and the Watergate explosion that wrecked the Nixon presidency was this basic truth about ourselves in America:

When public trust in government declines and affects the faith of millions of people in its principles and practices, the press is the institution that is least likely to benefit from the resultant disillusionment. Nor is the damage likely to be repaired very soon—a warning to the press in all its diverse forms that had better be heeded.

This was the manner in which I approached my last year with the Pulitzers to conclude an association of more than fifty years at Columbia. There would be many a visit and phone consultation in years yet to come. Of that I was sure. But after 1976, the tie would be broken. And so I determined my last task would be consideration for the correspondents who had been willing to stake their lives and their future well-being on their professional skills in reporting on a time of trial for the nation in Asia without parallel in our history.

To that end, I hoped the Pulitzer juries and the Pulitzer Prize Board, in its first year as the sole arbiter of the awards, would give such correspondents as Beech, Esper, Schanberg, Tamarkin, and any others like them the same consideration as the many candidates in more glamorous assignments among Pulitzer nominations in that year of 1976.

37 Auld Lang Syne

There is a sentimental notion abroad in America toward century's end that a university professor's last year of useful service is conducted from a roller coaster of pleasure.

That may well be for some who enjoy the salute of the multitudes of academe, but it didn't happen in quite that way for me during my leave-taking from the Pulitzers and the journalism school on Morningside Heights. To be sure, there were pleasantries and a few awards, but these scarcely lightened the work load.

The beginning of the end was pleasant enough on New Year's Eve before the spring semester of 1976, which would be my last as a combined teacher-author and prize-giver. After dining with friends on eastern Long Island, I'd put Dorothy to bed in the old house at Aquebogue. And out of habit more than anything else, I'd turned on TV a few minutes before midnight to relax to soothing band music and watch the shifting scene on a crowded dance floor.

I was by myself and the old homestead was quiet. Outside, there was a drifting light snow, but few cars were on the road. I noted in my diary:

> So I saw and heard the bicentennial year of 1976 coming in with Guy Lombardo leading his orchestra as usual in "Auld Lang Syne" at the Waldorf Astoria's grand ballroom in New York. And Ben Grauer, the old faithful, was reporting for the 35th straight year from a rainy Times Square where about 10,000 people were capering under umbrellas and waiting for the lighted sphere to drop beside the skyscraper with the passing of the old year.
>
> Somehow, feeling so alone, the old song hit me hard. I sat up awhile longer listening to the music. And when I got up this morning, New Year's Day turned out to be cold and clammy with a powdering of snow on the neighbors' rooftops. Dorothy's condition is unchanged but she will be going with me when I leave Columbia for Tennessee.

. . .

Under my agreement with the university authorities, I should have been relieved of my usual duties in the classroom so that I could concentrate on the Pulitzer Prizes for my last year as administrator. However, that didn't work out for 1976 any more than it had in 1975, for a rash of illnesses felled usually healthy faculty members for everything from nervous breakdowns to critical emergency operations.

While the annual cascade of journalism nominations swept into the Pulitzer office before the February 1 deadline, as a result, I divided my time between helping Rose Valenstein and Robin Holloway Kuzen with the cataloguing and fairly regular sessions for indisposed colleagues in their absences from their classes. That, alas, did not dispose of the still pending problem of electing my successor—an embarrassment to both of us, as witness the following:

> Jan. 19—Dick Baker came back from sabbatical leave today and I told him I thought he would succeed me, then asked if he would take the job. He said he would, so I shall arrange for an orderly transfer and hope that Joe Pulitzer and the board will vote to accept him. There is no one else whom I would now recommend. [1]
>
> As for Tennessee, Dean Hileman said the contract should be here soon but he now has a worse problem. Dozier Cade, the head of his journalism sequence, had a heart attack last night but all I could offer was help once I finished with the Pulitzers for 1976—and that wouldn't be for some time.
>
> Anyway, tonight at the Met Opera we heard Strauss's "Elektra," which I found tedious in performance, but Dorothy was as good as diamonds and more attentive than I.

My nights out, either at the opera or on Broadway, were the exception in a workaday arrangement from which I couldn't seem to escape. More often, my days were like this:

> Jan. 26—Busy cataloguing Pulitzer journalism entries—the last time I have to do that onerous job. Baker didn't show up; I'm sure he'll let the whole thing go hang before he does any cataloguing. Other extras will be hired to do it and perhaps he's right.
>
> Feb. 8—Heard from the University of Tennessee and all seems in order. There has been no argument over the contract mainly because I've been given everything I wanted. So now the arrangements are almost complete—a few more negotiations on various items and that's it. I've even been promised a nice place to live.
>
> Feb. 11—Finished assigning the various journalism juries to look over 856 entries with exhibits including the big one for Syd Schanberg

on Cambodia from the New York Times. Also got up the seating list for the luncheon and now it's up to Rose and Robin to do the stenciling, assembling, mailing, etc. The meal is ordered at the Faculty Club, the guests are invited, I'm finished with the organizing details and now let's have some prizes!

And I always thought that people a few days short of 70 were leading a serene, peaceful old age. Ha! I'm working one hell of a lot harder than I did when I was first married at 22 and doing the night shift on the city desk at the old, old New York Evening Post down on West Street in Manhattan.

Anyway, even though I expected nothing unusual for my seventieth birthday, Rose and Robin apparently decided during one of my frequent absences to teach somebody else's classes that I ought to be shook up just a little, which was thoughtful of them. And so, this was my birthday entry:

Feb. 17—I awoke at six with a shiver and a terrible nightmare that people were running all over our old house in Aquebogue—and then I realized this was the day I turned 70. So I got Dorothy up and dressed both of us, made breakfast and let in Mrs. Reams—wonderful Mrs. Reams, the nurse who stayed daytimes with Dorothy and usually kept her quiet.

When I left for school at 8:30, it was a gray, disheartening morning. When Robin came in she gave me a box of chocolates and Rose followed with a Mont Blanc pen and pencil set, so I kissed them both and thanked them for remembering my birthday. The sun came out and in the afternoon a lot of faculty and students showed up for a surprise party with birthday cakes baked by Rose's daughter, Ann. So I had all the usual, hugs and handshakes and even a few kisses from the girls and a red, red rose from one of them. [2]

In the afternoon, I went home and made an early birthday dinner, then took a chance and asked Mrs. Reams to dress Dorothy for a night out. I had tickets for the drama jury's recommendation for the Pulitzer Drama Prize, "A Chorus Line," and hoped Dorothy would be able to make it through the evening in an aisle seat. She did but coming home in a cab with her I had a guilty conscience. Anyway, it turned out to be a lovely 70th birthday." [3]

There was one belated birthday gift—something I hadn't expected. In making arrangements for the Gannett grant for *A Crisis for the American Press*, I'd assumed that would be more than enough to keep me busy in that first break-in year at Tennessee. However, three days before the arrival of the Pulitzer journalism jurors—the "Thundering Herd," I called them, this happened:

March 1—I have a new editor at Holt, Rinehart & Winston, Roth Wilkofsky, who proposed by phone this morning that I should do a fourth edition of my textbook, "The Professional Journalist," for Nov. 1. He said the trade wanted it, which helped. Anyway, I agreed to Nov. 15—after the Presidential election—and if all goes well the 4th edition will be ready before the Gannett book and I should have some extra income I'll need by then. Since 1960, the PJ has sold more than $100,000 worth in the first three editions.

The "Thundering Herd"—50 strong and full of vigor—took over our 856 Pulitzer journalism exhibits for March 4 and 5 with such a heartening show of spirit that I sent home the two juries that finished on the first day with the rest returning on the morrow. It was, in a way, a very subdued celebration of the sixtieth anniversary of the Pulitzer Prizes, so I didn't want to say anything more about leaving for Tennessee. However, President McGill insisted on a farewell appearance, so I made it as short as I decently could, thanked everybody once again, and was about to sit down when my jurors gave me another hand, standing up.

It was a nice way to end twenty-two years with the Pulitzers, particularly before a bunch of tough-minded newspaper people, most of them friends of years' standing.

What pleased me more at the end of the second day's session was a first-place recommendation for Syd Schanberg's great account of the fall of Phnom Penh as published in the New York *Times* on May 9, 1975. I had hoped the same international reporting jury also would recognize the vivid account of the capture of Saigon by George Esper of the Associated Press and the equally compelling story of the same event by Keyes Beech and Robert Tamarkin of the Chicago *Daily News*. A triple jury award (with Beech and Tamarkin sharing the Chicago *Daily News* Prize) would not have diminished admiration for Schanberg's epic, or so I thought.

But the international jury didn't see it that way, for it produced this summary judgment for the Pulitzer board:

> The jury feels that Mr. Schanberg's excellent and sensitive professional performance and his personal courage in covering this story make him the most distinguished candidate for a Pulitzer Prize in this category this year.[4]

Nobody, in any event, could argue with so emphatic a judgment, so it was forwarded to the Pulitzer Board without comment, along with the other jury recommendations for the year. That, too, was a fine way to wind up twenty-two years of association with the Pulitzer Prizes. Suddenly, all the extra work and the trials of the past two years at Columbia didn't seem to matter any longer. I was at peace with myself.

Events now began moving toward a climax at the annual Pulitzer board meeting on April 9.

Dick Baker, who had been absent from the school because of illness, came in on March 15 looking fit and cheerful as always to begin the change of administration for the Pulitzer Prizes—a pleasure for both of us. Next day, I completed arrangements with Holt, Rinehart & Winston for the fourth edition of *The Professional Journalist,* to be delivered Nov. 15 in manuscript.

The contract with the University of Tennessee arrived March 23 and, after sleeping on it, I signed it the next day before mailing it to Dean Hileman. Dr. Cade had recovered and was back at work, so I knew I would be arranging my courses through him. I had a momentary regret over leaving New York City, even so, because I knew the Tennessee stipend—and probably a lot more—would go for a new set of doctors, nurses, and maybe hospital treatments as well for Dorothy.

But as I wrote in my diary, "I feel that I must continue to be active in mind and body no matter what and this professorship in Tennessee seems to be my best possibility. So I've committed myself at least until June 30, 1977 after I leave the Pulitzers."

That was my situation the day before the final Pulitzer Board meeting when Joe Pulitzer and I had our annual lunch at the Carlyle to go over the agenda, as usual, and talk over whatever problems remained. But this time, there was a difference, as I noted in the following:

> April 8—After going through the few reservations he had about jury recommendations, Joe told me he wouldn't be staying on the board much longer. He said he wanted to retire from the Post-Dispatch, that he was now 63 and was bringing his half-brother, Michael Pulitzer, to St. Louis next year. He went on to call Mike mature, trustworthy and competent, said Mike was making more money out of his management of the Arizona Star than the Post-Dispatch made and could soon take over the P-D.
>
> That was the end of our last briefing, but neither of us made any move to retain some form of contact. To the end, it was an arms'-length relationship but always frank and above board.

There was no serious argument about any prize at the final board meeting next day with a lot of enthusiasm for the international reporting award to the New York *Times*'s Syd Schanberg, which pleased me very much. I had intended to try to make a final pitch for Esper of the AP and the two Chicago *Daily News* correspondents, but I saw it would be hopeless as Chairman Pulitzer seemed in a hurry to leave, or so I thought.

Actually, as I realized later, he was making adequate time for my ceremonial leave-taking and various honors I hadn't anticipated. There followed presentations of a hand-illuminated scroll from the trustees, a *festschrift* of letters from present and former board members, and Lee Hills made a special presentation of a thirty-pound antique gold plaque about my service with etched-in signatures of all board members. I concluded:

> April 9—The New York Times printed my retirement and the new Tennessee job plus a picture. President McGill toasted me at lunch and I responded. It was all handsomely done and I felt as if I were being cremated in style. For all their good intentions, I was relieved when it was over and Dick Baker was accepted as my successor. The Abel dispute also was settled by making him a member of the board without vote. So after 22 years, it's over.

Now the farewells began in earnest. At the New York apartment of one of the best and certainly the luckiest of this generation's war correspondents, Peter Arnett, there was a double leave-taking for Wes Gallagher, president of the Associated Press, and for me on April 15. A few days later, Gallagher's potential successor, Lou Boccardi, then the AP's executive editor, came to the Pulitzer office for my intensive ninety-minute instruction in the AP's computer revolution of news distribution—a useful and much-appreciated turnabout for one of his old teachers.

Then the Gannett Foundation, without any action on my part, arranged with the University of Tennessee to give me half my grant for *A Crisis for the American Press* upon my arrival at the Knoxville campus and the rest six months later. Old friends, one being Abe Rosenthal, then on his way to becoming executive editor of the New York *Times,* paused for a few hours to give me a much-appreciated lunch. Former students, too, surprised me with a collection of letters recalling in an overly generous way some remark or quirk of mine that may have influenced their conduct or their future.

These were the last few entries in my diary to conclude my twenty-two years with the prizes:

> April 28—Done! The last publicity piece for the 60th annual Pulitzer Prizes has been written. So has the last picture caption, the last letter

and the last instructions. This afternoon I took off for Aquebogue and do not expect to return until Monday when the 60th prizes will be announced—and my last. Strangely, I have no feeling about it. Like a marathon runner who keeps going after crossing the finish line, I seem to be a study in perpetual motion.

May 3—My last Pulitzer Prize announcement. It was peaceful, even sedate, when we released the press packets at 3 p.m., this time on President McGill's decision on taking over from the university trustees. Then there were photographs of me "awarding" the prizes by mailing the checks, letters and certificates, after which I turned over my files to Dick Baker and made myself available whenever necessary to answer the many questions I'm sure he will have for me.

May 4—The New York Times took notice of my Pulitzer Prize Special Award with a two-column headline and a picture, which led to more phone calls including one from Bill Hearst. He took me to the Banshees luncheon, sat Mayor Beame on his right and me on his left. And to continue my career as a retiree, I attended an alumni farewell party in the evening.

On May 11, the day before Commencement, President McGill asked me to come to his office where he presented me with my Pulitzer Prize Special Award and the hand-illuminated resolution of the trustees, both in handsome frames. It was a final going-away gift. But my last act was highly personal—a farewell lunch with Rose and Robin at Butler Hall with a bit of jewelry as a gesture of thanks for each of them."[5]

That night was Dorothy's alone, and Mrs. Reams dressed her in her nicest clothes after dinner for a D'Oyly Carte performance of *The Pirates of Penzance* at the Uris Theater, which seemed to hold her attention. And toward the end, I saw her lips moving as the chorus swung into the finale and I could swear I heard her murmuring the line of the lyrics that so amused her at one time "Go ye heroes, go to glory . . ." Of course, it might have been wishful thinking on my part. But I like to believe, when all the good-byes had been said, that she remembered just a little of who she had been since our marriage on Oct. 16, 1928.

As the curtain came down and we left the theater, I saw that she was smiling.

Southern Exposure

It was six years before I returned to Columbia and the Pulitzer Prizes. Even then, I stayed only for three days early in March 1982, as a member of the international reporting jury before going back to my teaching duties that year at the University of Florida.[1]

There had been major changes on Morningside Heights since my departure at the end of the 1975–1976 academic year. These included a new Columbia president, a new journalism dean, and a new Pulitzer Prize administrator.

The only remaining member of my administration during my 1982 visit was the ever youthful Robin Holloway Kuzen. Since the resignation and death of my successor, Dick Baker, it was easy to see that she had been handling the administrative office during the breaking-in period of the latest appointee, Bob Christopher, formerly of the New York *Daily News*.

Under the circumstances, I could understand the uneasiness of the few remaining journalism faculty people I knew as the fifty or so of the latest journalism jurors gathered in the World Room on March 1 at 9:00 A.M. One of my former associates murmured to me in greeting, "Don't you feel liberated, John?"

I wasn't sure what he meant and laughed it off when I noticed that the new administrator seemed to be fumbling around until Robin took over and calmly escorted us to the places where we were to do the reading of our exhibits and reach our decisions on prize recommendations during our three-day assignment.

Still, I could sympathize with the new administrator's perplexity over working with fifty editors and newspaper correspondents at once whenever called upon during their deliberations. It had never been easy for me in my earliest years as an administrator, certainly, and I wanted him to know it. So while I grinned and nodded my thanks to Robin for getting all of us started with such a modest show of activity, I also tried to give Christopher encouragement.

During this return visit to Columbia, I was determined to do nothing that would place a greater burden either on the newest Pulitzer operative or his superiors who together were responsible for the prizes.

My life, too, had changed since my departure for the South after leaving Columbia in the spring of 1976. At the end of my 1976–1977 academic year at the University of Tennessee, Dorothy had died. And in 1979, during a second multiyear teaching assignment in Knoxville, I had been married to JoAnn Fogarty Johnston, the widow of a Knoxville lawyer and the mother of two lively teenagers.

Since I already had received offers of other teaching assignments, my first problem was to decide on a permanent residence and that, so I thought, would have to be Aquebogue. I realized JoAnn and I might be moving fairly regularly to other universities and renting temporary housing for up to nine months or so. Even before my remarriage, I'd already taught for 1977–1978 at the University of Kansas, then returned to Tennessee for 1978–1981, and would be moving to Florida for 1981–1982.

JoAnn wasn't bothered. Nor were the children, who were away at private schools from early fall to late spring annually, except for vacations. Keeping up the old homestead in Aquebogue, therefore, became a necessity for all in our little family as our permanent abode. And of course it pleased me enormously that JoAnn and the children fell in love with the house that had been built in 1827.

JoAnn and I also used it as a convenient stopping-off place when we had reason to be in New York, Boston, or points in between. I remember once, when I was asked to lecture to the Nieman Fellows at Harvard, we drove north from Knoxville, stayed in Aquebogue on our way to Cambridge, took the Orient Point Ferry across Long Island Sound, and made the return trip along the same route.

It was useful, too, to be able to stay in Aquebogue when we had invitations in New York City. That happened once when I was voted into the journalistic "Hall of Fame" in New York by the Society of Professional Journalists/Sigma Delta Chi. But I liked it best of all when the laughter of children, the ones who became mine with my marriage to JoAnn, put new life into the old salt box. [2]

As for my return to Columbia after a six-year absence, I have never been quite sure of the reason for my recall and how it came about in 1982.

During my years at the Universities of Tennessee and Kansas, I'd seldom heard from the Pulitzer Prize office. When I did, it was just a routine inquiry about a prize won or lost of which I had some knowledge outside the files.

While I was in New York in 1981, however, Robin had managed to locate me through friends and told me in confidence that Dick Baker had become gravely ill and was likely to resign soon. She wanted me to know, I suppose, just in case she needed an administrative pinch hitter in a hurry. And yet, while I was deeply concerned about Professor Baker, I didn't think there was any chance I'd be pressed into emergemcy service, so JoAnn and I returned to Tennessee.

On the following Monday, the Pulitzer Prizes were announced for 1980–1981 but aroused so little comment at the University of Tennessee that I paid no attention to them. Then, two days later, the biggest Pulitzer scandal in years broke wide open. I recorded:

> April 15—The Pulitzer Prizes, announced Monday, created little stir until today when the Washington Post announced their Pulitzer Prize winner for the best feature, Janet Cooke, a 26-year-old black reporter, had faked her much admired story about an eight-year-old drug addict. The Washington Star had broken the story. The New York Times and Newsweek both were on the phone to me soon for background. But since it never had happened on my watch, there wasn't much I could tell them.
>
> April 16—The Washington Post is returning Janet Cooke's 1981 prize to the Pulitzer board by request.

Gradually, the sensation simmered down, and I thought it had been forgotten until, almost fifteen years later, there was a hollow echo of dissatisfaction from Ben Bradlee, who as the *Post*'s executive editor had been obliged by the Pulitzer board to return the Cooke prize. However, in an autobiography written in retirement, he belittled the Pulitzer Prizes and inferred some of his former associates on the board had been guilty of irregularities. In a New York *Times* book review thereafter, it was suggested that he had acted out of frustration over the Cooke affair. [3]

I'd long forgotten about it. At the time, unexpectedly, Dick Baker had asked me if I'd return to Columbia for the 1982 journalism juries. I didn't have the heart either to question him about the Cooke matter or ask him how he felt. I just said yes, I'd serve. He had been, after all, the best friend I ever had at Columbia.

Then came this additional request from a distinguished Pulitzer board member, Lee Hills of the Knight Newspapers: "May 8—Lee Hills phoned to say Joe Pulitzer wants him to propose recommendations for changes in the Pulitzer Prize procedures and he [Hills] asked me to do a first draft after reviewing 14 suggested changes. Will I never be out of this one?" [4]

That wasn't all. When Dick Baker resigned because of ill health soon afterward, I became involved in further dealings with the Pulitzer office as follows in the summer of 1981:

> July 2—Robin called and said Bob Christopher, who will be my latest replacement as administrator, will be resigning from the New York Daily News first. If he is a success at handling the prizes, maybe I can finally forget about the Pulitzers after 1982.
>
> July 16—The appointment of Bob Christopher, 57, as the new Pulitzer Prize administrator was announced today. I'm told the arrangement was that he had to quit the Daily News first to get the new job. However, the Columbia Journalism Faculty has refused to consider him for full-time teaching.

A bit more than a month later, on August 20, Robin wrote me in confidence that Dick Baker had cancer of the bone marrow and was undergoing therapy at Harkness Pavilion in New York City. Mercifully, his last illness was brief. He died September 2, and his last wishes were scrupulously observed. His funeral was private, his remains were cremated and scattered over the surface of the St. Lawrence River near the summer home where he and Marjorie and their son, Coleman, had spent many happy summers together. So in a way, my return to Columbia as a Pulitzer juror in 1982 was a testimonial to Dick's thoughtfulness. If he couldn't be around to patch up the Pulitzer procedures that Joe had asked Lee Hills to do, I assumed that he'd wanted me to be available, and I was glad to be of service.

So it happened that JoAnn and I flew to New York from Gainesville, where I'd spent the 1981–1982 academic year as a vsiting professor at the University of Florida. A Hertz rental car, with JoAnn driving, landed us comfortably in Aquebogue for the weekend with this heartening beginning:

> Feb. 26—Everything in the old homestead started up at a touch last night when we arrived from Florida after a long absence—the water pump in the basement, the heat from the basement furnace, the hot water, the lights and so on. It was almost as if we'd never been away.
>
> We had dinner at Brasby's down the road and JoAnn bought whatever food we needed for the week-end at the deli. This morning, we were lazy. But this afternoon, I pruned the roses in the garden and the wisteria behind the house. In the evening, to Dick Corwin's and Walter, his genius-of-all-works made a superb beef stew and an apple pie as a special for us. All in all, a lovely homecoming. [5]
>
> Feb. 28—A bright, sunny day, about 40 degrees, and I closed the old house with regret, JoAnn drove us to the Waldorf where we're staying during the Pulitzer judging and later turned in the Hertz rental. So to dinner and to bed early.

My return to Columbia after six years is best summarized in my general observations at the time:

March 1—JoAnn and I took off for Columbia by cab early and I met with the International Jury at 9 a.m. in the Journalism Building. I felt as if I'd been a stranger except, of course, for Robin. To lunch with the jurors and JoAnn stayed with Dick Baker's widow, Marjorie, and had lunch with her. In the evening, to a new rock opera at the Imperial, "Dream Girls," based on the Supremes, and I hated the loud, tuneless music even though I was impressed with the dancing. Back to the Waldorf at 11 p.m.

March 2—Our International Jury finished reading the exhibits and will vote tomorrow.[6] The only break in the routine was the presidential lunch at the Faculty Club. To the Metropolitan Opera in the evening and heard a superb performance of "Il Trovatore." Back to the Waldorf and JoAnn phoned the children to let them know we'd be back in Gainesville tomorrow night.

March 3—JoAnn stayed at the Waldorf to pack while I went to Columbia to wind up the jury sessions. After about an hour's discussion, we agreed unanimously to recommend splitting the prize equally between John Darnton of the New York Times and another correspondent from a different newspaper. Anyway, I enjoyed working with my colleagues, Creed Black, Claude Lewis and two ex-students, Fred Hartmann and Dick Oliver, and while JoAnn and I were comfortable at the Waldorf we were glad to get back to Gainesville that night.

In the rush of events that ended the academic year at the University of Florida, I took little notice of the Pulitzer Prize announcement that the international award had gone to Darnton of the *Times* instead of the split honor our jury had recommended. Nor was there any outburst of publicity in the southland for that year's prizes in general. Still, when Robin asked me to serve again, I couldn't very well refuse, although I had more than enough to do without that for the coming academic year.

Dean Arthur Brown at the University of Miami had just sent me a contract for 1982–1983 to teach journalism there, and I'd accepted primarily because I'd be working with another former student, Dave Gordon, who was the journalism director. JoAnn already had located the home of a doctor on sabbatical leave that we'd be renting at Coral Gables and was taking charge of all the other arrangements for leaving Gainesville.

In my book work, which now included a fifth edition of *The Professional Journalist,* my textbook, I'd thought of using a part of Janet Cooke's fake as an instructive warning to student editors but the Washington Post wanted a fee for the privilege, so I forgot about it. The big surprise was another long Asian lecture tour that summer for the International Communications Agency, the forerunner of the US Information Agency. Under the arrangements I approved shortly after our return from Columbia was this speaking schedule as a visiting American specialist:

June 1–8. Pakistan (Islamabad, Lahore, Karachi).

June 10–30. India (New Delhi, Bombay, Madras, Calcutta and points between).

July 2–7. Katmandu in Nepal in the Himalayas.

July 9–13. Colombo in Sri Lanka, the island republic that once had been Ceylon, a jewel in the British crown.

July 15–19. Thailand (Bangkok).

July 21–27. Manila and environs in the Philippines.

July 28. Tokyo and other major cities in Japan for an indeterminate period, depending on circumstances and arrangements for air travel to New York City with a Hawaiian stopover at the East-West Center.

My sponsors, who were familiar with my Pentagon record and my previous Asian tour, seemed to be interested primarily in my estimates of the growth of Chinese influence in the area, the decline of the Red Army after its disastrous experience with the Afghan rebels, and so on. As for my lectures abroad, if they caused my largely university audiences to support the United States after the Vietnam War, so much the better. But nobody expected miracles. I had insisted on JoAnn's presence on the trip and was paying her way to be sure there would be no bureaucratic objection.[7]

That, finally, was how we wound up a pleasant year at the University of Florida with Dean Ralph Lowenstein, his colleagues, and the students who founded a weekly community newspaper in one of my classes, *The CommuniGator,* which still appears on my desk elsewhere from time to time. To sum up my farewell:

> April 22—My last two classes at Florida. Then we had an open house, lunch and dinner for those who stopped by for the afternoon and evening at our campus home—32 students, the teaching staff and their families and our Florida friends, Faye O'Neal and Richard Lester. To bed early on our last night in Gainesville—and five weeks hence we're off to Asia once again.

As I had learned in my earlier tour in Asia, there was scant interest and even less knowledge among my new Asian audiences outside universities, during my travels from Islamabad to Tokyo in the summer of 1982, about the state of American letters, drama, and serious music. But there still was endless curiosity everywhere I went about the quality of life in America, the sense of turmoil that was projected from time to time by the federal government, and the manner in which decisions were made on distributing American largesse abroad in foreign aid and even military assistance.

What the Asian government audiences I addressed wanted to know principally was how to create a better press for their own countries in the United States, a subject in which I'm afraid I wasn't very helpful. As for the struggle for a free and independent press, I always had a polite hearing among Asians; but interest in that subject, as well as the Pulitzers, was close to zero, except among the usually hard-pressed journalists themselves in private and unreported sessions.

Militarily, from chiefs of state and whatever military people I was able to see, there was eagerness to learn what I had heard most recently of the Afghan guerrillas and the Red Army, but little except reserved but careful language about the growth of Chinese military power and competition for foreign trade. To conclude, I had to acknowledge in my report to my State Department superiors that the damage wrought by the Vietnam War to American influence and prestige across East and Southeast Asia might not be repaired for years, that Chinese military authority was rising, the Soviets declining, and Japan still remained the greatest competitor in the Pacific for the United States. The report was unremarkable—but honest.

To sum up my Pulitzer jury experiences in 1983 and 1984, while I was at Miami University and Syracuse successively, our proposals were ratified without argument by the Pulitzer board. That meant prizes for Thomas L. Friedman of the New York *Times* and Loren Jenkins of the Washington *Post* in 1983 and Karen Elliott House of the *Wall Street Journal* in 1984.

As for my teaching, except for a hurry-up substitute semester at the University of Tennessee in 1987, I bowed out with a great deal of satisfaction after my second year at Syracuse in 1985. It was one of the best I could remember from student performance to friendly association with my faculty colleagues, including the former dean, Henry Schulte, who had been in my early classes at Columbia.

My most cherished souvenir remains the Pulitzer Prize Special Award for my services to American journalism—a good way, to use the phase so often recalled by my students—to go with what you've got. [8]

Notes
Bibliography
Index

Notes

The Art of the Diarist

1. "Lyrics," by Oscar Hammerstein II (New York, 1949), 4.
2. *The Diary of Samuel Pepys, 1659–1669* vol. 1 (New York, 1942), 69. The entry was dated Apr. 18, 1661.
3. The authorized history was called *The Pulitzer Prizes: A History of the Awards in Books, Drama, Music and Journalism Based on the Private Files Over Six Decades* (New York: Columbia Univ. Press, 1974). The private files are the records kept by Columbia Univ. from the outset of its negotiations with both the first Joseph Pulitzer and the Pulitzer family after his death. My examination was complete. No essential fact was omitted. See also a quarterly publication, *The Columbia Library Columns*, vol. 6 no. 3; also, the latest issue of the Plan of Award and the Pulitzer Prize Board's membership, as contrasted with the Plan of Award and the membership of the Advisory Board on the Pulitzer Prizes when the history was published in 1974.

1. The Big Prize

1. Dean Ackerman liked to remind us that he was in the first class at the Columbia journalism school in 1912–1913, when it began as an undergraduate institution.
2. Ackerman became dean in 1931 and made the school a graduate institution in 1935. See Richard T. Baker, *A History of the Graduate School of Journalism, Columbia University* (New York, 1954), 104, 109–11.
3. The Liberty Window memorialized Joseph Pulitzer's successful campaign to mount Bartholdi's Statue of Liberty on Bedloes Island in New York harbor. I obtained the Window, once the city condemned the building in which it had been installed, by paying a previous mayor $1 at his suggestion. The Real Estate Board of the city later gave the university a Deed of Gift for the Window, after which it was relocated in the World Room of Columbia's Journalism building.
4. This was the second Joseph Pulitzer's last meeting. He died about a month before the 1955 board session, after which the third of the line, his older son, Joseph Pulitzer Jr., took his place by vote of the Pulitzer board.
5. I can only guess that the secretive way in which I became the board secretary and administrator of the prizes was based on uncertainty about my ability to do the job while carrying a full course teaching load and a night school class as well. University professors, like journalists, had to make do with scanty rewards in those years.
6. Lindbergh and the press never did get along.

7. For a life of the second Pulitzer, see Daniel W. Pfaff, *Joseph Pulitzer II and the Post-Dispatch.* (University Park, Pa., 1991). My copy is autographed by Joseph Pulitzer Jr., his son.

2. My View of the Prizes

1. Swope's evidence resulted in the conviction of a New York police lieutenant, Charles A. Becker, and four hired gunmen known as Lefty Louie, Dago Frank, Gyp the Blood, and Whitey Lewis for the murder on July 13, 1912, of a gambler, Herman Rosenthal, who was about to testify against Becker before a New York County Grand Jury. See E. J. Kahn Jr., *The World of Swope* (New York, 1965), 144–50. For his Pulitzer Prize, 183.

2. For a memorial to the New York *World* and its people, see John K. Hutchens and George Oppenheimer, eds., *The Best in the World* (New York, 1973).

3. For the background of the George Gershwin omission, see John Hohenberg, *The Pulitzer Prizes: A History* (New York, 1974), 106–7, 152, 207. The even more inexcusable omission was the refusal to honor the Gershwin folk opera, *Porgy and Bess,* now an established classic of modern American music.

4. The MacLeish story is in Louis Untermeyer, ed., *A Treasury of Great Poems* (New York, 1942), 1170–76.

5. The basis of my record of Margaret Mitchell's life and her work on *Gone with the Wind* came almost entirely from her admiring editor and publisher on the Atlanta *Constitution,* Ralph McGill.

6. For Carl Sandburg, see his autobiography, *Always the Young Stranger* (New York, 1952–53.)

7. General Romulo, who was one of my closest friends at the United Nation, told me the MacArthur story, and I knew all the rest about him from the time he won his Pulitzer Prize while he still was an American citizen.

8. Ernie Pyle's story is told at greater length in John Hohenberg, *Foreign Correspondence: The Great Reporters and Their Times* (New York, 1964), 355–65.

9. Joe Rosenthal's story also is in *Foreign Correspondence,* 372, 374.

3. An Atomic Crisis

1. The background of the Formosa Strait problem is in Dwight D. Eisenhower, *Mandate for Change* (Garden City, N.Y., 1963), 459, 469, 477–78.

2. Eisenhower, 461–63.

3. The Air War College trip is from my 1954 diary.

4. The book Baruch gave me was *My Own Story* (New York, 1957), written with Sam Lubell.

5. Salisbury received an ovation at the OPC for facing down charges of Communist sympathies. This 1956 Pulitzer Prize for his New York *Times* series, "Russia Re-Viewed," is a better measure of his work in Moscow.

6. Columbia's writing classes, where deadlines were strictly observed, was where our N-school students first were told how a night editor long ago had roused me from deadline paralysis by yelling at me, "Hey, go with whatever you've got. We're on deadline." The shock made a lasting impression on generations of students.

7. Colonel Boyd, who delivered the invitation for a Far East tour of duty for the Air Force, became a lifelong friend.

8. Ralph Bunche, the first black American to become a State Department division

chief, joined the United Nation as director of the Trusteeship Division in 1945. In 1950, he was awarded the Nobel Prize for helping bring at least a temporary peace to strife-torn Palestine with the end of the 1948–1949 Israeli war of self-defense.

4. New Times for the Prizes

1. The Pulitzers' background is from my own knowledge of the family.

2. Dulles's warning was called "brinkmanship" by his critics who accused him of going to the brink of war. See Townsend Hoopes, *The Devil and John Foster Dulles* (Boston, 1973), 265–83.

3. The induction of the new chairman is based on my diary notes.

4. The fiction jury's distinguished membership registered both annoyance and disappointment over their reversal. I could only report the board's action to them, as is evident in the latter stages of this narrative. I received a letter of acknowledgment from Faulkner that I treasure.

5. The Pulitzer board had to reverse the cartoon jury to grant their late chairman's request for a prize for D. R. Fitzpatrick.

6. Anthony Lewis survives as a New York *Times* columnist. I never had any part in the prize for former Sergeant Towery and never heard from him.

7. Professor Oscar Campbell of Columbia, the chairman of the drama jury, didn't think much of the Williams play. The Critics' Circle, however, already had given it their award.

8. If there was a leak to Murrow on the Towery award that gave him time to set up his cameras at the Cuero *Record,* I never did find out who did it and have no proof that there was an advance tip.

9. The New York *Times* for Apr. 24, 1955, reported Premier Jou's offer to negotiate.

5. Test for a Teacher

1. My Asian-Pacific mission lasted from June 12–July 23, 1955.

2. Ike's discussion of his "New Look" for the armed forces at the Pentagon is in Eisenhower, *Mandate for Change,* 447–55. My summary was based on data I received from the Air Force secretary's office.

3. Secretary Talbott was in high favor with the White House when he made his offer to me. See *Mandate for Change,* 448. My World War II reports remain classified.

4. For a Japanese view of the Pearl Harbor attack, see John Toland, *The Rising Sun* (New York, 1970), 216.

5. For Formosa Strait, see Hoopes, 264–83; also Eisenhower, 459–83.

6. This was my first trip to Taiwan although I'd had other work in what the British call the Near East, also in South, Southeast, and East Asia for many years.

7. Because I had so many Filipino sources at the United Nation, including several of my oldest friends, I always felt very much at home in Manila and was familiar with Filipino problems.

8. My reunion with former students in Tokyo was one of the most satisfying parts of my experiences in the Asian Pacific. Regarding my last interview with General Kuter before leaving Japan, it was my practice, before writing a government report, to discuss my conclusions with my principals before committing them to paper.

9. For Ike on the Talbott resignation, see *Mandate for Change,* 494; also the Pulitzer Prize-winning articles by Charles L. Bartlett in the Chattanooga (Tenn.) *Times* in 1956.

10. Secretary Douglas on several occasions discussed his interest in the US Air Force

Academy in Colorado with me. It was the main reason for most of my work for the Air Force during his regime in the Pentagon during the Eisenhower administration.

6. With Hearst in Moscow

1. My primary sources for the Hearst team's adventure are the three members of the group, "Young Bill," Joe Smith, and Frank Conniff, all of whom I'd known for years. The most complete account, of course, is their prize-winning exhibit in the Pulitzer files.

2. This account also is based on interviews with the team.

3. Joseph Pulitzer Jr. and W. R. Hearst Jr. are the sources.

4. My European arrangements are based on my diary entries, both the changes and the final decisions. But the whole thing was made possible only by my sabbatical leave in 1957.

5. My reports on the various missions I accepted and finished all were filed with the organizations named with special considation for the Air Force report filed from Europe.

6. The biggest surprise of all in my Pulitzer experience was the strenuous effort made by the chairman, Joseph Pulitzer Jr., to win a Pulitzer Prize for the son of William Randolph Hearst Sr., the first Joseph Pulitzer's great rival. I don't believe either knew the other at the time, and I never saw them together afterward. As the board's secretary, I took no part in the discussion.

7. Once the Air Force report was concluded, the European trip was a great pleasure. I have a picture book full of memories of the journey with Dorothy because it was one of the happiest times in our forty-nine-year marriage.

7. The Kennedy Prize

1. One source for Kennedy's background is James MacGregor Burns, *John Kennedy: A Political Profile* (New York, 1959).

2. Sources for Kennedy's researches include his introduction to the Burns campaign biography, from the preface to *Profiles in Courage,* and from my discussions with the senator's intimates. For the other prizes, a fuller account is in *The Pulitzer Prizes,* including fiction, 9, 258, and drama and history, 262–64 passim.

3. I was as surprised as other members of the Pulitzer board by Don Ferguson's dramatic and moving intervention. So far as I know, nobody, including Chairman Pulitzer, had any advance knowledge of the Milwaukee editor's plea for Kennedy.

4. I did not disregard Pearson's charges but made inquiries about the columnist's sources without avail. The published withdrawal of the accusation in Pearson's column disposed of the allegation. Kennedy's hand-written text was added evidence that the charge had been politically motivated.

5. My correspondence with Kennedy was left in the Pulitzer files at Columbia.

6. Burns's note is from my 1958 diary, entry of Feb. 3.

7. Kennedy's campaign plans are from Burns, 101–17 and 156–90 passim.

8. Remarks on a Catholic's duty in American public office are from Burns, 241–44.

8. A Question of Funding

1. I was greatly relieved that I never did have financial responsibility for the Pulitzer Prize Fund.

2. Douglas was the third Air Force secretary who had engaged me as a consultant during the Eisenhower years. Whatever work I did for the Pentagon had the approval of my Columbia superiors.

3. The Air Force budget cuts report is from Robert J. Donovan, *Eisenhower: The Inside Story* (New York, 1956), 52–54; also instructions to Ike's speech writer, 56.

4. "Up We Go" is still the AF Academy's fight song.

5. What the Wrights and Lindbergh did is history. The Arnold story is from Jack Raymond, *Power at the Pentagon* (New York, 1954), 49–50.

6. For FDR's air program, see Raymond, 48–52.

7. Ike's quote, "slugging with air," is from Raymond, 75.

8. Donovan is the source for Ike's estimate that the Air Force still had more than 40 percent of the military budget in the first year after his cuts.

9. The Academy spending controversy died away. I was continued indefinitely as an Air Force consultant during the Eisenhower administration and served occasionally when the work did not interfere with my Columbia duties.

9. The University Experience

1. *Sweet Bird of Youth* was one of Tennessee Williams's lesser works. I include it here as part of a widely varied university experience over nearly forty years.

2. Not all the comments on the Pulitzer drama prizes were favorable, as the Southern lady's view indicates. As for *Fiorello*, there were worse shows in the Pulitzer list, but most had much better ratings over the years.

3. Acheson, Truman's secretary of state, 1949–1953, was by no means the most disagreeable guest lecturer at Columbia. We once suffered through Fidel Castro early in his career.

4. Because of the prominence of the Van Doren family in academe, Charles's downfall became national news.

5. The dean who couldn't stand student criticism shall be nameless.

6. My attendance at the Council on Foreign Relations was a major attraction for me. The sessions nearly always were lively, the guests interesting.

7. Douglas Moore, the head of the Columbia Music Department, won his Pulitzer Prize for his opera, *Giants in the Earth*, in 1951, three years before I became affiliated with the Pulitzer Prizes. We spent many a happy new year with him and his family on eastern Long Island.

8. The bitter young instructor, whose complaint I overheard, came to Columbia at a time when the university was not very generous to newcomers. The position is much better today.

9. I managed to survive after a few difficult early years and have no complaints.

10. In the Public Interest

1. McGill was the source of the account of his prize-winning editorial.

2. He also recalled his warning about the Monday the high court would outlaw segregated schools.

3. The modern Supreme Court's views are discussed in the New York *Times*, sec. 4, p. 1, July 2, 1995.

4. For a fuller account of Buford Boone's adventure, see John Hohenberg, *The Pulitzer Prize Story* (New York, 1959) 91–95.

5. The Little Rock and Morin stories are told at length in Hohenberg, *The Pulitzer Prize Story*, 95–100, 101–6.

6. The other prize winners are listed in the historical record, Hohenberg, *The Pulitzer Prizes.*

7. Murrow's background is in Alexander Kendrick, *Prime Time: The Life of Edward*

R. *Murrow* (Boston, 1969). Friendly's views are in his *Due to Circumstances Beyond Our Control* (New York, 1967).

   8. Aubrey is quoted in Friendly, xi–xii. So is Friendly's response.

11. Shuffling the Prizes

   1. Changes in the Pulitzer board and the jury system are in the latest Plan of Award issued by the Pulitzer Prize Board at Columbia University.

   2. The discussion of criticism of the prizes is in Richard T. Baker, 1–10.

   3. For a more detailed discussion of jury reversals in 1960 and later, see *The Pulitzer Prizes.*

   4. Nobody, including Dean Barrett, ever named a particular juror or board member in their rumors of irregular conduct or produced evidence on which I could ask Chairman Pulitzer or the president of Columbia to proceed.

   5. The changes are listed in the minutes of the Pulitzer board meeting.

   6. I never did know the identity of the angry trustee. Apparently, his service was limited because I never saw him again.

   7. I was grateful that, remembering my beginnings in Seattle, the Univ. of Washington was willing to consider me among others as its next journalism dean; but I didn't want to leave New York at the time.

   8. If my Air Force service as a consultant did nothing more than start a long friendship between the Fishers and the Hohenbergs, that would have been worth the extra labors.

12. Presidential Politics

   1. The Kennedy-Nixon campaign in great detail is in Theodore H. White, *The Making of the President 1960* (New York, 1961). See also Arthur M. Schlesinger Jr., *A Thousand Days* (Boston, 1965).

   2. For the Khrushchev story at the United Nation, I prefer my own reporting as written herein. I saw and heard most of it. For another view, see Schlesinger, 72, 107–9, 114.

   3. These are my views and my conclusions about the three Kennedy-Nixon debates, which I saw in part and heard the rest via TV. For Schlesinger, 72–86.

   4. The New York *Times* for Nov. 10, 1960, carried the statistics on the Kennedy-Nixon election.

   5. White's Pulitzer Prize had to be delayed until 1962 because his book wasn't published until 1961.

13. Press versus Government

   1. Professor Rabi won his Nobel Prize in 1949.

   2. For the Baruch Plan, see Bernard M. Baruch, *The Public Years,* (New York, 1960), 360–81; for a more critical view, see Margaret Coit, *Mr. Baruch* (Boston, 1957), 560–87; for atomic energy, see Henry DeWolf Smyth, *Atomic Energy for Military Purposes* (Princeton, 1946).

   3. For Castro's beginnings, see Herbert L. Matthews, *The Cuban Story* (New York, 1961). I was as surprised as most of the students to see Castro in our big newsroom.

   4. The Jefferson anecdote is in Schlesinger. Kennedy's inaugural is from the text published in the New York *Times* the day after the 1961 inaugural, Jan. 21.

   5. See E. J. Kahn Jr., (New York, 1965) with a publisher's foreword signed by his friend, M. Lincoln Schuster.

   6. The analysis is based on my own knowledge with an assist from Turner Catledge.

7. The Storke editorial is in W.D. Sloan and J. B. Anderson, *Pulitzer Prize Editorials* (Ames, Iowa, 1980), 152–54.

8. The Bay of Pigs story is also related in Alexander deConde, *A History of American Foreign Policy* (New York, 1963), 333–38. See also James Reston's analysis in "*Deadline*," (New York, 1991), 293–94, 324–25. Schlesinger's view is understandably sympathetic, 267 et seq. Mine is somewhere between the two.

14. The Soviet Challenge

1. Khrushchev's diplomatic offensive against the United States began with the shooting down of Francis Gary Powers's U-2 spy plan. See David Wise and Thomas B. Ross, *The U-2 Affair* (New York, 1960). It continued with his Berlin squeeze, as related in Boris Dmytryshyn, *USSR: A Concise History* (New York, 1965), 306, 328. Khrushchev then moved toward renewed confrontation.

2. I had authority from the Pulitzer board only to visit Sarnoff and report on his proposal, not to warn him he had no chance of succeeding.

3. The 1961 Pulitzer board session went off without argument. Nagao became one of the few foreigners to win an award.

4. I was interested enough in the Berlin issue to visit the United Nation whenever I could. The quote from Kennedy on July 25 is from my notes. The construction of the Berlin Wall was a complete surprise.

5. McCloy enjoyed telling the story—a typical example of Khrushchev's brand of humor.

6. Joseph Pulitzer Jr. depended on me to keep him informed of developments in the Pulitzer Prize selection process. Our relationship was that of chairman and secretary.

15. Showdown

1. Swanberg's *Citizen Hearst* seemed to me to be a fair account of the publisher's life, but there was no pleasing the trustees who didn't like him.

2. Actually, the prizes for 1962 seemed to me to be stronger than usual. But the failure of Paris and Vienna meetings between President Kennedy and Premier Khrushchev, together with Khrushchev's rejection of an atomic test ban treaty, indicated danger ahead for all concerned. I have seldom seen graduate students in my classes quite as nervous.

3. Hilsman's briefing was on background on Aug. 24, 1962, at the State Department (meaning it was for use without identification of the source), followed by the first of ten speeches on the subject by Senator Keating beginning Aug. 31. Hendrix's reports in the Miami *News* added some details. See Elie Abel, *The Missile Crisis* (New York, 1966), 17–18. For Rusk's maneuvers, ibid., 25–26; for McCone, ibid., 17–18.

4. For Kennedy's announcement to the American people on Oct. 22, see Abel, 121–26.

5. The rest of the week of warning is detailed at length in Abel, 127–202, and is summarized in Dmytryshyn 329–30.

6. For Fomin/Scali, see Schlesinger, 824–30; Abel, 177–78.

7. For the Kennedy/Khrushchev correspondence, see Schlesinger, 826–28, 829–30; Abel 187–210.

16. The Greatest Sacrifice

1. Because I was in India on a State Department lecture tour on Nov. 22, 1963, I have deliberately avoided all but the barest reference to President Kennedy's assassination. For those who wish to reread that tragic story, I would recommend William Manchester,

The Death of a President (New York, 1967); Arthur M. Schlesinger Jr., *A Thousand Days,* and of course the Official Report of the Warren Commission. In the few pages of this chapter, all I am trying to do is to tell of the reaction among my audiences in India and Pakistan and of my wife's distressed outcry, "What is happening to our country?" I could not respond then—or now.

2. The quotation is from the beginning of the report For the Council on Foreign Relations of my travels: *Between Two Worlds* (New York, 1967).

3. During my first visit to Saigon in 1964, the resident American correspondents at the time filled me in on such details as the first visit of the attorney general, the battle with the Diem family, and all the other disappointments of the opening years of the Vietnam War.

4. The Bigart anecdote is in David Halberstam, *The Making of a Quagmire* (New York, 1964), 76; Beverly Deepe's remark was made to me.

5. The Halberstam piece is described in *The Making of a Quagmire,* 191. See also the New York *Times,* Aug. 15, 1963.

6. The Chicago *Daily News* had an excellent record in the Pulitzer Prizes. See Hohenberg, *The Pulitzer Prizes,* 78, 79–84, 181, 193, 304, 307, 352.

7. Albee won a drama prize in 1967 for *A Delicate Balance,* but he never thought the Pulitzer amounted to much because what he believed to be his best play, *Who's Afraid of Virginia Woolf?* was denied an award.

8. I heard the story many times over of Sulzberger's refusal to shift Halberstam when the president hinted at it. Halberstam verified it in *The Making of a Quagmire,* 268.

9. I finally did get to Vietnam in 1964 and 1970 for reasonably thorough visits with General Westmoreland and a number of correspondents.

10. On the flight of US jets to India, see Hohenberg, *Between Two Worlds,* 333.

17. Asian Dilemma

1. For Goldwater's campaign, see Theodore H. White, *The Making of the President, 1964* (New York, 1965). The Goldwater quotes on atom bombing are on 103 for his threat of Oct. 24, 1963, and 106 for his remarks in Wilton, N.H. He tried to "bury the bomb" later, see 325. For Kennedy's view of the Goldwater atom plan, see Schlesinger, 1018.

2. Quotes from *Foreign Correspondence* are on 451–52. Columbia Univ. Press published the book originally in 1964. Syracuse Univ. Press issued a new 1995 edition thirty-one years later.

3. Arnett won his Pulitzer in 1966 for his Vietnam reporting and was still covering the Bosnian war for CNN in 1995. Neil Sheehan won his Pulitzer in 1989.

4. The US government argued that reporters were falsifying the news by reporting so many defeats in Vietnam early on. Most of the reporters contended their facts were correct.

5. The first page reviews in *The New York Times Sunday Book Review* and the London *Times Literary Supplement* are suitably preserved in my files.

18. The Prizes and Vietnam

1. The Vietnam War's early stages are discussed in Hohenberg, *Between Two Worlds,* pt. 6, and in my *New Era in the Pacific* (New York, 1972), 283–332.

2. The quote is from Neil Sheehan's book, *A Bright and Shining Lie* (New York, 1988), 372, which won a Pulitzer Prize for nonfiction in 1989.

3. For summation of the 91 questionnaires correspondents filled out for me in Vietnam between June 3 and Sept. 3, 1964, see *Between Two Worlds,* 471–82. The journalists represented both American and non-American news organizations. The Council on Foreign Relations asked me to do this, and the correspondents responded of their own volition.

and probably will keep on telling it to the day I die because it was such a horrible experience for us both. She nearly always insisted on sharing both our risks and our good times in foreign travel.

5. Every newcomer to Vietnam was told the story of Ap Bac first of all, as I was in 1964, because it was so clearly an official American invasion of the truth of a defeat that might have been less noticed if the victory claim had not been so incredible.

6. See *Between Two Worlds:* for Witze, 296–97, for Zorthian, 295–97, 301–2; *Newsweek,* 298.

7. On President Johnson, General Taylor, and the New York *Times,* see Hohenberg, *Between Two Worlds,* 293–94.

8. See *Between Two Worlds:* for S. L. A. Marshall 311–12; for North Vietnamese troops in South Vietnam, 285–86.

9. Faas and Sawada also won Pulitzer Prizes for war photography.

19. Honors for the Duke

1. The record of the awards is in a white booklet, "The Pulitzer Prizes," issued periodically by the Pulitzer Prize board and obtainable from Columbia University. The latest I had at the time of this writing covered 1917–1991.

2. Duke Ellington's memoirs are in his *Music Is My Mistress,* published in 1973, the year before his death at seventy-five.

3. With regard to Chairman Pulitzer's hope for a more venturesome jury, I doubt if the board was ready then to break with precedent. Only one member had a professional background as a musician or music critic.

4. The decisive part of the public protest over the slight to Ellington came from William Schuman as a former music award winner and the president of the Lincoln Center for the Performing Arts.

5. The Duke was the most popular figure at Columbia during the 1972 commencement, when he accepted his honorary Columbia degree.

6. The jealousy of the Columbia music faculty in the Wuorinen case scarcely was to their credit when he was refused tenure and resigned.

7. Having a lifetime's interest in music in all its diverse forms, I followed the development of different kinds of American music (and noise) with the greatest interest, the basis for the discussion in this context.

8. If I had my way, Krock's farewell remarks would be engraved on a wall wherever the Pulitzer Prize board convenes for its annual vote on the prizes.

20. Fifty-Year Reckoning

1. Since the secretary of the Pulitzer board has no vote in its proceedings, I have no constraints upon me in attempting to stress the failures as well as the successes of the Pulitzer Prizes.

2. Even though TV news was ineligible for a Pulitzer in my time, the TV people usually covered the prize awards, as did radio.

3. As an old-fashioned liberal among the South's more conservative journalists, McGill's critical attitude toward the Ellington honor has always mystified his friends.

4. I don't know who proposed me as a board spokesman and don't really care. I had enough problems at Columbia without the added responsibility.

5. The diary entries accurately report my feelings at the time.

6. I did spend several summer months later at the East-West Center of the Univ. of Hawaii and thoroughly enjoyed the experience during a leave of absence from Columbia.

7. Except for the Navy ROTC hubbub, we were spared much of the early mob violence at Columbia that occurred elsewhere.

8. I think it only fair in a book of this kind to include the most persistent criticsm of the awards as well as to celebrate their general acceptance after fifty years. This is what I have attempted to do herein.

21. The Grand Show

1. Although I was deputized to invite five distinguished Pulitzer winners as speakers to replace President Johnson, who declined, I consulted President Kirk for his suggestions. He resolved my problem for me very neatly.

2. The impact of the Pulitzer awards is discussed at greater length in my book *The Pulitzer Prizes*.

3. The 1966 winners, like all the rest, are in the Columbia Univ. "White Books" of laureates, periodically issued by the university.

4. MacLeish was a three-time winner—for poetry in 1933 and 1953 and for drama with *J.B.* in 1959.

5. Warren's Pulitzer was awarded in 1947 for his novel *All the King's Men*.

6. Copland's prize was awarded in 1945.

7. Reston won his award in 1957.

8. The statement of the first Pulitzer's philosophy as a journalist is the most famous in a long record. The history of the first sixty years of the awards, which I was commissioned to research and write, contains the details of the origin and organization of the awards and the major developments during the first six decades.

22. Losing a Prize

1. Communist China and the Soviet Union, despite their joint help for the North Vientnamese cause, had a tense rivalry of their own. That, at least in part, may have accounted for the relatively brief Chinese period of encouragement toward a possible truce in the Vietnam War.

2. The "dirty little war" was the original phrase used by opponents of the conflict. It was stopped when the war became the longest and the worst fought in American history.

3. Salisbury's personal views are from his book, *Behind the Lines—Hanoi:* December 23–January 7 . . . (New York, 1967), 1–12.

4. Salisbury, 24.

5. My diary entries contrast with Salisbury's own expectation of a great adventure.

6. Dorothy stayed with friends, Colonel and Mrs. Syd Fisher, while she was in Paris —heaven to her because of her French heritage and her knowledge of the countryside.

7. I didn't expect student apathy toward Salisbury, a first-rate New York *Times* correspondent, just back from a major venture, but I was no expert at reading the student mind.

8. I have summarized the Salisbury articles that were submitted for a Pulitzer Prize and added his own point of view of the position as he expressed it to me when he came to Columbia to speak before my students.

9. If I have suggested tension in my account of the Pulitzer board vote on the Salisbury prize, that is what I intended. It was one of the most dramatic moments in my board experience.

10. The summary of the Pulitzer board discussion and vote for Hughes against Salisbury is from my own record of the proceedings. I also had known and admired Hughes's work; but the issue, to be frank, was whether the board was for or against Salisbury. As

for the trustees' discussion, that was relayed to me later by a person who had witnessed and heard the trustees' argument.

23. The Oldest Rebel

1. Quotes from an editorial are in Şloan and Anderson, 173.
2. Ibid., 168.
3. Knight's editorial was in the Akron (Ohio) *Beacon-Journal*, Feb. 21, 1954.
4. MAAG funding for the French in 1951–52 is related in Bernard Fall, *The Two Vietnams* (New York, 1963), 219–20.
5. The Kennedy briefing on the United Nation is from Burns, 83.
6. The Dulles quote on Navarre is in Fall, 122.
7. The Alsop-Bidault argument is in Joseph and Stewart Alsop, *The Reporters' Trade* (New York, 1959), 48–49.
8. Eisenhower's quote is from his *Mandate for Change*, 348–51.
9. The US billion-dollar investment in French rule in Indochina is from Fall, 227–28.
10. An Agence-France-Presse official described the end at Dien Bien Phu as an eyewitness.
11. The cartoon is from the St. Louis *Post-Dispatch*, May 8, 1954. It is in the Pulitzer Prize files.
12. Summation of the position in the Johnson regime is from individual comments to me from Messrs. Brown, Halberstam, and Arnett.
13. Mecklin's quote is from his *Mission in Torment* (Garden City, N.Y., 1965), 31–32.
14. From Knight editorial, "Haven't We Learned?," Apr. 4, 1954.
15. The Reischauer quote is from a Knight editorial, Feb. 5, 1967.
16. From US military communiqué in Saigon on casualties, Mar. 12, 1967, and Knight editorial, same day.
17. From Knight editorial, "Nation Faces Moment of Truth," Aug. 6, 1967, in Akron *Beacon-Journal*.
18. Knight criticism of Republicans is from Sloan and Anderson, 169.
19. McNamara's quote is from memorandum #118, Oct. 14, 1966, *Pentagon Papers*. (New York, 1971), 542–51.
20. LBJ's decision is from memorandum #129, May 19, 1967, *Pentagon Papers*, 577–85.
21. Knight editorial on nation being over-committed is in Hohenberg, *The Pulitzer Prizes*, 301.

24. Turnabout

1. The problems of a disunited American/South Vietnamese command in the Vietnam War and the hostile attitude of the home front are based on my diary record of my second visit to Vietnam in 1970.
The record of my first visit with General Westmoreland and my first field trip with him also are from my record. I was much impressed with the Ranger captain's anger over his cowardly troops.
2. I always thought it was a major error of the American high command to be trying to frighten the few young correspondents, some covering their first war. To complain to the Pentagon about them only served to antagonize them still more. And the Pentagon couldn't even attempt to persuade their editors to recall them, as President Kennedy tried to get the New York *Times* to recall or reassign David Halberstam.

3. The public view of the war is given at greater length in my *Free Press/Free People: The Best Cause* (New York, 1971), 344, passim.

4. The condensed account of the Tet offensive is based on the more detailed account in the 1995 edition of my *Foreign Correspondence: The Great Reporters and Their Times* (Syracuse, 1995, 279–81; see also Sheehan, 707—28.

5. President Johnson's recall of General Westmoreland and his broadcast to the nation are elaborated on also in the 1995 edition of *Foreign Correspondence*, 280—81.

6. Knight's quotations are from the Akron *Beacon-Journal*, Apr. 9, 1967.

7. The riots at the major party conventions and the disorders during the presidential campaign of 1968 were widely reported at the time. As for the riots in Tennessee, relatives and friends shared their memories with me. I had all I could do at the time to maintain order in my classes at Columbia.

8. The 1968 Presidential election figures are from records of the Election Commission.

25. The War at Home

1. President Kirk and Dean Barrett had resigned after the student strike on campus in 1968 and the disruption among both faculties and trustees. No matter how hard acting President Cordier and acting Dean Baker tried, it was difficult to maintain order at Columbia without permanent office-holders at top level.

2. I was fortunate to be able to keep in touch with Dr. Kirk after his resignation because his judgments were important in the designation of membership for the various Pulitzer Prize juries and other matters of administrative importance for the awards.

3. Because I had worked in New York City for so many years, I knew most of the leading critical figures in letters and drama, whether or not they had previously served on Pulitzer juries, and never hesitated to consult them when I had a chance. From long experience I knew perfectly well that neither I nor any individual board member could influence their judgment. It could have been disastrous for me if I'd ever tried.

4. Nixon's resistance, as history has shown, only stiffened the resolve of the North Vietnamese at the Paris peace talks.

5. One of the leaders of the Columbia College strike movement, so I learned, was the son of an old acquaintance of mine at the United Nation, a Tunisian correspondent for a French agency. That, however, didn't make life any easier for me, but at least we didn't have to face either mob violence or student guns.

6. The guarding assignments of federal and local police were publicized well in advance of the former president's funeral.

7. The Nixon reception was our first appearance at a formal White House celebration.

8. Anyway, it ended a fun week—and at the outset, I'd dreaded it.

9. Cordier approved the trip.

10. After the 1969 Pulitzer hold-for-release announcement, I never tried that tactic again regardless of provocation. There was too much chance for a leak or an embarrassing last-minute change by the trustees in the Pulitzer board's prize lineup.

11. Despite the Pulitzer Prize, Mailer's candidacy for mayor was an utter failure. He had no organization, no money, and little TV time to conduct so useless an independent campaign.

12. I was able to make the trip to Moscow in the summer of 1969 because I'd given up teaching at summer school.

26. Another World

1. The main part of this chapter is based on my diary notes covering 1968–1969; an article about the Czech/Russian experience that I wrote for the *Saturday Review,* Nov. 8, 1969, 78–80; and in *Free Press/Free People,* 350–73. Other notes and comment follow.

2. Solzhenitsyn's letter of protest was written in 1969.

3. The old Czech journalist was located in Prague through friends but, even so, he did not want to identify himself, fearing retribution from the occupying force.

4. The trip behind the iron curtain took about three months in the summer of 1969. I had covered the communications problems in Britain and Western Europe the previous summer.

5. The Soviets' fear of Communist China appeared to me to be genuine enough, but they used it merely to try to forestall questions about the Czech invasion, which appeared to embarrass them.

6. *Samisdat* at the time of my visit was a risky undertaking. In later years, when the underground opposition to the Kremlin's rulers gained strength, it was often a service from which an American correspondent could gain insights into the Soviet condition that otherwise were unavailable.

7. Solzhenitsyn was penned up in his home in Rostov until his departure, forced by the government, to his Vermont retreat. Otherwise, his foreign royalties for his books might not have been available to him.

8. My Pulitzer Traveling Scholarship was one of the three issued for graduates of the Columbia Journalism School class of 1927. To that $1,500 stipend while at the Univ. of Vienna, I added payments made by American and other correspondents who hired me sometimes as a temporary replacement. It was as a result of work for the old, old New York *Evening Post* from abroad that I was hired as night city editor when I returned in 1928.

9. Hochman's views were published under his byline in the Washington *Post* for a Sunday in late July, 1968. It was forwarded to me by Dixon Donnelly, an assistant secretary of state, who also helped with arrangements in London, Paris, and elsewhere.

10. The French visitors, all members of a closely-knit newspaper union, were not impressed with the general American practice of keeping correspondents' opinions out of the news unless they were assigned to do an opinion piece.

27. The Peace Riots

1. The Nixon doctrine was announced on Guam and published in the New York *Times* July 26, 1969, 1.

2. After the "War Moratorium" performance at the J-school on Oct. 15, 1969, it was repeated on university campuses elsewhere, Nixon's response was in the New York *Times,* Nov. 4, 1968, 1.

3. Hersh's sketch is based on his entry in *Who's Who in America,* 48th ed.

4. Hersh's first article is from the St. Louis *Post-Dispatch,* Nov. 13, 1969.

5. Added comment on Hersh disclosure is from his Pulitzer Prize exhibit for 1970.

6. Nixon's "State of the World" speech was in the New York *Times,* Feb. 19, 1970, 1. On Sihanouk's overthrow and the US invasion of Cambodia, see the New York *Times,* May 1, 1970.

7. The 1970 Pulitzer awards are from the Pulitzer Prize records. Nixon's speech was in the New York *Times,* Apr. 21, 1970.

8. My Apr. 28 diary entry was based on the *Wall Street Journal* and New York *Times*

editions of Apr. 28–29, 1970. The final report on campus disorders was compiled by the Carnegie Commission, published in the New York *Times,* Oct. 3, 1970.

28. Tragedy at Kent State

1. Giles's quote is in my book *The Pulitzer Prize Story II: 1959–1980* (New York, 1980), 1. Giles later became the executive editor of the Detroit *Free Press.*
2. The first report of the Akron *Beacon-Journal* was published May 4, 1970. It is reprinted in *The Pulitzer Prize Story II,* 189. The Filo picture, on 192, was published the same day in the *Valley Daily News* of Tarentum Pa., and the *Daily Dispatch* of New Kensington, Pa.
3. The quote is from the Akron *Beacon-Journal,* ibid.
4. The Carnegie report is in my *New Era in the Pacific;* 49–50.
5. In the case of the threat to the Pulitzer Prize announcement, I didn't take it too seriously. My relations with the students in the class of 1971 had generally been pleasant.
6. For the entire faculty, myself included, the end of school year was a nightmare, as the diary record shows.
7. The quote is from a prospectus submitted to the Ford Foundation and later included in the preface to *New Era in the Pacific.*

29. Rommy

1. Giichi Tanaka, a Japanese prime minister in the 1920s, was the author of Japan's expansionist policy.
2. Romulo's sketch is in *The Pulitzer Prizes,* 134–35. His interview was recorded at greater length in my Notebook no. 4, July 7–15, 1970. The Lopez interview follows in the same notebook.
3. The Marcos and Palaez interviews are also in Notebook no. 4.
4. The Sato and Nakasone interviews are in Notebook no. 2, June 18–21, 1970.
5. Seoul and Hong Kong visits are in Notebook no. 3, June 22–July 6, 1970.
6. Romulo, Soliven, Roces, and Escoda interviews are in Notebook no. 4.
7. Miyazawa's interview is given at length in Notebook no. 2.
8. The Watson incident is given in detail in Notebook no. 4.

30. Saigon Revisited

1. The count of army press agents was official, having been issued by the ambassador's office.
2. Despite his injuries, George H. Watson Jr., 1960 J, Columbia, survived his Vietnamese police beating but he was understandably reserved about his opinions of both the Vietnam government in Saigon and the American officials who had refused to give him a tetanus shot immediately after his injuries. His father, George H. Watson, Sr. had graduated from our school in 1922, five years before I did.
3. Shaplen's background is given in his book, *The Lost Revolution* (New York, 1955, 1963, 1964, 1965.) Arnett's is in an earlier note.
4. My views of Saigon were recorded at the time in my Notebook no. 4, July 7–15, under date of July 12.
5. The failure of the pacification program, as it was given by the American official in Pleiku, was fairly general at the time among officials and correspondents, despite the official line that the war still was being well fought.
6. The first impressions of Saigon Revisited, were based on my Notebook no. 4, date of July 12.

7. There were extensive day-to-day notes on correspondents' and other views in my Notebook nos. 4 and 5, the latter from July 16–27.

8. Bunker's views, as given at the time, are recorded in Notebook no. 5, July 16.

9. Khiem, Rosson, and Colby interviews are digested in Notebook nos. 4 and 5.

31. Life after Vietnam

1. Most US ambassadors to whom I talked in Asia confessed they were baffled by the Nixon doctrine as the president explained it on Guam.

2. Among Asian diplomats on my tour, the chief topic was the expectation of Taiwan's removal from the UN Security Council in favor of Communist China. To an old anti-Communist like Nixon, this was poison, and he avoided it until the last.

3. Jack Anderson, in a column distributed by the Bell-McClure Syndicate, Dec. 30, 1971, analyzed the reasons for Nixon's disastrous support of Pakistan against victorious India in their 1971 war. It was, Anderson said, a case of Nixon guessing wrong again. Mrs. Gandhi was slain Oct. 31, 1984.

4. The American two-Chinas policy was doomed to failure from the beginning of Nixon's term.

5. The class of 1971 at our school represented a lull in the storm of opposition to the Vietnam War.

6. I refrained from publishing my diaries on the prizes in general and the Pentagon Papers in particular for personal reasons. It was a twenty-year delay.

32. Turmoil at Columbia

1. McGill's "guarantee" was given publicly at a luncheon of the Pulitzer board Apr. 13, 1972. The trustees finally separated themselves from the prizes in 1975. The main point of contention came from trustees who favored the Nixon presidency; after his resignation, such contested awards ended.

2. The Pentagon Study Group was headed by Leslie Gelb, who later was a member of the New York *Times* staff and a president of the Council on Foreign Relations. The copies of the papers were distributed to the *Times*, Washington *Post* and others, by a disaffected member of the study group, Daniel Ellsberg.

3. The *Times*'s two exhibits came in just before the annual Pulitzer deadline for 1972, which was Feb. 1. There was not at first as much publicity about Jack Anderson's disclosures of American policy failings in the Indo-Pak War, but the two were linked by the respective Pulitzer juries.

4. I included references to my regular activities at Columbia and in the few evenings I had to myself to indicate that not all my life and my wife's were devoted to my working career.

5. The Papp complaint was not unusual. Broadway producers regularly argued with juries that disappointed them, but I know of no case in which allegations of questionable conduct were sustained against jurors, past or present.

6. There was so much uproar over the *Times*'s prize that the Talese protests were scarcely noticed in the news media.

7. Wallace Carroll served several times as a Pulitzer Prize juror, always with distinction and good judgment.

8. President McGill's request to have a faculty member sleep in the supposedly threatened Journalism building was an indication of the strain these demonstrations caused for a dedicated official who believed quite sincerely that these student strikes threatened the future of one of the oldest universities in the land.

9. The trustees' executive committee was reversed by the formal trustees' meeting that

reacted to President McGill's appeal for compromise. He later denied he had threatened to resign, then said he hadn't meant what he said in quite that way.

10. My Pulitzer Prize history was read and approved by President McGill and Joseph Pulitzer Jr., among others, before Columbia University Press published it in 1974. It turned out to be primarily a labor of love, but I never regretted the effort.

33. Watergate in Retrospect

1. Woodward had less than a year's experience as a reporter when he began work on Watergate and Bernstein, on the authority of his managing editor, Howard Simons, had nearly been fired before being joined with Woodward in their Pulitzer Prize-winning Watergate inquiry.

2. Much of the detail of Howard Simons's life and career come either from my knowledge of him as a former student in the Columbia journalism class of 1952 or from his Washington Post obituary on June 14, 1989. The latter credited him with an "important part" in its rise to national prominence. The Woodward quote was in this Simons obituary.

3. Nobody did Howie any favors either in college or graduate school. He had to earn his own way and was about to wind up writing science—he was good at it—when the Post's higher authorities brought him along with successive promotions to managing editor. That's when he was tipped off to the attempted Watergate break-in.

4. Luck was with Howie and the Post when James W. McCord Jr. turned up among the first suspects arrested in the break-in of the Democratic offices at the Watergate complex. Later, Vice-President Spiro Agnew was accused on a separate charge.

5. That was the story of the year, and the Post was voted the gold medal for public service.

6. The trustees' disclaimer did not avert still another clash with the Pulitzer board in 1974, as the next chapter demonstrates.

34. The Awards under Fire

1. Nixon's quote was from a speech before the National Association of Broadcasters in Houston, Mar. 19, 1974.

2. Clayton Fritchey in the Washington Star carried the Agnew quote and responded to it Apr. 24, 1970.

3. Ford became vice-president replacing Agnew on Oct. 12, 1973, and president replacing Nixon Aug. 9, 1974—the only unelected vice-president and president in our history.

4. As a New York Times book reviewer wrote, this was not an "approved" history of sixty years of Pulitzer Prizes in an ordinary sense.

5. There is no mystery about my source for President McGill's performance before the trustees. Several Columbia officials who attended filled me in.

6. I doubt if there was any legal basis for the trustees' vote to refuse to reappoint the Pulitzer board. The board had always been a self-perpetuation group, electing its own replacements subject only to their acceptance.

7. I once heard Chairman Pulitzer threaten to take the prizes to Washington Univ. in St. Louis. Others have said he also threatened once to ask Harvard to take custody of the awards. I do not know if he ever made good on either threat, and he never volunteered the information to me.

8. Barry Goldwater was reelected as a senator in 1969, a major influence in the conservative wing of the Republican Party.

9. Nixon's resignation made impeachment and trial unnecessary.

10. After his resignation, Nixon was treated as an elder statesman until his death in New York City April 22, 1994.

35. A Prize Solution

1. The previous record for journalism exhibits was a little more than 400. Many papers began sending in multiple exhibits.

2. Brucker's remarks were carried at length in the ASNE Bulletin for July 1, 1967.

3. I was in the middle of these continual exchanges between the board and the trustees, an awkward position for even a tenured Columbia professor in technical retirement, but I had no choice.

4. My invitation to teach at the Univ. of Tennessee came from Dean Don Hileman of the College of Communications, whom I had not previously known.

5. My suggestion for the prompt appointment of my successor was part of a Columbia press release. I did not want to serve beyond June 30, 1976, in any event.

6. Chairman Pulitzer, who managed large assets for the St. Louis *Post-Dispatch* and other properties as well as his own considerable fortune, often told me that he believed the Pulitzer Prize Fund could have been invested in a more profitable manner.

7. McGrory won the prize for commentary in 1975.

8. Knubel was the source for the maneuvering after the trustees' vote to separate themselves from the prizes.

36. Beyond Defeat

1. The final attack on Saigon by North Vietnam was as effective as it was surprising. The defense wasn't able to repel the foe.

2. The only explanation I have for the sudden collapse of Saigon, now Ho Chi Minh City, was that neither the small remaining army defenders of American soldiers nor the American public cared what happened as long as those who could get out did so safely.

3. Not many correspondents were left in Saigon at the end and three of them, Esper, Beech, and Tamarkin, managed to escape in safety in an aircraft.

4. My first experience at the Univ. of Tennessee in 1975 was a happy one, and I decided at once to stay beginning in 1976 if the authorities would have me. The answer, fortunately, was yes.

5. I was fortunate, too, that Dean Hileman and the Gannett Foundation agreed to handle my stipend for doing the new book, *A Crisis for the American Press* (New York, 1978). It all pointed to a renewed career and a new home in the fall of 1976.

37. Auld Lang Syne

1. Professor Baker's selection as my successor, and his agreement to do so, pleased me very much. We had been friends and colleagues for more than a quarter century.

2. My seventieth birthday surprise party at the Pulitzer office delighted me—a proper leave-taking from the two efficient ladies in my office who had made it possible for me to administer the Pulitzer Prizes while maintaining a professor's full course of studies for a score or more of graduate students in my classes.

3. I still had the notion that Dorothy somehow enjoyed a night in the theater, although her condition through Alzheimer's disease had reached an advanced stage that then made communication with her almost impossible.

4. The Schanberg prize capped my last session with the Pulitzer Prizes.

5. My farewells were done in style by both the university, my colleagues and students

in the J-school, and the Pulitzer board, the latter with the Pulitzer Prize Special Award for my services to American journalism.

Southern Exposure

1. When I returned to Columbia for three successive years of Pulitzer jury service for the first time, I was seventy-six and teaching elsewhere. I ended my work for the prizes in my eightieth year.

2. My new family and I easily adjusted to summers at the old homestead in Aquebogue, L.I.

3. I had no part in the Janet Cooke affair, and Professor Baker was too ill to be concerned.

As for Bradlee's unsubstantiated and undocumented charges against some of his fellow Pulitzer board members, including some of the most distinguished figures in American journalism, I would agree with the New York *Times* book reviewer who suspected he had been upset by the Janet Cooke affair (Book Review, Oct. 1, 1995, 11). In any event, neither Bradlee nor anybody else in my time, so far as I know, was guilty of such gross misconduct that would have disgraced not only themselves and the awards but a great university as well.

4. Lee Hills's procedural changes were adopted by the Pulitzer board.

5. JoAnn and I frequently stayed in Aquebogue on trips to New York and New England for my lectures.

6. Our Pulitzer jury acted quickly that first year. When I returned to my Florida classes, I found an offer for another year's teaching at Miami Univ., also in Florida.

7. During my Asian lecture tour, on which JoAnn accompanied me, Pam and Eric stayed at Aquebogue and were looked after by our neighbors during our absence. As a new and somewhat anxious father, it was hard being separated from them, and I was as happy as JoAnn was upon our reunion.

8. From the sunny Atlantic beaches near Miami back to two years of Ivy League experiences at Syracuse, JoAnn and I enjoyed the best of both worlds and I would hope that my students in both universities benefited. I did teach once more at Tennessee in an emergency during 1987. But after that, I busied myself almost entirely with my writing. For as long as my health remained good, JoAnn and I were comfortable in Knoxville.

It was a late marriage that worked for us and for the children.

Bibliography

The following sources are those that I have consulted in this and other works dealing with my twenty-two-year administration of the Pulitzer Prizes. They often amplified the primary sources of these diaries—the many friendships that grew out of my long association with the Pulitzer organization as well as those who strove for the awards and those who won them, as listed in the Notes and Comment.

Books

Abel, Elie. *The Missile Crisis*. New York, 1966.
Alsop, Joseph, and Stewart Alsop. *The Reporter's Trade*. New York, 1959.
Atkinson, Brooks. *Broadway*. New York, 1970.
———. *The Lively Years, 1920–1973*. New York, 1973.
Baker, Carlos. *Ernest Hemingway: A Life Story*. New York, 1969.
Baker, Richard T. *A History of the Graduate School of Journalism, Columbia University*. New York, 1954.
Barrett, James W. *Joseph Pulitzer and His World*. New York, 1941.
Baruch, Bernard M. *My Own Story*, New York, 1957.
———. *The Public Years*. New York, 1960.
Berger, Meyer. *The Story of* The New York Times, *1851–1951*. New York, 1951.
Brown, John Mason. *The Worlds of Robert E. Sherwood: Mirror to His Times*. New York, 1965.
Browne, Malcome W. *The New Face of War*. Indianapolis, 1965.
Brustein, Robert. *The Theatre of Revolt*. Boston, 1962.
Burns, James MacGregor. *John F. Kennedy: A Political Profile*. New York, 1959.
Butler, Nicholas Murray. *Across the Busy Years*. 2 vols. New York, 1935, 1939.
Carter, Hodding. *Where Main Street Meets the River*. New York, 1952.
Childs, Marquis, and James Reston. *Walter Lippmann and His Times*. New York, 1959.
Coit, Margaret. *Mr. Baruch*. Boston, 1957.
Compton, Arthur H. *Atomic Quest*. New York, 1956.
Cooper, Kent. *Kent Cooper and the Associated Press*. New York, 1959.

331

Cox Commission Report. *Crisis at Columbia.* New York, 1968.

Curti, Merle. *The Growth of American Thought.* 2d ed. New York, 1951.

DeConde, Alexander. *A History of American Foreign Policy.* New York, 1963.

Dmytryshyn, Boris. *USSR: A Concise History.* New York, 1965.

Donovan, Robert J. *Eisenhower: The Inside Story.* New York, 1956.

Emery, Edwin, and Henry Ladd Smith. *The Press in America.* New York, 1954.

Eisenhower, Dwight D. *Mandate for Change.* Garden City, N.Y., 1963.

Fall, Bernard. *The Two Vietnams.* New York, 1963.

Friedel, Frank. *America in the 20th Century.* 5th ed. New York, 1982.

Friendly, Fred. *Due to Circumstances Beyond Our Control.* New York, 1967.

Frost, Robert. *In the Clearing.* New York, 1962.

Gassner, John, ed. *Best American Plays, five ser., 1938–1963.* New York, 1939, 1946, 1951, 1957, 1963.

———. *Theatre at the Crossroads.* New York, 1960.

Gaver, Jack, ed. *Critics' Choice: New York Drama Critics' Circle Prize Plays, 1935–1955.* New York, 1955.

Gelb, Arthur, and Barbara Gelb, *O'Neill.* New York, 1960.

Gould, Jean. *The Poet and Her Book: A Biography of Edna St. Vincent Millay.* New York, 1969.

Gramling, Oliver. *AP: The Story of News.* New York, 1950.

———. *Free Men Are Fighting.* New York, 1942.

Groves, Leslie R. *Now It Can Be Told: The Story of the Manhattan Project.* New York, 1962.

Halberstam, David. *The Best and the Brightest.* New York, 1969, 1970, 1972.

———. *The Making of a Quagmire.* New York, 1964.

Herblock [Herbert A. Block]. *Special for Today.* New York, 1958.

Higham, John. *History.* Englewood Cliffs, N.J., 1965.

Hofstadter, Richard. *The Progressive Historians: Turner, Beard, Parrington.* New York, 1970.

———, and Walter P. Metzger. *The Development of Academic Freedom in the United States.* New York, 1955.

Hohenberg, John. *Between Two Worlds.* New York, 1967.

———. *A Crisis for the American Press.* New York, 1978.

———. *Foreign Correspondence: The Great Reporters and Their Times.* New York, 1964, 1995.

———. *Free Press/Free People: The Best Cause.* New York, 1971.

———. *New Era in the Pacific: A Study in Public Diplomacy.* New York, 1972.

———. *The Professional Journalist.* 5th edition. New York, 1983.

———. *The Pulitzer Prizes: A History.* New York, 1974.

———, ed. *The Pulitzer Prize Story II, 1959–1980.* New York, 1980.

Hoopes, Townsend. *The Devil and John Foster Dulles.* Boston, 1973.

Hughes, Glen. *A History of the American Theatre.* New York, 1951.

Hutchens, John K., and George Oppenheimer, eds. *The Best in the* World. New York, 1973.

Ireland, Alleyne. *An Adventure with a Genius.* New York, 1920.

Johnson, Gerald W. *The Lines Are Drawn.* Philadelphia, 1958.

Kahn, E. J. Jr. *The World of Swope.* New York, 1965.

Kendrick, Alexander. *Prime Time: The Life of Edward R. Murrow.* Boston, 1969.

Kennedy, John F. *Profiles in Courage.* New York, 1956.

Laurence, William L. *Men and Atoms.* New York, 1959.

Leckie, Robert. *Conflict: The History of the Korean War.* New York, 1962.

Lie, Trygve. *In the Cause of Peace.* New York, 1954.

McGill, Ralph. *The South and the Southerner.* Boston, 1959.

MacLeish, Archibald. *Poetry and Experience.* Boston, 1961.

Mailer, Norman. *The Armies of the Night.* New York, 1968.

Manchester, William. *The Death of a President.* New York, 1967.

Martin, Harold H. *Ralph McGill, Reporter.* Boston, 1973.

Matthews, Herbert L. *The Cuban Story.* New York, 1961.

May, Henry F. *The End of American Innocence.* New York, 1959.

Mecklin, John. *Mission in Torment.* Garden City, N.Y., 1965.

Morison, Samuel Eliot. *The Oxford History of the American People.* New York, 1965.

Morris, Joe Alex. *Deadline Every Minute: The Story of the United Press.* New York, 1957.

Nowell, Elizabeth. *Thomas Wolfe.* New York, 1960.

Parrington, V. L. *Main Currents of American Thought,* 3 vols. New York, 1927–1930.

Pfaff, Daniel W. *Joseph Pulitzer II and the* Post-Dispatch. University Park, Pa., 1991.

Pulitzer, Joseph Jr. *A Tradition of Conscience.* St. Louis, 1965.

Raymond, Jack. *Power at the Pentagon.* New York, 1954.

Remmelkamp, Julian S. *Pulitzer's* Post-Dispatch. Princeton, 1967.

Reston, James. *Deadline, a Memoir.* New York, 1991.

———. *Sketches in the Sand.* New York, 1967.

Salisbury, Harrison E. *Behind the Lines—Hanoi: December 23–January 7.* New York, 1967.

Sandburg, Carl. *Always the Young Stranger.* New York, 1952–1953.

Schlesinger, Arthur M. Jr. *A Thousand Days.* Boston, 1965.

Schorer, Mark. *Sinclair Lewis, an American Life.* New York, 1961.

Seitz, Don C. *Joseph Pulitzer, His Life and Letters.* New York, 1924.

Sergeant, Elizabeth. *Robert Frost, the Trial by Existence.* New York, 1960.

Shaplen, Robert. *The Lost Revolution.* New York, 1955.

Sheaffer, Louis. *O'Neill, Son and Artist.* Boston, 1973.

Sheehan, Neil. *A Bright and Shining Lie: John Paul Vann and America in Vietnam.* New York, 1988.

Sloan, W. D., and L. B. Anderson. *Pulitzer Prize Editorials.* 2d. edition. Ames, Iowa, 1980, 1994.

Smyth, Henry DeWolf. *Atomic Energy for Military Purposes.* Princeton, 1946.

Swanberg, W. A. *Citizen Hearst.* New York, 1961.

Stuckey, W. J. *The Pulitzer Prize Novels.* Norman, Okla., 1966.

Thompson, Lawrance. *Robert Frost: The Years of Triumph.* New York, 1970.

Thomson, Virgil. *American Music Since 1910: 20th Century Composers.* New York, 1970.

Toland, John. *The Rising Sun.* New York, 1970.

Truman, Harry S. *Memoirs.* 2 vols. New York, 1956.

Tuchman, Barbara. *Stilwell and the American Experience in China, 1911–1945.* New York, 1971.

Turner, Frederick J. *The Significance of Sections in American History.* New York, 1933.

Untermeyer, Louis. *A Treasury of Great Poems.* New York, 1942.

Wise, David, and Thomas B. Ross. *The U-2 Affair.* New York, 1960.

White, Theodore H. *The Making of the President* ser. for 1960, 1964, 1968, 1972. New York, 1961, 1965, 1969, 1973.

Periodicals

Ackerman, Carl W. "Handbook of the Advisory Board of the Graduate School of Journalism," later called succcessively the Advisory Board on the Pulitzer Prizes and currently the Pulitzer Prize Board.

———. "Pulitzer Secrecy," letter to the editor, *Saturday Review,* July 14, 1951.

Baker, Carlos. "Forty Years of Pulitzer Prizes." *Princeton University Library Chronicle* 18 (Winter 1957): 42–45.

Bendiner, Robert. "The Truth about the Pulitzer Awards." *McCalls,* May, 1966, 82ff.

Clemons, Walter. "The Pulitzer Non-Prize for Fiction." *New York Times Book Review,* June 6, 1971, 55.

De Voto, Bernard. "The Pulitzer Prize in History." *Saturday Review,* Mar. 1937, 12–14.

Hohenberg, John, ed. Pulitzer Prize issue of *Columbia Library Columns* 6, no. 3 (May 1957).

Hutchens, John K. "Time: 4:24 p.m. Prizes: Pulitzer. *New York Herald Tribune Book Review,* May 8, 1955, 2.

Leonard, John. "Pulitzer Prizes Fail-Safe Again." *New York Times Book Review,* May 14, 1972, 47.

Mathews, William R. "Recollections of the Pulitzer Committee." *Arizona Daily Star,* May 22, 1966.

Maydeck, Robin, and others. "What's Behind the Pulitzer Prizes?" *Seminar* quarterly, issued by Copley Press, Sept. 1971, 34ff.

Mizener, Arthur. "The Pulitzer Prizes." *Atlantic Monthly* 200 (July 1957), 42–44.

Monroe, Harriet. "Pulitzer Award System." *Poetry* 30 (July 1927), 210–16.

"Watergate Three, The," *Time,* May 7, 1972, 82.

Unpublished Material

Ackerman, Carl W. "Pulitzer Prizes vs. Ivy League Colleges." Partial MS in Ackerman Papers Collection, Library of Congress.

Krock, Arthur. Seven-page MS for Copley Newspapers that was included in a letter to John Hohenberg, Mar. 19, 1971, and left with the papers in the Pulitzer collection at Columbia Univ.

Robinson, William Reynolds. "Joseph Pulitzer." Ph.D. diss, Columbia Univ. Libraries.

Index

Symbols are used as follows:
* Pulitzer Prize winner
† Prize-winning work
‡ Pulitzer juror
§ Pulitzer board member

Abel, Elie,‡ 191, 200, 223, 249, 260–61,
    276–78, 302
Abrams, General Creighton, 194
Acheson, Dean,* his likes and dislikes,
    70
Ackerman, Dean Carl W.,‡ xii, 4, 7, 13
Adams, Edward T.,* 200
Advisory Board on the Pulitzer Prizes
    (later Pulitzer Prize board), 3–4, 80–
    81, 117, 124; Duke Ellington affair,
    146–47, 149; Pentagon Papers, 247–
    64; student peace riots, 199–201,
    218; Watergate, 265–72. *See also*
    individual awards
Agnew, Vice-President Spiro, resignation
    of, 273–74
Air Force Academy, JH report on, 61–67
Air War College, Formosa Strait crisis
    and, 15, 27
Akron (Ohio) *Beacon Journal,** 181,
    184, 185–88; reports on Kent State
    riots and tragedy, 220–26; wins a
    Pulitzer, 253
Albee, Edward,* 124, 161
Alabama, University of, riot over black
    student, 75
Alsop, Joseph, 182
Amalrik, A. A., 207
Amanpour, Christiane, 79

American Society of Newspaper Editors
    (ASNE), 249, 254, 284
American Specialist program, JH role in,
    121–27
American Vietnam combat deaths, 226
Anderson, Jack,* 258–60
Anderson, Major Rudolph, 115
Ap Bac, battle of (Vietnam), 139
Aquebogue, Long Island, JH home, 247,
    305
Apartheid reporting prize, won by J. L.
    Hoagland, *Washington Post,* 253–
    54
*Arkansas Gazette,** attacks desegregation
    rioters, 76
Arnett, Peter,* 225, 237–38, 302;
    Vietnam War reports of, 79, 139,
    143, 158, 163
Ashmore, Harry, 76
Asian correspondence, a view of the
    future, 250
Associated Press: and the Pulitzer Prize,
    34, 50, 105, 136, 148, 158, 292;
    Pulitzer Prize winners between 1954–
    1976 include Edward Adams, 200;
    Peter Arnett, 79, 139, 143, 158, 163;
    Malcolm Browne, 132–33; Horst
    Faas, 143–48; Relman Morin, 76;
    Joe Rosenthal, 12; Jack Thornell,
    177
Atkinson, Brooks,* 134–35, 197, 200
Atomic control at the United Nations,
    109–10
Aubrey, James, on TV and prizes, 78
Austrian State Treaty, in Hearst team
    report, 39–40

335

Baker, Carlos,‡ 26, 50
Baker, Richard T.,§ xii, 80, 222–23; his death, 304; replaces JH, 289, 301
Baldwin, Hanson W.,* 174
Barber, Samuel,* 145
Barkham, John,‡ 249
Barnes, Hewlett, 82
Barrett, Edward W., 82–83, 85
Baruch, Bernard M., 16, 110
Bassett, Leslie,* 152
Bay of Pigs, 97–100
Beech, Keyes,* 292
Beecher, Bill, 241
Beichman, Arnold, 141–42
Berlin blockade, 103, 106–8
Bernstein, Carl,* and Watergate, 6, 164, 265–72
Berryman, John,* 148
Beveridge, George, 71, 77
Bigart, Homer,* 122
Bingham, Barry,§ 105
Block, Herbert L.,* 6, 77
Boccardi, Louis D., 302
Bohlen, Charles (Chip), 39
Bolshoi Ballet, 40–41
Boone, Buford, 75
Boston Globe, 153
Bowles, Chester, 125
Boyd, Julian,‡ 50
Boyd, Colonel Max, 18
Bradlee, Benjamin C.,§ 199, 300
Brandt, Mayor Willy (Berlin), 107
Bremner, John, 267
Brezhnev, Leonid, receives Nixon in Moscow, 277
Briggs, Major General Buster, 66
Broder, David S.,* 271
Brown, Dean Arthur, 308
Brown, Francis,§ 26, 50
Brown, John Mason,§ 68, 85, 124
Brown, Robert U., publisher of Editor & Publisher magazine, 15
Browne, Malcolm W.,* AP reporter in Vietnam, 132–33, 136, 158, 237
Brucker, Herbert, Pulitzer board critic, 284
Bunker, Ellsworth, 192, 193, 237, 242
Burns, James MacGregor,* 50, 253
Butler, Nicholas Murray,§ xii, 9, 145
Bunche, Ralph, 20

Butterfield, Alexander, 274
Byck, Sylvan,‡ 26

Cable News Network (CNN), 79
Califano, Joseph A. Jr., 267
Calley, Lieutenant William L. Jr., in My Lai massacre, 215, 217–18
Campbell, Oscar J.,‡ 26
Campus peace riots. See Peace riots, student
Canham, Erwin D,§ 50, 72, 197
Carmody, Nancy, 253, 254
Carnegie Endowment for International Peace, 72
Carpenter, Frank, 92
Carroll, Wallace,§ 26
Carter, Elliott,* 189
Carter, Hodding,§ 24
Castro, Fidel, and Bay of Pigs, 98–101, 110, 116
Catledge, Turner,§ 100, 176, 285
Cat on a Hot Tin Roof (Williams),† 24–25
Catton, Bruce,* A Stillness at Appomattox, 5
Central Intelligence Agency (CIA), 267–68
Chambers, Lenoir,* 84
Chicago Daily News,* 77, 123, 153
Chicago Tribune,* 105, 269, 271
China under Mao, 248
Chinese University of Hong Kong, 69, 224, 249
Christian Science Monitor,* John Hughes's prize, 176
Christopher, Bob, 304
Citizen Hearst (Swanberg), prize denied for, 109, 117
Clifford, Clark, replaces McNamara as secretary of defense, 194
Columbia Graduate School of Journalism, affected by student riots, 191, 198, 222–23
Columbia Unversity, affected by student riots, 189–92, 196–98, 218, 222–23
Columbia University Press, 130, 223
Conniff, Frank,* 39–42
Conrad, Paul,* 163
Considine, Bob, 15, 41
Cony, Ed,* 105

Cooke, Janet, prize withdrawn, 306
Copland, Aaron,*‡ 148–49, 165–66
Cordier, Andrew W.,§ 189, 190, 191, 196, 216
Council on Foreign Relations, 71, 128, 129, 131–32, 136, 144, 157
Cox, Archibald, 274
Cronkite, Walter, 162
Crumb, George,* 150
Cuban missile crisis, 110–17
Cuero (Texas) *Record,* 25
"Czech Spring," 204–5

Davidovsky, Mario,* 150
Davis, Brigadier General Ben, commander of the Thirteenth Air Force, 32
Davis, David Brion,* 162
Dean, John W. III, 270–71
Deaths, combat. *See* American Vietnam combat deaths
Deepe, Beverly, 122
"Deep Throat," 268–69, 270–71
De Gramont, Sanche (Ted Morgan),* 105, 163
Delany, Kevin, 267
Democratic National Committee and Watergate, 267–72
Des Moines *Register,** 6
Dispatch News Service, breaks My Lai massacre story, 215–16
Diary of Anne Frank, The, 45
Dien Bien Phu, French loss of, 182
Dobrynin, Anatoli, 112, 116
Dole, Robert, 268
Donald, David Herbert, 105, 162
Donoghue, Bill, 92
Douglas, Secretary of the Air Force James H. Jr., 37, 61–67
Dreiser, Theodore, 8, 159
Dulles, Allen, 182
Dulles, Secretary of State John Foster, 23, 27, 182, 229
Dunning, Bruce, 241

East-West Center, 69, 224–25
Eberhart, Richard,* 152
*Effect of Gamma Rays on Man-in-the-Moon Marigolds, The,** 253
Ehrenburg, Ilya, 207

Ehrlichman, John D., 270, 275
Eisenhower, President Dwight D.,§ 14–15, 29–30, 37, 98–99, 226
Ellington, Edward K. (Duke), xi, 145–49
Ellsberg, Daniel, makes public the Pentagon Papers, 255–71
Ervin, Samuel J., 270
Escoda, Tony, 234
Esper, George, 202
Eunson, Bob, 34
Evans, Colonel Pug, 32
Eyer, Ronald, *Newsday* music critic, in Ellington affair, 46, 149

Faas, Horst,* 143, 148, 259
Fall, Bernard, 173
Faulkner, William,* 8, 9, 124, 145
Feis, Herbert,* 105
Felt, Admiral Harry, 140
Ferguson, J. D.,§ proposes *Profiles in Courage,* 50
Fetterman, John,* 200
Filo, John Paul,* photographs Kent State tragedy, 221
Fiorello,† 69, 83
Fisher, Colonel Sydney G., 86, 169
Fitzgerald, F. Scott, 159
Fitzpatrick, D. R.,* 25
Florida peonage exposé, 8
Florida, University of, 69, 307
Flowering Peach, The, loses Pulitzer Prize, 24–25
Fomin, Alexsandr, 115
Ford, President Gerald R., 274, 280–81
Ford Foundation, 224, 249
Foreign Correspondence: The Great Reporters and Their Times (Hohenberg), 117, 130–31, 139–45
Formosa Strait crisis, 14–15, 18–19
Frankel, Max,* 162
Friedman, Thomas L.,* 310
Friendly, Al, 162
Friendly, Fred, 78–79, 156
Frings, Ketti,* 159
Frost, Robert,* 159

Gandhi, Indira, JH's last meeting with, 251–52
Gannett Foundation, 296, 302

Gassner, John,‡ 124
Gershwin, George, 9
Gershwin, Ira,* 9
Gill, Brendan,§ 197
Giles, Bob, 220
Gilroy, Frank,* 148
Goldwater, Barry, on Nixon, 128, 129–30, 278
Goltz, Gene,* 148
Gordon, Dave, 308
Gordone, Charles,* 223
Graham, Katharine, 265–72
Grapes of Wrath,The (Steinbeck), 11
Grau, Shirley Ann,* 148, 162
Gromyko, Andrei,109
Guns of August, The (Tuchman),† 260

Halberstam, David,* 123, 125, 132–33, 136, 140, 158, 236
Haldeman, H. R,, 269, 270, 271, 275
Hammarskjold, Dag (UN secretary general), 16, 111n
Hammerstein, Oscar II,* xi, xiii, 160
Harriman, Governor Averell (New York), 92
Harron, Robert, 18
Harvard University, effect of peace riots on, 198, 199, 200
Hastings, John, 253–54
Hawaii, University of, 69, 224
Hickam Air Force Base, Hawaii, 31
Hearst, William Randolph Jr.,* xi, 39–42, 109, 303
Hearst, William Randolph Sr., 10, 39
Heinzerling, Lynn,* 105
Heiskell, John N., 76
Hellman, Lillian, *Toys in the Attic* loses drama prize, 83
Hemingway, Ernest, 153, 159
Henderson the Rain King (Bellow), loses prize, 83
Hendrix, Hal,* 110
Herblock. *See* Block, Herbert L.
Hersh, Seymour M.,* 214–16, 217, 223, 225
Higgins, Marguerite,* 123
Hills, Lee,* ‡ 134, 159
Ho, Robert, 233
Ho Chi Minh, 153, 192–93, 201, 226
Hochman, Jiri, 210

Hofstadter, Richard,*‡ 134, 159
Hohenberg, John: about this book, xi, xii, xiii; attends first Pulitzer board meeting, 3–7; Berlin blockade crisis, 103, 106–8; Cuban missile crisis, 112–17; decides to remain at Columbia, 31; economies in the Pulitzer Prizes, 59–60; farewell lunch, 303; Faulkner's prize, 145; Formosa Strait crisis, 13–18; jury reversals, 83–87; notifies John F. Kennedy that board did not question that he wrote *Profiles in Courage*, 47–55; offered outside jobs, 20, 29–30; Pacific inspection trip, 33–36; planning for fiftieth anniversary of prizes, 156, 161; produces Vietnam War report, *Between Two Worlds*, 171; publication of *Foreign Correspondence*, 133–34; reaction to JFK assassination, 121–27; receives Pulitzer Prize Special Award, 303; records last Vietnam prize, 294; releases Pulitzer Prize record on Pentagon Papers prize, 256, 257–63; report on USAFE, 42–46; on rise in TV news and decline of newspapers, 74–79; sees Kennedy win presidency, 89–94; shocked at Bay of Pigs fiasco, 97–100; sixth Asian mission, 227–35; stories of George Gershwin, Margaret Mitchell, Carl Sandburg, Archibald MacLeish, and Carlos Peña Romulo, 8–12; and student peace riots, 191, 196–97, 210, 218; study of press behind iron curtain, 201; surveys Vietnam correspondence and nearly loses his wife, Dorothy, to a Vietcong bomb, 136–44; trustees of Columbia vs. Pulitzer board, 276–80; trustees separate themselves from prizes, 293; Vietnam and Washington, D.C., interviews for survey of war coverage for Council on Foreign Relations, 137–39, 142–44; on Watergate, 265–72
Hohenberg, Dorothy Lannuier: Asian trip and reaction to Kennedy assassination, 126–27; attends her last Broadway show, 303; effect of Alzheimers and her death, 305: helps

New York police catch a robber, 172;
    with JH in Europe, 42–45; second
    Asian trip, 226–32; unhurt in Saigon
    hotel bombing, 137–38; White
    House visit, 200–201
Hohenberg, JoAnn Fogarty, xiii, 305–8
Hohenberg, Simon, Holocaust victim,
    209, 210
Hong Kong, 71, 233
Hotel Caravelle, Saigon, bombing at, 237
House, Karen Elliott,* 310
House Judiciary Committee. See US
    House Judiciary Committee
How to Succeed in Business Without
    Really Trying,† 109
Huang, General J. L., of Taiwan Air
    Force, 32
Hughes, John,* wins Pulitzer after a
    board fight over a prize, 176
Humphrey, Hubert, his presidential
    campaign disrupted by peace rioters,
    195
Hunt, E. Howard, 269

India–US relations at time of Kennedy
    assassination, 125–27
Inside the German Empire (Swope), 9
International Communications Agency.
    See US International Communications
    Agency
In the Days of McKinley (Leech), 83,
    159

Jackson, Robert H.,* photographer of
    murder of Kennedy assassin, 133
Johnson, President Lyndon B.: defends
    Vietnam policies, 132, 133–34;
    General Westmoreland demands
    more troops for Vietnam, 184–85,
    187–88, 189; increases Vietnam war,
    128–29; meets Kosygin, 206; and
    Nixon elected president, 198; peace
    talks fail, 205; recalls Westmoreland,
    193–94; refuses to attend Pulitzer
    Prize celebration, 147–50; responds
    to critics, 141; and student riots, 96–
    97, 189, 197–99; Tet offensive, 192;
    and Tonkin Gulf incident, 137–38
Jones, Howard Mumford,* 148

Jones, Howard P., offers JH post at East-
    West Center, 157
Joplin, Scott,* 149
Jury protests about Pulitzers, 85

Kann, Peter B,* wins Pulitzer for reports
    on Indo-Pakistan conflict, 258
Kansas, University of, 69
Kapitsa, P. L., 207
Karmin, Monroe,* 177
Kaufman, George S.,* shares Of Thee I
    Sing prize, 9
Keating, Senator Kenneth, 111
Keepers of the House, The (Grau), 162
Kennan, George F.,* Russia Leaves the
    War, 48
Kennedy, John F.: anti-Nixon campaign
    of, 89–91; assassination of, 121–27;
    and the Bay of Pigs incident, 97–100;
    and the Cuban missile crisis, 112–17;
    first Pulitzer winner to seek and win
    the presidency, 53–55; Profiles in
    Courage wins prize, 47–50; as a
    senator, 52–53; students cover his
    election, 93–94
Kennedy, Robert F., 115–16, 122–23
Kent State tragedy, 220–26
Kerr, Walter,‡ 197
Khiem, Tran Thiem, South Vietnam
    leader, 242
Khoman,Thanat, the view from
    Thailand, 251
Khrushchev, N. S., 37; Berlin blockade,
    103, 107–8; and the Cuban missile
    crisis, 112–17; and Hearst team
    interview, 39–42; persecutes writers,
    207–8; threats made at the United
    Nations, 97–100; at the United
    Nations after U-2 spy plane incident,
    88–89
King, the Reverend Dr. Martin Luther
    Jr., 153
Kirk, Grayson:§ asks JH to report on
    proposed TV prize, 103–5; as
    Columbia president and Pulitzer
    board member, 5–7; and Ellington
    receives honorary degree at
    Columbia, 149; leaves Columbia,
    189; proposes rule for Pulitzer board,
    124; at Pulitzer fiftieth anniversary,

Kirk, Grayson (*continued*)
163; quoted on Bay of Pigs incident, 99; quoted on peace riots, 197, 201; receives Ellington case protests, 148; services of evaluated, 195
Kleindienst, Richard, G., 271
Knight, John S.,* 163, 181, 184, 185–88, 201, 205
Kohlmeier, Louis,* 148
Kolodin, Irving,‡ 149
Korean rivalry, 231–32
Krock, Arthur,*§ 7, 24, 25, 151
Ku Klux Klan and White Citizens' Councils, exposés of, 8, 76
Kuter, General Lawrence, US Far East Air Force commmander, 32–33
Kuzen, Robin Holloway, 298, 303, 304, 306

Laird, Secretary of Defense Melvin, 200
Laurent, Michel, 259
Lee, Harper,* 105
Leech, Margaret,* 83, 159
Lewis, Anthony,* 25
Lewis, Sinclair, 158
Liddy, G. Gordon, 269
Lindbergh, Colonel Charles A.,* 6
Lippmann, Walter,* 109–10
Livingston, J. A.,* 148
Lodge, Henry Cabot Jr., 48
Loesser, Frank,* 9
Logan, Joshua,* 159
Loh, Gene, city editor, *China Daily News,* Taipei, 33
Lon Nol, seizes power in Cambodia, 217
Lopez, Andrew,* 84
Lopez, Salvador, 72, 229
Los Angles *Times,** wins public service award for drug exposé, 84
Lott, Milton, loses a Pulitzer, 24, 26
Louisville *Times and Courier-Journal,* 177, 200
Lowenstein, Dan Ralph, 309
Lucas, Jim* 6
Luening, Otto C.,‡ 150
Lyons, Leonard, 24

MacArthur, General Douglas, breaks news of a Pulitzer award, 11

McCarthy, Senator Joseph R. Jr., ridiculed by Herblock, 77
McCloy, John J., 107–8
McCone, John A., 111
McCord, James W. Jr., 269, 270
McGill, Ralph,*§ xiii; criticizes Ellington jury, 155, death of, 196, 203; warns the South, 75, 109; wins prize, 74
McGill, William J., Columbia president,§ 253, 256; agrees to separate trustees from the Pulitzers, 284–89; backs Pentagon Papers prize, 257–63; negotiates with trustees, 264, 268; presents JH with Pulitzer Special Award, 303; truce with the trustees, 281–82; upholds two prizes against the trustees, 276
McGinley, Phyllis,* 105
McGrory, Mary,* remarks on Nixon's downfall, 288
McKeel, Sam, 267
McKelway, Ben,§ 136
McLaughlin, John, 36
MacLeish, Archibald,* remarks at Pulitzer celebration, 162–64

Macmillan, British Prime Minister Harold, 114
McNamara, Secretary of Defense Robert S.: quits Pentagon, 194; role in Vietnam War reporting, 122–23; seeks negotiated settlement and orders preparation of Pentagon Papers, 186–87
McQuary, Joan, 130
Magruder, Jeb Stuart, 270
Mailer, Norman,* 199
Malamud, Bernard,* 162
Malik, Adam, view of from Indonesia, 251
Mao Zedong, in the Formosa Strait crisis, 15
Marcos, Ferdinand, 229, 230
Marshall, Brigadier General L. A., quoted on Vietnam War, 142
Mason, Alpheus T., 50
Mattingly, Garrett,* wins special Pulitzer, 83
Maxwell, W. D.,§ 123
May, Edgar,* 105

Menon, Krishna, an Indian view of China, 28
Menotti, Gian-Carlo,* 145, 159
Meredith, James, 177
Miami *Herald,* 177
Miami *News,* 110
Miami University, 69
Michener, James A., 83, 160
Miller, Arthur,* 161
Miller, Dave, 241
Miller, Gene,* 177
Miller, Perry,* 152
Milwaukee *Journal,* 177
Mitchell, Attorney General John N., 269, 270
Mitchell, Margaret,* *Gone with the Wind* wins a prize, 10–11
Miyazawa, Kiichi, Japanese critic of the United States, 234
Mollenhoff, Clark,* 77
Molotov, Vyacheslav, interviewed by Hearst team, 40
Moore, Douglas S.,* 72, 171
Moosa, Spencer, 33
Morgan, Ted. *See* De Gramont, Sanche
Morin, Relman,* wins a Pulitzer for a phone call, 76
Morison, Samuel Eliot,* 83, 159
Morris Agency, William, 117
Mosel, Ted,* 105
Mosely, Philip, 73
Moyers, Bill, 161
Mulligan, Hugh, 241
Murrow, Edward R., 26, 78
My Lai tragedy, 214–16, 217, 226

Nagao, Yasushi,* 106
Nakasone, Yasuhiro, 231–32
Nation, the, 101
National Association of Broadcasters, 273
Nehru, Jawaharlal, 125
Nelson, Jack,* 82
Nevins, Allan,* 49, 159
New Era in the Pacific: A Study in Public Diplomacy, 225
Newsday (Long Island),* 6, 223
Newsweek, quoted, 140–41
New York *Daily News,** forecasts rise of Fidel Castro, 77–78

New York *Times:** individual awards to Brooks Atkinson, 134; Hanson Baldwin, 174; Thomas Friedman, 310; Max Frankel, 162; David Halberstam, 123–25, 132–36; Anthony Lewis, 25 (while on staff of Washington *Daily News*); James Reston, 96–97, 106; A. M. Rosenthal, 84, 162–63; Harrison Salisbury, 17, 73, 169–70; Pulitzer public service award in the Pentagon Papers disclosure, 257–63
New York *World* (Pulitzer's newspaper) merged to form New York *World-Telegram,* 9
Nieman Foundation, 267, 272, 305
Nixon, President Richard M.: attacks Pulitzer Prizes, 273; and Cambodia, 216–19; debates John F. Kennedy, 90–93; faces House impeachment, 276–78; and My Lai tragedy, 214–16; new attacks elsewhere, 212–13; peace riots resume, 218, 254; resigns Aug. 18, 1974, 280; "Vietnamized" the war, 198; vows he would not be the first president to lose a war, 194–95; and Watergate, 264, 265–72, 279
Nixon, Pat, 261
Nobel prizes, 159, 207, 208
No Place to Be Somebody (Gordone),† 223
North Atlantic Treaty Organization (NATO), 112
Nuclear test ban treaty, 206

Obst, David, 214–16
O'Connor, Edwin,* 50, 109
Odets, Clifford, loses drama prize, 21–22, 24–25
Of Thee I Sing,† 9
O'Neill, Eugene,* 48, 159
Organization of American States, 112
Orr, Carey,* 105
Oswald, Lee Harvey, 126–27
Ottenberg, Miriam,* 84

Pacific defenses of the United States, 249
Padover, Saul, 43–45

Palach, Jan, 205
Pasternak, Boris, 207
Patrick, John,* 5
Peace riots, student, 189–91, 196–97,
    199, 218–19; Kent State tragedy,
    219–21, 224, 236. See also under
    individual universities
Peace seminar at Columbia, 3, 15, 17
Pearson, Drew, 47–50
Pelaez, Emanuel, 229
Penn, Stanley,* 177
Pepys, Samuel, xi
Persichetti, Vincent,‡ 150
Petersen, William E., Columbia trustees'
    chairman, 259, 262–63
Philadelphia Bulletin, 6
Pham Van Dong, North Vietnam
    premier, 175–76
Philippines Herald, 11
Piston, Walter,* 145, 159
Poats, Rutherford, 34
Polk, James R.,* 213, 275, 276
Porter, Katherine Ann,* 124
Porter, Quincy,*§ 6
Portland Oregonian reporters Wallace
    Turner and William Lambert,* 77
Professional Journalist, The
    (Hohenberg), 250
Profiles in Courage (Kennedy),† 47–50
Providence (R.I.) Journal and Evening
    Bulletin, 273, 275, 276
Public Broadcasting Service (PBS), 79
Pulitzer, Joseph I, xiii, 167
Pulitzer, Joseph II,§ 5–7, 21
Pulitzer, Joseph Jr.:§ bars TV prize, 105;
    as board chairman, 22; changes
    procedures of board, 26–27; draws
    protest over slight to Duke Ellington,
    149–50; keeps Columbia J-deans off
    Pulitzer board, 277; separates
    Columbia trustees from Pulitzer
    board, 284–89; shakes up a music
    jury, 145, 146; supports prize for
    Hearst team, 41–42
Pulitzer, Michael E., xiii, 21, 301
Pulitzer, Ralph, 83, 84
Pulitzer Prize board. See Advisory Board
    on the Pulitzer Prizes
Pulitzer jury's rule on reversals, 26
Pulitzer prizes, general: changes in prizes,
    80–81, 117, 124, 146–47, 148–49;

effect of Columbia riots on, 197–99,
    218–19, 221–24; funding of prizes,
    60; plan of award, 25; special
    meeting of Pulitzer board, 152–60;
    war-reporting prizes, 225–26
Pulitzer Traveling Scholarship, 209
Pyle, Ernie,* 12

Quarles, US Air Force Secretary Donald,
    36, 43–45
Quill, 249

Rabi, I. I., 95–97
Reischauer, Edwin O., 184
Republican National Committee, 268
Reston, James,*§ 106, 166–67, 197, 271
Richardson, Elliot L., 271, 274
Roces, J. P. (Chino), 234
Rodgers, Richard,* 160
Roethke, Theodore,* 5
Rogers, Secretary of State William P.,
    200
Rome, Harold, 10
Romulo, Carlos P.,* 11, 224, 227–29,
    234
Roosevelt, President Franklin D., 199,
    226
Rosenthal, A. M.,* 84, 162–63, 302
Rosenthal, Joe,* 12
Rosson, General W. B., 242
Royster, Vermont C.*§ 151, 260
Ruby, Jack, 127
Ruckelshaus, William D., 274
Ruder, Mel,* 148
Rusk, Secretary of State Dean, 71, 111,
    123, 132

Sackler, Howard,* 197, 200
St. Louis Post-Dispatch,* xiii, 21–22,
    25, 60n, 214–16
Saint of Bleecker Street, The (Menotti),†
    15, 25
St. Petersburg (Fla.) Times,* 153
Salinger, Pierre, 129
Salisbury, Harrison,* defeated by John
    Hughes for another Pulitzer, 176–77,
    224; reports from Hanoi criticized,
    169–70; White House critical of him

and the New York *Times*, 171, 174–76; wins Pulitzer for Moscow reports and observes Formosa Strait crisis, 17, 73

Samisdat (Moscow and Czech underground press), 206–7

Samuels, Ernest,*§ 148, 162

Sandburg, Carl,* 11, 159

Santa Barbara (Calif.) *News-Press,* 101

Sarnoff, Robert, 104–5

Sato, Eisaku, Japanese prime minister, 228, 231

"Saturday Night Massacre," 274

Saturday Review, 248

Sawada, Kyoichi,* 143

Scali, John, 115

Schanberg, Syd,* 294–96, 300

Schell, Jonathan, 212–13

Schlesinger, Arthur M. Jr.,* 152, 162, 167–68

Schuller, Gunther,‡ 149

Schulte, Henry, 30

Schuman, William,* 148

Scott, US Air Force Brigadier General Bob, 36

Selective Service Board, 19

Sergeant, Winthrop,‡ 146–49

Sessions, Roger, 151

1776, 19, 24–25

Shaplen, Robert, 236–37

Sheehan, Neil,* 137, 139, 144; obtains Pentagon Papers for the New York *Times,* 257–63; quoted on Vietnam War, 212–13; wins a Pulitzer for *A Bright and Shining Lie,* 263, 271

Sherman, Thomas B.,‡ 146, 149

Sherwood, Robert E.,* 159

Ship of Fools, The (Porter), 124

Shu, General, Taiwanese army chief of staff, 33

Sihanouk, Prince Norodom, 216

Sirica, Judge John J., 269, 270, 274

Simons, Howard, 264, 265–72

Sluman, Colonel Curtis D., 34

Smith, Governor Alfred E., 88

Smith, Howard Van,* 77

Smith, J. Kingsbury,* 39–42

Smith, Merriman,* 133

Smith, Major General Sory, 32–36

Society of Professional Journalists/Sigman Delta Chi, 85, 305

Soliven, Maximo, 233

Solzhenitsyn, Aleksandr, 204, 205, 207, 211

Sorenson, Theodore, 49

Soviet Union, reporting from, 37, 39–42, 88–89, 97–100, 103, 107, 205, 206, 207; a Czech view of, 209–210

Stafford, Jean,*§ 162, 222

Statue of Liberty window, 3

Steinbeck, John,* *The Grapes of Wrath,* 11

Stevenson, Adlai E., 18, 98–100, 113

Stone, Marvin L., 34

Storke, Thomas M.,* 101

Strohmeyer, John,* 162

Student performance at Columbia J-school, 69, 70–71, 91–93

Students for a Democratic Society (SDS), 191, 197–99, 218

Sulzberger, Arthur O. (Punch) Sr., 125, 162, 201

Swanberg, W. A., 109

Swope, Herbert Bayard,* 9, 152

Syracuse University, 69, 310

Szulc, Tad, 101

Taft, Senator Robert A., 70

Taiwan defense, 13–20

Talbott, Secretary of the Air Force Harold, 29–30, 36

Tamarkin, Robert, 292

Taylor, General Maxwell D., 141

Tennessee, University of, 7, 69, 294–96, 301

Tet offensive, 192

Thailand, proposed spread of war to, 136–37

Thant, UN Secretary General U, 114, 248

Thomson, Virgil,*‡ 124, 260

Thornell, Jack,* 177

Time, calls on Nixon to resign, 274

Times Literary Supplement, 135

Toland, John,* 162, 253

Topping, Seymour, 170, 182

Towery, Roland K.,* 25, 162

Trimble, Vance,* 84

Truman, President Harry S, 162, 199, 226

Trustees of Columbia University: *Citizen Hearst* prize denied, 109; failed attempt to dissolve Pulitzer board, 276; objection to a prize for the Pentagon Papers story, 257–64; objection to Watergate prize, 265–72; pick John Hughes over Harrison Salisbury for a prize, 176; separated from prizes, 284–89; their Pulitzer authority defined, 25, 105
Tuchman, Barbara,*‡ 124, 260
Tuohy, William,* 199
TV news prize proposed, 78–79, 104–5, 117, 153
TV war coverage, 236

U-2 spy plane, 8, 110, 112–14
Unger, Irwin,* 148
United Press International (UPI), 106
University, JH's experience at, 68–73
US House Judiciary Committee, 277, 278
US International Communications Agency, 308–9, 310
US Supreme Court, 278
Utica (New York) newspapers, 77

Valenstein, Rose, 223, 249, 261, 298, 303
Van Doren, Charles, 70
Variety, 249
Vermillion, Bobby, 34
Vu Van Thi, South Vietnam ambassador, 173
Vietcong, 121, 128, 192
Vietnam, North, 121, 174–76, 236
Vietnam, South, 121–24, 212–13, 214–16, 217
Vietnam War, 121–22, 125, 128–29, 132–33, 136–44; antiwar protest movement and, 216; General Abrams replaces Westmoreland, 193–94; and the invasion of Cambodia, 216; more US troops sought for, 184–85, 187–88; and Nixon elected president, 198; Nixon's pacification program, 212–

13; and North Vietnam, 174–76; Phnom Penh falls, 293; Saigon falls, 292; student riots about, 91, 96–97; Tet offensive in, 192

Wagner, Mayor Robert F. (New York City), 7
Wall Street Journal, 105, 163, 177, 218, 258, 260
Wang, Taiwan Air Force General Tiger, 32
Ward, Robert W.,* 150
Washington *Daily News*, 25
Washington *Post*, 6, 264, 265–72, 306
Washington *Star-News*, 273, 275–76
Watson, George, 235, 241
Watergate, xi, 160, 264, 265–72, 274, 275, 281, 284
Watts, Richard,‡ 197
Westmoreland, General W. C., 138–39, 184–85, 187–88, 192, 193–94
Wharton, Edith,* 159
White, Jack,* 273, 275, 276
White, Theodore H.,* 94, 109
Who's Afraid of Virginia Woolf? (Albee), 124
Wilder, Thornton,* 159
Wilkins, Ford, 34
Willenson, Kim, 191
Williams, Tennessee, 68, 159
Williams, William Carlos,* 124
Witze, Claude, 140
Wolfe, Thomas, 159
Woodward, Bob,* 6, 264, 265–72
World Room, Columbia University, 4–7, 199, 304
Wuorinen, Charles,* 149–50

Yevtuchenko, Yevgency, 207, 210
York, Brigadier General Robert, 139
Yu, Frederick T. C., 233
Yu, Nancy, 33

Zorin, Valerian, 114
Zorthian, Barry, 140